THE 1973 YEARBOOK OF AGRICULTURE

93d Congress, 1st Session

House Document
No. 93–29

HANDBOOK
FOR THE
HOME

U.S. DEPARTMENT
OF
AGRICULTURE

LCC No. 73–600300

For sale by the Superintendent of Documents,
U.S. Government Printing Office, Washington, D.C. 20402
Price $5.70   Stock Number 0100–02960

FOREWORD

EARL L. BUTZ

Secretary of Agriculture

Handbook for the home, the 1973 Yearbook of Agriculture, is a guide to helping families use their incomes to best advantage. It suggests ways that families can live fuller, more secure, and more satisfying lives, and helps them avoid costly pitfalls of all kinds. It gathers a great wealth of consumer material into some 400 compact pages. This is a book for families. It centers around the home—whether home is a suburban house, a country place, or a city apartment. The Yearbook's subjects also cover family activity outside the home.

Family living costs, family records, and family money management plans are among the book's early chapters, in the section on *Families*. A money management plan is a device to help you get maximum use from your money, as our authors stress. Families are faced with making deliberate, conscious choices regarding the patterning of their way of life. Every way of life has certain benefits as well as costs. Families need to choose wisely so that the style of life they pick will give them the greatest benefits with the lowest costs.

Safety in the home is discussed in the Yearbook's opening section. Nearly as many people are injured from accidents in the home as from traffic accidents and work accidents combined. Hazards include falls, fires, and chemicals. Improper handling of food is another hazard. Food safety is of prime concern to homemakers. Handled improperly, food can cause illness even though it was safe to eat when purchased or first prepared. Live safely—and you give yourself a good chance to live longer.

As you make a quick run through the book, you will be treated to a variety of highlights from the chapters, and the authors' thoughts. Take crafts, for instance, one of our nation's great heritages, and a chapter subject. We were born to be creative in a world rich in design, rich in natural resources, rich with innovative people. Hopefully this book will serve as a springboard to families' creativity—not just in crafts but in their homes, gardens, furnishings, and communities. As we get more involved in the complexities of large institutions and organizations—and engage in standardized, routine jobs—we have a greater need for individual creativeness within our own households.

Family camping has captivated over 40 million Americans, so there is a chapter titled, *Hey, Just Look What's Happened to Camping!* Gardening started with the Garden of Eden, and it's still going strong as a family activity. Undoubtedly it will continue as long as there is a civilized way of life. The relaxation of growing our own plants helps us shed the worries and pressures of our hectic age. The book has two chapters on gardening.

Our dwellings provide the stage upon which the private drama of American families is enacted. In the *Dwellings* section everything from site selection to remodeling is discussed, including financing a home, insurance, legal angles, foundations and basements, electricity, shade trees, climate control, second homes, and taking the work out of housework. One important pointer in this section is to check very carefully for possible soil problems on any homesite you are considering. Otherwise you take a needless gamble, perhaps with your entire lifesavings. Repairing damage due to soil-related failures can be most expensive.

Your choices and decisions in home furnishings will reflect, naturally, your needs, likes, and dislikes. But, as the *Furnishings* section in the Yearbook points out, it is wise to use some accepted principles to guide you. Carpets, clothing, appliances, sewing equipment, and lighting are examples of subjects in this section. Carpeting is one of the most expensive items in your home, and should be selected with extreme care. This holds true, as well, for major appliances. The chapters on appliances give lots of good tips.

Changing fashions often make clothes old hat before the wear life of a garment is over, as a chapter on the role of clothing observes. Understanding the fashion cycle—the gradual rise, peaking, and eventual decline in popular acceptance of a style—will help you be a wise consumer. It may prevent you from investing in quality that will long outlast the fashion value of your clothing. Another chapter notes that careful attention to labeling can increase satisfaction with apparel and household textiles.

Some of the more important values we seek today involve being part of a community of people who share common goals, and can and will work together to achieve them. Increasingly, we are placing a higher value on the quality of life. But realization of a higher quality of life for everyone won't happen without a lot of hard work, as the *Communities* section notes. There is a need for plans, and plans need to be carried out.

Present concern about quality of life and the environment has arisen in part as a citizen protest. Great resources and great opportunities have not been translated into the good life implicit in the American dream. What is at stake is too important to be left to the experts. A new partnership between citizens, their public and private agencies, and their government can lead the way.

The textbooks don't say it, but a Yearbook chapter does: Most real environmental planning at the community level begins with worry. "Yes, we were worried," one citizen is quoted. "Our town was changing and we were afraid that our natural resources would disappear under the bulldozer." This town did something about it—inventorying its natural resources, and adopting subdivision control regulations.

Land and outdoor recreation go together like ice cream and apple pie, in an author's words. When the land includes a body of water, it's even better. Land and water and trees make a near perfect combination. If you have one or more of these resources, some U. S. Department of Agriculture agencies will likely be able to help you—or tell who can help you—develop recreational facilities for your community.

This Yearbook cannot begin to go into full detail on the many subjects it covers. It can only give highlights. So *Suggested Further Reading* lists are given at the end of many chapters. The Yearbook's readers are also referred to such valuable sources of information as State Extension services, trade associations, public utility companies, consumer magazines, and consumer columns in newspapers. The more knowledgeable consumers this nation has, the better will be our way of life.

PREFACE

JACK HAYES

Yearbook Editor

Does this sound familiar as an indication of the new consumerism: "The housekeeper has been asking for information on many home matters. She has asked what is needed for an adequate diet. She has sought to know the wearing quality of textiles used for clothing and house furnishings, and the best methods of cleaning and preserving such textiles. She has sought help in water supply, plumbing, heating, ventilating, and lighting. She is looking for information about the comparative energy required for performing household tasks by different methods."

Well, compressed somewhat, that paragraph was in the 1913 Yearbook, 60 years ago. Those words still are most timely. The 1973 Yearbook of Agriculture covers much of the same information needs—in today's setting. It also steers the homemaker—and her husband—to where they can get more information.

Of course, the 1973 Yearbook goes far beyond the 1913 statement. And incidentally, the 1913 Yearbook merely outlined homemaker needs, but made no attempt to fill them. You'll find that the longest section by far in the '73 book is devoted to DWELLINGS, including choosing a builder, noise control, mobile homes, and house plans.

Most of the 1973 Yearbook authors are either with USDA or the State universities and land-grant colleges, and their chapters are based in the main on Federal or State research. The chairman of the 1973 Yearbook Committee is with the agency administering USDA funds in support of university research.

While the agriculture establishment for many years has been carrying on consumer activities, including issuance of a vast number of consumer publications, the Yearbooks of Agriculture have entered this area in full measure quite recently.

Four Yearbooks from the last eight years should prove of special value to consumers. These may be obtained from the Superintendent of Documents, Washington, D. C. 20402. Enclose a check or money order for the amount indicated when ordering.

- *Consumers All*, 1965, $2.75. A how-to book covering most practical questions a family could think of.
- *Outdoors USA*, 1967, $2.75. A combination guide to outdoor recreation, conservation handbook, and primer on beautification.
- *Food for Us All*, 1969, $3.50. Practical know-how on food for every homemaker.
- *Landscape for Living*, 1972, $3.50. Down to earth advice for the home gardener.

Simple Home Repairs . . . inside is another publication of special value to homemakers that you may order from the Superintendent of Documents. Send a check or money order for 40 cents.

Readers of the 1973 Yearbook may also wish to obtain a copy of *Consumer*

Information, an index of selected Federal publications of consumer interest. To obtain a free copy, request it from Consumer Information, Public Documents Distribution Center, Pueblo, Colo. 81009.

This Editor's Preface can't wind up without noting that the 1973 Yearbook is a cooperative venture—planned by a talented Committee, written by knowledgeable authors, the type set by a private contractor, and the printing done in the Government Printing Office. Overall book production was designed by Dudley Kruhm of the Typography and Design Section, Government Printing Office, under the direction of Robert McKendry, Superintendent. Howard Behrens of the same Section created the cover.

Bruce Beacher, of the Cooperative State Research Service, was chairman of the 1973 Yearbook Committee.

Subcommittee chairmen for the four sections of the book were Jeanne Priester, Extension Service, FAMILIES; Robert Yeck, Agricultural Research Service, DWELLINGS; Enid Tozier, *Virginia Polytechnic Institute and State University,* FURNISHINGS; and John Barringer, *Rural Electrification Administration,* COMMUNITIES. Robert Birch, *National Agricultural Library,* served as an advisor.

Other Committee members were:

Kate Alfriend, *Office of Communication*
Landy Altman, *Agricultural Research Service*
Albert Arnst, *Forest Service*
Warren Bailey, *Economic Research Service*
Robert Dugan, *Farmers Home Administration*
Cozy Ellison, *Fort Valley (Ga.) State College*
Lyman Henderson, *Agricultural Research Service*
Helen Johnson, *Rural Development Service*
August Kehr, *Agricultural Research Service*
F. Glennon Loyd, *Soil Conservation Service*
George Schladt, *Farmers Home Administration*
Helen Souders, *Agricultural Research Service*
Val Weyl, *Animal and Plant Health Inspection Service*
Joel Wheeler, *Office of Management Services*

CONTENTS

91/DWELLINGS

FAMILIES

Computerized Families Are on the Horizon, But You and I Will Still Call the Shots

TODAY'S FAMILIES have both the freedom and responsibility to determine and control everyday activities. No longer need family events just happen; *they can be decided.* Decisions made by families on a day to day basis determine the quality of life possible for each of us since it is in the family that individual personality and character are formed. Here the values, skills, and discipline necessary for living in the larger world are shaped.

Popular literature is rampant with descriptions of family breakdown, fears concerning values the family appears to be perpetuating, and threats of the family's extinction by emerging technological and social forces. Evidence does exist of marked changes in the way of life of today's families. Different attitudes regarding sexual relationships, size of family, ways of rearing children, and male and female roles prevail.

Despite the attention given to change wrought by technological development, much remains the same. Trends suggest that the time-honored values of equality, work ethic, free enterprise, private property, freedom of choice, individualism and personal worth show considerable stability. How these values are adapted and reinterpreted in everyday situations is changing. The changes do not herald the family's demise. Rather they call for a different and increasingly more important role for the family.

Understanding what is happening to our population, income, and mobility provides some basis for predicting what will be happening in the family, and offers clues for planning the future.

Population will continue to increase in the 1970's, but its rate and mix will change. If present trends prevail, the rate of population growth will decrease. Women will continue to outnumber men. Children under 5 will decrease due to reduced birth rates. The over 65 age group will increase because of improved health practices and economic assistance.

There will be more "empty nest" households and fewer "full nest" households due to the declining birth rate and earlier age at which children will leave home.

Family income, contrary to current pessimistic economic predictions, is expected to rise. Average family incomes in 1970 prices will rise from about $11,000 in 1970 to about $15,000 in 1980. No longer restricted to purchasing for mere survival, the family will face a new complexity in its decision-making in distributing its increased money resources among the many things it wants as opposed to what it needs.

Families are on the move, and the move seems to be both from the farm and the city. The hard core farm and metropolitan population is decreasing. If present trends continue, by 1985 nearly half of our population will be living in suburban areas around metropolitan centers.

The migration of urban families into rural areas and farm families to the urban fringe will result in a breakdown of the traditional stereotypes once held of racial and ethnic groups. This new intermingling of families representing different life styles will introduce new flexibility and broader acceptance of variation in patterns of everyday living.

We can see for ourselves that our neighbors, even though they may eat and rear their children differently, are in many ways like us. Use of the same consumer markets and educational institutions will reduce the differences and encourage acceptance of diversity

AUTHOR BEATRICE PAOLUCCI is a Professor in the Department of Family Ecology, College of Human Ecology, Michigan State University.

Day care centers.

in family standards, attitudes, and life styles.

Present day biomedical advancements are changing the family. We now have information that makes it possible to determine when someone will be born and to some extent when he will die.

Separation of sexual activity and procreation have made family planning possible. More effective contraceptives, more easily obtained abortions, and genetic counseling provide the knowledge and the mechanics for child spacing and birth control. Through medication it is possible to prolong the life of the sick and aged.

Regardless of scientific information, religious attitudes and ethical considerations will play a large part in helping families make these important life and death choices.

Along with biomedical advances, technological gains in both industry and agriculture are changing the family. Technology has made it possible for machines rather than people to produce

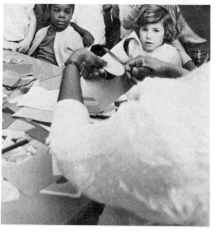

an abundance of material goods. Technology also has made it possible for a smaller number of farmers to produce an abundance of food.

Rather than depending upon one another because of what we produce, we are becoming dependent upon one another for what we know. This change from a dependence on production to a dependence on information will reshape work and consumption patterns. It has

3

made a difference in where families live and how they use their time.

Because of these changes, families are and will be faced with making deliberate, conscious choices regarding the patterning of their way of life. Every way of life has certain benefits as well as costs. Families will need to choose wisely so that the style of life they select will give them the greatest benefits with the lowest costs.

The traditional family grouping of wife as homemaker, husband as breadwinner, and their children will remain dominant, although the people in the family may change because of divorce, separation, and remarriage.

The family with dual careers, both husband and wife working, will increase—particularly among the young and better educated. The husband and wife family, with no children, will also increase.

Some couples will choose to remain childless. Others will spend the major part of their lifetime with no children present because of possibilities for spacing and limiting family size.

An increased number of single parent families will be formed as a result of divorce, death, abandonment, or the choice of the unwed to rear their children alone. In most cases, the single parent family will have an employed woman as its head.

Because of increased acceptability, more individuals may remain unmarried and establish single households. The single adult living alone will establish close kin or simulated kin networks, relying upon and sharing with others economic and emotional resources, fulfilling parent-like roles in an "aunt/ uncle" capacity.

Among the young, there are some who will choose to live in a commune arrangement where several couples and their children will share a common house, eat together, and divide housework and child care.

Among the elderly, primarily for economic reasons, married and/or unmarried individuals may share a common dwelling, resources, and depend upon one another for companionship and emotional support.

These different family forms will present different issues and problems for family members. Families will need information for wisely selecting the family pattern they want to pursue.

The patterns of interaction and consumption within the family and the relationship the family has with nonfamily groups and organizations will differ. Whether both parents work, how many adults are present to care for children, what the income is, all make different demands on family members.

If the woman works outside the home, the family is likely to be more democratic and its members more involved in sharing household tasks. The new feminism will have two effects: an increased awareness of women's decision-making role within the family and society, and a drive on the part of women for more personal satisfaction through greater independence, self-expression, and personal achievement.

Many women will rediscover their personal autonomy and satisfaction in the wife-mother role in the family. This role will take on greater economic significance as society begins to place dollar value on family functions such as caring for children and production of services for family members.

The woman's contribution to the family will become increasingly important and complex because of the information needed for decision making and the knowledge that the productivity and health of family members depends upon the quality of choices she makes.

The changing role of women assumes a corresponding change for men in attitudes and role identity. A more equal sharing of the decision making and more equal division of labor in the family are obvious changes. The male as authority figure and head of household may disappear. Children, as well as women, will become more directly involved in family decision making, will share the growing equality of the family, and will have a less dependent relationship with their parents.

4

Snowmobiles at Lake Tahoe. Precautions are being taken to prevent pollution of the lake as a result of winter sports activity.

Many women will work outside the home, for economic as well as personal reasons. The woman's employment will affect family spending decisions. Functions performed by her for her family will be delegated to the market place and will require family dollars.

The family will be faced with buying such services as care of infants, children, the sick, aged or disabled; household cleaning, counseling of family members, managing of credit, interior decorating, laundry, as well as ready-made clothing and meals away from home.

As the family buys more products and family services, it will be faced with making new kinds of decisions. This will require processing a large amount of information. Along with how to perform a homemaking skill and purchase material goods, families will want to know how to purchase a family service.

Information will be needed about judging the quality of service, determining direct cost of the service as well as indirect costs (such as transportation costs of taking a child to a day care center), and consequences to family and society of delegating some decision-making to an out-of-family agency.

Purchasing family services will alter the choice-making function of the family in a marked way. Buying services once produced by the family no doubt will also bring changes in the closeness of the family group and the dependence of family members upon one another.

Families will need to learn to turn to the computer for assistance. With the increasing amounts of information a family is required to process, the home computer outlet will become a necessity for both decision making and family record storage and retrieval.

A home communications revolution is predicted with the arrival of the home computer terminal. It will serve as a source and processor of information. A virtually infinite amount of information from many sources will be at the instantaneous disposal of the family for more efficient decision making.

The computer will plan meals, turn lights on at appropriate times, keep track of family members' schedules, calculate budget information, and oversee credit, spending, and bank accounts. Just as home equipment frees the homemaker from the labor of housekeeping, the computer releases family members from some repetitious managerial duties.

The home terminal may serve as a home education center for children's homework and as part of the lifelong learning program of parents and elderly family members.

The change which will have the most immediate effect on family decision-making will be increased discretionary time. This does not necessarily mean more free time, but rather some choice about how family members will use time. It is predicted that the workweek will be shortened to four days by 1985. Currently, longer vacations and earlier retirement are a part of many professional and union goals.

For economic reasons many families will decide to use this "free" time to hold a second job. With the increasing interest in personal development, a segment of the time might be chosen by some to develop alternative interests through life-long education programs that will facilitate career changes, to increase their skills for effective citizenship, to pursue an interest in the creative arts, and to learn new skills to enhance their family living. A renaissance of the home arts of cooking, sewing and gardening is already underway.

With leisure time a possibility, recreation and participatory sports will increase dramatically, placing a severe stress on existing recreational areas and threatening the natural environment at large. The family will be faced with serious value decisions concerning maintaining the natural environment, increasing economic growth, and pursuing environmentally damaging recreational activities.

Today more than in the past the family will be in a position to choose its style of living and in so doing shape the quality of life possible for each of us. As it chooses the resources it will use to carry out its way of living, the family will determine too the quality of the environment.

From the home and family radiate the warmth and concern that keep people human. Home represents the safe harbor from the stresses of everyday living. It is the harbor where each person can feel he has value to himself and to others. The society of the future will have need for richer, more creative, more supportive family ties. The day to day decisions made do make a difference.

This Yearbook is dedicated to providing you with practical information for making those choices. The nation—its international and national image, prosperity, and health—is a reflection of the well-being or lack of well-being of the family. The quality of life achieved in individual families directly affects the total society. For in its simplest and probably most important form, a nation is no more than a reflection of the sum of the homes of America.

Family Living Costs: Some Figures and Tips to Help You Plan

FAMILY LIVING is big business! Expected life earnings of a high school graduate are near $400,000 and those of a person with 2 years of graduate school after college are over $600,000.

How a family uses $400,000 to $600,000 during a lifetime depends upon many things. The management and economic principles of successful businesses also apply in the home but may or may not be followed. Family decisions are made in a social setting. Here personal relationships, communication, tradition and custom, attitudes and beliefs, as well as knowledge and skills, influence family resource management.

Each family is uniquely different. How it lives and spends its money is influenced by its values, goals, income, education, stage in the family life cycle, and residence location.

AUTHOR JOSEPHINE H. LAWYER is a family resource management specialist with the Extension Service.

6

It is important that your family understand its priority values. For example, how important is health, knowledge, security, economy, or comfort to your family? Such values establish a framework from which all decisions are made.

The statement "People don't plan to fail, they just fail to plan," relates to one's goals. A family that agrees upon what it wants to accomplish, and works toward it, is more likely to secure what it wants.

Be realistic about goals. Select those you can expect to reach. Plan goals that can be accomplished within one or two years, and others to be achieved within five or more years in the future. Review goals annually and make adjustments when there is a major change affecting the family.

Family needs and living costs change throughout life. The family life cycle diagram is a concept used to help families visualize time segments more realistically. Notice the short period without children; the long period with children; and the longer period after children have left home.

Income is one of the most important determinants of your family's living standard.

Household income usually increases until the head of the household reaches late middle-age, and decreases after that.

The table, with Bureau of Census figures, shows income and age-related differences:

Money Income of Households, 1970

| By age of head | Mean °|
Years	Income
14–24	$ 7,115
25–34	10,313
35–44	12,193
45–54	12,858
55–64	10,573
65 and over	5,418

° *Mean income is total income for the group divided by the number in the group.*

THE FAMILY LIFE CYCLE

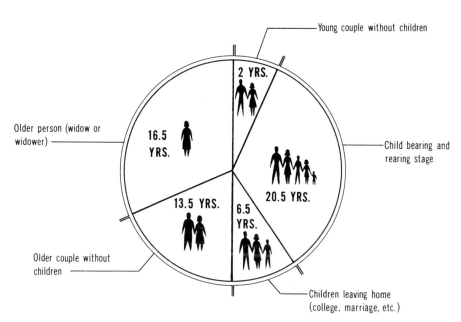

Young couple without children

2 YRS.

Older person (widow or widower)

16.5 YRS.

Child bearing and rearing stage

13.5 YRS.

6.5 YRS.

20.5 YRS.

Older couple without children

Children leaving home (college, marriage, etc.)

A major reason more families have higher incomes today is that 55 percent of all households have one or more people in the labor force. The Conference Board estimates that close to 45 percent of all adult women work compared to less than 35 percent in the early 1950's. Forty-two percent of married women work.

Education influences your family's income and how it is spent. The Bureau of Census reports the mean income of households by education of the head in 1970:

Elementary ....$ 5,747 to $ 7,253
High School ....$ 8,757 to $10,422
College ....$11,761 to $15,980

The number and age of family members also influence your family living costs. Generally, costs rise as children grow, and reach a peak during high school and college years. Food costs are typical as these Bureau of Labor Statistics figures show:

Average cost of food plans at three cost levels in April 1973

Cost for one week
Low   Moderate   Liberal
Family of 2:
20–35 years .....$21.90....$28.00....$34.40
55–75 years .....$17.90....$23.50....$28.30
Family of 4:
Preschool
children ....$31.70....$40.60....$49.30
School children..$36.70....$47.30....$58.10

Where your family lives also makes a difference in living costs. Generally, both income and living costs are lower in the South. While the average median income was $10,290 in 1971, it was $8,980 in the South, $10,703 in the West, $10,785 in the North Central, and $11,020 in the Northeast. Median income means that half the people make more than that figure and half make less.

In 1970, living costs were 5 to 10 percent below the national average in Dallas and Atlanta; 5 to 15 percent above in San Francisco, Chicago, and New York; about 20 percent higher in Hawaii; and 35 percent higher in Alaska.

Management skills and consumer competency can help you get the most from your income and other resources. Your success depends upon ability to:
• plan and control spending
• use credit to advantage
• choose adequate insurance protection
• select, maintain, and use consumer goods and services that meet family needs
• plan and build financial security

Today most goods and services are purchased with income. The family that reaches more of its social and economic goals is one that plans how it will spend, then controls and adjusts its plan as needed. The family knows how much money it has, and allocates it to get the most satisfying level of living it can afford.

Although spending is a family affair, there are records which can be useful when reviewing your spending.

The table shows how many families at different income levels spend their after-tax income:

	Percent of Income
Housing	27–30
Food	19–25
Transportation	14–17
Clothing	9–13
Medical care	6–7
Recreation	4–5
Personal care	2–3
Tobacco and alcohol	3–4
Education	1–3
Miscellaneous	3–6

Americans in 1971 spent 79 percent of their personal income, saved 7 percent, and spent 14 percent for personal tax payments.

The Bureau of Labor Statistics has calculated three living standards for an urban family of four consisting of a 38-year-old man, a wife who does not work outside the home, a boy and a girl.

In autumn 1971, the Bureau estimated the family needed $7,214 for a low cost budget, $10,971 for an intermediate cost budget, and $15,905 for a higher cost budget.

The proportion of the budget estimated for food ranged from 20–27 percent; housing, 20–25 percent; personal taxes, 9–16 percent; Social Security, insurance, contributions, 9–10 percent; clothing and personal care, 11–12 percent; transportation, 7–9 percent; medical care, 4–8 percent.

Credit is a useful resource, especially when purchasing expensive items. However, every family has a debt limit related to its income, ability to increase income, and its present spending.

Credit advisors differ in recommendations of a family's installment debt limit, in addition to payment on a home mortgage.

Examples are: A family should not be indebted for more than
• 20 percent of a year's after-tax income.
• what 10 percent of their after-tax income would pay up in a 12- to 24-month period.

You can use credit to advantage by shopping for it and making as large a downpayment as possible.

If you are a credit union member, or have savings in banks or savings and loan associations, you can usually obtain credit at lower costs than from other lenders.

Always compare total finance charges and annual percentage rates before deciding where you will purchase credit.

A short repayment period is one way to reduce costs. For example, a family with 8½ percent interest on a home loan of $18,000 would pay $13,900 interest over a period of 15 years, $19,480 in 20 years, or $31,810 in 30 years.

Some financial advisors suggest downpayments of 10–25 percent on a home, 25–30 percent on a car, and 10–20 percent on furnishings and equipment.

Consider saving in advance for costly purchases. If regular amounts were deposited in a savings account, you would save this interest, plus 12–36 percent which you might pay for using credit. Paying cash could save as much as $500–$600 on a car.

Most families have some insurance, and many feel they would like larger amounts. Since several types are needed, it is important that you be realistic about what you can afford.

A family's need for life insurance changes over time. A breadwinner with small children usually has greater liabilities than after children are grown. He needs to investigate differences in types and costs of term and other insurance, and to consider combinations which will provide adequate coverage throughout life.

A homeowner needs to increase insurance coverage as the home appreciates in value.

Due to increasing medical and legal costs, a car owner needs greater liability protection than in the past. He may not be aware that he can buy several times the minimum lability coverage for a few dollars more than for the smaller premium.

You can become a more competent consumer when you consciously follow management and economic principles as you select, maintain, and use goods and services. These apply, regardless of what you purchase, but are especially important when the cost is large:
• *Plan what to buy.* Each decision to buy means that you do not have that money for something else. Fit purchases into the family's spending plan. Anticipate and set aside money for large future purchases.
• *Decide where and when to shop.* Buy from reputable dealers. Learn merchandising practices and use them to your advantage. Example: Dealers may give a greater discount on an automobile during the off-season.
• *Know how to buy.* Get information on cost, quality, grades, guarantees, annual percentage interest rate (if item is to be financed), and expected performance. Make price and feature comparison (especially on expensive items).
• *Be a responsible consumer:* Know about and use laws and regulations that protect consumers. Understand consumer rights and assume consumer responsibilities.
• *Develop family business skills:* Maintain a good credit record. Understand

9

contracts and other legal business forms. Develop a workable system for family business papers, spending, income tax records, etc.

Today's family needs to prepare for financial emergencies and security. Economic, social, technological, and political change continuously affect your income. People are also retiring earlier and living longer.

A recent University of Michigan study indicated that less than half the Nation's families have $500 in savings, yet all face risks such as accidents and illness.

Financial experts vary in recommendations of what a family's emergency savings should be. Money to cover 3 to 6 months living expenses is often suggested.

Inflation is a reality with which all must cope.

Rising prices and rising taxes cut incomes of those on fixed incomes 50 percent from 1940 to 1950, 28 percent from 1950 to 1967, and another 25 percent from 1967 to 1972.

From 1962 through the first 10 months in 1972, average consumer prices on the goods and services bought by urban wage earners and clerical workers increased 38 percent. Cost of food eaten at home increased 33 percent while that eaten away from home increased 53 percent. Housing increased 40 percent, transportation increased 29 percent, apparel and upkeep increased 34 percent, and medical care increased 58 percent.

Most financial experts advise families to first set aside regular amounts and build adequate savings in banks, savings and loan associations, and U.S. Savings Bonds. Then some suggest buying real estate, particularly a home, as a hedge against inflation. After this, families may decide to invest in shares of American business.

How do you start a financial security plan? First, study future financial needs for children, education, retirement, etc. Include expected inflation in your estimates. Then develop a plan which commits part of your income to your future.

Some suggest 5 to 10 percent of after tax earnings for this purpose.

The sooner your family starts its financial security plan the better. Through compounding of interest, reinvestment of interest, and appreciation in property and business values, you can attain financial security providing you start early enough.

Someone has said that ability to plan consciously may be man's most distinctive feature. Certainly how you plan to use income and other resources is directly related to your success in reaching family goals. Family living is big business. Each family member is part of the management team.

For further reading:

Consumer Product Information Center. *Planning for the Later Years,* 020A, Public Documents Distribution Center, Pueblo, Colo. 81009, 35 cents.

How to Live on Your Income, The Readers Digest Association, Inc., Pleasantville, N.Y., 1970.

Planning Your Financial Future, U.S. News & World Report, Inc., Washington, D.C. 20037, 1972.

The Time-Life Book of Family Finance, Time Inc., New York, 1969.

Keeping Records; What to Discard

Who was it that said, "Never put off until tomorrow what you can do today"? Perhaps it was Aristotle, or Confucius, or Abraham Lincoln. They were all wise men. We suspect that the author of these words (really Lord Chesterfield) had run into a snag with his family record system and was vowing to turn over a new leaf for the morrow.

Most of us could profit from this same advice, when it comes to family records. When, for example, was the last time you couldn't put your hands on an important paper you knew you had carefully put away someplace? How much time do you spend trying to straighten out your family business affairs, especially at income tax time?

How, in fact, do people decide what records are important to keep and what can be discarded? How do they decide where these records and papers should be stored? Even though each family must work out its own system, some general guidelines can be helpful. As a starter, you could ask yourself a few questions.

• How easy or difficult would it be for other family members to figure out your record system? Or do you have a system?

• Who in the family besides you knows where to turn for necessary information about the family assets and obligations? Do you have a listing of the people who are important contacts? For many families such a list would include: tax counsel, attorney, banker, broker, insurance representatives, employer, all creditors and debtors, perhaps others.

• Are you sure that title to family property and possessions is held in the best way for all concerned?

A good record system will provide a bird's-eye view of what happens to the property after you are out of the picture, or when your spouse dies. Other changes in family situations can alter your plans also, for example divorce or separation, children reaching the age of legal maturity, perhaps a long illness, accident, lawsuit, natural disaster, loss of job, retirement.

• What happens if your house is burglarized, or if there's a fire and records are destroyed, or if you just plain lose track of important papers? Which ones can be replaced, and how do you go about replacing them? Which ones cannot be replaced, and what do you do about these?

AUTHOR CONSTANCE BURGESS is Extension Consumer Education Specialist, Cooperative Extension Service, University of California.

Every family has some important records. Each of us has a birth certificate, or should have an acceptable substitute. Since there are many occasions when the information on your birth certificate will be needed, it is important that you keep it in a safe place, preferably in a safe deposit box.

By the same token, there will be a death certificate for every person someday. These will be needed occasionally and should also be kept in the safe deposit box.

While it is possible to get duplicate copies of birth and death certificates for a small charge, it may take weeks to do so.

Other family-type records that are important documents, and that ought to be kept in your safe deposit box, include marriage certificates, divorce or other legal papers regarding dissolution of marriage, adoption papers, citizenship records, service papers, and any other document that is either government or court-recorded.

The original copy of a will, in most cases, is kept in the safe of the attorney who prepared it. This is highly desirable, since it may save complications later. The client receives the two carbon copies, one of which may be put into his or her own safe deposit box. However, there could be a legal delay in getting this copy at the death of the person involved. The third copy, therefore, should be kept at home where it is readily accessible.

Some of your important papers, for example investments, are of a business or financial nature. Certificates for securities are non-negotiable (can't be sold or legally transferred) until they are signed by the owner. Nevertheless, such certificates can be lost or stolen, and the signature can be forged. In either case replacement involves both cost and delay. Such certificates then, when not left with the broker, should be kept in the owner's safe deposit box.

Government bonds can be replaced without cost, but there will be a delay of several months. Thus it is best to keep these in the box, also.

Among other investment-type documents that require safekeeping are papers that serve as proof of ownership, such as deeds for real estate, other mortgage papers, important contracts, automobile titles (if this applies in your State), leases, notes, and such special papers as patents and copyrights.

If you don't have a safe deposit box, you ought to consider getting one. The yearly rental, at your bank or savings and loan company, is only a few dollars. For many families the smallest size is adequate, though larger sizes are available at slightly higher charges. Some savings institutions make these boxes available at no cost to depositors.

If you do have a safe deposit box, is it large enough to hold all of the items that ought to be in it—and small enough to keep out the things that don't need to be there? This is a business investment for many families, and often the rental can be claimed on their income tax. It should not be used as a catch-all for souvenirs and unimportant papers.

A guideline as to what goes in and what stays out of your safe deposit box might be: Put it in if you can't replace it or if it would be costly or troublesome to replace.

Many items can be replaced rather easily. Copies of insurance policies can be obtained from your insurance companies. Copies of cancelled checks are available at your bank, usually.

Generally speaking, the following additional items do not need to be kept in a safe deposit box: income tax returns, education records, employment records, bank books, social security cards, guarantees, burial instructions, old love letters.

Are you a saver of papers and records and receipts and cancelled checks? Some people are such avid savers that they take over the garage and park their car on the driveway!

It isn't necessary to keep all cancelled checks. Utility bills and charge account bills show the balance owed. If you paid last month's bills, only the current amount due will be listed. When you pay bills by personal check,

you can call on the bank for proof that your check was cancelled.

On the other hand, it's important for you to keep any checks and other receipts that may be needed for income tax purposes or as proof of payment on installment debts.

The Internal Revenue Service has 3 years in which to audit Federal income tax returns. However, this limit does not apply in unusual cases. If you failed to report more than 25 percent of your gross income, the government has 5 years to collect the tax or start legal proceedings. Also, there are no time limitations if you filed a (proved) fraudulent return or if you failed to file a return.

Time limitations for State income taxes vary from State to State, so you'll want to find out what the law says in your State.

Among your important records will be a household inventory. Before this is of much value, in case of fire or burglary, you'll need to supply some details. Be sure to list the item, date bought, purchase price (not including credit charges), model number if it applies, brand name, dealer's name, and general description (color, size, style, electric or gas, etc.). Don't forget to include a realistic lump sum in your list for clothes and jewelry if you don't itemize these.

This information serves a triple purpose. It helps you to determine the value of your possessions so you can have adequate insurance protection. It is helpful if it becomes necessary for you to make an insurance claim. And it can help the police to find stolen goods following a burglary. Some families take pictures of their rooms to help identify possessions.

It's a good idea to make several copies of your household inventory. One copy should be put in your safe deposit box; and you may wish to give a copy to your insurance company. The third copy can be kept in a convenient place at home.

Have you tried filling out a net worth statement, as a means of keeping tabs on yourself and your family possessions? Such a record provides a good overall picture and can be prepared in an hour or less. When done on an annual basis, you can see quickly whether you are getting ahead financially or falling behind and, in either case, how fast.

An accurate net worth statement can serve as a point of departure for the year ahead. If you're not making as much progress financially as you had expected to, you can decide together whether to stay on course or to change directions for the coming year.

Where are you going to find a net worth form that will meet your needs? Try your county Cooperative Extension Service office. Or ask at your bank. Better yet perhaps, you can make one to fit your family. All you do is list your assets, list your obligations, and subtract the debts from the assets. Hopefully the plus side of the ledger will get larger each year and the minus side smaller. But there may be good reasons why you'll fall behind sometimes, such as when you buy a new home or when other expenses are heavier than usual.

NET WORTH STATEMENT *

Assets

	197__	197__	197__
Cash: on hand	$	$	$
saving accounts			
checking accounts			
House, market value			
Other real estate, value			
Household furnishings, value			
Automobile(s), blue book value			
Life insurance, cash value			
Stocks and bonds, today's value			
Money owed you			
Other assets			
Total	$	$	$

Obligations

	197__	197__	197__
Mortgages, balance due	$	$	$
Installment debts, balance due			
Credit cards, balance due			
Charge accounts, owed			
Other debts, total owed			
Total	$	$	$

Net Worth

(assets minus debts)	$	$	$

° Prepared on the same date each year, such as January 1.

Keeping records should be a family affair, rather than the responsibility of just one member of the household. It is important that everybody concerned be in on the decisions that affect the future of the family. Each person needs to know:

• What emergency numbers to call if the need arises.

• Who the legal and financial advisers are, and how to reach them by telephone.

• Where insurance policies are located.

• Where a copy of each individual will is located.

• What documents are in the safe deposit box.

• Where other records are kept, including the household inventory, cancelled checks and other income tax information.

In the final analysis, you and your family can function best within a framework that is meaningful for you. Some families find it easier to discuss their business affairs together than others do. The family that develops a satisfactory system for keeping records is likely to do a more realistic job of planning for the future.

Managing Money For Your Family

ARE YOU LIVING up to your income? From the income they now receive, many families could raise their level of living 10, 15, or 20 percent by using a financial plan. Such a plan is a guide specifically tailored for your family's needs, desires, and resources. And you are the best designer of the plan for your family.

A financial plan helps you choose between the more important and less important uses for your money. You identify money that now goes for "fuss and stuff" and direct it to more important uses. These leaks may be keeping you from getting what you really want.

It helps you establish priorities for your goals because it provides a financial means to the goals and tells you when you can reasonably expect to reach those goals. But it should not be considered a mandate. Change your plan when situations change and when new opportunities present themselves.

A plan gives you a sense of security. You can build into your plan the ability to ease the effects of a financial haymaker or to snap up a bargain. You can plan for college educations, your retirement days, repairs, automobile replacement, or whatever you want.

Without a plan, you may fall into the costly trap of having someone else manage your money through unnecessary installment plans, other loans, and the interest you pay for them. On the credit treadmill there is no reserve for repairs, replacements, or other emergencies. In these situations a family often resorts to unplanned use of credit. A spending plan is helpful in making decisions as to when to use credit. It helps you decide if you can assume additional obligations and to plan for the cost of the credit.

A financial plan is a wonderful device for helping you get maximum use from your money, but it will not do this automatically. You must draw up the plan yourself and then make it work for you.

There is no average or "proper" amount to be spent for clothing, food, housing, and other items. What you spend depends on the size of your family; income; the age of family members; where you live; your needs, goals, and individual likes; your health and other resources available.

A plan does not insure that all financial hazards are adequately met or avoided. It can cushion the blow and

AUTHOR HILDA DAILEY is Extension Specialist, Home Management, Extension Division, Virginia Polytechnic Institute and State University, Blacksburg.

help you make financial decisions in time of stress or opportunity.

There are several parts to a plan. These could be called steps but one step does not necessarily follow another. They need to be developed simultaneously. The plan consists of a list of your family goals and priorities; the amount of income your family has to use; a record of how income is now being used; a periodic evaluation of progress and review of goals.

A great deal of discussion and thought is needed before you write your spending plan. List the things you want or would like to do. Your children may have something to add. Your list will probably include both real needs and whimsical or fun items. The more definite you make your goals the easier you can achieve them.

Now decide which ones should receive highest priority. You can also begin listing the approximate cost and when you plan to reach each goal. It may be helpful to set up a timetable. It could include *soon* (within the next 3 months), this year, next year, 5 years from now, and 15 years from now.

The details of distant goals may be vague but you should start now making definite preparation for reaching them. A distant goal can also be clear cut. For example: "Saving for retirement" is vague but "Have $5,000 in a savings account by 1980" is a well-defined goal.

By setting up a time schedule and defining your goals as clearly as possible you will reach them faster and with less effort.

The next step in making a financial plan is to determine how much money you will have available to use to reach your goals. Most families find they can plan best in terms of a year. You may wish to begin with 6 months if this is your first plan.

Income may come from many sources. Include salary, wages, tips, net earnings from a business or farm, interest from savings accounts, dividends from investments, and extra money from odd jobs. Include earnings from all family members. A child may use his earn-ings as spending money, but it is contributing to family income.

Write down your total income and subtract income taxes. This is the amount to use in making your plan. If your income is irregular, determine the minimum amount and the maximum amount that you expect. Use the minimum to plan for needs and the most important wants. You can list in order the other priorities should your income go above the minimum you expect.

The next step is to find out how you are using your money now. Begin keeping a record of your expenditures and savings. Each month add the amounts you have spent for each category. The categories will vary from family to family but the more common ones are savings, food, clothing, household operation, tranportation, recreation, gifts, contributions, housing, personal development, medical care, and personal spending money.

Total the amount spent in each category for 3 months. This will give you an idea of what you will be spending on a yearly basis.

Now you can begin to make changes in your spending and savings to bring them in line with accomplishing your goals.

You can now set up your financial plan. Remember the plan includes your goals, income, and expenses.

Decide on the goal you will work toward first and decide how you can attain it. If the goal is to get out of debt, look for ways you can cut expenses or earn extra income to increase payment on debts. Or you may look for ways to avoid using credit until all bills are paid.

Your goal may be to purchase a certain item. Select the amount you will save each payday and consider it like any other bill you must pay.

This action in itself helps you to get the most value for your money. First it provides the cash to obtain the goal and second it helps stop the leaks in your spending. The $10 put in savings cannot be spent for "fuss and stuff."

Your goal may be to accumulate an

emergency fund. Every family needs one. First make a list of emergencies that you will plan to finance from this fund. They may include such expenses as equipment repairs, car repairs, small medical bills, unexpected necessary travel, or money to take advantage of an unexpected opportunity.

Now, decide on the amount you will need in this fund. Decide how much you will put into the fund each payday. If you need $300 you can put $10 a month into the fund and it will take you 30 months to reach your goal. But emergencies probably will not wait 30 months! You may not have enough in the fund to pay the total cost, but it's a beginning. That is better than taking the whole expense out of one pay check. Worst yet is having to borrow, because this would increase the initial cost.

Start with $1, $10, or an amount you will not really miss. You can increase the amount later. Trying to save too much is futile. You will be borrowing from yourself when you run short of cash.

Once you break your commitment, it is much easier to break it again and again. Saving a comfortable amount each payday is the secret. Think of your savings quota as a fixed cost like rent or an installment payment.

When you reach your stated amount, reward yourself. One idea is to use the next payment to treat yourself. The following payment can then be directed to another goal. Of course, when you must draw from this fund, begin replacing that amount on a monthly basis.

Another suggestion to include in your plan is preparation for irregular expenses that are a certainty—taxes, insurance premiums, licenses, organization dues, etc. Add the annual cost of these and divide by 12. Put that amount into a fund each month. You will have the money to meet the expenses when they are due. One of these probably will come due before you have accumulated sufficient money, but you will be further ahead than if the total bill had to be paid out of a single paycheck. Before the year is out you will be breaking even with the fund.

This method does away with the worry and scrimping to meet irregular bills.

Now you are ready to list the expenses that remain the same month after month. Yours may include rent or mortgage payments, installments, electric bills on the budget plan, music lessons, and pledges. They are considered fixed expenses.

After you list your savings and fixed expenses, you are ready for your day-to-day living expenses. Unless you have been keeping fairly accurate records you will need to estimate or wait until you kept records for a few months. These variable expenditures are usually for clothing, food, recreation, education, medical care, gifts, furnishings and equipment and household operation.

In making your plan, allow some leeway. Do not plan to use every dollar. You will not spend exactly the amount you plan. You will have some unexpected expenses. Prices change and sales occur, so do not try to balance every dollar. You do need some uncommitted dollars to make the plan work.

If your plan is too strict you will take all the fun out of managing money. Developing a financial plan and using it as a means to reaching goals is like a game. It is a challange to see how much you can do with the money you have to use.

For most people the less desirable aspect of the plan is keeping records. There are ways to simplify this activity.

Keep records simple. Set up your record sheet to show what you need to know about your family. For example, some families have one column for food. Some families set up a column for food at home and another for food away from home. Some families list all clothing in one column, and some list clothing for each member of the family separately. Make the record sheet fit your family.

You can ease the job of record keeping by designating one person to

	Last Year	Budget For This Year	Jan.	Feb.	March	April	May	June	July	August	Sept.	Oct.	Nov.	Dec.
Income:														
Fixed Expenses: Mortgage or Rent														
Insurance—Auto and other property														
Insurance—Life														
Taxes														
Licenses, Fees and Dues														
Installment payments														
Emergency Fund														
Day-to-Day Expenses: Food														
Clothing														
Personal Items														
Furnishings & Equipment														
Operating Expenses														
Auto and Transportation														
Medical and Dental														
Education														
Recreation														
Contributions														
Gifts and Miscellany														
Regular Savings or Plans for Special Events:														
TOTALS														

17

record the amounts spent and saved. Or one might read out the amount while another writes. Use a spindle to hold receipts or notations until you record them. Try putting grocery receipts together and record only the total for the month. If you decide to separate food items from other items bought at the grocery store, circle nonfood items and enter the total for those circled. Record pocket money, allowances, or "spending money" as such and do not try to account for every penny.

Time spent on keeping records will pay valuable returns. These could be equivalent to an extra job or a pay raise. Besides a planning aid, they are useful when you prepare your income tax form.

Monthly income and expenditures need not balance to the penny. Some months you may spend more than your monthly income. It is important that you balance income and outgo in the long run.

At the end of the year your income should equal your savings plus expenditures for the year. If you continually spend more income than you have, you are treading on dangerous ground.

Some professional managers have a term: cash flow accounting. It simply means keeping the amount of money coming in from every source roughly equal to the amount going out for every purpose (non-essentials and savings as well as essentials.)

The account is only a tool to use to show how you are actually using your money. Having this information helps you find a way to attain your goals. So the account is only a part, but a vital one, of your financial plan.

In the process of setting up your plan you have discovered that either your income covers expenses and savings, they are the same, or needs and wants are greater than income. If the income covers all needs and future goals, you have no problem. You may wish to consider uses for your surplus money.

More than likely your needs and wants are greater than your income.

Take a new look at each part of your plan.

Where are you spending money that is less important than some other expenditures? Decide what is least important, important, and most important. Now look for ways to trim each of the flexible categories—food, clothing, transportation, gifts.

You may consider:
• A less expensive item
• Saving to pay cash to avoid credit charges
• Doing maintenance jobs on your home, car
• Using community services, recreation, library
• Buying less clothing, recreation, transportation
• Creating gifts, recreation

Review savings and investments to increase return, or insurance to reduce cost. You may use one vacation for home projects, or daily trips; switch to a cheaper car; convert an endowment policy or a limited-pay policy to cheaper life insurance.

Look realistically at the way you are using your money now. Are the things you are buying really as important as the big things you want, such as getting on a cash basis, more security, or adequate income for retirement? A lot of money can slip away and rob us of many big pleasures.

If your income still does not cover your important needs and wants, you might consider ways to increase your income.

Finally, do not expect a plan to work perfectly. Your wants and needs change. New situations develop. Your plan should be evaluated every few months. You may give it a thorough evaluation at the end of a year. It is good to see how much progress you have made and where you hope to be financially at the end of the next 12 months.

Do not try to do too much too fast. Do not expect miracles! You will only become discouraged and give up the whole idea.

If the plan does not work, maybe it

needs to be changed or maybe you should try a little harder to make it work. Look for some solution. Use the plan to guide you but do not become a slave to it.

Several times, savings have been referred to as the tool for accomplishing future goals. After a family has decided on a savings plan, the decision on how to invest wisely must be made.

Life insurance is a way to provide immediate financial protection for the loss of income through the death of the breadwinner. Once children are expected, the need arises for life insurance. Life insurance is usually purchased to cover the cost of the funeral, the expenses of the last illness, and to provide income for the survivors.

In planning for this type of financial protection be sure to consider all resources the survivors will have to use (earning ability as well as financial), the amount of income that will meet necessities, and finally the cost of such a program. Concentrate insurance dollars on the breadwinner and buy the type of insurance that will give the most protection for the cost.

A saving account is the second leg of the stool for a savings program. It is here where a family keeps the money that it may need immediately or plans to use within the near future.

After the family protects itself with insurance for the survivors and a savings account, it is then ready to invest in other possible channels. At this point a family needs to consider these channels in line with its distant goals, and the economy.

As you evaluate these ways to invest, give the source a test.
1. How safe is the principal?
2. How much risk can you afford to take?
3. What income yield can you expect? Depend on?
4. In case the need arises, how fast and easily can you sell the security?
5. How much management and care does this investment require?

Life insurance, savings accounts, and Government bonds have fixed value. They lose buying power during inflationary periods. However, they should form the basis of a family's savings program.

Some family finance professionals strongly suggest that a family should have 2 to 6 months' income reserved for emergencies.

After this is accomplished, a family is ready to consider other types of investments.

In times of inflation, your home may be one of the best protections against inflation. Of course, home ownership is not for everyone and all homes do not appreciate. Some lose value. In the sequences of selecting investments, a home is often chosen after life insurance and savings accounts.

Common stock, variable annuities, and real estate—either in a growth area or rental property—are the best investments for protection against inflation. These are the ones that can appreciate, but of course you must select them carefully.

In addition to life insurance and savings accounts, other investments that are *not* good hedges against inflation include fixed annuities, municipal bonds, shares in a credit union, preferred stock, and corporate bonds.

A list of your goals, a record of savings, expenditures, and income, and a plan for reaching these goals make up your family's financial plan. Your plan will help you direct your dollars where they will give you the most value.

For further reading:

U.S. Department of Agriculture publications:

A Guide to Budgeting for the Family, Home and Garden Bulletin No. 108, Washington, D.C. 20250, 1970.

A Guide to Budgeting for the Retired Couple, Home and Garden Bulletin No. 194, Washington, D.C. 20250, 1971.

A Guide to Budgeting for the Young Couple, Home and Garden Bulletin No. 98, Washington, D.C. 20250, 1971.

Consumer Choices
In a Free Economy

IN A GAME based on it, you pass go and collect $200 so that some day you can live the good life by charging everyone who stops at your hotels. It brings you football via satellite, plenty of free parking, and instant Dutch chocolate breakfast.

It's the enterprise economy in which millions of business firms compete ultimately for your consumer dollars. The economy was created to serve consumers and cannot function without you. You need to actively and intelligently participate in it in order to improve its performance.

The enterprise economy is both a simple idea and a subject of great unnecessary mystery. Every American family consumes its products and services and most of them also earn all or part of their income from private business firms or producers. Many Americans fare well in the system, but the good life eludes others. There are many good selfish reasons to understand the basis of the trillion-dollar-plus economic machine as it affects you.

An economy's purpose is to produce goods and services so that members of the society can take care of their material wants, ranging from cola drinks to hospital insurance. Business enterprises use workers, managers, machinery, money, land, as well as the services and products of other organizations, to produce and deliver what consumers will accept. It's a system of money exchanges as producers must pay for all of their needs. The producers' payments become income for workers, managers, landowners, and the lenders and owners who supply much of the lump sums of money needed to operate a business. Some large companies need $100 million lumps at a time to finance their growth and improvements.

Producers and providers of services actually constitute a very complex set of enterprises. A few of them are government owned such as the Tennessee Valley Authority or the Postal Service. Machine tool companies and aircraft manufacturers are among those who sell only to government or private enterprises and not to consumers.

Goods sold to consumers are logically called consumer goods and all others are considered to be producer goods. Many enterprises make or manufacture neither producer nor consumer goods, but instead may distribute goods (such as retailers and wholesalers), store them (such as warehouses), finance them (such as banks) or just advertise them. Manufactured goods would have no value or usefulness if they were not shipped, financed, stored, or made known to other producers or consumers. These activities are necessary in the economy, but they also add to the costs and ultimately to the prices paid by consumers.

Money is especially important in a modern economy. You and every other consumer can testify to that when the cashier totals the tab at a restaurant or the rent comes due, but the need for money is even more basic.

If you were a farmer or painter also, you might be able to make payments in the form of turnips or by painting an office sometimes, but money is a simpler way to pay. Money is better as a medium of exchange or for making payments because it has an agreed upon value to both parties, it is a useful measure or standard of value, and it is a means of deferring payments until a later date (credit). Wouldn't you rather be paid in money than in rivets from a bridge you helped build, a supply of balloons you helped manufacture, or bushels of turnips you helped farm?

Money is important because producers need more money at times than their sales will generate. They use many

AUTHOR LEE RICHARDSON is Director for Consumer Education, Office of Consumer Affairs, Executive Office of the President.

financial institutions and individual sources for credit, as do consumers.

Producers borrow money from lending institutions and individuals and repay interest and the amount or principal of the loan. Sometimes, these loans are a special long term type called bonds, but they have to be repaid. Producer financing costs ultimately are borne by consumers in the prices that they pay.

Producing enterprises obtain money without promising to repay the original amount from owners, but owners share in the profits when and if they occur. Sometimes there are no profits because consumers stop buying products such as Edsels and Packards.

Money received for productive services is the starting point for most households to determine their future courses as consumers. However, there is money available to them as credit from banks, savings and loans associations, mutual savings banks, credit unions, consumer finance companies, and even other individuals who will lend, temporarily, some of theirs. American consumers owe several hundred billion dollars for homes, autos, vacations, educations, refrigerators, and cotton dresses. For the use of the money on credit for a few days or for a few decades, consumers pay billions of dollars each year in interest and other finance charges.

Consumer credit is important to virtually every household, yet, many consumers today have serious difficulties in using credit. Major mistakes can affect one's credit reputation and limit the ability to obtain needed credit in the future.

Financial institutions sometimes accept deposits which consist of money that consumers or producers, including governments, may not need to have physically in their possession. A check drawn on a deposit account in a bank has the effect of requiring the bank to transfer ownership of the money. Financial institutions accept deposits in other forms too, such as savings accounts for which they pay the savers interest or dividends.

Whether checking or savings accounts are the source of the money, the financial institutions invest or lend the money for purposes such as building bridges, buying fertilizer for turnip farmers, or financing a home.

An economy like the United States is quite complex in detail, but consumers, producer enterprises, and money are its central elements. An economy is always in motion as money, goods and services flow continuously in exchange between its participants. If consumers were to decide not to buy anything, the system would collapse as the desire for autos, vacations, and dresses ceased, workers became unemployed, and families with no income had to produce all of their needs themselves. Indeed as stated earlier, the economy was created to serve consumers and cannot function without them.

Consumers don't always share fully in the American dream of prosperity and security. Much of the problem arises out of the fact that some families do not receive adequate income.

In a complex, continuously moving, and changing economy, millions of Americans suffer from periods of unemployment, an inability to earn sufficient money for household needs, or other problems related to income. Low income quickly becomes a problem of insufficient goods and services to meet needs and wants.

Even the relatively prosperous family normally wants more goods and services than its income and credit allow. You need only consider all of the places you might go next weekend, all of the interesting products available at your favorite stores, or all of what you would like to present to loved ones, to verify that your own wants too are limited by income.

Low, medium, and high income families further limit themselves as they all make mistakes in spending their money. Sometimes the mistakes are serious and U.S. society is now turning its attention to consumer problems as never before. This new emphasis is often called consumerism and it emphasizes protective

21

490-100 O - 73 - 3

laws and education to help consumers.

Consumers have a responsibility to themselves, immediate family, and other persons in preventing and eliminating mistakes. A responsibility exists both to learn about and act upon possible mistakes in using unsafe toys, highly flammable materials, non-nutritious foods, and excessively expensive credit. The possibilities of problems are as extensive as the choices faced in selecting from among literally hundreds of thousands of products and services available to U. S. consumers.

The important principle for consumers is found in the expression "let the buyer beware," a warning which means that consumers are literally on their own. Consumerism will not change the basic need for consumers to make their choices intelligently, to use caution in any transaction, and to be resourceful in solving consumer problems.

Your mistakes in making consumer choices are your consumer losses and they have the same deadly effect on you as lower income. Consider the basic steps by which pennies and hundred dollar bills can be cared for and made to work harder to improve your standard of living.

Prevention is the best consumer cure. The consumer must take the responsibility to first determine objectives and plans. Some consumers allow producers to convince them that they need garbage disposals, asparagus, and a cure for dandruff without exercising critical judgment. You as a consumer should have a road map that determines the basic needs of food, housing, savings, transportation, emergencies, insurance, education, entertainment, etc. If this road map or budget can barely be met with the available income and credit, then there is simply no logical way to detour or take side trips for other expenditures.

Few consumers learn this lesson because few want to learn it.

A second way to improve consumer choice is to use good buying strategies and tactics to carry out the basic plan. Prices, quality, and convenience can vary greatly in buying food, auto insurance, or dandruff treatments. A watermelon is a better buy at certain times of the year because of transportation costs. A used car may be adequate for many purposes. A turnip is nutritious. Air conditioning may not be necessary every night in July.

The variety and choice available makes your personal consumer decision process complex, but the potential savings and improvements are huge compared to poor results from not shopping harder. A great deal of sorrow can be avoided by obtaining reliable information in consumer education courses, consumer magazines, numerous books and pamphlets from private and government sources, and the experiences of friends.

Unfair and deceptive practices of a few businesses would largely disappear if consumers practiced self-defense and refused to deal with disreputable companies. Such defense means being well-informed.

The consumer inevitably makes mistakes despite good plans, strategies, and tactics. Chemical products may cause injuries. A seller fails to deliver. A contractor uses poor workmanship. A repairman doesn't repair a faulty appliance. A turnip decays. Consumers can remedy some producer mistakes by notifying the conscientious sellers and others by reporting or taking action against the not so conscientious.

When the problem arises out of a mistaken use or misuse of the product, then the experience at least should teach prevention the next time.

As nothing is free in an economy, there are some items that become hidden costs for the consumers who ultimately pay all of the bills. Shoplifted cameras, coats, and razor blades are paid for by increased prices for other customers. Bruised, pinched bananas and other produce raise the costs for sellers and thus the prices for groceries. Carelessly unscrewed lids on baby food jars not only increase the costs through spoilage, but also can pose a serious health hazard. The consumer's demands for free carryout or delivery, no-interest credit cards, and other services are hidden in merchandise prices.

A complex economy requires consumers to actively participate in general economic affairs and the shaping of the many relationships between producers and government. Consumers elect the legislators who make the laws. Consumers should present their problems and views direct to producers as well as to government officials where needed. Consumers can assist in improving product safety, helping maintain reasonable prices, and raising the quality of goods not only by buying wisely, but by addressing themselves to economic and consumer problems.

It's a mutual responsibility among consumers to seek to maintain or restore competition among producers and to improve the ways in which producers make and sell their products and services.

And who knows? This may lead to a better turnip.

Are You a Sharp Consumer? Try This Check List

Nothing pleases the consumer more than the realization that a purchase has proved worthwhile. However, the tremendous assortment of products and services at the marketplace is causing perplexing problems for today's consumer. Of prime importance is the decision-making capability to use money for goods and services that provide maximum satisfaction.

Good decision making begins with a clear appraisal of the needs and wants of your family.

Ask yourself: What is important to us now and in the future? Do we have specific facts about the product or services we are considering? What order

of priority do we want to give these needs and wants?

Recognizing the difference between needs and wants and the conflicts they cause in the use of resources can help you set priorities. A need actually is a *lack of something* which, if allowed to continue, can harm the individual. For example, lack of proper food can result in physical illness. In contrast, wants are *desires for goods and services* we develop as we observe what others do and want.

Your values influence decisions which determine the actions you take as you manage your resources to obtain what you want in life. Values provide the force that makes people work toward goals. An understanding of your values provides a basis for setting goals for the use of all your resources.

The family or person that identifies values, sets goals, and plans the use of resources will achieve a balance of wants, needs, and resources.

Earning money is important, but how you use it is more important. Good shopping habits can help you increase your buying power to reach more goals with your money.

When making a decision about any major expenditure for goods or services you may be frustrated by the number of choices you have. This chapter incorporates a check list to help you be a more effective consumer.

Sometimes a purchase is disappointing because the item failed to live up to claims made about it. Take your complaint to the seller when this occurs. If he doesn't help, try the manufacturer or contact a consumer protection agency or organization.

Other times a product disappoints you because circumstances change. In our fast-moving society new information and products appear daily. At times you will prefer new products and features,

AUTHOR DORIS M. MYERS is a State home management specialist, Texas Agricultural Extension Service, Texas A&M University, College Station.

or you will find new facts which change your mind about the best product for you.

Accept these changes. Respect decisions you made yesterday—remember they were based on information and products available at the time. Be flexible with your decisions to allow for change.

Some buying decisions are more important than others.

To help you decide whether you need to spend time and effort, ask yourself these questions:

• How much money is involved?
• What risks are involved?
• Can you afford to make a mistake?
• What are the consequences if a mistake is made?
• How long will the consequences be felt?
• Is the purchase urgent?
• Can you do without it?

Major buying decisions concern purchases which involve a large amount of money, must last a long time, and are expected to give much service.

Make it a rule to "sleep on" a major purchase. The offer should be just as good the next day. The extra time and thought put into making decisions will pay off in satisfaction.

Minor buying decisions involve smaller amounts of money and usually have a shorter life expectancy.

Being an effective consumer in today's world involves time and energy, a willingness to seek information about products, as well as decision-making and money management skills. Manufacturers provide products to meet consumer demands.

Only by assuming the responsibility of planning, shopping carefully, and following manufacturers' instructions, can consumers continue to find quality products to meet family needs.

The kind of consumer you are today may well determine not only your economic prosperity but your economic survival as well.

Analyze family expenditures to see if a major purchase will fit into the family budget.

Check List for Effective Consumer Practices

Do you plan your purchases for a year or more in advance? (For example, purchases such as a car, carpeting, family health insurance?)
Yes ☐   No ☐

Do you set up a savings plan far enough in advance to pay cash or make a large down payment? (This practice allows you to buy when goods and services are on sale. Large down payments or cash purchases save paying interest.)
Yes ☐   No ☐

Have you considered a savings plan for items you will need to replace? (Few purchases can be made only once in a lifetime. By considering the life expectancy of major purchases, cash can be saved to replace them.)
Yes ☐   No ☐

Have you figured how these purchases fit into your overall plans for using family income? (Consider total family expenditures now and in the near future to be sure that all fixed expenditures can be met.)
Yes ☐   No ☐

Will this be a long-term or continuing expenditure? (For example, some life insurance policy premiums are paid until a certain age or through a lifetime. Expenditures such as a home improvement loan or home mortgage may be paid monthly for 5 to 30 years.)
Yes ☐   No ☐

Do you take into consideration what you have on hand before shopping? (By buying products that complement what you already own you can avoid disappointment and dissatisfaction. For example, a new lemon yellow refrigerator may make your old coppertone range look very out of place.)
Yes ☐   No ☐

Have you identified needs and wants before going to buy? (For example, you may need a car, but want the most expensive features.) Yes ☐   No ☐

Have you thought about taking care of *needs* first? (If wants will fit into the overall budget, they, too, can be satisfied. Buying choices made today affect the future choices you make. For example, buying a color television-record player-radio combination commits you to future expense for repairs and maintenance, possibly restricting choices in other areas of future spending.)
Yes ☐   No ☐

Have you determined the *real cost* of the item you choose to buy? (Real cost is what you have to give up or do without to afford this purchase. As you think about your needs, identify the requirements to satisfy them.)
Yes ☐   No ☐

Do you expect your purchase to last a long time? (Durable, high-quality products can be expected to last longer than poorly constructed, cheaper products.) Yes ☐   No ☐

Have you made a detailed list of all the features you expect to get? (Color, size, style, model, construction, durability, appearance, ease of use and care, safety features, and storage requirements.) Yes ☐   No ☐

Have you considered installation, operating and service costs? (Be certain that adequate, reasonably priced service will be available for equipment and other items. For instance, a car purchase is only a fraction of the total cost resulting from depreciation, maintenance and repair, and other operating expenses.) Yes ☐   No ☐

Have you rated the desired qualities and characteristics in order of importance to you? (This serves as a check when you shop. It helps you avoid impulse buying. Be willing to compromise on less important points when necessary.) Yes ☐   No ☐

Have you decided how much you have to spend? (Study the total spending for all family needs to see where you stand. The amount of money you have determines how many extra features, special characteristics, and perhaps the quality that you can afford. Be realistic in the amount of money you can spend.) Yes ☐   No ☐

Above, shopping for credit is important. Right, shopping for a car is a family affair. Below right, read and understand the warranty before buying a large appliance.

Will you use credit? (If credit, what type: 30-day charge account, revolving charge account, monthly installment plan, or personal loan to make cash payment?)   Yes ☐   No ☐

Will you pay cash? (Cash is usually the preferred method; however, credit lets you use the item while making payments.)   Yes ☐   No ☐

Is the item worth the interest cost you pay for credit? (It is easy to overbuy or to spend more than you can afford with use of credit. Assume no more debt than you can safely repay out of current income.)
    Yes ☐   No ☐

Have you taken enough time to shop for the right buy? (Shopping in a hurry may result in hard-to-live-with choices. Making last minute purchases can be an expensive habit. There are more than financial resources involved in making a purchase.) Yes ☐   No ☐

Do you shop when you are tired? (Shopping when you are fatigued, depressed, or not well physically may lead to poor choices, impulse buying, or overbuying.)   Yes ☐   No ☐

Do you have transportation to the marketplace? (Weigh the cost of travel against other features when you choose a place to buy. For major purchases, it may pay to travel considerable distances to find what you want. But beware of the "false economy" of traveling to three or more stores for a "special" at each. Yes ☐ No ☐

Do you have the knowledge and skill to be an intelligent consumer? (The more you know about prices, quality, advertising techniques, store reputations, brands, even plain arithmetic, the more you'll get for your money.) Yes ☐ No ☐

Do you study with care exactly what you need and how much you can spend? (Comparing costs of needs and your available money before shopping can help you avoid the temptation of impulse buying.) Yes ☐ No ☐

Have you pinpointed reliable dealers where you can shop and compare products? (Reliable dealers will stand behind the products and services they sell. Be careful about door-to-door salesmen who do not have a permanent address.) Yes ☐ No ☐

Have you gathered facts about the type product you want to buy? (The more you know about products, the more likely you will choose one that meets your needs.) Yes ☐ No ☐

Have you studied catalogs, labels, hangtags and booklets for descriptive information on features, use and care instructions, and cost of products? (They let you know what is available and provide the basis for making quality and cost comparisons between competing products.) Yes ☐ No ☐

Do you judge advertising by whether it appeals to your emotions or gives you facts concerning quality, performance, and use? Yes ☐ No ☐

Have you studied consumer information booklets and magazines and contacted resource people who can advise on the choices of goods and services? (Contact business firms, manufacturers, trade associations, independent testing agencies, and government units. The Federal Government has publications for sale. Your county extension agent has information to help you in making shopping decisions. The county agent can also direct you to other sources of help.) Yes ☐ No ☐

Have you discussed your future purchase with friends, neighbors, and other individuals who own similar products? (They can share their experiences with a particular item. Find out how often the item is used, whether it performs well, how long the owner has had it, and if services and parts are readily available. Yes ☐ No ☐

Have you studied the sales contract and warranty to learn what service can be expected from the product, the retailer, and the manufacturer? (When buying mechanical or electrical equipment, as well as many other products, the main concern is to find a product that will operate without trouble. Be sure you get a product that will wear well and, above all, one you can get repaired when needed.) Yes ☐ No ☐

Do you cull your choices to the few that best fit your needs? (Consider the pros and cons of each. Use your list of desired characteristics to help you decide which product combines the greatest number of features you need.) Yes ☐ No ☐

Do you compromise on your choices? (Accept the fact that whenever you decide to buy a particular item, you may have to give up something else you want. Be sure the total features, characteristics, and cost of the item you choose are more important than the products you give up.) Yes ☐ No ☐

Do you accept your decisions as the final word? (Sometimes the choices seem about evenly balanced. Questioning "what might have been" often leads to frustration and dissatisfaction. If you spend time and effort in making an important buying decision—then be confident the choice was right for you.) Yes ☐ No ☐

Have you learned anything that will help you with your next purchase? Yes ☐ No ☐

Some Pointers
About Nutrition

Everytime you eat something you make a nutrition decision. You accept or reject the food available to you at meals at home or when you "raid the icebox." Or you select food for yourself at the many places in the community where food can be purchased, such as supermarkets, drive-ins, restaurants, food counters in drug stores, and the like. Over time, these selections make a difference in how you look, feel, and how well you can work and play.

When a good assortment of food in appropriate amounts is selected and eaten, the consequences are more likely to be a desirable level of health and enough energy to allow you to be as active as you need and want to be. When choices are less than desirable, the consequences are likely to be impaired health or limited energy or both.

Studies of diets of individuals in the United States show that food selection is a highly individual matter, even among quite young children. Furthermore, far too many individuals of all ages are making poor choices day after day and are either now living with the consequences or one day they will be.

Nutritionists and workers in allied professions have, for many years, been concerned about helping people learn to select and enjoy a wide variety of food combinations that can add up to a good diet.

If asked, most of you would probably say you believe you are well fed—that the choices you make are good ones. After all, you are not really sick, neither are you hungry. Some of you may be a little sheepish about the extra poundage you are carrying around.

However, if further questions are asked, it usually adds up to the fact that you may be shorting yourself. Milk and milk products (cheeses, ice cream, buttermilk, yoghurt) are often slighted. Then you may skip many fruits and vegetables, particularly those that are good sources of vitamins A and C. These include dark green leafy vegetables and deep yellow ones (vitamin A), and citrus fruits and vegetables such as cabbage, tomatoes, green peppers (vitamin C).

Every American has the right to choose to be uninformed about nutrition as well as to be informed. If you believe that you are well fed, attitudes, habits, and information cannot be forced upon you, as likely as not.

There are life situations, however, that tend to cause you to want to know how to make the best choices. For example, you are leaving your parents' home and are setting up your own apartment. For the first time you are completely responsible for the household food supply. Some of you realize for the first time what a responsibility this really is, especially if you do not have unlimited funds.

You probably patronize a supermaket and are faced with literally thousands of choices. If you are not careful, you can easily overspend. Furthermore, although all your choices are perfectly good foods, no matter how you combine them, they may not add up to a well balanced diet that will help you be and do as you aspire. A food guide such as U.S. Department of Agriculture Leaflet 424, *Food for Fitness*, would help you make your choices. And USDA's Home and Garden Bulletin 183, *Your Money's Worth in Foods*, will help you get the most nutrition for your food dollar.

Now, you are to be a family. The first baby is coming and both young expectant parents are concerned that this new life they are bringing into the world have the best possible start.

AUTHOR MARY M. HILL is a nutritionist in the Consumer and Food Economics Research Institute, Agricultural Research Service.

A number of older people eat well-balanced meals, just as they did when they were younger.

Most of you are willing to seek and take advice on food selection at such a time.

During the first years of your child's life, many of his attitudes toward food and his food preferences are being established. Those around him regularly —whether parents, relatives, or baby-sitters—communicate their attitudes and their preferences whether they mean to or not.

This is a very important period because it is the time when the child is willing to taste anything, inedible as well as edible. This is the time to learn to enjoy a wide variety of foods, particularly those that in later years appear to be shunned.

Illness strikes! It may be any one of a number of diseases that require modifications in diet, such as a painful or discomforting allergy, diabetes, or a heart attack. These are often frightening situations and you will seek all the help you can get.

If as a young child you have learned to eat and enjoy a wide variety of foods, then you still have a good variety to choose from even when you have eliminated the "no no's" that your condition requires. On the other hand, if you have limited yourself to a relatively few favorite foods, now is the time to develop a spirit of adventure and at least taste foods you have previously rejected. Try it, you might like it!

Are you fighting the "battle of the bulge"? This means you know you are eating more energy-producing food than you are using up in activity, and you want to do something about it. If you are only about 10 to 15 pounds over your normal weight for your height and body frame, you can do something about it on your own. Usually, the best way is to cut down on calories (energy) and increase activity.

If you are more than 10 to 15 pounds overweight, you should consult your physician to learn whether you have other difficulties that should be checked or treated at the same time.

All persons throughout life need the same nutrients, but in varying amounts. This is true for young and old alike. We do not outgrow our need for nutrients as some older people seem to believe. Many older people eat as they have for years and are as healthy and active as ever.

Others are living in isolation and are much less active, may have physical problems which make food purchasing, food preparation, and even eating such monumental problems that it hardly seems worth the trouble. Many of these people want and need help and often do not know how to find it. USDA has developed a *Food Guide for Older Folk* that has much helpful information for

29

the elderly who are taking care of themselves, including recipes for one- and two-member families.

The plans for the further implementation of the *Older American Act* will attempt to seek out these people, provide some meals and sociability, and through its educational dimension will offer help not only in food selection but in purchasing, storing, and preparation.

Since food selection is such an individual matter, the homemaker cannot be held totally responsible for all the choices made by various family members especially since more and more choices are being made away from home and often without her knowledge.

I have indicated situations that tend to influence family members to want to learn more about nutrition. Unwilling students seldom learn very much.

Help in achieving nutritional health is available to patients through local hospitals, and to the public through State extension services and their county home economists. Helpful publications are available from the same sources and from the Office of Communication, U.S. Department of Agriculture; the U.S. Department of Health, Education, and Welfare; and such industry sponsored groups as the National Dairy Council, National Livestock and Meat Board, Cereal Institute, and Sunkist Growers, to name a few.

Everyone needs to know how to select food wisely. Some of you may want to know why these selections are important to you. You can get lists of recommended reading from State extension services, State health departments, and local colleges and universities as well as government agencies. Many evening classes in adult education in nutrition are available in local high schools, community colleges, and universities.

With family members, even quite young ones, going in all directions and more and more food being eaten away from home, just what can parents do to help themselves and their children eat and enjoy a good assortment of foods in appropriate amounts?

First, they can make a good assortment of foods available in the home. One way to do this is to follow a reliable food guide such as USDA Leaflet 424, *Food for Fitness—a daily food guide*, mentioned earlier, which groups foods according to similarity in nutrient value.

Children can hardly be expected to eat foods that a parent or other family member refuses even to taste. Parents can set an example and expect children to at least taste foods each time they are served.

Day care facilities should be chosen with care. Parents need to investigate the variety of foods served and the experiences that are provided to help children learn to enjoy food.

Then children can be encouraged to at least taste all the foods served in day care and school feeding situations. These are excellent places for young children to extend the variety of foods they will eat. One of the big problems in school feeding has been that parents have not always realized that new or unfamiliar foods were served for this purpose.

Since we know that milk and milk products and fruits and vegetables are the nutrient sources most likely to be passed over as snacks in away from home eating, they should be emphasized at home. Cheese, raw vegetables, and fruits that can be eaten out of hand are good choices when youngsters are on the run. Milk, ice milk, ice cream, and cereals make good "sit down" snacks. Carbonated beverages should at least be limited in the home.

Parents can concern themselves with the curriculums in the schools their children attend. Sequential programs in nutrition education throughout the school career have an excellent potential for improving nutrition decisions of family members.

Well-conceived educational experiences for young children can:
• Influence the development of wholesome attitudes toward food and a willingness to taste new or unfamiliar foods
• Help extend the variety of foods that

30

Above left, elementary students try out tacos as part of a nutrition program. Right, toddler enjoys learning to eat. Left, snacking in a day care center.

children will eat and thus help develop good food practices
• Help them identify and report the foods they eat
• Lay the foundation for an understanding of the relation of food to health

Well-conceived educational experiences for older children can:
1. Help to maintain wholesome attitudes toward food
2. Continue to help develop and maintain good food practices
3. Help children discover for themselves that food makes a difference in health and performance
4. Help children differentiate among the various nutrients and begin to understand their functions and sources

In the secondary schools, nutrition experiences can be included in health, science, biology, and chemistry courses as well as in home economics. Here the earlier work can be reviewed, enriched, and given added depth so that students completing the program will have the facts upon which to make judgments for themselves. They will make their choices, good or bad, knowing what they are doing and what they might expect the consequences to be.

They will know that food is good, that it contains nutrients which perform certain functions in the body, and what kinds of food and what quantities are appropriate for various family members. They will also know that food *per se* has no magic or spiritual qualities.

Few school systems in the United States today provide such a curriculum, although its effectiveness has been amply demonstrated. Parents should at least voice their concern so that the nutrition decisions of family members in generations to come will not be a matter of whim or of uninformed persuasion.

Special Problems
Of Families: How
To Obtain Help

WHEN THE FAMILY HOME catches on fire, call your local fire department for help.

When somebody tries to break into your home in the middle of the night, call your local police department.

When the electricity line into your home is knocked down by a falling tree or an ice storm, call your local utility company.

All of these situations are common, at some time, to most American families. And there is a common place to turn for help in any community.

But other troubles can hit any family in the United States—at anytime—and there is no common place to turn for help when a family cannot help itself. The help may be there, but it is hard to find, hard to give it a name, and sometimes not available to all persons in the community.

In addition, the help or service may exist in one community and not another. It may be called one thing in one place and have another name in the next county. In some localities, the help or service is provided by public agencies; in others, by private or voluntary organizations, or all three.

For instance:

• Where do you go for outside help if your husband deserts your family and leaves you to feed the kids and pay the bills from an empty bank account?

• Where do you go for help if your wife is suddenly hospitalized for a serious mental illness and there is nobody to take care of the children while you work as a traveling salesman?

• Where do you go for help if you are a 14-year-old with parents who refuse to let you do your thing and make your life intolerable, so you decide to leave

home and go on your own in a nearby city?

• Where do you go if you realize that your neighbor is beating and neglecting her child?

• Where do you go if your son admits he is on drugs and is willing to accept outside help since he is convinced you can't help him?

When families have troubles like these—bigger troubles than they can handle themselves or through their own economic resources—they DO have somewhere to turn for help. Varying from community to community, from State to State, there is, first of all, a wide variety of public agencies where troubled families can receive the services they need.

This public—or governmental—system of providing help to individuals and families unable to meet their own problems grew out of earlier development of private (or voluntary) organizations in the 18th and 19th centuries, such as church bodies and fraternal organizations which began to help their members meet special needs. The services they supplied ranged from operating insurance organizations to providing baskets for the poor to operating day camps for the children of poor urban families.

Along with growth of such voluntary services, certain basic needs were met by designated public bodies. Provision of bed and food for the destitute ("the poor farm"), of a free burial for the deceased, of free medical services at the municipal or county hospital . . . all of these public services paralleled the growth of voluntary ones.

The big change came with the explosive effects of the Great Depression on many families. By the early 1930's, America was filled with over 15 million persons unemployed and with thou-

AUTHOR WALTER J. ANGRIST is Director of the Office of Public Affairs for the Community Services Administration, Social and Rehabilitation Service, Department of Health, Education, and Welfare.

sands in a state of semi-starvation. Private and voluntary service organizations just could not handle the flood of persons in need of help. Local and State public agencies assumed the burden, but also began to crack under the financial strain of just helping to meet the barest needs of individuals and families.

Out of that kind of escalation came Federal intervention—in the form of the "Social Security Act of 1935."

Contrary to popular belief, this law did much more than provide the beginning of a nationwide annuity or insurance base for those who work, contribute, and then reach retirement age. Provision also was made in the law for cash assistance payments to destitute families with children—and also for certain services in behalf of all children in need of protection. Later amendments to that Act—particularly in the sixties—added Federal financial support for State-rendered social services to those in need.

Since 1935, Congress has made hundreds of changes and additions to the Act as the Federal-State welfare system gradually developed out of the original dependent children "afterthought" included with the original Social Security legislation. Today, the Act takes up 1,456 printed pages!

While each State operates its own public social services system under the Social Security Act, it receives Federal funds to help pay the costs each year. Each State, if it desires, can include services supported by Federal funding provided under other legislation. Or it can operate completely separate agencies for different groups of people needing the same services.

This system—of providing help in the form of services—really is a nonsystem. There is variation, from State to State, on who is eligible for free help (by right of low income, for instance) and there is no pattern among States on what if any fee system should be available for those who can afford to pay for the services. There also is the aggravating problem of a particular public service available in a State or county just to those who are destitute, while other public services are available for all who seek them, without regard for income. Here is the way the list of social services is split between special income eligibility and eligibility for all:

For the poor

Day care for children of eligible mothers who desire to work or who must seek work in order to retain their income maintenance cash grant.

Homemaker services, when the mother is ill or hospitalized, or otherwise unable to take care of her family.

Homemaker services for the elderly and the permanently disabled.

Family planning services.

Services to help prevent births out of wedlock.

Protection services for the elderly who are too feeble to manage their own personal affairs.

Foster care for the elderly unable to continue in their own homes but not requiring institutionalization.

Special services to the blind.

Home-delivered hot meals services, primarily for the elderly.

For all

Information and referral services (helping people to find the service they need in their community).

Child welfare services, including protective services for children who are abused and/or neglected by their parents (or others).

Care for homeless children.

Adoption and foster home services for children (when they can no longer be properly cared for by their parents, or due to the death of parents).

Temporary shelter services for runaway and delinquent children.

The entire range of public social services, when a major disaster strikes a community, to all families with children without regard for income eligibility, during the period of crisis.

Each State differs in determining exactly who is eligible for free public social services and each State offers a different total list of services. Despite that patchwork quilt arrangement, the Social Security Act is the social service base for the Nation, with the Federal Government paying a major share of the States' costs.

Additional Federal-State services are funded and provided under other Federal legislation, such as special service programs for the elderly under the Older Americans Act and services to the disabled under the Vocational Rehabilitation Act.

Besides the public system in your community, your county, and your State, there also is some—if not a great amount—of available help from another system. That, too, is a nonsystem called the "voluntary" sector. Within that grouping are such familiar organizations—supported through individual donations and gifts, plus fees—as the Boy and Girl Scouts, YMCA, YWCA, Family and Children's Service, Red Cross, Senior Citizen Service Center, Legal Aid Society, the Travelers Aid Society, and many more.

Along with those familiar service agencies, there also may be a number of specialized organizations that are less visible. These may offer special services to alcoholics, young unmarried pregnant women, drug addicts, etc. Depending on location, there also may be installations of the Veterans Administration, the Social Security Administration, and other Federal agencies which provide services to special groups.

And then there is a third nonsystem of organizations providing a variety of services either to member groups or to all who need and seek them. These include the church-related social agencies, the ethnic and fraternal groups, the community service clubs (such as the Kiwanis, Rotary, Lions), along with loosely knit neighborhood groups and associations. All provide some kinds of services to families in trouble.

Now, how do you find help, when you require it, in YOUR community,

assuming that you or your family just cannot meet your own needs or solve your own problems?

It's not easy, but it can be done. Most Americans, in most communities, can find most of the kinds of help they may need within their local area. But in the face of the intricate "nonsystem" described above, where do you start?

In just about every city in the Nation, there is a classified phone directory called the "Yellow Pages" and if any public, voluntary, or private (for profit) services agencies exist, they will be listed under the heading: "Social Service Organizations."

Using the Washington, D.C., directory as an example, the organizations under this heading number in the hundreds and range from Big Brothers of the National Capital Area Inc., through Family Service, to Young Adult Rehabilitation Council. In your phone book there may only be four agencies listed where you can call for help, or there may be 400. The longer the list, unfortunately, the more difficult it is to decide from organization names which one can help you with your particular problem.

Strangely enough, the best place to call or see is your county or local public welfare office (in some areas called social services or public assistance), whether you can or cannot afford to pay for the help you need. Under the Social Security Act, all Federally-funded local welfare agencies provide information and referral services without regard for welfare eligibility by reason of poverty, et cetera.

If you don't want to call the welfare office, the yellow pages can still prove useful.

Here's the way it might work, assuming you no longer can cope with feeding the children and keeping them in line and managing to run your home as a working mother without a husband in the house. In addition, suppose you need special help with your teenager. She refuses to come home in the evenings at a set time and you are convinced she is in bad company.

34

You look in the phone book under "Social Service Organizations" and you spot a listing for *Family and Children's Service* (perhaps it is called "Community Child Welfare Agency" or some similar name).

Upon explaining your problem and asking for help, you are told that this agency only serves those with an income level far below your own. But the agency refers you to, say, Lutheran Social Services, which provides counseling and other services to families with children without regard for income. An early appointment is made for you and professional help is waiting.

After you meet with the agency, you may find that they also want to bring in your daughter's school guidance counselor. And they also may help you to involve her in a teen club that carries out community service projects during the weekends. Finally, the agency may be able to locate part-time, daytime homemaker help to ease your overall burden.

But suppose you drew a blank after a half-dozen trial-and-error phone calls. Where else to turn?

If you are church affiliated, your minister or priest is one of the best informed professionals in town, when it comes to helping you find the social service help you need. (Even if you do not have a church affiliation, he will be glad to help.)

Others in the community who will be able to point you in the right direction include such persons and organizations as lawyers or a legal aid society, county agents in rural areas, the mayor's office, local police (or the sheriff's office), the labor union office (if you are a member-family), the family doctor, your insurance agent, the United Fund (or the Community Chest, Red Feather) agency.

Just a word about a very special problem: the problem of where a non-English-speaking person or family can be sent for help. Because of the increasing awareness of such a problem, a number of self-help organizations have recently come into existence in communities where there are a recognizable number of ethnic minorities. These groups may or may not be affiliated with so-called "language churches." In either case, the community generally will know of such groups and you can refer such problems to them. Where no such organizations exist, city hall or local police may be the best way to find a bilingual person in the community who can help.

Sometimes, the best referral agent is as close as the home down the block—if a neighbor has experienced a problem similar to yours.

Most communities can help meet most of the special crisis needs of a family if and when it has exhausted its own capabilities without success. The system of help—social service—is truly a nonsystem made up of a wide variety of public, voluntary, and private organizations where help may be found. The best first step is a call to the nearest public welfare agency, where information and referral services are available to all. The phone book is the next best step.

Along with the Federal-State services system, many counties and cities provide additional services at the local level. These might include mental health centers, crisis intervention units in public hospitals, police intervention in family arguments, special court services for juvenile delinquents, and school district social workers and guidance counselors.

Safety in the Home: Guarding Against Falls, Fires, and Other Hazards

ACCIDENTS are the major cause of death for all young people under 35 and the fourth most frequent cause of death for all age groups in this country —fourth only to heart disease, cancer, and stroke. Each year some 115,000 Americans lose their lives in accidents, over 400,000 are permanently crippled, and at least 11 million are disabled for a day or longer.

Each year about 55,000 of our fellow citizens lose their lives and 2 million suffer disabling injuries in traffic accidents. Over 14,000 meet death and 2.3 million are seriously maimed in accidents at work. And 28,000 deaths and over 4 million serious injuries result from accidents in the home.

Did you notice from the above statistics that nearly as many people are injured from accidents in the home as from traffic accidents and work accidents combined?

Statistically, by far the most common types of home accidents are falls. Each year over 10,500 Americans meet death in this way, within the four walls of their home, or in yards around their house. Nine out of 10 of the victims are over 65, but people of all ages experience serious injuries as a result of home falls. It is impossible to estimate how many injuries result from falls, but they must run into the millions.

Falls can be a problem for all ages. In the process of growing up, children or teenagers often will fall. Fortunately their bodies are supple, so they may suffer only skinned knees, bumps, and bruises. But in an older person, the same fall may cause a broken arm, leg, and hip or other injury that requires hospitalization or medical care. As you get older you may not fall any more often, but the results usually are more serious and may even be fatal.

Preschool children are often killed by falls from open windows and porches when their normal curiosity and the urge to climb lead them to dangerous exploration. Therefore, it is a parent's responsibility to keep small children away from stairways, open windows and porch railing; and to install gates, bars, and other means of protection whenever possible.

Adults fall because they don't look where they're going, are in a hurry, careless, or thinking about something else. Running or taking two steps at a time invites falls. Perhaps you're guilty of trying to save an extra trip up the stairs by loading your arms with bundles or boxes that keep you from seeing where you are going. You may find it's safer to make an extra trip.

It is difficult for anyone to see in the dark, yet many persons try to get around their home without the use of lights. In the dark anyone can forget the coffee table in the middle of the living room, the last step on the stairs, the small rug near the bed, or the toy left on the steps. Other causes of falls are water and grease spots on the floor; toys or boxes on the stairs; extension cords, hairpins or paper clips on the floor; a torn place in the linoleum or loose throw rugs on the floor.

Also, the bathroom's combination of water, soap, and slippery surfaces creates special hazards for all ages. A few inexpensive items such as a suction-type rubber mat or saftey strips in the tub, a non-slip mat on the floor, and bathtub handholds can go a long way toward eliminating falls in the bathroom.

The death and injury toll from falls is highest during the fall and winter months as wet leaves, water, sleet, snow or ice on the steps and sidewalks are particular hazards. A fall on the same

AUTHOR PHIL DYKSTRA is Manager, Home Department, National Safety Council.

level can be just as dangerous as a fall down the stairs or from a higher level. The second major cause of home deaths is fires. Over 6,000 such deaths are reported each year; nearly half of those who die are 65 and over, or young children under 4. Add to that an estimated 250,000 disabling injuries. The International Association of Fire Chiefs report that fires strike an average of 1,500 homes every day, or over half a million homes per year.

property damage becomes severe, the toxic gases released by a fire can wipe out a family. A cigarette or match dropped on bedding or upholstery will produce gases which may bring about unconsciousness or cause death by suffocation before the smoldering materials can even burst into flame.

A great number of fires in the home are caused by carelessness or such

---

Occupational Safety And Health Act

ROBERT O. GILDEN [*]

THE 1970's BROUGHT A NEW dimension to the working places and the farms of America. The reason: enactment of the Occupational Safety and Health Act (OSHA) of 1970 "to assure so far as possible every working man and woman in the Nation safe and healthful working conditions and to preserve our human resources."

The act applies to employers engaged in a business that affects interstate commerce. This includes farmers who employ one or more workers at any time during the year, but excludes the immediate family.

To assure compliance with the act, a national consensus of work safety and health standards has been developed and inspectors employed. Citations of non-compliance may be issued and penalties imposed. Recordkeeping and reporting have been required.

Administration of the act has been the responsibility of the Department of Labor. The National Institute of Occupational Safety and Health of the Department of Health, Education, and Welfare is charged with determining safe health standards. State governments are being encouraged to

set up and enforce their own safety standards, providing their plans meet Federal qualifications.

Because agriculture was not represented in the development of most national safety standards and because of the different types of working conditions found in agriculture, only four safety standards were initially applied: Sanitation in Temporary Labor Camps, Storage and Handling of Anhydrous Ammonia, Pulpwood Logging, and Slow-Moving Vehicle Emblem.

Currently committees are setting up additional standards for agriculture. These will be issued only after hearings to which the public may respond. Standards under development are: Organophosphate Insecticides, Roll-over Protection for Agricultural Tractors, Housing for Temporary Occupancy by Agricultural Employees, and Guarding of Equipment.

As one looks at the accident statistics in agriculture, standards in respect to personal protective equipment, noise, dusts, tools, working surfaces, petroleum, electrical and livestock handling will be under consideration.

Safer and healthier working conditions are on the way throughout America.

---

[*] Executive secretary, National Advisory Committee—Safety in Agriculture.

---

age of 1,500 homes every day, or over half a million homes per year.

Leading causes of home fires are: combustible materials too close to fires, falling asleep while smoking, starting fires with flammable liquids, and defective heating or electrical equipment.

Of those that die from home fires each year, many are the result of burns and panic, but most are caused by deadly smoke and gases. Even before

thoughtless acts as tossing away a lighted match or cigarette, allowing rubbish to accumulate, overloading electrical wires, improper storage of flammable liquids, or misuse of heating and cooking equipment.

Few families go to bed at night without first checking to make sure that the doors and windows are locked, but overlook a very basic fire safety rule— sleep with your bedroom doors closed.

37

Nighttime fires are the most serious because the family is asleep and the discovery of fire is usually delayed. The design of most homes is such that fire-produced gases can easily reach the bedrooms where your family is sleeping and cause death before the flames travel that far.

A closed bedroom door gives you extra protection by delaying the gases and fire, thus giving you a few extra minutes to escape.

At the first sign of fire in a home, it is essential for everyone to get out of the house, particularly children and elderly persons who may need assistance.

Not everyone instinctively flees from a burning home: children often panic and hide in closets or under beds. Being prepared or knowing what to do in case fire breaks out can mean the difference between life and death. Assemble all members of your family and go over these procedures:

• Make sure everyone sleeps with his bedroom door closed.

• Draw out a floor plan of your home. Mark an escape route and an alternate route from each room in the house. Very young children and elderly persons should receive careful consideration when mapping out family escape plans. Both groups will need special assistance in escaping from home fires.

• Agree on a way in which any member of the family can sound an alarm. It is likely that fire may block hallways and prevent you from reaching other bedrooms. Pound on a wall, yell, use a whistle or any other method that will awaken members of the family who are asleep.

• Instruct family members not to waste time getting dressed or collecting prized possessions. Speed is essential in escaping from fire.

• Make sure that every family member knows how to test a door. If the panels or knob are warm, keep the door closed and use an alternate escape route. If not, brace foot and hip against the door and open cautiously to prevent super-heated air from blowing it open.

If no hot air or smoke greets you, it is probably safe to pass through.

• If you are forced to remain in a room, stay near a slightly opened window. Place towels or cloths in the door-cracks. To reach the other side of a smoke-filled room, crawl with your head about 18 inches above the floor.

• Decide on a meeting place outside the house where everyone will assemble as soon as they are outside.

• Call the fire department once everyone is out of the house. Use a neighbor's phone or a call alarm box. Speak clearly and plainly, making sure you give your full name and address.

• Hold a practice drill once you have set up escape routes, and then repeat drills periodically.

About 2,000 deaths and over 100,000 disabling injuries each year are the result of clothing fires. The most frequent victims of clothing fires are children and elderly people. Children are burned when their clothing is ignited by matches or cigarette lighters, stoves and heaters, or outdoor fires. Adults set their clothes on fire using stoves carelessly, warming themselves at fireplaces or heaters, or falling asleep smoking.

Medium and heavy weight smooth fabrics, fabrics that burn slowly, or fabrics that are flame retardant or treated with a permanent flame retardant finish are wise choices when selecting clothing or decorating fabrics.

Close fitting garments are less hazardous from a fire standpoint than loose fitting ones. Flowing robes, flaring skirts, blousy sleeves, and ruffles and frills on garments are more likely to be ignited in situations involving careless use of fire. Therefore, garments worn by men and boys are usually safer than those worn by girls and women.

Another major cause of accidental home fatalities and injuries is poisoning. Each year nearly 2,000 individuals die from poisoning; over 200 of them are children under 5. It is estimated that over 800,000 non-fatal accidental poisonings occur each year, one-third of which involve youngsters under 5. Most of these accidents are caused by

Aspirin is a frequent cause of poisoning of young people.

swallowing such common household products as medicines, bleaches, solvents, insecticides and cleaners.

Points to remember:

• Keep all household products in their original containers.

• Read the label each time medicine is taken; follow directions implicitly.

• Take only medicines prescribed for you; give others only those medicines prescribed for them and in the exact quantity prescribed.

• Give and take medicine only in a well-lighted room—never in the dark.

• Avoid taking medicines in front of children. Children tend to imitate their parents; they like to try what they see other members of the family doing.

• Always call medicines by their proper names. Most children have a craving for sweets. In their inexperience, it is easy for them to mistake medicine and other harmful substances found in the kitchen, bathroom, or yard, for something good to eat. This is particularly so when the parents, in order to persuade their children to take needed medicines, refer to the drugs as "candy."

One simple rule to prevent children from being harmed is to keep poisons out of their reach. Your own best

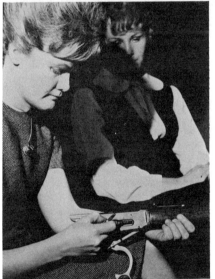

Top, guns, bows, and arrows locked up in a cabinet. Ammunition is stored separately, in a locked drawer. Above, keep guns pointed in a safe direction, and make sure guns in the home are unloaded.

means of preventing poisoning accidents is to read the label and follow directions.

The problem of firearm safety in the home is especially difficult because

39

most people are not aware it is a problem. They accept the fact that safety should be taught to those in the hunting field and to people handling guns on a range, but not in the home where there is no intention to discharge a firearm.

Annually, more firearms accidents occur in the home than occur in the hunting field, on a range, and all other places combined. A Metropolitan Life Insurance Company statistical bulletin listed 173 firearm fatalities in the home. Forty-nine of these fatalities occurred while playing with a gun, 25 while examining or demonstrating, and 22 while cleaning and repairing. All of these fatalities could have been avoided if the guns had been unloaded before being brought into the home and the ammunition and guns stored in separate places.

Other points of gun safety which are important:
• Treat every gun as if it were loaded.
• Keep the gun pointed in a safe direction.
• Keep guns in a locked rack or cabinet, and ammunition in a locked drawer.

Pools are another prime cause of accidents. Over 13 million families in this country own either an in-ground, above-ground, or wading pool. Each year over 700 persons drown in home accidents, and at least 230 of these deaths are in home swimming and wading pools. You may say "That doesn't concern me since I don't have a pool at home"; however, about one-third of the victims drowned in a neighbor's pool.

Drowning accidents need never happen; they could be prevented in nearly all cases. To prevent these accidents involves action of several types: first of all, making sure there is adequate physical protection for your backyard water areas; secondly, providing qualified supervision for children; and thirdly, making sure all family members learn to swim and know some basic rescue techniques.

Although fencing or other physical barriers won't prevent all accidents, a fence that can't be hurdled or easily climbed should be constructed around all types of pools. Some fences are easy to climb, such as a horizontal basket weave fence, and are no deterrent for curious, energetic children. Gates and doors should have self-closing and self-latching mechanisms placed out of reach of children.

Other supplementary protection devices and safeguards are such items as pool covers, alarm systems to warn of intruders in the water, floatlines, depth markings, rescue devices and, in general, a well-designed pool.

Qualified and constant supervision is another factor needed to prevent home drownings, especially for children under 5 and non-swimmers. A trip to answer the phone, to fix a snack in the

Thousands of families enjoy backyard pools, but many drownings occur when safety measures are not observed.

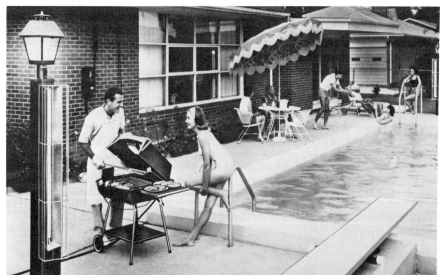

kitchen, or a friendly chat with the neighbor across the fence is enough time for anyone to drown.

When pools are not in use, their gates should be locked. Small plastic pools should be emptied and turned over. Even a few inches of collected rain water in one of these pools could cause a drowning.

This by no means covers all the myriad of accidents which may, and do, occur in the homes of this nation. We American are very ingenious when it comes to ways of maiming ourselves—even in the so-called safety of our homes. However, we have tried to cover some of the major types of injuries which show up in accident reports most frequently.

What about *your* home? Is it really safe? Don't wait until an accident happens. Start your own safety campaign right away. Make a survey for danger spots. Brief your family in safety rules. Equip your home with a first-aid kit and learn how to use it. Guard yourself and your family against the sudden, unexpected, painful, and often fatal accidents that happen at home.

Live safely—and you'll give yourself a good chance to live longer.

Safe Handling Of Food, and Home Storage

Safe handling of foods in the home should be of prime concern to homemakers. Foods that are handled improperly can cause illness even though they were safe to eat when purchased or first prepared. You should be aware of the danger and know how to keep food wholesome.

Foods can become unsafe due to the growth of bacteria, which are widely distributed in the soil, water, and air. However, not all bacteria are harmful.

Bacteria grow rapidly when provided with the right surroundings—food, moisture, and warmth.

"Food poisoning" includes both true food poisoning and bacterial food infections. True bacterial food poisoning is caused by a poison, or toxin, which is released into the food or is formed in the intestine by some bacteria. In bacterial food infection, disease-producing bacteria enter the body in contaminated food and set up infections in the digestive tract or bloodstream after having been swallowed.

In both situations, a large number of bacteria must be present in the food to cause illness. Large numbers of bacteria in food mean that the food has been mishandled through contamination or holding the food at improper temperatures. Contamination can be a result of poor sanitary habits in food preparation.

One kind of food infection results from eating food in which large numbers of Salmonellae bacteria are growing. The toxin of the bacterium *Staphylococcus aureus* produces staphylococcus poisoning. Perfringens food poisoning is due to the bacterium *Clostridium perfringens* which forms a toxin in the intestine. Botulism is caused by one of the most powerful poisons, the toxin of the bacterium *Clostridium botulinum*.

Salmonella infection and staphylococcus poisoning are characterized by a number of symptoms including nausea, vomiting, diarrhea, and abdominal cramps. In perfringens poisoning all the above symptoms may be present with the exception of vomiting. The toxin of *Clostridium botulinum* attacks the nervous system and often causes death because the person cannot breathe properly. Other symptoms include double vision, inability to swallow, speech difficulty, and progressive respiratory paralysis.

AUTHOR CAROLE A. DAVIS is a home economist, Consumer Use of Foods Staff, Consumer and Food Economics Institute, Agricultural Research Service.

Foods most frequently involved in Salmonella food infection and perfringens food poisoning are meats, poultry, fish, and foods kept for several hours in the temperature zone of rapid bacterial growth, 60°–120°F.

Custard or cream-filled baked goods, poultry, poultry dressing and gravy, meat sandwiches, meat salads, and dairy products are foods commonly associated with staphylococcus poisoning.

Low or medium acid canned vegetables, fruits, meats, sausage and fish may be involved with botulism. Danger signs in cans are bulging lids, off-odor, leakage, or contents bubbly and spurting out on opening the can.

Food from containers showing any signs of spoilage should be discarded immediately without tasting.

You can help protect your family from foodborne illness by—
• Stressing personal hygiene for all members of your household
• Making sure all dishes, utensils, kitchen equipment, and work surfaces are clean
• Taking simple precautions in storing, preparing, cooking and preserving food

Strict cleanliness of person and surroundings is the best way to prevent the contamination of foods and the spread of foodborne illness in the home. A household member who has an infectious disease or infected cut or skin infection should be discouraged from handling, preparing, or serving food.

Keeping foods cold inhibits bacterial growth and toxin production. Generally, prompt cooling and proper refrigeration of foods can hold the number of bacteria in foods to a safe level and no ill effects follow. The hazard lies in holding foods for any length of time above refrigeration temperatures and below serving temperatures of hot food. For further information, see the food temperature guide.

Certain foods need special care. Always hold uncooked and cooked foods containing eggs in the refrigerator. If eggs are cracked, or unpasteurized frozen or dried, be sure to use them only in products that are to be thoroughly cooked. Store unfrozen raw meat, poultry, and fish in the refrigerator.

Thaw frozen raw meat or unstuffed raw poultry in the refrigerator or immerse the package in its watertight wrapper in cold water. Thaw until meat is pliable. Stuff fresh or thawed meat, poultry, or fish just before roasting.

Directions on the package of all prepared or partially prepared frozen foods should be followed exactly. Heating the specified time helps to assure that the food will be safe to eat.

Keep hot foods hot, above 140°F., and cold foods cold, below 40°F. Food may not be safe to eat if held for more than 3 or 4 hours at temperatures between 60° and 120°F., the zone where bacteria grow rapidly. This includes all time during preparation, storage, and serving. Some bacterial growth may occur between 40°–60°F. and 120°–140°F.

Serve hot foods soon after cooking or refrigerate promptly. Freeze cooked food to be kept for more than a few days. Heat leftovers thoroughly before serving.

Maintain strict sanitation in preparing food for the home freezer. Keep all food to be frozen—and everything that touches it—clean.

Home canned vegetables, meat and poultry may contain the toxin that causes botulism if improperly processed. A steam-pressure canner must be used to can meat, poultry, and vegetables, except tomatoes. A boiling-water-bath

Before using a pressure canner, check carefully to be sure it is in good working order.

TEMPERATURE OF FOOD
for control of bacteria

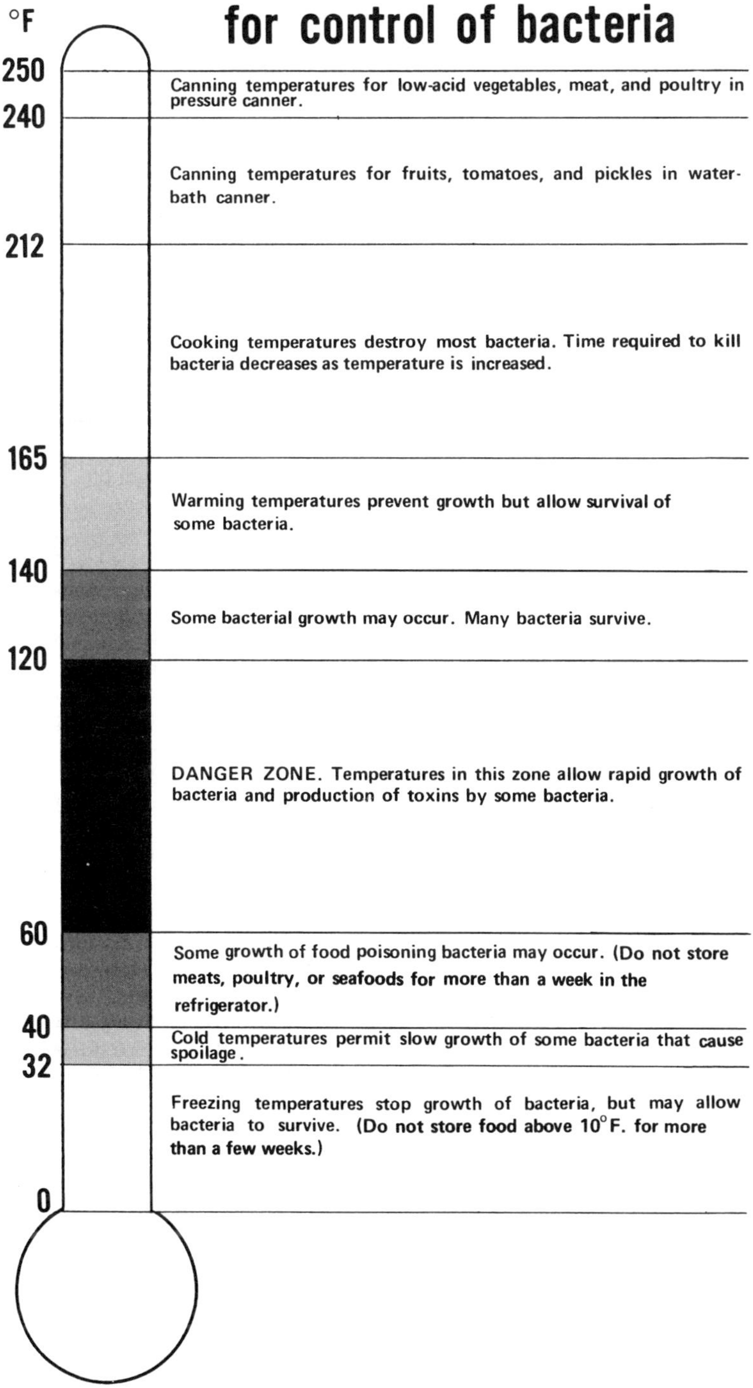

°F

250

240

Canning temperatures for low-acid vegetables, meat, and poultry in pressure canner.

Canning temperatures for fruits, tomatoes, and pickles in water-bath canner.

212

Cooking temperatures destroy most bacteria. Time required to kill bacteria decreases as temperature is increased.

165

Warming temperatures prevent growth but allow survival of some bacteria.

140

Some bacterial growth may occur. Many bacteria survive.

120

DANGER ZONE. Temperatures in this zone allow rapid growth of bacteria and production of toxins by some bacteria.

60

Some growth of food poisoning bacteria may occur. (Do not store meats, poultry, or seafoods for more than a week in the refrigerator.)

40

Cold temperatures permit slow growth of some bacteria that cause spoilage.

32

Freezing temperatures stop growth of bacteria, but may allow bacteria to survive. (Do not store food above 10°F. for more than a few weeks.)

0

43

canner, an oven, or an open kettle will not heat these products enough to kill the bacterial spores of *Clostridium botulinum* within a reasonable time. There is no danger of botulism if these foods are canned properly in a pressure canner. Be sure that the canner is in perfect order and that each step of the canning process—including time and temperature directions—is followed exactly.

There is a great possibility of microbial contamination of certain equipment that comes in close contact with food being prepared. Such equipment includes all cutting, dicing, slicing, grinding, mixing equipment, and cutting boards.

Because raw foods may contain bacteria not often present in the cooked product, it is important to thoroughly cleanse all utensils and surfaces between use for raw items and cooked foods to prevent contamination of the cooked food.

Dismantle equipment, such as blenders, so that parts coming in contact with food can easily be cleansed and sanitized. Thoroughly clean all utensils and work surfaces with hot soapy water after each use. Bacteria can be destroyed by rinsing utensils and surfaces with chlorine bleach in the proportion recommended on the package. Cutting boards, meat grinders, blenders, and can openers particularly need this protection.

Promoting food safety begins when buying food. Make grocery shopping your last stop before returning home so that perishable groceries can be refrigerated or frozen as soon as possible. Chances of maintaining good quality in foods during storage are increased if the initial food quality is high.

Shop with the idea of using foods immediately rather than storing for long periods. Buy only amounts of foods that you can store properly and use within the time of optimum quality.

Buy fresh fruits and vegetables that are bright colored, and free of defects and bruises. Do not choose overripe produce. Lettuce and other greens should have firm, crisp leaves and no signs of wilt. Handle fresh fruits and vegetables carefully to prevent injury.

Buy meats that are graded and have been USDA inspected. Check the thermometer in the meat case to see that meats are held at temperatures of 40°F. or below while on display.

Buy packages or cans of food that are in good condition. Avoid packages that are torn or improperly sealed, and cans that are leaking, dented, rusted, or bulged at the ends.

Frozen foods should feel firm, and not thawed. An ice coating on the outside of the package is an indication of some previous thawing. If food has softened, chances are it has already lost quality. Be sure the color of fruits and vegetables in plastic bags is bright and natural. Buy frozen foods that are stored below the frostline in the freezer.

Many products are now dated to give an indication as to the length of time they may be sold. Dairy products, packaged meats and cheese, and other packaged foods are among dated foods. Become familiar with date coding used in your locality and purchase foods accordingly.

Select frozen foods and other perishables last when shopping so they will have less time in which to warm up. Be sure ice creams and frozen juices are placed in insulated bags at the checkout counter. All cold foods should be placed together in bags. The volume of cold products will help to provide a cooler environment than when cold foods are interspersed among room temperature items.

Low temperatures are required in the storage of many perishable foods. Low temperatures retard quality loss and delay spoilage by slowing the action of natural enzymes, and by slowing the growth of spoilage organisms that may be present.

The amount of moisture and degree of temperature needed to retain quality in storage varies with different foods. Most fresh, perishable foods keep longer in the refrigerator. But certain varieties of apples and of vegetables such as potatoes, onions, hard rind squashes, and eggplant keep well in a cool, dark place. A few fruits and vegetables can be kept successfully at room temperature.

Green leafy vegetables need cold, moist air to retain their crispness. If you do not have adequate hydrator space in the refrigerator, plastic bags or plastic containers with lids may be used to keep food moist. Any refrigerated food that may lose quality through drying should be kept covered.

Refrigerate shell eggs promptly. They lose their mild flavor quickly at room temperature. To insure best quality and flavor, use eggs within a week.

Most fats and oils need protection from air, heat, and light. Butter, fat drippings, and margarine need to be stored tightly wrapped or covered in the refrigerator. Vegetable oils in small quantities may be kept at room temperature. For long storage, keep oils in the refrigerator. If they solidify, they will become clear and liquid after they are warmed to room temperature. Most of the firm vegetable shortenings and lard have been stabilized by hydrogenation and can be kept at room temperature without damage to flavor.

Fruits are fragile and need special handling to keep them from being crushed or bruised. The softened tissues permit entrance of spoilage organisms that quickly cause loss of quality. Sort fruit before storing. Injured fruit will contaminate sound, firm fruit. Because temperature is an important factor in ripening, do not place unripe fruit in the refrigerator.

Unripe apples are best held at cool room temperatures (60°–70°F.) until ready to eat. Store ripe apples in the refrigerator. Allow unripe apricots, nectarines, peaches, avocados, bananas, pears, and melons to ripen at room temperature, and then refrigerate. The skin on bananas will darken, but the flesh will remain flavorful and firm.

Store unwashed and unstemmed berries and cherries covered in the refrigerator to prevent moisture loss. Citrus fruits are best stored at a cool room temperature. They may also be stored uncovered in the refrigerator.

After canned fruits or canned juices have been opened, cover and store in the refrigerator. They can be safely stored in their original containers, but for better flavor, storage in glass or plastic is recommended.

Store meat, poultry, and fish in the coldest part of the refrigerator. In manually defrosted refrigerators the coldest area outside the freezing unit is the chill tray located just below the unit. The area at the bottom of the cabinet is the warmest. The door and hydrator storage areas are usually warmer than the rest of the refrigerator. The temperature in frostless and self-defrosting refrigerators is fairly uniform throughout the cabinet. The temperature should be 40°F. or lower in the general storage area of the refrigerator.

Loosely cover fresh meats, roasts, steaks, and chops, and use within 3 to 5 days for best eating quality. Ground meat is more likely to spoil than roasts or chops because more surface area on the meat has been exposed to the air and mechanical equipment. Use ground meat within 1 or 2 days.

Store poultry and fish in their transparent wrap in the refrigerator and use within 1 or 2 days. Store variety meats in the refrigerator and use within 1 or 2 days.

Store fresh milk and cream in the

Always cleanse a cutting board thoroughly, especially between use for raw and cooked foods.

Maximum Home-Storage Periods to Maintain Good Quality in Purchased Frozen Foods

Food	Approximate holding period at 0° F.	Food	Approximate holding period at 0° F.
Fruits and vegetables		*Meat—Continued*	
Fruits:	*Months*	Cooked meat:	*Months*
Cherries	12	Meal dinners	3
Peaches	12	Meat pie	3
Raspberries	12	Swiss steak	3
Strawberries	12	*Poultry*	
Fruit juice concentrates:		Chicken:	
Apple	12	Cut-up	9
Grape	12	Livers	3
Orange	12	Whole	12
Vegetables:		Duck, whole	6
Asparagus	8	Goose, whole	6
Beans	8	Turkey:	
Cauliflower	8	Cut up	6
Corn	8	Whole	12
Peas	8	Cooked chicken and turkey:	
Spinach	8	Chicken or turkey din-	
Baked goods		ners (sliced meat	
Bread and yeast rolls:		and gravy)	6
White bread	3	Chicken or turkey pies	6
Cinnamon rolls	2	Fried chicken	4
Plain rolls	3	Fried chicken dinners	4
Cakes:		*Fish and shellfish*	
Angel	2	Fish:	
Chiffon	2	Fillets:	
Chocolate layer	4	Cod, flounder, had-	
Fruit	12	dock, halibut,	
Pound	6	pollack	6
Yellow	6	Mullet, ocean	
Danish pastry	3	perch, sea trout,	
Doughnuts:		striped bass	3
Cake type	3	Pacific Ocean perch	2
Yeast raised	3	Salmon steaks	2
Pies (unbaked):		Sea trout, dressed	3
Apple	8	Striped bass, dressed	3
Boysenberry	8	Whiting, drawn	4
Cherry	8	Shellfish:	
Peach	8	Clams, shucked	3
Meat		Crabmeat:	
Beef:		Dungeness	3
Hamburger or chipped		King	10
(thin) steaks	4	Oysters, shucked	4
Roasts	12	Shrimp	12
Steaks	12	Cooked fish and shellfish:	
Lamb:		Fish with cheese sauce	3
Patties (ground meat)	4	Fish with lemon butter	
Roasts	9	sauce	3
Pork, cured	2	Fried fish dinner	3
Pork, fresh:		Fried fish sticks, scallops,	
Chops	4	or shrimp	3
Roasts	8	Shrimp creole	3
Sausage	2	Tuna pie	3
Veal:		*Frozen desserts*	
Cutlets, chops	9	Ice cream	1
Roasts	9	Sherbet	1

refrigerator and use within one week for best eating quality. Keep dried milk in a tightly closed container. Store evaporated milk at room temperature until opened, then place in the refrigerator. Tightly wrap cheeses and keep in the refrigerator.

Store breads in the original wrapper in a breadbox or the refrigerator. Although bread keeps its freshness best at room temperature, in hot, humid weather store bread in the refrigerator to protect against mold.

Cereals, flours, spices, and sugar keep best at room temperature, away from the heat of a range or a refrigerator unit. Tightly closed containers will keep out dust, moisture, and insects.

A storage temperature of 0°F. or lower is necessary to maintain the best quality in frozen foods. Unfavorable changes in eating quality take place more rapidly in food stored at temperatures above 0°F., causing foods to lose color, flavor, characteristic texture, and nutritive value.

Check your freezer to be sure the temperature is 0°F. or lower in several spots. Regulate the temperature control to maintain the warmest spot at no more than 0°F., if possible.

The freezing compartments of home refrigerators are not designed to give a temperature of 0°F. Hold frozen foods in these compartments only a few days. In refrigerator-freezers where temperatures can be maintained at 0°F. or lower in the freezer cabinet, food may be kept for the same storage periods as in a freezer.

Place food in your home freezer promptly after arriving home. Rotate the food in the freezer by placing the most recently purchased products underneath or behind foods that were already in the freezer.

The table gives suggested maximum home storage periods to maintain good quality in purchased frozen foods. These times are for foods that have been subject to good commercial freezing, handling, and storage before you purchased them. Recommended periods are approximate.

Occasionally, frozen foods are partially or completely thawed before it is learned that the freezer is not operating or that the door has been left open. You may safely refreeze frozen foods that have thawed if they still contain ice crystals or if they are still cold— below 40°F.—and have been held no longer than 1 or 2 days at refrigerator temperatures after thawing. Partial thawing and refreezing may reduce the eating quality of foods, particularly fruits, vegetables, and prepared foods.

Be sure to defrost the freezer before a collection of frost reaches a depth of one-half inch over a large area of the refrigerated surfaces. Defrost also when frost starts to accumulate on packages that have been stored in the freezer only a few hours. Excess frost on freezer walls or shelves reduces storage space and may cause the storage temperature to rise several degrees.

Store green leafy vegetables and tomatoes in refrigerator hydrator.

Guidelines for Handling Pesticides and Other Hazardous Materials

MOST PEOPLE THINK their homes are safe, but frequently they are not. Statistics show a large proportion of accidents occur there. In 1971, the National Clearinghouse for Poison Control Centers reported 136,051 cases of poisoning in and around the home.

These poisonings—often to children—resulted from swallowing or otherwise ingesting common materials such as medicines; cosmetics; kitchen, laundry and cleaning aids; garage and workshop items such as paints and varnishes; and miscellaneous materials such as pesticides, moth balls, deodorizers, rust preventives, and typewriter cleaners. In some cases the poisonings resulted from inhaling fumes.

Home safety is your responsibility. There is an old saying: "A good home is a happy home." This also implies that a good home is clean, orderly, healthy, well managed, and safe. A safe home is one with a place for everything and everything in its place.

Is your home safe? The question deserves serious thought. A home that met safety requisites in the past may not pass them tomorrow due to aging of the property and new requirements.

If you have qualms about your home's safety, now is the time to evaluate the situation and take any corrective action needed immediately.

Check around the various rooms in your house to determine the variety of hazardous materials present that could result in accidents or in death. Review the following list so you will have a better idea of what to look for. Common potential poisons generally found in the home are:
• Medicine cabinet items such as prescription medications, cough sirups, aspirin, boric acid, camphorated oil, oil of wintergreen, rubbing alcohol and liniments, laxatives, antiseptics, and iodine.
• Cosmetics such as depilatories (hair removers), shaving creams and lotions, colognes and perfumes, nail polish and remover, cuticle remover, astringents, permanent wave solutions, sun tan creams and oils, hair lotions, creams and shampoos.
• Laundry and cleaning aids such as bleaches, drain cleaners, dyes, detergents, dry cleaners, floor and rug cleaners, ammonia, furniture polishes and waxes, metal and jewelry cleaners.
• Garage and workshop items such as paints and varnishes, shellacs, paint thinners and removers, insect sprays, rat poisons, auto polishes and waxes, plastic menders, gasoline, kerosene, certain chemicals (acetic acid, for example) used in photography, leather preservatives, moth balls and crystals, pesticides, deodorizers, rust preventives and removers, and typewriter cleaner.
• Volatile substances, those which tend to vaporize and give off fumes or odors. These materials may also be flammable, and for maximum safety should not as a rule be stored indoors.

In this category are gasoline, alcohol, many cleaning and polishing agents,

If a PESTICIDE is accidentally swallowed, call a doctor at once

AUTHOR L. C. GIBBS is Program Leader, Pesticide-Chemicals, Extension Service.

Coauthor Ovid Bay is Program Leader for Information, Agriculture and Natural Resources, Extension Service.

Keep PESTiCiDES out of reach of CHILDREN

disinfectants, paints and varnishes, solvents and others.

Paints of this type usually carry label instructions regarding use, handling, and storage, and it is the responsibility of the individual to follow them.

Another safety aspect is that these materials should always be used in well-ventilated areas. Indoors, windows should be opened widely so that fumes will not concentrate.

• Pesticides are toxic chemicals used to control or repel insects, plant diseases, rodents, weeds, nematodes, and other pests. They are available in a number of different forms and concentrations such as liquids, solids, gases, powders, dusts, and granules. Insecticides are for control of insects, fungicides for plant diseases, herbicides for weeds, and rodenticides for rodents.

Safe use of pesticides is the responsibility of every purchaser. Your responsibility begins when you buy a pesticide and ends only when all the material has been used and the empty containers disposed of safely. Some pesticides retain their potency long after they have been applied. They should be stored, handled, and applied with respect for their dangerous nature.

The label of the pesticide container, by law, clearly lists the precautions needed for safe use. Before buying a pesticide, read the label to be sure the precautions are understood and they can be followed. Many pesticides used on food crops have limitations on the time intervals required between last application and harvest.

Store all pesticides where they cannot possibly be contacted accidentally by children or pets. A sturdy locked cabinet in a toolshed which is isolated from the house is an ideal place to store them. Remember to keep them locked at all times except when in use.

Observe the following precautions in using pesticides:

Read the label carefully and completely and be sure you understand it fully. Follow it explicitly.

Never stir any chemical solution with your hands. Be sure to wash clothing and equipment thoroughly after *each* use.

Do not eat, drink, or smoke while mixing or applying pesticides. Wash hands and face immediately after working with pesticides.

Rinse and drain all empty pesticide containers with water or other diluents being used in your spray operations. Each container should be rinsed three times and the residue poured back into your spray tank before you dispose of it.

Crush empty pesticide containers and bury them 18 inches deep in soil where they will not contaminate water supplies. If you burn the containers, stay out of the smoke. Do not burn containers for volatile substances such as 2, 4-D. Never burn aerosol containers.

If you live in an apartment, wrap empty rinsed containers in several layers of newspaper, crush, and/or puncture

Before using a
PESTiCiDE
remove pets ·· their
food and water from
the area

the container (except aerosols) and place them in your garbage container.

Mix only the quantity of pesticide you need for a specific job. Avoid storage if possible. Protect labels so they won't become lost or illegible. Never use unlabeled pesticides.

Avoid applying pesticides that might contaminate wells, ponds, streams, and water supplies.

Dispose of leftover spray materials in a safe manner. The best way to do this is to use up the material for its purpose.

Store chemicals in a separate locked storage area. Keep all chemicals out of reach of children, pets, and irresponsible persons. Label the storage area and never allow small children to play in or around a mixing, storage, or disposal area.

Apply pesticides only on quiet days when the wind is at a minimum and blowing away from susceptible plants.

Buy only as much pesticide as you need for a single season.

Household cleaning supplies are frequently stored in a cupboard in the kitchen, and in many cases under the kitchen sink. Storage under the sink is perhaps one of the worst places for materials of this nature, especially those which are poisonous.

If you store them under your kitchen sink or in cabinets where they can be reached by small children, you are asking for trouble. Inventory the materials that are accessible to small children

whether you have any kids or not, for the simple reason that your grandchildren or other children who might be visiting you could get into them and be poisoned accidentally. Cans and bottles seem to attract small children, and those containing toxic materials contribute significantly to the total number of cases of accidental poisonings and deaths.

Most households have a rather large number of medicines of various types located in the medicine chest, kitchen cabinets, and in hall closets. Here again safety, as far as your home is concerned, can be insured if you will check to see that all of these materials are stored on high shelves out of reach of small children and that no materials are retained which do not have a label on them.

Many medicines and other hazardous materials today have a safety cap which is referred to as a childproof lid. Even so, they still should not be left out where children can reach them. Frequently many of these materials are kept on nightstands around beds. This is a bad practice. Keep all medicines in places where small children can't get at them.

Paints, varnishes, and paint removers of certain types are hazardous and contribute substantially to the number of poisoning accidents and deaths. Some of these materials are extremely toxic. Instructions and precautions are given on the containers for their safe storage, handling, and use. Observe directions on the label and store containers where

Don't keep
PESTiCiDES
in places like this

Wrap PESTiCiDE CONTAINERS before Disposal

they are unavailable to persons who should not have access to them.

Household insects seem to have an incredible ability to escape extinction. Cockroaches, for example, which have been on the earth millions of years longer than man, can subsist on any kind of food. They thrive in all parts of the world. Some species prefer man's home to other habitats. Once they enter it, they use countless instinctive tricks to keep from being killed or evicted.

You can help control household pests by systematic house cleaning. However, the best way to rid your home of practically all insect pests and to keep it free of them is by a combination of good housekeeping practices and proper use of the right insecticide. It is easier to prevent pests from infesting your home than it is to get rid of them after they are established.

Household insects seek available food in places where they can hide and breathe. If you eliminate these attractions from your home, the insects will look elsewhere for them. Here are some basic rules to follow:

Practice sanitation. Many household insects live on spilled food and organic matter that has not been completely cleaned up. They breed, multiply, and hide in small areas where food is left in the cracks and crevices of cupboards, walls, floors, and around baseboards. They also hide in seldom used storage cabinets, behind kitchen drawers, and behind wash tubs and around water pipes and toilets.

Keep these places clean. Frequent scrubbings with hot water and soap or a detergent will do the job. Scrub surfaces *before* treating them with pesticides, of course.

Dispose of garbage, bits of foods, crumbs, scraps of fabric, lint, and other waste materials that insects may eat or in which they can breed. Keep all foods in tightly closed containers that are clean outside as well as inside.

Before purchasing dry foods, examine packages carefully for evidence of breaks and signs of insect infestation. Don't let insect pests hitchhike into your home.

Cockroaches and silverfish often enter the house in the crevices of cardboard containers used in transporting groceries or other materials. Don't leave these used containers in the kitchen or basement where unwanted pests can escape and infest your home.

Permanently seal up places where insects can enter. You may not be able to close them all, but you can close most of them. Calk the openings and cracks around wash basins, toilet bowls, water pipes, drain pipes, etc. Fill in the cracks around the baseboards and between the floor boards. Cover openings where rats or mice may enter. See that windows and doors are closed and tight fitting. When the windows are open, be sure that screens are in place firmly.

Keep PESTiCiDES Away From FOOD, DISHES, POTS, or PANS

As previously indicated, pesticides can be applied in many different forms and ways for a variety of different purposes. This will help you know how to select and apply the right pesticide properly:

Surface sprays are designed for use on surfaces in the home where insects are likely to crawl. Spray particles are coarse and are used to dampen or wet surfaces. When the spray dries, a thin deposit of insecticide remains for several weeks and the deposit will kill insects which crawl over it. You can buy these sprays in pressurized containers; or you may buy a liquid insecticide and apply it with a household hand sprayer that produces a continuous coarse spray.

Space sprays leave little residue and generally should not be used as surface sprays. Aerosols are entirely too fine for surface application. You can buy space sprays in pressurized containers, or you can buy a liquid insecticide and apply it as a space spray with a household hand sprayer having a nozzle that produces very fine particles.

If you use one of these products for spraying a kitchen or pantry, place all cooking and eating utensils and food where they will not be contaminated by falling particles.

Observe approved pest control practices at all times. Application of pesticides may be needed to supplement good housekeeping. Follow directions and heed precautions on the label.

Avoid inhaling
PESTiCiDE
sprays or dusts

using
PESTiCiDES?

Read the Label

Space sprays and aerosols are designed for space application. They are especially effective against mosquitoes, house flies, and other flying insects. They may also be used to penetrate the hiding places of insects such as roaches, and to drive them into the open where they can be killed with surface sprays or dusts.

The particles, or droplets, of space sprays are much finer than those of surface sprays and persist in the air for a short time. The particles of an aerosol are even finer than those of a space spray, and float in the air for a longer time.

Hazardous Materials Safety Checklist

Do you always read the label before using hazardous material and follow directions? ....Yes ☐ No ☐

Do you store hazardous materials in their original labeled containers? ....Yes ☐ No ☐

Do you keep hazardous materials out of the reach of children, pets, and irresponsible people? Yes ☐ No ☐

Do you avoid smoking while using hazardous materials when directions so indicate? ......Yes ☐ No ☐

Do you avoid inhaling hazardous materials and wear protective clothing and masks when directed to do so? ....Yes ☐ No ☐

Do you avoid spilling hazardous materials on your skin and wash immediately when they are spilled accidently? ....Yes ☐ No ☐

Do you wash hands thoroughly after handling hazardous materials and before eating or smoking? ....Yes ☐ No ☐

Do you cover food and water containers of pets when using hazardous materials such as pesticides which might contaminate them? ....Yes ☐ No ☐

Do you always dispose of empty hazardous material containers so they pose no hazards to humans, animals, wildlife, or valuable plants? ....Yes ☐ No ☐

Do you wash contaminated clothing before reuse when this is directed? ....Yes ☐ No ☐

Do you always observe label directions to keep the residues of hazardous materials, such as pesticides applied to plants, within the limits permitted by law? ....Yes ☐ No ☐

Do you store your hazardous materials in locked cabinets and in a well-ventilated storage facility? ....Yes ☐ No ☐

NOTE: ALL ANSWERS SHOULD BE "YES"

Liquid insecticides or dusts may contain the same active ingredients and both can be used for surface application. Dusts, however, can be blown into cracks, corners, and other places difficult to reach with sprays. Insecticides may also be applied to surfaces in liquid, cream, or paste form with a paintbrush. This method often permits more accurate placement of the material than spraying or dusting, and is particularly recommended where only spot treatment is needed.

Poison baits may be used to control rodents and some other pests. However, they are generally more hazardous to humans and pets. If you use a poisoned bait, handle it with extreme care. Follow the directions and observe all safety precautions that are on the container label.

Follow Directions..
Every time you use a
PESTiCiDE

53

490-100 O - 73 - 5

What's Being Done About Drug Abuse

A STEAMING CUP of coffee, a frosty mug of beer, a couple of aspirin, a tranquilizer, a marihuana cigarette, and the innocent looking white powder that is heroin have one thing in common: they are drugs.

Few people have used all of them. But most of us in recent years have become aware of the increasing use of drugs of all kinds, and particularly of the mood-altering drugs which have caught the fancy of many young people to a degree which endangers them and alarms their seniors.

Less than 10 years ago, the average American knew little about drugs and had little desire to know more. Probably most people had heard that some jazz musicians and rock singers smoked marihuana, that a few artists and writers had experimented with what they called "mind-expanding" drugs, and that addiction to heroin was a problem in the ghetto. But few realized that drug abuse was at that very moment filtering from isolated groups into the mainstream of American life.

Today, heroin addiction is still most prevalent among the black, the poor, and the alienated. But it is also found in middle-class suburban neighborhoods, and use of the drug has penetrated high school and college campuses. Like all narcotics, heroin is highly addictive; once its users become addicted they are driven to continue taking the drug, less for pleasure than to avoid the misery of withdrawal symptoms. It is estimated that over half a million Americans are addicted to heroin.

Over 20 million have tried marihuana at least once, and use of the drug is steadily increasing among young people, at increasingly early ages. Marihuana is not addictive and has not been shown to produce serious physical or psychiatric problems at present social levels of use. However, even moderate smoking of marihuana may impair motor performance sufficiently to lead to motor vehicle accidents. And the issue of long-term, chronic use and its effects remains unresolved.

LSD appears to have declined in popularity, at least among adults. However, some college and high school students continue to experiment with this and other drugs which produce hallucinations.

Heroin is an opiate. LSD is a potent hallucinogen, and marihuana is medically classified as a mild hallucinogen. All three are illegal, and in the minds of many they are the dangerous drugs of today. Certainly heroin is the most degrading of drugs. And marihuana is the illegal drug most commonly used. However, the misuse of drugs which can be manufactured and prescribed legally is also a source of growing concern.

Amphetamines have been used to excess as pep pills and diet pills. Potent methamphetamine, injected intravenously, can cause addiction and death.

Barbiturate sleeping pills are addicting and, in one sense, more dangerous than heroin since sudden withdrawal from heavy use of barbiturates can cause death. The combination of barbiturates and alcohol can have the same result.

Tranquilizers are also overused by much of our population, and recently the sedative methaqualone has become popular among some young people.

Perhaps half a million people are directly affected by use of these drugs. Often they are obtained and used illegally, but there is an ample, legal supply available: prescriptions for mood-altering drugs have accounted for

AUTHOR SHEILA CARROLL is with the Office of Communications, National Institute of Mental Health, Department of Health, Education, and Welfare.

nearly a fourth of all the prescriptions issued by physicians in the course of a year.

These figures make us reflect on our drug-taking habits as a nation. There is reason to fear not only that drugs are taken too freely and prescribed too easily, but also that their very abundance is creating a climate in which drug abuse cannot help but flourish. This climate, or drug culture, is further nurtured by an ever-growing variety of over-the-counter medicines, temptingly packaged and advertised.

Americans of all ages are using drugs in greater variety and in greater numbers than ever before. Virtually every category of pharmacologic agent that has some sort of effect on mood is being misused at this time.

It seems today that if a chemical can be abused, it will be abused. And, since the use of all sorts of drugs in the next 10 years is expected to increase manyfold, we have no reason to believe that the problem of drug abuse will soon disappear.

When we explore the causes of drug abuse, we should remember that many of today's drugs are thousands of years old—for example, marihuana, alcohol, and opium. Throughout recorded history man has used pleasure-giving and pain-killing substances for comfort and protection against the hardships of life and its strains.

What is new is the explosion of experimentation with drugs among our young people and—concurrent with drug use—the disinterest shown by a segment of youth in such traditional activities as schooling and jobs.

Drug users say they take drugs to feel good. Feeling good may mean euphoria, or dreamy languor, or vivid hallucinations.

Drugs can provide excitement. They also can provide refuge from teenage growing pains, or from a hopeless cycle of sordid poverty, the anxieties and stresses of a turbulent existence, the frustration of a mechanized society, or an empty life.

In some young people drug taking has been attributed to rebellion and hostility toward authority, be it their parents, school, or the establishment world in general. For others, drug use is a way of avoiding or at least postponing the often painful process of growing up, making decisions, and assuming adult responsibility.

Despite the popular notion of the evil "pusher" who lures the young into drug use or addiction, most users try drugs out of curiosity and first obtain them from friends. In many schools and social groups, drugs are "in," and this pressure—"peer pressure"—is probably the most important single factor in the initiation of drug use.

Because drug abuse is such a complex problem, it must be dealt with in a variety of ways. One is law enforcement. Unfortunately, illegal drugs are widely available almost everywhere, and many adults may not realize that it is often easier for a teenager to get marihuana than to get a six-pack of beer.

Traffic in drugs ranges from the international smuggling and sale of heroin by criminal syndicates to a marihuana trade conducted largely by amateurs and small-time operators.

Strenuous efforts are being made by the Department of Justice to cut the international traffic in which profits are astronomical. The Department of State has persuaded Turkey to greatly reduce cultivation of the opium poppy from which heroin is derived, and is negotiating with other countries to reduce foreign production and export of dangerous drugs.

At home, Federal, State, and local law enforcement agencies have increased their efforts to trace and eliminate drug traffic, with heavy penalties now focused on the big pushers of drugs. New, stringent legislation is directed toward preventing the illicit distribution of useful, legal drugs which can be misused.

Legal controls, even if they were multiplied many times over, cannot be a total solution for the drug abuse problem. We must also treat and rehabilitate those among us who have been snared by drugs and use every means at hand to prevent our children from joining that all too large segment of our population which misuses drugs.

Until recently, treatment for drug abuse meant treatment for addiction to a narcotic, usually heroin. For years, the results were discouraging and it appeared that the majority of addicts suffered from an incurable disease. Now a variety of treatments offer new hope.

All of these treatments are based on recognition of the fact that narcotic addiction is a stubborn disease and that when addicts are taken off drugs the battle for recovery has only just begun.

Some succeed when, after a period of hospitalization, they join a treatment program in which they are given close supervision and assistance in rebuilding their lives over a period of months or years. Others, in increasing numbers, are turning to methadone treatment programs.

Like heroin, methadone is a narcotic

Identifying Drug Users

WALTER WOLMAN and
E. M. STEINDLER [°]

Detecting drug abuse is not a simple matter. A youngster who wears his hair differently, changes his manner of dress, and begins to associate with new friends probably is undergoing modifications in his attitude and life style. Such changes, however, are commonly seen in the adolescent years and do not always mean that drugs are being abused.

It may be helpful for a parent to become acquainted with the more usual signs of the physical and behavioral effects of certain drugs, if he understands, at the same time, that such signs are by no means conclusive. They may indicate physical or emotional disorders.

Drugs most frequently abused are narcotics, sedatives, stimulants, and hallucinogens. They all have either a depressant or excitatory effect on the central nervous system of the body.

Persons under the influence of narcotics, such as heroin, generally are drowsy and apathetic, and have little interest in what is going on around them. If, however, they have been taking the drug on a regular basis, tolerance—which builds up rapidly—can reduce the magnitude of such symptoms.

When a person has been taking heroin or another narcotic long enough to develop physical dependence, a characteristic withdrawal syndrome appears from 8 to 12 hours after the last dose. The most frequent signs, mild at first and becoming more and more pronounced as time goes on, include running nose, watery eyes, yawning and perspiration—as in a bad cold or flu. During the second day following withdrawal, stomach cramps, vomiting, diarrhea, and muscle spasms causing uncontrollable kicking and twitching are usually experienced.

Although not particularly dangerous, the withdrawal period for a narcotic-dependent person can be highly discomforting and painful, and medical help should be sought to relieve distress.

Sedative drugs, such as barbiturates, also have a depressant effect on the central nervous system. But like alcohol, with which they have a cross-tolerance, they can cause giddiness, talkativeness, and agitated behavior during the early intoxication state. These signs are displaced by grogginess, drowsiness, and sleep as time goes on.

Pronounced intoxication effects do not normally occur if the sedative is taken in small therapeutic doses. And it is only through taking larger amounts regularly over a long period of time that physical dependence develops. If that happens, however, it is essential that the person

[°] Department of Mental Health, American Medical Association.

and it relieves the "drug hunger" which causes many addicts to relapse. Because it is longer and slower acting than heroin, a daily dose of methadone permits addict patients to hold jobs and resume normal living.

Another still experimental treatment method offers great promise. This is the use of narcotic antagonists, chemicals which set up a form of blockade in the nervous system and prevent narcotics from having any effect at all. Antagonists are not addictive. They may prove highly useful in treating addicts, and in preventing addiction in young experimenters who are in danger of becoming "hooked."

Help for people who abuse non-narcotic drugs comes in many forms, institutional and informal.

Hospital emergency rooms are geared to treat barbiturate overdosage and acute drug reactions for which prompt medical treatment is essential. Free clinics manned by professional volunteers offer a variety of medical services

who discontinues use be hospitalized and observed closely, because withdrawal from barbiturates in such a case can be dangerous and even fatal unless expertly controlled.

Amphetamines, or pep pills, cocaine, and drugs which resemble amphetamines, such as methamphetamine (speed), are stimulants. Extreme restlessness, irritability, aggressive behavior, and rapid speech can characterize the intoxication period. Fatigue, exhaustion, and severe depression result when effects of the drug wear off. Because tolerance develops very rapidly to most of the effects of amphetamines, the chronic—as opposed to the beginning or infrequent—user will show few signs of drug taking. This is not true of the user of cocaine, because that drug does not produce any significant degree of tolerance.

Drugs such as LSD and mescaline are in the hallucinogenic class. They are so termed because the more prominent effects of intoxication include perceptual distortions resembling hallucinations. An individual on "a trip" is clearly disoriented with his surroundings. If the delusions he is experiencing are frightening and threatening, rather than pleasurable, he may be panic-stricken and act in unpredictable ways.

Marihuana often is classed as a mild hallucinogen, but it rarely produces the acute feelings of dissociation that the more potent substances do. Marihuana effects can be either stimulant or depressant, depending mainly on the mood of the user when he takes it, his companions, and the physical surroundings. When intoxicated, the user can be light-headed, outgoing, and cheerful, or he can be drowsy, withdrawn, and sullen.

With low to moderate doses of weak marihuana, such as commonly used in the United States, there are few discernible after effects, although physical and psychological impairment as a result of long-term use is a possibility still under study.

Unless a person is experiencing the effects of a drug at the time or, in the case of narcotics and sedatives, the effects of drug withdrawal, it is extremely difficult to tell who is a drug abuser and who is not. Signs of regular drug taking, however, include:

• Needle "tracks" along the veins of the arms and legs, which indicate intravenous administration probably of heroin or amphetamines.

• Loss of interest in other forms of recreation because of preoccupation with drugs.

• Inability to concentrate for long periods of time.

• Impaired judgment and memory.

• Increased appetite because of food deprivation during intoxication.

Although some persons have their favorite drug and stick to it, many take a combination of substances, either at the same time or in sequence. Some don't really know what they are taking because drugs sold illicitly in the street seldom are what they are touted to be—they often contain cheaper substitutes, adulterants, and contaminants. For these reasons it is important to obtain professional medical care for anyone who is "under the influence" and unable to help himself, so that an appropriate diagnostic examination can be made.

and counseling to the youthful, floating, drug-using population.

Telephone "hot lines" give emergency advice and sustaining comfort to anonymous callers.

At "rap sessions" in storefront clubrooms, church cellars, and other movable informal meeting places, young people discuss their "hassles" and hear out each other's problems. Many adolescents and young adults who view the older generation with skepticism or hostility find comfort and companionship in these meetings. Often, in addition, they develop an incentive to "get their heads together" and find an active, challenging alternative to drug taking.

Treatment services need to be expanded in our communities—not only to help those already hooked on drugs —but as an integral part of our preventive efforts.

Drug abuse is like a communicable disease; it spreads—by example, by word of mouth, and by imitation. Drug abuse is certainly increasing, but so is the number of young people who have tried drugs and want out. As we provide treatment services for them, these young people become able to tell other youth that the drug scene is not as great as they thought it was, before they got hooked. And, of greater importance, they are believed by their contemporaries before experimentation becomes a habit.

Parents can help prevent drug usage by example, by knowledge, and by understanding. If they are to talk to their children about drugs, they must be informed—usually they know far less about drugs than do their children. Ideally, before their child is tempted to experiment, they will have been able to explain to him the futility of the drugged life and—what is even more convincing to young people—the actual damage that a drug abuser does to his body.

Ample informational material on drugs is now available. For a starter, you might want to read *Answers to the Most Frequently Asked Questions* *about Drug Abuse* and/or *Tips on Drug Abuse Prevention for the Parents of a Young Child*, obtainable free from the National Clearinghouse for Drug Abuse Information, P.O. Box 1080, Washington, D. C. 20013. Additional reading material and information about films and educational programs also can be obtained from the National Clearinghouse.

Parents may panic when they find evidence that their child is using drugs but this emotion, though understandable, is not likely to help. Drug experimentation does not necessarily mean that a youth has a psychological problem and "needs help." Most adolescent drug abusers are not regular users. Nor are their parents necessarily to blame for their experimenting with drugs, since pressure from their peers is far more convincing to many young people than advice from parents.

While parents have a duty to speak their minds on the subject if drug abuse occurs, their greatest influence will come from the example they set. If they use legal drugs to excess and dole them out unthinkingly, they are training their children to view "pill popping" as normal. If they use alcohol as a crutch, they will have a difficult time in persuading sons or daughters to desist from drug usage.

While the parents' action is legal and their children's is not, they are setting examples of escapism which may be imitated. As adults, they have the opportunity to discourage—by example and not merely words—the "magic potion notion" that drugs can be the remedy for all ills and that a random sampling or overuse of chemicals will bring instant happiness.

Handcrafts: A Creative Approach to Living

CREATIVITY IS FUN and a personal responsibility.

What if we were never allowed to be creative? Creative in thought? Creative in action? Without creativity, the world would come to a complete standstill! Nothing new tomorrow, no progress, only thoughts of the past.

What if everyone looked alike, thought alike, and acted alike? Would it be peaceful or boring? How long peaceful? And, how very long boring?

What if our whole exterior environment were all bright green? Green skies, green clouds, green soil? What if our whole near environment, our homes, were all bright green: green walls, green glass, green floors, green furnishings! No lights and darks or dulls, just bright green! How would you like it for a week, a year, a lifetime?

What if everything were smooth: smooth trees, soil, shrubs, clothing, upholstery—all as smooth as glass!

What if all lines were straight: Tree limbs, furnishings, clothing! What if all shapes were triangles: houses, trees, chairs! And, what if all forms were round: You, me, the dog, the house! How boring!

We were born to be creative in a world rich in design. Rich in natural resources. Rich with innovative people who consider creativity fun and a responsibility, not to be slighted in a world of rich endowments by God, nature, and man's creative urge.

The fantastic everchanging colors: brilliant oranges, reds, yellows, and

AUTHOR MIRIAM E. MC GREW is a Related Art Specialist with the Cooperative Extension Service at The Pennsylvania State University, University Park.

rusts of autumn. The subtle jewel-like quality of icicles glistening in the sun and drip-dripping, each minute changing that icicle's form and texture and finally nothing but a memory of beauty. Fabric designers and sculptors are constantly aware of nature's changing design.

A spider weaving his fantastic structural trap to feed himself and his young. Strong enough to catch a fly, weak enough to be destroyed by a thoughtless child. Weavers spin their own webs in new and fantastic arrays—delicate enough for a baby's baptismal robe or a brilliant, sturdy poncho.

Clay, nature's earthy vein, waiting for a creator to change it into beautiful pottery. Earth's substances—each has its special combination for our potters to create objects both functional and decorative.

Design requires creative thought, experimentation, decision making, and organization before it can be developed into a finished product. The hands of the creator must be guided by the eye to develop the craftsman's creative ideas.

Stimulating? Frustrating? The wastebasket is the artist-craftsman's best friend—used extensively until he has disciplined his ability, thought, and action into a creative product which is now "a part of him." His own ideas, his own skill, his unique expression become a creative object worthy of the time it took him to create it.

Usually the only reason people say they are not creative is that they are afraid to try. Many fearful people resort to kits. The product result is not unique, not theirs. When they have weaned themselves from kits and begun to work with their own ideas and to develop their skills, then they become craftsmen. Crafts, like all other professions, take lots of time to learn.

For those who still feel they are unable to create unique, beautiful designs, the folk and traditional and ethnic crafts furnish a wide field of expression. Reproductions of our early culture require fascinating research in libraries. Au-

59

Craft demonstrations.

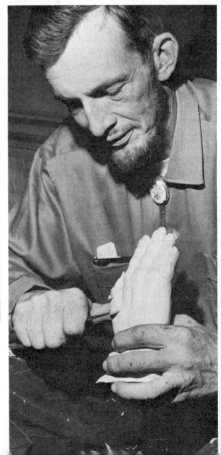

thentic reproductions must be executed exactly as they were done in the past.

Crafts are one of the rich heritages of our nation. In pioneer days, the itinerant craftsman traveled from home to home, selling his wares and earning his bed and board by weaving fabric or a coverlet or handcarving wooden items for the kitchen or barn.

If people become involved in these early crafts and have done sufficient research in books and magazines and discussed early methods (many are not on record) with the eldest members of their family or community, they may become interested in "trying their hand." They may wish to make corn-husk or apple dolls, dressed and doing an early activity. If they live in a wooded area and like to collect the unusual from nature's wonders, they may begin to reproduce the pine and nut "Kissing balls" and Christmas wreaths. If the male member of their family loves to hunt, they may create with feathers.

Feather wreaths were made at an early date. These were possibly made with a circle of twined grapevine or willow whip with moss wedged between. Tin ware, weaving, stitchery, horn work, are only a few of the early crafts possible for a folk and traditional craftsman.

The 1976 Bicentennial celebration will furnish a ready market for folk and traditional crafts. Crafts of the highest quality which are authentic reproductions and give the historical background will be in demand by the Bicentennial consumer. Folk and traditional craftsmen who love to demonstrate their work will be in great demand during the Bicentennial.

What are folk crafts? "They are objects which are made in communities which have developed through the years with some influence by outside cultures, yet still maintain a tradition in technique and design in the production of crafts. The folk crafts also are produced by hand, but the tools with which the craftsman works are more sophisticated or advanced than the tools used by indigenous craftsmen. These crafts could also be called 'country crafts.' "—David Van Dommelen.

The consumer often asks, "What is a craft?"

"Craft: A trade, occupation or profession requiring manual skill and training, combined with a knowledge of and creative use of the principles of art." —Legal definition.

"Craft: An article which is as unique and as individual as the hands and tools which created it."—*Village Crafts.*

"A craftsman is one who creates out of basic materials from his own design or from established forms, by his own skill and the best technique of his craft, an object which fulfills its purpose to the satisfaction of the user and the beholder."—Pennsylvania Guild of Craftsmen.

"Neo-crafts (contemporary) are produced by craftsmen who are not tied to traditional techniques or designs. The work they produce is often advanced and has a sense of 'fine art' to it. Often the materials are new, or new combinations are used along with old and new techniques blended together. These craftsmen are constantly searching for new ways to express their craft and they are deeply involved and committed to a personal approach to designing."— David Van Dommelen.

How will a person know if he has created? When it happens, he will be thoroughly exhausted, yet he may not have moved from his chair. He will be pleasingly exhausted. The great feeling he has had when he has worked hard at any rewarding task: the kind of fatigue that allows him to sleep soundly and awake to a new day of creative effort. He will know!

Creative contemporary craftsmen not only have all the rich natural resources and related contemporary subject matter, but they also have manmade materials and efficient, fast equipment to aid them in their creativity. Their products are only limited to their imagination, skill, and knowledge of design.

Each State, in fact each region of each State, has thousands of creative

craftsmen spending endless hours developing quality crafts, both decorative and functional for today's consumer.

Today's consumer wants unique and beautiful handcrafted objects to wear and for his home environment. Each consumer is an individual different from all others. He prefers objects which are unique and he demands quality.

Craftsmen today are meeting this demand and people and homes are showing great change as a result of the unique handcrafted items available.

Crafts are big business. No longer does a good craftsman have to work in a job he dislikes all day and then try to create at night and on weekends. He has earned his professional status by hard work and is now a respected, contributing member of today's society.

Part of the fun of being a craftsman is meeting other craftsmen. They are interesting, exciting people, young or old. They love to share their ideas and resources, and to help others find markets for their work. They enjoy teaching others their special skills.

Craftsmen have helped educate consumers to make wise choices. They help

Top photos, craft displays; one at top right shows Cumberland Mountain quilts. Above, home weaving for supplemental income.

them become aware of the design and techniques involved. They inform the consumer of certain standards to require when purchasing a handcrafted item. They help them relate their choice to its intended use. They often involve the consumer in trying the craft himself and thus another craftsman begins a new and exciting field.

Some crafts are done in leisure time for pleasure or for supplementary income. More and more are done seriously for total income. Learning the marketing of crafts is important to all those who wish to earn a living by their talent and skill.

Craftsmen often form small groups and exchange ideas and resources. As this group expands to include more members with like interests and standards, a small craft organization is formed. Later these groups may become a chapter of a State guild if they have maintained standards required by the guild. Many new opportunities are then available: training workshops in special media, craft marketing techniques, craft fairs and sales, festivals, TV appearances, demonstrations, and teaching others.

State art councils help in partially subsidizing local arts and crafts festivals. Often they will help a new organization with some beginning workshops. Some State arts councils help with marketing training.

Both guilds and small craft groups working together bring special status to a region of their State. They draw crowds of tourist consumers to attend their festivals and fairs. This boosts the economy of the area considerably because the tourists not only buy crafts, but they also use the restaurants and motels and other services of the area.

Historical villages, country stores, privately owned craft shops, and galleries are a few of the outlets that have developed in abundance to sell the quality products of local craftsmen. Some buy outright, others consign from the craftsmen.

Some States are lucky and have craft centers and cooperatives which also are local outlets for the best crafts of the State.

Craftsmen also sell at home. However, unless they are very well known, this limits their exposure and their income.

Regional craft fairs sponsored by the American Craft Council usually include about 500 craftsmen who sell both wholesale and retail. Dealers come from all over the country to get the best for their shops and their consumers.

Crafts are big business now. Consumers are more aware and appreciative of the handcrafted items. They will drive any distance to attend a craft fair or festival or to visit special craftsmen and buy their products.

American craftsmen have integrity. They create their own designs, their products have quality, and they are unique art objects. Some may become cherished antiques of the future!

In my home state, the Pennsylvania Cooperative Extension Service has worked closely with Area Resource Development agents, State and county agencies, local county craft organizations, the State Guild of Craftsmen, the American Crafts Council, Federal agencies, Pa. Council on the Art.

Pennsylvania Extension has played an active role in developing the full potential of the crafts industry. We have stressed creative use of our rich natural resources and urged craftsmen to relate their products to Pennsylvania history and environment.

Craft training workshops are taught by professional craftsmen who not only know their skill but also are experienced in marketing techniques. These workshops are held from 6 to 10 p.m., four nights a week. Over half of the participants are men. The workshops are open to anyone from high school to the still enthusiastic elderly.

Many Pennsylvania craftsmen live on farms and have developed their studios in barns or in a renovated granary. The privacy of an isolated farm is important to them.

Pennsylvania received a great deal of help from William Seymour, Craft Spe-

63

cialist with the Farmer Cooperative Service, U.S. Department of Agriculture, in Washington, D.C. Mr. Seymour kept Pennsylvania constantly informed of what other States were doing to help craftsmen develop a quality industry and coordinated special resources and craft events.

Mr. Seymour also coordinates the Interagency Craft Committee which is made up of various Federal agencies involved in arts and crafts development. The combined vision and efforts of this committee, whose responsibility is to promote the development of American arts and crafts, will help States develop a sound, long-range plan.

Future American arts and crafts centers in each State would not only sell quality crafts of the respective State but would also have craft training workshop areas. They would make it possible for more people, young and old, to learn crafts from professional teachers, and also furnish an established outlet for their products.

Hopefully, if we continue to develop a quality craft development program, we may have a national center for American arts and handcrafts in Washington, D.C. An international sale of quality American arts and crafts in foreign countries is also a possible long-range goal.

Creativity is fun and a personal responsibility, not only for the creator, but for the individual consumer. Awareness of beauty is a special gift to man. It gives him a reason to live and express and to enjoy life.

Ukrainian egg decorating demonstration.

Craft Organizations:

Pa. Guild of Craftsmen, 13 chapters
Contact: Mrs. Harriet Beech
Rural Delivery 3
Gettysburg, Pa. 17325
Revised Constitution, Contemporary and Traditional Crafts.

Village Crafts
Contacts: Mrs. Pat Macneal
R. D. Box 42
Rebersburg, Pa. 16872

Mrs. Ruth Coleman, Director
921 Tressler
Boalsburg, Pa. 16827
Craft Training for Elderly and their low income families.

Peters Valley Craftsmen
Peters Valley
Layton, N.J. 07851
Craft Village, Training and Sales
Department of Interior, National Park Service.

American Crafts Council
44 West 53rd Street
New York, N.Y. 10019
Largest crafts organization in the U.S.

World Crafts Council
U.S. Section
American Crafts Council
29 West 53rd Street
New York, N.Y. 10019
International crafts organization—70 countries

State Council on the Arts
Governor's office of each State

National Art Endowment
806 15th Street, Northwest
Washington, D.C. 20506
Nancy Hanks, Chairman
National Council of the Arts
Clark Mitze, Director
State and Community Operations
National Endowment of the Arts

Appalachian Regional Commission
Department of Agriculture
Washington, D.C. 20250
John Souder, Coordinator of Craft Programs

Farmer Cooperative Service
U.S. Department of Agriculture
Washington, D.C. 20250
William Seymour, Craft Specialist

Wood carving studio in a converted Pennsylvania farm granary.

The American craft industry potential is unlimited. Consumer demand continues to increase rapidly. Success is imminent if all continue to work together toward a long-range goal and maintain creative skill, enthusiasm, and integrity.

For further reading:

American Crafts Council. *Craft Shops, Galleries, U.S.A.,* 44 West 53rd Street, New York, N.Y. 10019.

Bank of America. *The Handcraft Business,* Small Business Reporter, Department 3120, P.O. Box 3700, San Francisco, Calif. 94137.

Crafts Horizon Magazine, 44 West 53rd Street, New York, N.Y. 10019.

Encouraging American Craftsmen, Report of the Interagency Crafts Committee by Charles Counts, Superintendent of Documents, Washington, D.C. 20402, 45 cents.

Farmers Cooperative Service. *The Cooperative Approach to Crafts,* FCS Information 78, U.S. Department of Agriculture, Washington, D.C. 20250.

Lyons, Mary. *Crafts for Retirement,* American Crafts Council, 44 West 53rd Street, New York, N.Y. 10019.

Mosley, Johnson, and Koenig. *Crafts Design,* Wadsworth Publishing Co., Belmont, Calif. 94002.

Nelson, Norbert N. *Selling Your Crafts,* Reinhold Publishing Co., 430 Park Avenue, New York, N.Y. 10022.

Prerau, Sydney. *Taxes and the Craftsman,* American Crafts Council, 44 West 53rd Street, New York, N.Y. 10019.

Robinson, John W. *Gift and Art Shops,* Small Business Bibliography (revised) No. 26, Small Business Administration, Washington, D.C. 20416.

Seymour, William R. *American Crafts, a Rich Heritage and a Rich Future,* Farmer Cooperative Service Program Aid No. 1026, U.S. Department of Agriculture, Washington, D.C. 20250.

Small Business Administration, *Handicrafts and Home Business,* Small Business Bibliography (revised) No. 1, Washington, D.C. 20416.

————. *Specialized Help for Small Businesses,* Small Marketeers Aids No. 74, Washington, D.C. 20416.

The Unicorn. Books for Craftsmen—4, Box 645, Rockville, Md. 20851.

University of Wisconsin. *The Arts in the Small Community—A National Plan,* 216 Agricultural Hall, 1450 Linden Drive, Madison, Wis. 53706.

————. *The Arts and the Small Community,* Vol. I and II, 216 Agricultural Hall, 1450 Linden Drive, Madison, Wis. 53706.

Yager, Francis P. *Craft Cooperative Bookkeepers,* Farmer Cooperative Service, Washington, D.C. 20250.

Hey, Just Look What's Happened to Camping!

Family camping has captivated over 40 million Americans, and it has captured the imaginations of 32 million more. It has been described as the "biggest single growth industry in the booming travel/leisure market." Camping ranges from backpacking to rolling homes with complete creature comforts. It is both an end in itself and a magic carpet to a wide variety of other forms of outdoor recreation, and its growing popularity fits both changing life styles and the mobility of modern Americans.

Camping was once a June to September activity for the young and hardy. Today, it is a year-round fascination for big and small families, retired couples, the affluent, and the budget watchers, as nearly 800 manufacturers provide a camping rig to fit every pocketbook and camping need.

During the 1960's, the number of camping vehicles produced each year—travel trailers, camping trailers, truck campers, and motor homes—grew from less than 100,000 units to nearly half a million. The recreational vehicle industry forecasts a minimum of 7.5 million of these camping units will be in use by 1980.

Until the 1960's, most campgrounds were owned and operated at public expense. In decades past, the campground "ranger" was the symbol of backwoods knowledge and authority. For up to 10 months of each year he may have been an area's only human resident. Today, nearly two-thirds of the Nation's 15,000 campgrounds (800,000 campsites) are commercially operated and many include such conveniences as laundromats, supervised recreation programs, and babysitting services.

Since the mid-1960's, campground franchising has become a significant force within the industry. Today approximately 50 companies grant campground franchises; and the largest of these has over 500 campgrounds.

Camping in the cold-weather States is no longer just a summer activity. Today we have insulated clothing and insulated camping vehicles with modern heating plants and freezeproof plumbing. Along with this goes surging interest in snow-vehicle travel, cross-country skiing, downhill skiing, and even old-fashioned snowshoeing. These factors have combined to extend the camping season to 12 months for many campers and campground managers!

If you happen to be one of an estimated 7.5 million families in the United States that has considered, but postponed, your first camping vacation or recreational vehicle trip, you may be finding it difficult to resist the flood of new low-cost camping equipment and the increasingly common offers of fully-equipped campsites for rent.

For the beginning camper, borrowing or renting the equipment is undoubtedly the best way to try camping at minimum cost. Borrowing has always been a big business, but in recent years camping equipment rentals have become an important segment of the industry—particularly equipment which is all set up and ready to use right on the campsite of your choice. One in 10 campers now rents his equipment.

Even before borrowing, renting, or buying your first camping rig it pays to visit a camping equipment show to see what modern-day camping is all about. The 1971 camper market survey found that a third of all potential campers had

AUTHOR WILBUR F. LA PAGE is a Forest Service research project leader, and chairman of the Family Camping Federation's research committee.

COAUTHOR WALTER S. HOPKINS, formerly Chief of the Branch of Outdoor Recreation Research, Forest Service, is an Associate Professor of Forestry at Oregon State University.

COAUTHOR J. RICHARD WILLIAMS recently retired as Executive Director of the North American Family Campers Association.

Family at a campsite.

already visited at least one of these equipment extravaganzas.

Whether your camping interests tend to focus on lightweight backpacking in the wilderness, the comforts and conveniences of a $25,000 motor home, or any of the dozens of options in between, camping shows in major cities all across the country can be one of the best places to find the answers to your camping questions.

Among the major categories of equipment that you will find displayed at almost any camping show are:

TENTS: Tents continue to dominate the camping scene. A survey conducted for the Coleman Company indicated there are approximately 6 million tent owners (having 7.5 million tents) in the United States. That's half the total number of households that went camping in 1971. However, about a third of the tent owners also own a recreational vehicle of some kind.

Tents are found in a variety of sizes, colors, and shapes, and in a price range of less than $50 to around $200. Aside from the specialty tents designed for lightweight backpacking and winter use, most tents come equipped with an easily erected exterior frame, awnings, mosquito-proof windows with storm flaps, and a sewed-in floor.

Tent sizes refer to the dimensions of the floor: 8' x 10', 9' x 9', and 9' x 12' are the common sizes. In addition to floor size, tent shape plays an important role in determining the amount of living space in a tent. Within a comparable size class, cabin tents—because of their straight walls—have considerably more living space than umbrella tents.

Tent campers who wish to "smooth it" rather than "rough it" will need additional basic equipment. Most important are good sleeping bags (approximately $25 each) plus air mattresses ($10) or cots ($10). Also needed are a gasoline stove ($20) or one burning propane gas ($30) and a lantern ($15 to $25) using the same fuel as the selected stove. Essential is an ice chest ($5 plastic to $20 aluminum). Choose these items carefully. Consider practicality, durability, convenience, safety —and only then, economy.

But some campers aren't satisfied just to pitch a tent and rough it. They crave all the comforts of home while communing with nature. To appease that demand, American ingenuity has developed the recreational vehicle, a roving room on wheels. Five types of recreational vehicles are recognized, with amenities ranging from primitive to deluxe: pickup covers, camping trailers, travel trailers, truck or pickup campers, and motor homes.

PICKUP COVERS: This type is perhaps the simplest and lowest cost way of beating the pitch-a-tent routine or flopping on the ground in a sleeping bag with an air mattress. A cover is a simple roof over the pickup bed, with or without a door at the rear. This "dog house" can be prettied up with windows and metal trim. It provides an adequate shelter for two sleeping bags or cots placed on the pickup bed. Usually the weatherproof compartment contains no fold-out devices or special gimmickry.

CAMPING TRAILERS: A camping trailer (tent trailer) represents the next step up in luxury and convenience above the tent. While traveling, it's a compact box on wheels which, upon arrival, opens up into a tent sleeping 4 to 8 persons.

The camping trailer offers the convenience of a carrying case with an already-mounted platform for the tent. The range in price is from about $350 to $2,000; the more expensive models will include stoves, sinks, refrigerators, toilets, and detachable awnings and screened rooms for additional living space.

Known as "pop-ups," most camping trailers are equipped with simple devices by which one person can raise and lower the tent. Because they collapse to a low profile, camping trailers are easily towed behind almost any automobile.

Approximately 100,000 camping trailers were produced in 1972 and sold at an average price of $1,000. "Pop-ups" tend to be the most readily available rental recreational vehicle. Rental fees start at around $65 per week.

TRAVEL TRAILERS: Travel trailers represent the largest single segment of the recreational vehicle industry, with about 200,000 units produced in 1972. These vehicles range in size from about 12 feet in length to 32 feet, and sell from $700 to $17,000; 20-foot or 21-foot models are most popular, and the trend has been toward increasingly

sophisticated "self-containment"—toilets, hot showers, complete mini-kitchens, space-heaters, and air conditioning.

A travel trailer is heavier and less compact than a camping trailer, and more skill is required to maneuver it in and out of a campsite. But it has the big advantage of walk-in livability. No unfolding, unpacking, and rearranging is necessary.

Another advantage in using a travel trailer is that the tow vehicle can be detached quickly and used separately for running campground errands or going "downtown."

A recent variation of the basic travel trailer is the fifth wheel hitch, which means pulling the trailer with a pickup truck instead of a car. The hookup resembles the common tractor-trailer hitch, with the pickup bed serving as the anchor point. The front of the travel trailer is designed with a gooseneck projection to accommodate the coupling hitch underneath.

TRUCK CAMPERS: Pickup or truck campers are equipped much like the travel trailer except that they are built to slide onto the bed of a pickup truck. Many of the larger, more fully equipped units are permanently attached to the frame of a ¾-ton truck.

Truck camper units range in price from $1,000 to about $10,000, with the average unit selling for around $2,000 plus the cost of the pickup truck.

Together with pickup covers or caps—the empty shell which fits onto a pickup body to provide sleeping shelter only—this segment of the industry accounted for another 200,000 units in 1972.

MOTOR HOMES: These self-powered homes on wheels represent the smallest, most expensive, yet the fastest-growing segment of the recreational vehicle industry. About 60,000 units were produced in 1972 and sold from $5,000 for a simple van conversion to over $25,000. Motor homes, in lengths up to 36 feet, combine the comfort and the self-containment of a travel trailer, with the convenience and driving ease of a pickup.

WHERE TO CAMP: Camping equipment shows (and dealer showrooms as well) are not only good places to find out *how* to camp, they can also be an important source of ideas about *where* to camp. With nearly one million camp-sites in 18,000 campgrounds in the United States and Canada, novice campers and "oldtimers" alike increasingly need new ways of locating and evaluating campgrounds before they undertake their trips.

Several different State, regional, and national campground guidebooks are now published and updated annually. Some of them are as large as a Manhattan phone directory. The Woodall Publishing Co., Rand-McNally, the American Automobile Association, and others have extensive programs of campground inspections for their annual directories of public and commercial campgrounds in North America.

According to Woodall's listings, there are twice as many campsites on private land as now exist on all national parks, national forests, and State parks combined. Not only do the private developments outnumber the public, most are newer and contain more modern conveniences. But many public park systems have also "gone modern." Oregon's State Park System and several others are well along toward providing full utility connections (water, electricity, sewer) at every camping site.

HOW IT ALL STARTED: Growth of the commercial campground industry in America closely parallels that of the recreational vehicle industry. As the campground industry rapidly matured, it went through at least three distinct "generations" of camping developments.

The first "generation" of private campgrounds, which actually started before World War II, was characterized by small "Mom and Pop" developments of less than 50 campsites, built with an average investment of less than $20,000. As more and more people went camping, and recreational vehicles became increasingly common, new, well-equipped campgrounds began springing up. The second generation of commercial campgrounds began about 1964 when the first generation was at the peak of its growth. This was the generation of big business entering the camping field. The continued expansion of the recreational vehicle industry had begun to attract the attention of large investors, landowning corporations, motel chains, and oil companies.

While most first-generation campgrounds had been developed as a source of extra income on land already owned by the developer, new investors were looking for land to buy in the right locations for attracting campers. At the same time, franchising entered the scene—providing chains of campgrounds all across the country, reservation services, and high quality standards.

Second generation campgrounds were bigger, averaging nearly 100 campsites, more expensive to develop (from $50,000 to $100,000 each), and they offered a larger array of services and facilities such as campground stores, recreation halls, laundromats, and supervised recreation programs. Full utility connections for recreation vehicles became common, with half or more of the sites having at least an electrical connection.

The late 1960's and early 1970's saw the introduction of commercial camping's third generation, the "resort campground." Because of large development expense (often $1 million and more), most resort campgrounds are found in Florida and similar areas where a year-long camping season is assured. However, there are a few in such Northern States as Maine and Michigan.

These "campgrounds" contain the ultimate in services: marinas, gas stations, restaurants, movies, water sports, golf and tennis, sports instruction, craft and souvenir shops, baby tending, and even discotheque bars. Characteristically built on exceptionally attractive water bodies, these campsites have fees that vary from as much as $16 for a waterfront site to a low $5 or $6 well back from the water.

One of the most recent innovations in third-generation campgrounds is the

69

A variety of recreational vehicles and tents at campsites on the national forests.

condominium campground where you buy your campsite and pay an annual maintenance fee for campground upkeep. The condominium offers some of the comfort and convenience of a second home, without the high initial investment and taxes that characterize most resort communities. You may even be able to rent the site to others when you are not using it.

If the convenience and personal service of commercial campgrounds is not important to you, there are literally thousands of developed campsites in the national forests, national parks, and State parks in America. Many of these are within or adjoin some of the most spectacular scenic areas in America. A few municipal and county parks also have developed campgrounds which are open to the general public.

The National Forest System, alone, has more than 5,000 campgrounds containing almost 82,000 individual campsites. The National Park Service provides an additional 28,000 campsites at over 400 locations.

In contrast to resort, condominium, and other destination type campgrounds, an excellent system of overnight camping accommodations is available along major interstate highways. These campgrounds are sufficiently removed from the noise of the turnpike to provide a quiet night's rest. But instead of tennis courts and other recreational opportunities, these campgrounds offer a variety of services aimed at helping to speed the traveler on his way: restaurants, dumping stations, auto services, propane refills, and equipment repairs.

An atmosphere of warmth and congeniality pervades most campgrounds. Getting acquainted, comparing equipment, and sharing ideas and stories is part of the experience.

For those times when you prefer solitude, you might try "houseboat camping," or wilderness backpack camping in one of the 90 designated wildernesses in the National Wilderness Preservation System. The latter offer a diversity of experiences from canoe

camping in the Quetico-Superior region of northern Minnesota to a pack trip into the Pecos Wilderness of New Mexico's Santa Fe National Forest.

Camping, because of its diversity of forms and appeals, seems to have something to offer nearly everyone. It combines the American's appreciation for the outdoors with his fascination for gadgets and motor vehicles. The camping market's growth of the 1960's has not been without its problems of campground crowding and littering, highway congestion, inadequate facilities and services. However, most of its participants are thoughtful, upstanding citizens, and like America itself, the camping market's strength is in its diversity.

For further reading:

Ade, Ginny. "Commuter Campgrounds," *Holiday,* March/April 1972.

Chaplin, Red. *Tips for New Campers.* What to look for in buying equipment and commonly asked questions answered. Published by North American Family Camping Association, 76 State Street, Newburyport, Mass. 01950. Send stamped self-addressed envelope. 1972.

Cunningham, Jerry. "Wilderness Gateway," a monthly column on backpack camping appearing in *Better Camping,* Woodall Publ. Co., Highland Park, Ill.

Family Camping Federation of America. Reports of the First and Second Annual American Camping Congresses, Chicago, Ill. Martinsville, Ind., 1971–72.

LaPage, W. F. *Camping Market Research for Developers,* a collection of camping market research reports, pub. by USDA Forest Service, Upper Darby, Pa. 1972. (No charge).

Miller, James Nathan. "Those Rolling Homes Away From Home," *Reader's Digest,* January 1973.

Riviere, Bill. *The Camper's Bible,* Doubleday, Inc., Garden City, L.I., N.Y. Good basic paperback on camping techniques.

Gardening Galore—
Bring the Outdoors
Inside: Terrariums,
Bonsai, Hybrids

Gᴀʀᴅᴇɴɪɴɢ started with the Garden of Eden. Undoubtedly it will continue as long as there is a civilized way of life. In fact, the more sophisticated and advanced our culture becomes, the more we seem to need the relaxation of growing our own plants.

Gardening can be an easygoing hobby, a scientific pursuit, an opportunity for exercise and fresh air, a serious source of food to help balance the family budget, a means of expression in art and beauty, an applied experiment in green plant growth, or all of these things together.

You may be a city dweller whose yearning for green plants is satisfied by minigardens in the house or patio. A shut-in who can enjoy container grown plants. A homeowner in the suburbs whose garden is a basement. Or you may be someone in the wide open spaces who is letting loose his full yearn for creativity.

Gardening has no bounds, no space limitations, no requirements that cannot be met readily in today's world. Not really needed are power tools, large areas of sunshine-bathed land, or even a strong back. A gardener is not restricted by any age limitations, training requirements, or any social background from doing "his thing." And many physically handicapped persons can garden.

Here are a few ideas on gardening for fun and health.

You can grow plants or seedlings in

Indoor gardens can beautify many areas of a home.

any room in your home from basement to attic. Cool, efficient fluorescent lighting has made gardening inside feasible. Through indoor gardening, plants can live from the small germinating seed to full maturity without once seeing the sun.

ᴀᴜᴛʜᴏʀ ᴀᴜɢᴜsᴛ ᴇ. ᴋᴇʜʀ is Staff Scientist, Vegetables and Ornamentals, National Program Staff, Agricultural Research Service.

Indoor lighting of a container garden with a circular fluorescent light.

Estimate of light requirements of some common plants:

Low	Medium
Most ferns	Schefflera
English ivy	Dumb Cane
Pothos	Rubber plants

High	Very High
Norfolk Island Pine	Most flowering plants
Citrus	All vegetable plants
Coleus	Begonias
Caladium	African-violets
	Orchids

Illumination in foot-candles at various distances from two or four 40-watt standard cool-white fluoresent lamps:

Distance from lamps (inches)	Two lamps (Used 200 hours)	Four lamps mounted 2 inches apart	
		Used 200 hours	New lamps
	Ft.c	Ft.c	Ft.c
1	1,100	1,600	1,800
2	860	1,400	1,600
3	680	1,300	1,400
4	570	1,100	1,300
5	500	940	1,150
6	420	820	1,000
7	360	720	900
8	330	660	830
9	300	600	780
10	280	560	720
11	260	510	660
12	240	480	600
18	130	320	420
24	100	190	260

But it is in the basement that gardening indoors has really blossomed. Plants may be grown in a wide range of structures in the basement. One man grows seedlings successfully in an old refrigerator. He merely placed a discarded 14 cubic foot refrigerator on its back on four cement blocks. Lights were installed in the door.

For indoor gardening, the light level determines the type of plants you can grow. Plants can be classed in four groups of light requirements: low (50 to 200 foot-candles), medium (200 to 500 foot-candles), high (500-1,000 foot-candles), and very high (over 1,000 foot-candles). A foot-candle of light is the measure of light intensity given off by one candle at a distance of 1 foot from the point of light.

The tables may be helpful to you in determining light requirements and how to meet them.

Here are a few rules that must be observed to grow most plants indoors:
• Provide proper light equivalent.
• Give the plants light for 14 to 16 hours each day.
• Provide a temperature of about 60° to 65°F. for the dark period and 70° to 75°F. during the light period.
• Keep the plants on the dry side—avoid overwatering. Plants suffer more from too much water than from too little water.
• Underfeed rather than overfeed. Preferably use a slow release fertilizer or organic fertilizer.
• Use an artificial soil that can be purchased. These artificial soils are usually 50-50 peat moss and perlite or vermiculite.

73

Water gardening can be fun. From left to right are English ivy, aluminum plant, and peperomia.

Water gardens are easy and satisfying. A simple water garden for a sunny window is a vine grown from a sweetpotato. Merely suspend the bottom half of a sweetpotato in a bottle filled with water. The bottom of the sweetpotato is the half which has no stem scar. Roots will form rapidly on the bottom half and sprouts on the top half.

Another simple water garden is the stem end of a carrot, cut with about 1 inch of the carrot, and placed in a shallow container of water. The stem will sprout into a beautiful green growth that will be a welcome sight in a bright, sunny window at any time of year.

You can grow attractive water gardens by sticking cuttings into various forms or shapes of styrofoam, and placing the arrangement in a shallow container of water. You may want to add wisely chosen colorful or attractive dried material to the living plants.

Plants that can be used in these arrangements are aucuba, ivy, grape ivy, peperomia, philodendron, and pothos. One arrangement was cleverly worked into a small bird's nest, with a colorful toy bird on the nest.

More venturesome gardeners might try growing mushrooms indoors in cool, dark basements. The propagating material used to grow them is called spawn, and the pasteurized organic material is called compost.

In recent years a few nurserymen and seedsmen have been offering for sale trays containing mushroom compost especially prepared for home use, which appear to be the solution to many of the problems of growing mushrooms at home. The trays include spawn.

It is recommended that the amateur grower purchase these prepared trays instead of attempting to make his own mushroom compost. They are prepared for the nurserymen and seedsmen by commercial mushroom growers who are equipped to compost manure economi-

74

cally on a large scale, to pasteurize the compost effectively, and grow spawn in the trays.

Full directions for growing mushrooms are furnished along with the trays. If the directions are carefully followed, and the trays placed in a cool, damp location, moderate yields can be expected—usually between a half pound and a pound per square foot of tray space.

Once the mushrooms begin to appear on the trays, they will continue to develop for about 60 days.

As mushrooms do not need light for normal development, they can be grown in a basement room or shed where it would be impossible to grow green plants. Growing space must be available in which the temperature can be maintained under 65° F., and the humidity of the air kept moderately high.

Some ventilation is necessary, but the number of air changes normally occurring in the average basement will usually be sufficient for a few square feet of mushroom bed.

Indoor container gardening is another activity you might like. Growing plants in containers can be fun for youngsters as well as the not so young. Containers that may be used are limited only by your imagination—aquariums, old bottles, canning jars, plastic toys, china pottery, or concrete tubs on a patio.

Vegetables can be grown in pails, tubs, baskets. They may be grown on doorsteps, balconies, porches, carports. You need only your choice of a container, artificial soil, and seeds. Artificial soil is free from disease organisms and

Top photo, plants going into a water garden should be cut on the stem just below the node—the point where a leaf originates. Center photo, arranging pothos leaves in florists foam in a container. Each node should be inserted into the foam so the preformed root can develop rapidly. Bottom photo, cut flowers have been added to the arrangement of pothos leaves. They should be watered every three or four days to maintain freshness.

Mums are excellent plants to supply color for container gardens, either in minipots or in larger containers with other plants.

weed seeds, and is very lightweight and portable.

Tomato or leaf lettuce plants grown in a suitable container will not only be decorative and fun to grow but result in great salads. Onions, peppers, and even a cabbage plant may also be grown in a container.

Terrariums are glass-enclosed gardens. Fish tanks, brandy snifters, old bottles of any size, even quart fruit jars may be used. Terrariums can be fashioned as a base for a lamp, and thus provide light to the plants as well as beauty to a room.

Many native and cultivated plants are suitable for growing in a terrarium or bottle garden, especially those that require high humidity—African-violets, ferns, coleus, ivy. You can collect plants that are ideally suitable in the woods, if you are lucky enough to have woods to wander in.

Place a layer of gravel or pebbles, in the bottom of the container for drainage. Dig moss from the woods to line the sides of the container below the soil level, with the moss placed against the glass. Then put in a 2-inch layer of synthetic soil (or if you wish, ⅓ garden soil, ⅓ peat moss, and ⅓ sand).

Plant, using sticks, wires, or any other convenient tools to put the plants in place. Avoid getting dirt on the inside glass walls or the plant leaves. Water lightly if needed and cover with glass or plastic to close the container. Once planted, the terrarium rarely needs water, only indirect sunlight or artificial light.

Gardens in miniature are fascinating, and provide opportunity for expressing your artistic leanings. They run the gamut of miniature rock gardens, landscapes, portable rock gardens, miniature herb gardens, miniature roses, cactus gardens, and miniature bog gardens with insect-catching plants. Even well chosen woodland flowers can be developed into a small wild flower garden for a city dweller.

The Brooklyn Botanic Garden has published a handbook on miniature gardens which gives detailed instructions for this very satisfying activity. It can be obtained by requesting "Handbook on Miniature Gardens," Manual No. 58, Brooklyn Botanic Garden, 1000 Washington Ave., Brooklyn, N.Y. 11225. The price is $1.25.

A discussion of container gardens is not complete without a mention of bonsai. The Japanese word bonsai means "tray planting." This method of growing plants is so popular that bonsai societies are springing up in many metropolitan areas.

In theory, bonsai trees and plants are dwarf growing because their roots are restricted either by pruning or by being grown in a very small container. Plants 100 years old may be less than a couple of feet high.

The simplest bonsai garden is developed by growing trees or shrubs from seeds sown directly in a selected shallow container of 2 to 4 inches in depth. The seeds—when allowed to grow for a few years, and thinned, pruned, or trained in various shapes—take on the appearance of a forest in miniature. Tree seeds such as pines, spruce, Japanese maples, and ginkgo may be used, or shrubs such as holly and boxwood.

Top, getting a terrarium together. Seven specimens were used in this 16-inch bubble. Soil may be covered with bark chips for more pleasing appearance. Above, terrarium made to be viewed from one side. Soil was graded low in front, high in back.

Others may wish to buy plants for their bonsai hobby. Dwarf conifers are sold by many nurseries. With persistence, the leisure-time gardener can find miniature plants of all decriptions, especially from firms dealing with rock garden plants.

Most libraries will provide a wealth of books dealing with bonsai.

Plant hybridization can make a fine hobby for an advanced gardener. Hybridizing plants to create new types is an activity that many people are trying. It is usually done to bring together, in a single plant, two or more unlike characters in the parent plants. There are virtually unlimited opportunities with almost all plant materials.

Techniques of cross-pollinating plants are easy to learn and little equipment is needed. Amateur plant breeders have developed many of the beautiful plants available to us today—African-violets, daylilies, roses, gladiolus, azaleas, and rhododendrons are only a few.

Some vegetables may be good crops for the leisure time gardener to experiment with.

PERFECT FLOWER

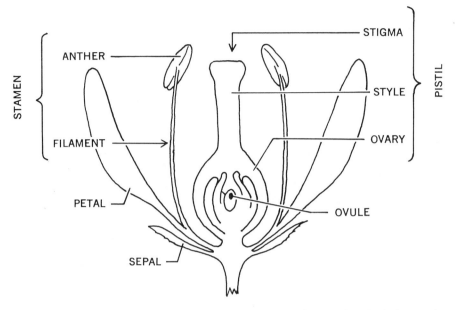

Parts of a flower. The flower shown here is a perfect flower; that is, it has male and female reproductive organs. The stamen is the male organ and the pistil is the female organ.

A careful study of the structure of flowers and the sexual reproductive organs of the plants to be hybridized should be made before any work is attempted. See the sketches with this chapter.

The following equipment is helpful, if not essential, in cross-pollination work.

A hand lens
A pair of tweezers
A small camel hair brush for pollen transfer
A box of tags with strings for attaching
A pencil
A supply of small bags.

Cross-pollination consists of transferring pollen of one plant to the stigmas of a flower of another plant. To assure that only the desired pollen will fertilize the ovules of the selected female parent, its own pollen must be prevented from reaching its stigmas.

Where possible this is best done by emasculation. Remove the anthers from the flower of the female parent with tweezers or other instrument before the anthers have shed their pollen (in case of perfect flowers—those with both male and female reproductive organs). Then cover the remainder of the flower with a small paper or cellophane bag to prevent insects, wind, or other agents from placing undesired pollen on its stigmas. In case of imperfect flowers, emasculation or anther removal is not necessary; the cover alone will prevent crossing.

When stigmatic surfaces of the emasculated or depollinated flower of the female parent have become receptive (usually indicated by stickiness of the surfaces), pollen from the desired male parent should be applied to the sticky surfaces. A camel hair brush is handy for this job.

A tag with a record of the cross should be attached to the stem of the

IMPERFECT FLOWER

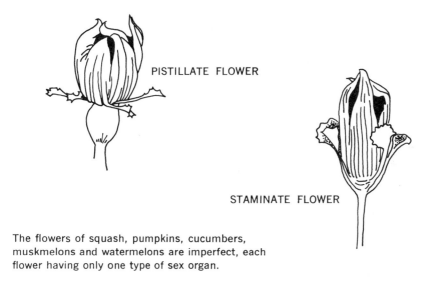

PISTILLATE FLOWER

STAMINATE FLOWER

The flowers of squash, pumpkins, cucumbers, muskmelons and watermelons are imperfect, each flower having only one type of sex organ.

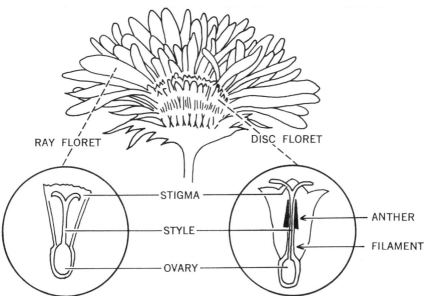

RAY FLORET

DISC FLORET

STIGMA

STYLE

OVARY

ANTHER

FILAMENT

Cross section of chrysanthemum. Flowers, such as chrysanthemums, zinnias, marigolds, and daisies are made up of clusters of florets.

flower. The flower should be covered again for a few days to assure that no undesired pollen reaches the stigmas until fertilization has taken place.

Fertilization is indicated by development of the ovary. Seed resulting from the cross will produce hybrid plants.

If fertilization has failed, the entire

flower will fall off within a few days, in most cases.

Generally speaking, plants within the same species can be successfully crossed. However, now and then crosses between varieties within a species may fail. Crosses between species are often unsuccessful, but a few such crosses may succeed.

For the leisure time gardener, many other activities may be of interest. Briefly, here are a few:

Build a plastic greenhouse, or even a more permanent glasshouse. For information obtain CA-34-134 List of Sources of Information on Greenhouses from the U.S. Department of Agriculture, Washington, D.C. 20250.

Develop an espaliered tree or shrub. The shaping of trees and shrubs on a trellis or against a wall is an art which is becoming more popular in this country. It requires only judicious pruning and can be mastered if you are a determined gardener. Before starting the project, try your library for books on the subject.

Join a plant society, plant arboretum, or a horticultural society. Gardening is more fun if you share your experiences with others. You can find names and addresses of such organizations in the Directory of American Horticulture. This book is available in most libraries.

Build a foyer garden or table garden. These gardens are decorative and provide many hours of enjoyment.

Tweezers are handy for removing the anthers—a necessary step in cross pollination of plants. A camel hair brush may be used to apply pollen from another plant to produce hybrid seed.

For further reading:
U.S. Department of Agriculture publications—

Minigardens for Vegetables, Home and Garden Bulletin 163, Washington, D.C. 20250.

Selecting and Growing House Plants, Home and Garden Bulletin 82, Washington, D.C. 20250.

Growing Ornamentals in Urban Gardens, Home and Garden Bulletin 188, Washington, D.C. 20250.

Building Hobby Greenhouses, Agriculture Information Bulletin No. 357, Superintendent of Documents, Government Printing Office, Washington, D.C. 20402, 25 cents.

43 Million Volunteers
Do a Zillion Things
For Their Communities

THE VOLUNTEER MOVEMENT in America—43 million strong and growing—appears to contradict the old saw that "you can't get something for nothing." Volunteers spend their time and energy on projects that benefit someone else. The service agencies they work with can't as a rule offer remuneration. The people they help can't give anything in return. These millions of volunteers do something for nothing.

Nothing tangible, at least.

A housewife looking in on shut-ins by phone finds personal satisfaction, knowing she has brightened a lonely day.

A suburbanite coaching a basketball team made up of inner city youngsters gains in sensitivity to their special problems.

A women's league provides babysitters for disabled youngsters to give parents relief from the demanding care these children require. And benefits from the knowledge that it is filling a desperate community need.

Something for nothing? In a way, yes. In a way, no.

A barrage of news about social tensions, world problems, urban blight, rural poverty, and personal tragedies reaches us daily. It can be overwhelming. People ask, "Is there ever any *good* news?" Volunteers have an answer for them because they have discovered the truth in another old saw—that by giving, you receive. By doing something, however small, to solve another person's problems, volunteers have learned that they can also begin to solve some of their own problems, their community's, and society's.

That's good news. Volunteer efforts may not make the front page of the major dailies, but they cause a dramatic difference in the lives of both those being helped and those giving a hand.

Small wonder then, that a fifth of our total population is already volunteering. And the National Center for Voluntary Action believes that millions more citizens would like to become involved but aren't sure how to go about it, aren't sure what they have to offer.

There are as many recipes for volunteering as there are for barbecuing, and more are being written every day. But each volunteer starts with roughly the same basic ingredients.

The first is time.

Service agencies sometimes classify volunteers according to the amount of time they can give. A permanent volunteer works on a regular basis (either part-time or full-time) with no set date on which he or she intends to end volunteer service. A retired accountant, for instance, walked into a volunteer center in Chattanooga, Tenn., 6 years ago and offered his services. He's been keeping the books there ever since.

Temporary volunteers work for a specified period of time. For example, a teacher might spend the summer months working at a camp for inner city youngsters, then return to a regular position. Intermittent volunteers want to help but can't offer their services on any regular, scheduled basis. Instead they are available for a specific project.

Available skills constitute the biggest batch of ingredients that any volunteer adds to his or her own volunteer recipe. These can range from being able to talk on the telephone to managing a fund raising campaign. Some programs need people who can listen, some need those with teaching experiences, clerical skills, a knack for crafts, or an ability to write.

Can you cook, sew, drive a car, coach a sport, read to people, work well with

AUTHORS KATE ALFRIEND AND BONNIE KREITLER are information specialists in the Office of Communication.

Above, USDA workers in New Orleans play Dixieland jazz for institutionalized children and for senior citizen groups. Right, retired teacher runs a drama program for young children in Staunton, Va.

youngsters? You can volunteer. In fact, volunteer programs run on the premise that no one is unskilled and everyone has something to offer.

Another set of ingredients might be loosely termed "available capital." Do you have a phone? Could you provide transportation for those without a car? Do you have a rare blood type? Add these to your volunteer recipe.

The final ingredient is a decision about whether formal or informal volunteer projects will suit you best. Your office might decide to put on a music program for a local nursing home around Christmastime—a very informal volunteer effort. Someone else might be interested in joining forces with a formally organized program such as Foster Grandparents.

Many people look close to home when volunteering. Museums, libraries, legal aid societies, drug abuse centers, ecology groups, schools, nursing homes, settlement houses, youth groups, cooperative extension services, and institutions for the handicapped make only

Participant in RSVP feeds elderly patient at infirmary in Madison County, New York. RSVP, based on the program SERVE (Serve and Enrich Retirement by Volunteer Experience) developed in New York City, is federally funded under ACTION. In Madison County it operates through the Cooperative Extension Service.

a partial list of the community groups with volunteer help. Contacting each one individually is a tedious business. In some communities you can simplify this by going through a volunteer placement bureau.

Over 235 communities across the nation currently have either a voluntary action center or a volunteer bureau. These groups are coordinating bodies for local service agencies that need volunteer support, providing them with technical aid in various areas, helping them avoid duplication of effort, and motivating volunteers. They also function as a placement service for people who aren't sure what volunteer opportunities there are or what sort of volunteer work they are suited for.

Voluntary action centers are affiliated with the National Center for Voluntary

Action (1735 I St., N.W., Washington, D.C. 20006). In addition to its other services, this privately-supported, nonprofit parent organization makes case histories of successful volunteer efforts available to those looking for solutions to similar problems.

Volunteer bureaus are affiliated with the United Way of America located at 801 N. Washington Street, Alexandria, Virginia 22314. Both parent organizations will provide lists of their affiliate groups and will also help local groups interested in starting a volunteer bureau or voluntary action center in their community.

If your community doesn't have a volunteer bureau or voluntary action center, check with either the local health and welfare council (or its equivalent) or the local branch of the United Way or Community Chest. They may not operate a volunteer placement service, but they will at least be able to provide a list of the agencies they serve. You should also be able to learn about the areas of greatest need in your community.

Volunteers form the mainstay of many Red Cross and Salvation Army programs. Both often look for help via the volunteer clearinghouses already mentioned. But in communities where no other group coordinates volunteer placement, a direct call to one of these agencies may guide you to local needs.

Extension Service offices are located in nearly every county in the United States, and the agents there can guide you to volunteer projects. County agents are not only aware of the many State programs using volunteers which operate in their counties, but also receive information regularly from groups such as the National Center for Voluntary Action. They can give you a lot of leads and frequently can place you in their programs.

Look up the county Extension office in your local phone book or call your county government offices for the number.

Churches, women's leagues, Jaycees, and many other civic groups organize local community service efforts. These are often of short duration, but some have ongoing programs that would welcome the support of non-members. One of these projects might match up your skills with a community need.

ACTION is a Government agency set up in 1971 as a citizens service corps to enable Americans to volunteer their services both at home and abroad. ACTION's programs are all formal volunteer efforts and since some of them include stipends for volunteers, purists claim they are not true volunteer programs. Still, ACTION offers those who want to serve others some unique opportunities they won't find elsewhere.

The Peace Corps, Volunteers in Service to America (VISTA), the University Year for Action, the Foster Grandparents program, the Retired Senior Volunteer program (RSVP), the Service Corps of Retired Executives (SCORE), and the Active Corps of Executives (ACE) are all under ACTION's umbrella (806 Connecticut Ave., N.W., Washington, D.C. 20525).

In recent years, many volunteer agencies have realized America has a great wealth of "senior power" waiting to be tapped. Special programs utilizing this pool of talent have sprung up.

On a national level, for example, ACTION operates the Retired Senior Volunteer Program (RSVP) which places older citizens in local volunteer projects, and the Service Corps of Retired Executives (SCORE) which gives retired businessmen and women the opportunity to offer their professional services and guidance to small businessmen who need advice.

State education departments are using the skills of retired teachers and teacher-aides in adult education programs to help undereducated individuals.

Many of these new programs for senior volunteers carry an added benefit—a small stipend or wage to supplement the meager fixed income which many of them must live on. These stipends not only help the volunteer, but can also help the community by

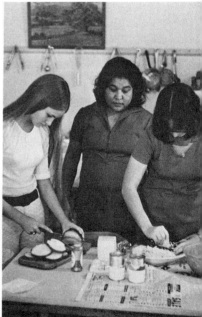

Volunteer homemakers trained in an Extension program to aid low-income families conduct a cooking class for youth group and a dressmaking class.

making the difference between someone who is dependent on the community and someone who can actively contribute to it. The stipends and wages can boost the senior volunteer's feeling of self-esteem as well as economic independence.

Green Thumb is one work program that offers rural senior citizens some pay. It is sponsored by the National Farmers Union (1012 14th St., N.W., Washington, D.C. 20005) under a grant from the U.S. Department of Labor. Retired persons with farm or rural backgrounds who are 55 or over and have incomes below the poverty level are employed on projects involving restoration of historical sites, creation of parks and recreation areas, and beautification of communities. Others take on community service and outreach efforts. They work 3 days a week for a small hourly wage, earning up to $1,600 a year.

ACTION's Foster Grandparents Program uses low income persons over 60 to provide companionship and guidance to mentally, physically, or emotionally handicapped children in institutions. This agency also uses senior volunteers in its Peace Corps and VISTA programs. Retired teachers can earn added income as part of the Teachers Corps (Office of Education, Washington, D.C. 20202).

Information on other paid volunteer opportunities for senior citizens is available from both the Department of Labor (Washington, D.C. 20210) and from the Administration on Aging (U.S. Department of Health, Education, and Welfare, Washington, D.C. 20201).

Volunteers are acknowledged as the backbone of many vital community services. They fill in where government funds and programs leave off, enriching the lives of their fellow citizens and their own lives as well.

Forty-three million Americans have found that volunteerism is a solution to problems, a way to make changes. They think that doing something for nothing is well worth their while. Care to join them?

Insurance for Your Health, Car, Life

IF YOU HAVE NO interest or concern for your family's financial security, the following information will be of no value to you.

How would your family react emotionally and financially toward a long-term illness? A legal suit brought against you because of inadequate car insurance? Or the death of the breadwinner of your family?

Insurance, whether it be health, car, or life, is protection for you and your family against risk.

Good health is one of the most valuable things in life, but good health is not a product that remains the same throughout life. By having adequate health insurance, the risk of financial disaster from a long-term illness can largely be relieved.

It is often very hard to sort out the facts and obtain the kind of health insurance you are seeking because health insurance contracts are detailed and not the easiest to understand. If you will look for the following six items, you will be likely to get the essential in your health insurance plan:

• What are types of expenses that are covered by the policy?

Every policy covers certain kinds of expenses, and these expenses will be subject to certain conditions. Hospital indemnity, which is one of the simplest forms of health insurance, will pay only a fixed amount while you are hospitalized. If you receive outpatient treatment, you probably will collect nothing.

• How much will the policy pay?

AUTHOR CHARLOTTE GEORGE is a State Family Economics and Management Specialist at the University of Missouri-Columbia.

490-100 O - 73 - 7

The glowing ads give the top payments possible, but few policyholders receive the top payment. To be safe about what the policy does and does not cover, get a copy of the actual policy and study it.

When the ad for a health insurance plan says, "Up to $20,800 extra cash when you're in the hospital" and "Get $100 tax free each week," stop and do some thinking and figuring. To collect the $20,800 at the benefit rate of $100, you would have to be hospitalized for 4 years!

Not considering maternity, mental, and TB cases, only 15 out of 100 people are hospitalized during any one year. The average hospital stay is 8 days. Those with the highest hospitalization rate stay an average of 12 days.

Look at other methods designed to limit payments. These might include deductibles, copayment provisions requiring you to pay a portion of the expenses, and the specified amount allotted for various kinds of operations.

Always find out what the limits and restrictions are in any policy. If you are paying $50 per day for your room, plus drugs, X-rays, and operating room expense, and the indemnity policy pays $14 a day, you are going to be left with the remainder of the hospitalization expense.

• Is there a waiting period before benefits go into effect?

Usually, individual policies (in contrast to group policies) have a clause stating that you can't collect during the first 2 years for an illness you had before you enrolled in the plan, or you may not receive benefits even though you didn't know about the condition at the time.

Be alert to such clauses as "benefit builder" period. Be sure you get the details. In some policies there may be more than one kind of waiting period in the policy.

• Is the policy renewable?

If a policy is stated as noncancellable, the company can't cancel until the premium period lapses on the policy. However, the company can refuse to renew the policy. Few companies offer a truly noncancellable policy.

When reading the ads and policies you will find that the company can cancel, refuse renewal, or raise premiums if it does so for all policyholders of the same "class." What is a "class?" It can mean all people in the same State with the same coverage, or all people in a group of the same age. Some companies guarantee renewal but maintain the right to raise rates on a class basis.

• Does the coverage supplement Medicare?

Services such as dental treatment, eyeglasses, medical appliances, and drugs not supplied by a hospital are not covered by Medicare. If the policy being considered to supplement Medicare concentrates its benefits on hospitalization or on services covered by Medicare, it still isn't going to provide the coverage needed. The policyholder will have some uncovered costs to face.

• Is the company licensed in your State?

You can protect yourself more adequately and efficiently to some extent by insuring with companies licensed by your State. If you have a complaint against a company licensed in your State, the State insurance department can proceed against the company with more ease.

In considering a given company, be sure to find out if the company is licensed. Your State insurance department will be able to provide this information.

When starting your health insurance program, begin with basic coverage. There is no policy that will cover all the potential costs. Begin with an insurance that pays for a range of major costs—hospitalization and surgery. Then choose a reliable "major medical" policy that is designed for covering the costs of serious illness.

Before buying any insurance, whether it is through a group protection or an individual policy, review carefully the insurance coverage you already have. Remember, group protection usually provides more comprehensive coverage at a lower rate.

If you are nearing 65, it is particularly important to review what you have, because many policies reduce benefits when you qualify for Medicare. If you are interested in learning more about the Medicare program, ask for a free copy of *Your Medicare Handbook* at the Social Security Administration Office in your area.

Shopping for auto insurance can present many problems and leave you very distraught. However, if you know the basic features to look for, you can shop with more confidence and are likely to get more for your money.

Auto insurance can be bought in the form of a bundle of coverage or each section in the bundle can be bought separately.

Liability is the core of an auto policy. With liability coverage the insurance pays for bodily injury and property damage to others when you are legally responsible for the accident.

Claims against you may be settled out of court; or if court action is brought against you, the company will defend you. The protection covers you, resident members of the family, and others who drive with your approval. You and members of your family are also covered when driving another car with the owner's consent.

Liability coverage is stated separately for bodily injury and property damage. The maximum coverage is generally stated in a form such as 10/20/5. This indicates the company is liable for up to $10,000 for any one person injured; up to $20,000 for all injuries in the same accident; and up to $5,000 for damage to the other car, fences, and other property. For damages exceeding these amounts you are responsible.

Liability coverage pays for other people's injuries—not yours. Medical payments cover you and your passengers' medical fees regardless of who was to blame for the accident. Medical payments coverage is sold in amounts ranging from $500 to $5,000. The limit is for each person injured, so with a

$500 plan, four people would collect a total of $2,000.

The uninsured motorist coverage offers protection to you, your spouse, and resident children if you are struck while driving or walking by an uninsured or hit-and-run-driver.
• The coverage applies only when the other driver was to blame for the accident
• The insurance applies only to bodily injury in most States
• Bodily injury payments generally are limited to minimums of State liability regardless of the face value of the basic policy

Collision pays for damage to your car when you hit another vehicle or an object like a tree, telephone pole, etc.

Collision coverage is usually sold in the form of $50, $100, or $200 deductible. If you collide with a tree, do $150 damage to your car and you have $50 deductible, the company will pay $100.

The larger the amount of deductible, the less the premium. In most instances by buying a $100 deductible collision rather than $50 you can cut about 20 percent of the collision premium.

The company keeps its responsibility to the "actual cash value" of the car. This means that if your car is worth $700, that is the most you can expect to receive on a collision claim. Regardless of how dear to your heart the "old crate" is, the company will not spend $800 to repair it. Consider the value of your car. It may be unwise economically to buy collision coverage for an old car.

Losses caused by fire, wind, theft, vandalism, collision with animals, explosions, flood, and lightning are covered by the comprehensive coverage feature. Comprehensive does provide limited coverage for personal effects left in the car. If you have a homeowner's insurance policy, there may be additional coverage for personal effects left in your car. Discuss this with the agent who sold you the homeowner's policy.

Accidental death and dismemberment coverage pays a lump sum for death in a car accident, loss of a limb, blindness, fractures, and dislocations, plus a disability benefit each week. This accidental death often overlaps coverage from liability and other insurance. Therefore, you are spending premium money for overlapping coverages.

Premium rates vary by locality and State and according to the loss experience of the company. But these factors are heavily weighed according to:
• The purposes your car is used for: pleasure, business, or farmwork. Business takes the highest rate and farmwork receives the lowest
• Age (teenagers are considered a high risk)
• Marital status (a young married man is considered a better risk than a young bachelor)
• Whether you drive to work, and the distance to work if you do
• Total mileage. A car driven over a certain distance in a year is often subject to a higher insurance rate

Special rating factors can help trim premiums. Some of the examples for you to explore are:
1. If your son or daughter ranks in the top 20 percent of his class, or is on the dean's list, ask the company if it has a good-student discount
2. Encourage your young person to take driver training. Generally, that will qualify him for a driver-training discount
3. If another car is bought for the family, include the car on your policy. This will entitle you to a multicar discount on the second car
4. Check with the company about the age a young driver passes from the high premium category to the lower premium adult category, and remind the company when he reaches this age
5. When buying a car, find out if the car is subject to the "souped up" car surcharge
6. Check on companies offering the "safe driver" plan. If you have an "accident or traffic violation free" driving record, you can realize considerable savings on your auto insurance premium.
7. Remember there is no best company. Be knowledgeable about the types of coverage available and do some cost comparing among two or three companies

Our present auto insurance system depends largely on the person at fault paying for the damage. The "fault" system has been under criticism as being inequitable and costly in settling claims.

Today, several States are considering the no-fault system in which injured persons are paid up to certain amounts for medical expenses and loss of income by their own companies regardless of who is responsible for the accident. In States where the no-fault system has been enacted, a reduction of premium rates has occurred. The U.S. Department of Transportation has recommended that all States adopt a no-fault system. Some Congressmen are urging that the Federal Government make such a system mandatory throughout the country.

Life insurance is financial protection for dependents against financial loss as a result of the breadwinner's death. Because of the dependence on cash by today's families, life insurance is a way through which families can gain protection and financial security.

Life insurance is not a savings plan or an investment plan. Neither is it the answer for building an educational fund for children. Life insurance is often sold for such purposes, but there are better ways for obtaining these objectives than through life insurance.

When the breadwinner dies there are many financial problems a family must face. The problems usually come in this order:
—Burial expenses and any medical expenses not covered by health insurance
—Adequate funds to meet the family's living expenses until the wife and/or the children can make employment arrangements
—Educational funds for children

Regardless of the frills and fanfare about life insurance policies, there are four basic types of life insurance: term, straight life, limited payment life, and endowment.

Term insurance provides pure protection while the other three have a savings feature. But remember the basic principle is to gain the most protection for the family at the lowest cost should the breadwinner die.

Term insurance is a type of life insurance which provides pure protection only. As the name implies, the policy covers the owner of the policy for a term of 1, 5, 10, or 20 years. At the end of the term, the coverage stops, and the policy has no cash value. It is wise to buy a "renewable term" policy. This allows the policy owner to renew the policy for another term without another physical examination.

Term insurance is the type of insurance that gives the family the greatest amount of protection for a limited period for the least cost. It generally is best to buy term insurance on a reducing coverage basis so that it can be reduced or terminated as dependents become older and no longer require as much protection.

Term insurance can be increased to the maximum protection as each child is born or can be decreased to no insurance on the father as the children become economically independent. Several term policies rather than one or two large policies can be bought. This allows the policyholder to increase coverage or to drop policies to best meet his needs. Buying term insurance in this way also allows for convenient distribution of premium dates.

Straight life insurance provides for a certain amount of coverage throughout life. It differs from term insurance in that straight life combines a decreasing amount of protection with an increasing amount of savings in the policy. Because of the savings element as well as the protection in the straight life plan, the premium for a certain amount of straight life at a given age is higher than the premium for term insurance.

The premium for straight life remains the same through the length of the policy. In the early years, the policyholder is actually paying more for the cost of protection. The extra portion of the premium is what builds up the savings element of the policy.

In a straight life policy the terms "face value" and "cash surrender value" are often used. The face value is the amount payable at the insured's death. The cash surrender value is the amount of savings that has built up in the policy.

The cash value increases while the policy is in force. The insured may cash the policy in at any time, but this will terminate the policy and the protection stops. If the insured desires, he may borrow the cash value from the company. But when the policy is borrowed from, the coverage is reduced until the loan is repaid.

Limited payment life insurance is comparable to straight life except that the policyholder pays the premiums on the policy in a given number of years. Usually the premiums are for 20 or 30 years, or by the time that the insured is age 65.

After the policy is paid up, it remains in force for the rest of the insured's life, unless he wishes to withdraw the cash value. If the policy's cash value is withdrawn the coverage stops.

Premiums for limited payment life insurance at a certain age are higher than premiums for straight life. The reason for the difference is that all the premiums are paid within a given number of years.

Families that have very high incomes in their early years and whose income may decrease in later years may want to make use of the limited payment life insurance policy. The average family would not possess ample funds and would have difficulty purchasing enough coverage to meet its needs.

The other type of life insurance is the endowment policy. Savings is the primary emphasis in an endowment policy, but some protection is also included. The primary purpose is to build up a certain amount of money in a given

number of years. Endowment insurance can be purchased on the basis of 10, 15, 20, 25 or 30 years, or mature to cash at a given age. When the endowment policy has reached a point at which the cash savings is equal to the amount of the face value, the policy matures.

At this point with the total cash available to you, the protection portion is zero and the coverage ends.

The premiums are much higher for endowment policies than other types because of the emphasis placed upon savings.

When purchasing life insurance there are many important factors for you to consider other than the four basic types of insurance just discussed. When you and your family are establishing a life insurance program, consider these very important factors:

1. Buy the policies which will give the most protection at the least cost
2. Insure the right family members
3. Consider the family's financial needs
4. Buy the insurance from companies that are financially sound and are represented by honest, well-trained agents

Let's consider some examples of individuals at various stages in the life cycle and the kinds of life insurance needs for their particular situation.

Jerry is single and has no dependents. Probably the only life insurance he needs is enough to cover his debts and burial expenses.

Insurance can be purchased at a lower rate during the young years, but by buying while young, the premiums are paid for a longer period of time. In the end, the amount paid in for premiums is about the same. Secondly, he is paying for protection that really isn't necessary.

Suppose that Jerry marries Jeannette, who is a college graduate and is working. Perhaps enough insurance would be needed to cover their debts and burial expenses.

Later, Jeannette has quit work and their first child is on the way. They have purchased a home with a small downpayment and a 30-year mortgage. The situation regarding life insurance takes on a different look. There are dependents who need financial protection. Do they need insurance? That is not the question! The question is, how much insurance is needed?

As the family increases in size, it is essential to add more insurance on the father or the breadwinner to protect the dependents. When the children are young and depend upon the family for financial needs, that is the time families with modest income have difficulties providing enough life insurance on the father to protect the mother and the children.

Families with modest to average incomes should insure the breadwinner or breadwinners first. When considering the amount of insurance for the mother with dependent children, substitute child care is a need that should be planned for until the children can care for themselves. The death of a small child would have no effect upon the income of the family. Perhaps a policy to meet funeral expenses would be sufficient for the young child.

Families should consider the other resources available. Social Security benefits are available to most people with dependent children through age 18 and to widows when they reach age 62. Also, families should strive toward savings to be used for emergencies and have some stocks and/or real estate that will increase in market value during inflationary times.

As the children become financially independent of the family, the emphasis on family financial security will shift from protection to saving for the retirement years. Every family situation is different and it is important that each family give adequate thought and study to planning its financial future.

Yes, it really does make a difference what happens to you and your family in financial stress or tragedy! The road to happy family living is not always easy. However, with the responsibility of providing financial security comes your right and responsibility as an American consumer to choose adequate insurance protection for your family.

DWELLINGS

A Complex of Factors Determines Our Family Housing Requirements

Oᴜʀ ᴅᴡᴇʟʟɪɴɢs provide the physical stage upon which the private drama of American families is enacted. There children are conceived, loved, reared and nurtured. There dreams are spun and goals set. There family members are maintained in sickness and in health. And there highly significant decisions are made—on the number of children to be born, a life style to pursue, goods and services to consume, and what to attempt tomorrow.

In a literal sense, the house, apartment or mobile home is the private world of America. Most of us must share streets and highways, schools and churches, and places of work and shopping centers. But for the majority of us our dwellings are the end of public sharing. So a major prerequisite of wholesome, satisfying family life is decent and livable housing. In no small way, the health and viability of this nation depend on the quality of the family's private envelope—the dwelling.

Housing, no less so than families, is infinitely complex and varied. Family needs, life styles, goals and aspirations are so varied as to require an ever increasing demand for a variety of housing forms. Assuming "houses are for people," major ways in which families vary must be kept to the forefront.

A number of needs and requirements are common to all families, although each has its own list of priori-

AUTHOR JAMES MONTGOMERY is Professor of Gerontology and Housing, Department of Management, Housing and Family Development, College of Home Economics, Virginia Polytechnic Institute and State University, Blacksburg.

ties and its own interpretations. Among them are protection from the elements, insects, vermin, animals, and people; health, sanitation needs; and storage. Also, space needs to be provided for furniture and equipment to facilitate such activities as food preparation, eating, sleeping, housekeeping, lawn care (where this is a family responsibility) entertainment, play, and personal improvement.

Families should be versed in how they want these needs to be met and how to communicate their desires to those who design and build housing.

Beyond these basic and tangible considerations are several others, largely of a social-psychological nature, which are also very important but less well understood by families and by those who provide our housing. Among them are the family situation, personal needs in housing, and use of mechanization and technology.

First off, let's take up the family situation.

As families traverse the life cycle—young families, founding families, teenage families, post-parental families, old families, broken families, including the widowed—housing needs differ widely. This variable greatly affects the demands for the amount and organization of space, furnishings and equipment, care and maintenance, day-to-day activities, health and safety, and the home's location in relation to neighborhood and community services and supports.

A family with children may place a high priority on being near schools, for example, while an older couple may choose housing in terms of proximity to health services and to a shopping center.

That style to which a family, a "single" or an aged widow aspires also has great bearing on housing needs. Those families oriented toward leisure, recreation and "where the action is," have housing requirements quite different from those who are oriented toward a more intimate and self-directed type of living.

Money also affects needs and especially, ability to satisfy needs. Rising housing costs greatly deter a family's ability to secure the type of shelter that it wants. In 1972 mobile homes constituted 67 per cent of all new homes costing less than $20,000, while conventionally built houses accounted for only 33 per cent of the homes in this price category. Rising housing expectations are colliding with rising housing prices.

Where a family decides to live—open country, village, small city, central city or suburb—also affects needs and their fulfillment. To illustrate, utilities may be a serious problem to country residents, while in cities the need for open spaces and privacy assumes greater significance.

Now let's turn to personal needs in housing.

All of us, regardless of age, sex, race or creed, need to think well of ourselves. And in no small way we evaluate ourselves in terms of the way in which we think other people feel toward us. In our society, often impersonal, we judge people by the clothes they wear, the cars they drive and the dwellings they occupy.

A few years ago a study was made that examined self-attitudes which a group of older low-income persons held *before* and then *after* moving into a well-designed housing complex for the aged. The researcher found that on the average a person's self concept became more positive after moving into better housing. A part of this can be attributed to housing—and a part to the increased opportunities to become involved with other persons and to make new friends.

In our society all of us need privacy, although the kind and amount needed varies from person to person. Man seems to have a basic desire to become involved and then to withdraw into his own private world. Children need privacy for the pursuit of hobbies, study, daydreaming, and to escape the presence of disapproving parents. Husbands and wives must have a measure of privacy if the union is to be fruitful and enduring. And there are times when each member of the family needs a space, a corner or a room in which to retreat.

In housing, privacy doesn't "just happen"—it must be consciously planned. As we increasingly live in mechanized homes in noisy neighborhoods, privacy will become more difficult to achieve. In earlier days rural families usually had privacy, even if the rural poor often had little. But today, with noise and people all about us, greater effort must be made to secure privacy.

Man is a social being. Therefore, he needs an opportunity to interact with others. At an early age children find playmates, teenagers have their peers, and the parents make and entertain friends.

The handicapped and the aged no less so than other persons also need an opportunity to interact with others. The term "shut-in" implies a sick, afflicted or aged person who is forced to function in a limited life space. We now know that one of the problems most common to the handicapped and the very old is loneliness.

Housing, then, has much to do with the quality and frequency of entertaining, the extent to which we interact with nearby persons, and how we get to town. Of even greater importance is the way in which the house affects the relationship between husband and wife, parents and children, and brothers and sisters. The size, location, floor plan, condition and the nature of furnishings and equipment all affect the ways in which family members relate to one another and to outsiders.

Still another common need of individuals and families is a feeling that they are attached and belong to the small part of the world in which they live—a house, neighborhood and/or community. Pride in our immediate environment is related to rootedness. One doubts that persons turn upon or otherwise abuse housing if they feel a part of it.

Perhaps a beginning of feeling a part

Melrose Towers in Roanoke, Va., has 212 apartments for senior citizens. Photos show a quilting class, an efficiency apartment, and a lounge.

of our place is to have housing which is satisfying and to have access to friends or potential friends.

A basic characteristic of man is the need to exercise some degree of mastery over his environment. We need to be able to make our own imprint on one or more aspects of the environment, to shape it or control it to our liking.

Evidence of this need is easy to illustrate. In most any home one finds one or more of the following: gardening, papered or painted walls, color schemes, objects of art, and spaces for hobbies and other creative outlets. As we move more into crowded areas, with small lawns or none at all, and into rented quarters where we are forbidden to paint or fix up, it becomes more difficult to make an impact on our environment.

Efforts must be made to provide an opportunity to be creative. Perhaps one reason why so many American families wish to own a single-family house is to maximize their opportunity to make changes of their own choosing—to paint, have pets, furnish and to garden (or not garden) as they see fit.

One cannot help but ponder the consequences of public housing (and private rental units, for that matter) which often provide such limited opportunities for creativity or environmental mastery. In the long range, the degree to which a family is free to individualize its dwelling depends upon the landlord, money, opportunity, and the family's talents.

As we become more involved in the complexities of large institutions and organizations, and engage in standardized, routine jobs, the greater will become the need to be creative in the home environment.

Straws in the wind suggest that effective human beings need to experience a variety of stimulation. In former days, rural folk lived close to nature which provided such a variety. The seasons, the weather, sounds, temperatures, fragrance and smell once provided a virtual parade of change. Such is still the case in open country and small towns. But in our large cities the variety of nature has often been overshadowed and muted by noise, fumes, crowds, streets, and buildings.

For many persons—especially small children, the handicapped, the ill and the aged—psychological stimulation or a wholesome variety of environmental stimuli rests with the dwelling. Moreover, for the housewife who works at home all day, for students who study at school, and for wives and husbands who work at an office or factory, home is potentially also a very important way of getting a needed variety of stimulation.

Research one day may verify what many women have known for years—that it is important to paint, re-arrange the furniture, engage in spring cleaning, and grow flowers in and around the house. As the nation becomes more urban in character and more populous, greater efforts will have to be made if homes are to provide more psychological stimulation.

The poor, and nursing home residents who frequently live in drab circumstances, especially need more stimulating environments.

Finally, let's turn to mechanization and technology.

Consumers increasingly are demanding mechanization of their dwellings which make them more and more dependent upon factory-produced items—refrigerators, heating and cooling systems, laundry equipment, and personal care equipment. These in turn are placing increasing demands upon utilities and services that must be provided by the public or by corporations.

These conditions bring into the picture—besides producers, consumers, and those who provide the utilities—another force to be reckoned with: the regulators of housing. Building codes, zoning orders, and subdivision controls are common. Beyond these are newer agencies concerned with the quality of the environment—pollution monitors, licensing agencies, and environmental protection programs.

Barn-inspired weekend house of redwood board and batten, with extra outdoor room joined to main house by deck.

Thus, while a family decides how the enclosed space and lawn will be used, it is more dependent than ever before on external factors. Therefore, of necessity traditional decision-making prerogatives are being abridged. In the final analysis, then, housing production and housing usage have become very much a part of modern technology —which in turn has rendered housing highly dependent upon complex forces of our political and economic life.

The story of housing outreach does not stop here. Increased incomes, more leisure, and building and transportation technology have enabled many families to fulfill a variety of wants and needs by owning a second home.

Some 3 million Americans own a second home—the realization of a dream formerly entertained largely by the rich. These second homes are a part of our increased interest in family vacations and are often located near places where there is swimming, skiing, fishing, hiking and "roughing it with nature."

It is not very surprising that second homes are on the increase as a result of crowded urban conditions, rising incomes, shorter working hours, greater leisure, and increasing efforts of families to do things together.

Another adjunct to housing has been the rapid increase in camping. More than 4½ million families own (or rent) a recreational vehicle—tent campers, travel trailers and motor homes. Home away from home has been applied to motor homes which are self-powered and self-contained units.

The growing popularity of recreational vehicles and tents have brought heavy usage to public parks and have resulted in a rapid growth of private campgrounds.

In camping one observes an ancient desire for new experiences, the satisfaction of curiosity, and the pursuit of meaningful family activities. Perhaps the most advanced examples of mechanized housing in the world today are motor homes which, while termed self-contained, are also the most dependent of all forms of shelter—they need roads, gasoline, water, electricity, waste disposal, and a rented plot for the night.

This chronicle of housing needs and their satisfactions has stressed variations and dependence on markets, services and utilities that no longer are to be reckoned with by the family's own resources.

Housing production, distribution, financing, usages, utilities and services involve more than a father, his sons and neighbors. It is now a piece of the technological web which overlays all forms of modern life.

Folkways, tradition, and simple skills no longer are adequate to aid families in procuring housing. Building materials, furnishings, and equipment are products of the industrialized economy.

Therefore, families must become more diligent in understanding their own housing needs and more adept in knowing where to secure technological information prerequisite to making rational decisions. Fortunately, they have access to countless stores of valuable information—the Cooperative Extension Service of the U.S. Department of Agriculture, U.S. Department of Housing and Urban Development, the consumer magazines, and trade publications.

These must take the place of folk wisdom which no longer suffices. And the fact that a given family will occupy a number of homes throughout the life cycle suggests that their need for housing information is endless.

Housing, as stated earlier, is the hub of the family's private world. The nature of housing has a direct effect on the quality of family life. It affects health, time and energy required in rearing a family and caring for its members, the way in which the family members relate to one another, self-related attitudes, morale, and satisfaction with one's station in life. It also affects the way in which one family relates to another, to the neighborhood, and to the community.

True, we cannot weigh or measure with great accuracy the ultimate impact of housing on human behavior. But the present state of knowledge, limited as it is, suggests a significant relationship between housing conditions and the quality of life.

Families do not want, expect or require dwellings that are identical. Poor families are more interested in securing clean, safe and reasonably comfortable housing than in, say, finding quarters that are especially psychologically stimulating. At the same time, many families having greater incomes can take basic shelter for granted and proceed to satisfy "higher" level needs in housing.

Nevertheless, as a nation we are being more and more concerned with housing that does far more than support physical survival. In other words, essentially all American families are upgrading their housing goals and expectations. And the dominant housing image remains the single-family house.

In view of the subjective nature of housing needs, families would do well to ponder and then define what they really want and need in the way of housing. Society would be well advised to support research to determine and then transmit the best data we are able to ascertain to designers, planners, housing producers and other housing decision makers.

Housing now being provided no longer stems from traditional wisdom and skills. Therefore, as a nation we should make every effort to improve the fit between housing needs and structures.

Only when families are more articulate in identifying their needs, when research reduces guess, when builders become more sensitive to human needs and when public policy is founded on needs, will the nation have a variety of good housing designed, built, and serviced in line with family purposes.

For further reading:

U.S. Department of Agriculture. *Wood-Frame House Construction*, Agriculture Handbook 73, Superintendent of Documents, Government Printing Office, Washington, D.C. 20402, $2.25.

———. *Selection and Use of Wood Products for Home and Farm Buildings*, Agriculture Information Bulletin 311, Superintendent of Documents, Government Printing Office, Washington, D.C. 20402, 60 cents.

———. *Simple Home Repairs . . . inside*, Extension Service Program Aid No. 1034, Superintendent of Documents, Government Printing Office, Washington, D.C. 20402, 40 cents.

What Can A Family Afford to Spend For Its Housing?

For years, prospective home buyers have been asking what they can afford to spend for housing. Answers, if any, usually were expressed in vague generalities. In many instances, mortgage lenders gave contradictory opinions.

This can be attributed to slow development in the home mortgage lending field.

During the early 1900's, mortgage lenders relied principally on the amount of the loan being restricted to a low percentage of the value of the property. Private lenders were the principal sources of home mortgage loans. As additional safety factors, they imposed their own ideas regarding the conditions under which they would grant loans. This resulted in many conflicting rules and lending practices.

Two of these rules received wide acceptance. The most common one required that monthly mortgage payments of principal and interest not exceed a week's salary or 25 percent of the borrower's monthly income. That rule is still used by some lenders. The other rule required that the cost of the home being financed not exceed two and one-half times the borrower's annual income.

Since the advent of the higher percent of loan to value for home mortgages (due mainly to governmental guarantees), lending practices have become more stable. Methods used for

AUTHOR WYATT W. DAWSON is a consultant in mortgage credit, credit reporting, and related matters, in Arlington, Va. He served 31 years with the Federal Housing Administration, retiring as Chief of the Mortgage Credit Section.

analyzing the acceptability of mortgage risks have become far more sophisticated.

These advancements have included the responsibility of the borrower as a prominent part of the loan security. They have proven the old rules-of-thumb to be totally unrealistic in mortgage credit evaluation.

The improved methods of analysis, which nullified the old rules and guidelines, make it relatively simple for the prospective home buyer to accurately estimate the amount that can safely and comfortably be spent for housing.

The chart with a "do-it-yourself" procedure is designed to help reach this decision. It consists of a simple accumulation of financial information, making income and expense estimates, and drawing your own conclusion as to the housing expense you can afford. Prospective home buyers are encouraged to work up these estimates. The results will be most informative.

This information and estimates should be tabulated in four parts. Part One is designed to determine the *Dependable Monthly Income*. Part Two covers *Total Monthly Obligations* (exclusive of housing expense) *and Salary Deductions*. Part Three details the *Present Monthly Housing Expense*. Part Four provides for estimates of the *Proposed Monthly Housing Expense*.

It is easier to evaluate the individual's financial position in terms of monthly obligations to monthly income than to deal with a conglomerate of monthly, semiannual, and annual obligations and income. All the estimates should be reduced to a monthly basis.

A word of caution: do not allow enthusiasm for homeownership to modify very realistic estimates of income and expense.

PART ONE—DEPENDABLE MONTHLY INCOME should include only those amounts which are well established or can reasonably be expected to continue during the early years of housing obligations.

Overtime cannot usually be depended upon unless it is a definite requirement of the type of employment and is regularly received. Unpredictable overtime income is of little help when the mortgage payment is due now. Also, it is well established that overtime is the first to go in times of economic stress, nationally, locally, or when the employer has financial difficulty.

Commissions and gratuities may be included if they represent part of the salary arrangement and are regularly received. In such cases, the monthly average should be used.

A secondary job salary may be included as dependable income if it is well established and does not increase the total working hours beyond a reasonable amount.

Bonuses and other income contingent upon the employer's earnings are not usually dependable for the monthly regularity of mortgage payments.

A spouse's earnings can be included provided this employment has been established as a pattern of the family life. That is particularly true for a wife if after having children she continues with her employment.

Earnings of minors in the family cannot safely be relied upon for long-term obligations.

If income from real estate is involved, include only the net amount received after all related expenses are paid.

All other income should be evaluated on the average monthly amount and regularity received.

Addition of the foregoing estimates provides the Total Dependable Income.

PART TWO—MONTHLY OBLIGATIONS AND SALARY DEDUCTIONS represent a tabulation of the known amounts rather than estimates.

Federal, State, and Other Income Taxes will include salary withheld, payments on anticipated taxes, and any other form of income taxes. Local tax authorities can provide information if needed.

Personal Property Taxes will include those assessed against household and any other personal property. Real estate and automobile taxes should not be included.

Retirement Payments will include social security payments, employment retirement payments, and any annuities being purchased.

Insurance Premiums and Insurance Loan Payments should include life insurance, policy loans, hospitalization and health, household and other miscellaneous policies. It should not include insurance on real estate or automobiles.

Automobile and Transportation Expense should be tabulated under a separate part of monthly obligations so as to identify differences caused by relocating the home. Material changes must be considered in the final comparison of the present and new housing expense. This tabulation should include automobile loan payments, automobile-related insurance of all kinds, taxes and license, maintenance, and fuel. It should include any other type of job-related transportation regularly used.

Other Accounts, Notes, and Installment Payments includes all obligations not included in previous tabulations (except real estate and housing obligations). List the average monthly payment on open charge accounts, personal notes, and installment contract payments.

Subtract the total of Monthly Obligations and Salary Deductions from the Total Dependable Income. The result will be the amount of income available for Housing and All Other Living Costs.

PART THREE—PRESENT MONTHLY HOUSING EXPENSE should also represent a tabulation of known amounts rather than estimates. It applies to rental or home-owned property.

Rent (or Mortgage Principal and the Interest Payments if home is owned) will be listed unless the home is owned clear of debt.

Mortgage Insurance Premium will apply only when the home is owned and financed by an insured mortgage loan.

Taxes and Any Special Assessments will apply in homeownership cases.

Heat and Utilities will include the amounts paid as a tenant or a home owner.

Maintenance expense usually applies to homeowners only.

Subtract the total of Present Monthly Housing Expense from the previously determined Housing and All Other Living Cost. The result will be the amount remaining for All Other Living Costs (and savings) at the present time. This will be a vital factor in estimating how much the family can afford to spend for housing.

PART FOUR—PROPOSED MONTHLY HOUSING EXPENSE will include estimates of the same items considered under the present monthly housing expense.

Mortgage Principal, Interest, and Other Monthly charges, comprising the cost of financing a new home, will necessitate some inquiry for proper estimates. Local banks and lending institutions can readily provide the amount of monthly principal and interest payments required to liquidate the proposed loan in a specific number of years. Other monthly charges may vary between lenders. It would be advisable to compare and make estimates on the most favorable charges.

If the proposed home to be purchased is an existing property, most of the housing expense items can be obtained from the present owner, lender, tax collector, and utility companies. If government mortgage insurance is involved in either existing or proposed construction, the lender having the loan or loan commitment can usually provide reliable estimates of all items comprising proposed monthly housing expense.

Taxes and Special Assessments for proposed construction (if not available through a formal or government appraisal) can be made with help from the tax assessor and by neighborhood comparisons.

Hazard Insurance cost can probably be accurately estimated by your insurance broker. The mortgage lender selected may require certain insurance coverage at a cost which he can quote.

Heat and Utilities cost estimates can be developed with help from the sources, the architect if new construction, or by asking owners of similar properties in the neighborhood.

Maintenance Expense of property being purchased should be as accurate as possible as it can be a substantial amount in older properties and in certain types of construction. If proposed construction is involved, estimates from the architect (if any) or the appraiser should be reliable.

Subtract the total of Proposed Monthly Housing Expense from the previously determined Housing and All Other Living Costs. The result will be the amount remaining for All Other Living Costs (and savings) under the proposed housing expense.

You have now developed the two key factors for determining what you can afford for housing, the amount left for all other living costs under your present housing arrangements, and the amount left for all other living costs under the proposed housing costs.

At this point, the amount left under the proposed housing cost should be adjusted by any material difference in automobile and transportation expense due to the new location.

Consideration should also be given to the cost of moving to the new home, purchase of any additional furniture or carpeting, and any significant expenditures for draperies or other items not included in the purchase price of the home.

Each family establishes its standard of living through preferences in food, clothing, housing, education, automobiles, and many other things. This is limited by income, number of dependents, any abnormal medical expenses, and other obligations having priority. Many families with the same income have wide differences in the way it is allocated.

This is why the application of rules limiting housing expense to a percentage of income has no validity. It is the reason why the standard of living established by each family is the best basis

100

ESTIMATING INCOME AVAILABLE FOR HOUSING

PART ONE

DEPENDABLE MONTHLY INCOME
Head of Family's Base Pay — $ _____
Head of Family's Other Earnings
Spouse's Base Pay — $ _____
Spouse's Other Earnings — $ _____
All Other Dependable Income — $ _____
    TOTAL DEPENDABLE INCOME — $ _____

PART TWO

MONTHLY OBLIGATIONS AND SALARY DEDUCTIONS
Federal, State and Other Income Taxes — $ _____
Personal Property Taxes (Other than real estate and
    automobiles) — $ _____
Retirement Payments (Including Social Security) — $ _____
Insurance Premiums and Insurance Loan Payments
    Life — $ _____
    Policy Loan Payments — $ _____
    Hospitalization — $ _____
    Household and Other Insurance (Exclude
    home property and automobile) — $ _____
    Total — $ _____
Automobile and Transportation Expense
    Loan Installment Payments — $ _____
    Insurance — $ _____
    Taxes — $ _____
    Maintenance and Fuel — $ _____
    Other Job Related Transportation
    (If regularly used) — $ _____
    Total — $ _____
Other Accounts, Notes, and Installment Payments
    _____ — $ _____
    _____ — $ _____
    _____ — $ _____
    Total — $ _____

TOTAL MONTHLY OBLIGATIONS AND SALARY DEDUCTIONS
Deduct Total **MONTHLY OBLIGATIONS AND SALARY DEDUCTIONS**
from **TOTAL DEPENDABLE INCOME. The results will be the amount
of income available for HOUSING AND ALL OTHER LIVING COSTS**

PART THREE

PRESENT MONTHLY HOUSING EXPENSE
Rent (or Mortgage Principal and Interest Payments
    if you own your present home)
Mortgage Insurance Premium, if owner — $ _____
Taxes and Any Special Assessments, if owner — $ _____
Hazard Insurance, if owner — $ _____
Heat and Utilities paid as Owner or Tenant — $ _____
Maintenance, if owner
    TOTAL PRESENT MONTHLY HOUSING EXPENSE — $ _____
Deduct PRESENT MONTHLY HOUSING EXPENSE from
HOUSING AND ALL OTHER LIVING COSTS.
**The results will be the amount left for ALL OTHER
LIVING COSTS on the basis of the PRESENT
HOUSING EXPENSE** — $ _____

PART FOUR

PROPOSED MONTHLY HOUSING EXPENSE
Principal, Interest, and Other Monthly Charges on the
    Proposed Financing — $ _____
Taxes and Special Assessments — $ _____
Hazard Insurance — $ _____
Heat and Utilities — $ _____
Maintenance
    TOTAL PROPOSED MONTHLY HOUSING EXPENSE — $ _____
Deduct PROPOSED MONTHLY HOUSING EXPENSE from
**HOUSING AND ALL OTHER LIVING COSTS in PART
TWO. The results will be the amount left for
ALL OTHER LIVING COSTS on the basis of the
PROPOSED HOUSING EXPENSE. Compare this figure
with the amount left for all living costs under
the present housing expense.** — $ _____

for determining what the family can afford for housing.

In reaching your decision, keep in mind that any downward adjustment in the standard of living to which you and your family have become accustomed is a most difficult undertaking.

Assuming that your present housing expense leaves a sufficient amount for your present standard of living and savings, a lesser amount of housing expense would be a welcome improvement. This frequently happens in moves from rental to home-owned properties.

If the proposed home requires an increase in housing expense, the amount of increase you can afford may be determined by a number of calculations and adjustments.

In some instances, the family may have been accumulating a significant amount of savings under its present housing expense. Perhaps the family would like to invest part of these monthly savings in home-owned property. Translating this additional monthly expenditure into mortgage payments would indicate the amount the mortgage financing could be increased for a more expensive home.

For example, a $50 a month increase in the mortgage payment, on the basis of a 7 percent, 30-year term, would provide about $7,500 more mortgage money to be used for a better home. Your banker or mortgage lender can assist you in translating other amounts of monthly payments into increases in mortgage amounts.

A more expensive home could also be purchased without disturbing living standards, if the monthly mortgage payments are kept the same by investing a larger downpayment.

If you own your present home, the same results could probably be obtained by selling or trading it in on a more expensive home.

When neither monthly savings nor additional downpayments are available, increased housing expense would have to be accomplished by reducing present living costs. If there is a sufficient amount of truly nonessential items in these costs that could be diverted to housing, there would be no problem. If only partial reductions can be made, purchase of a less expensive home may be indicated, with intent to trade-up when income permits. In such cases, be sure that the amount of housing improvement which can be obtained through these partial reductions justifies the cost of buying, financing, and moving to the new home.

If present needs demand more housing (due to size of the family, relocation, or other reason) without additional income, consider carefully which, if any, living costs can be abolished or reduced to defray the expense. In some instances, temporary rental, rather than a home purchase, may be indicated.

There are no satisfactory guidelines for cost of housing for newlyweds starting new households. Until definite characteristics are established, housing expense should be kept within safe limits as to income.

If you itemize deductions in your income tax returns, give consideration to the deductible items of interest and taxes. Mortgage payments on high percentage loans to value include very substantial amounts of deductible interest.

You are now aware of the details of your dependable income and expenses. A clear knowledge as to source of funds needed for housing expense will be rewarding.

Enjoy the benefits of your home without excessive financial burdens.

Home Sweet Home: The Choice Is Yours, And Not Just Once

Housing needs change over time as people get married, and have children who grow up and eventually leave the home. Traditionally, the "housing ladder" was: unfurnished apartment, furnished apartment, single family dwelling. The rate of progression depended upon the earnings and savings of the family. The ultimate goal was a house with a fenced yard, lawn, and flowers.

Housing now comes in many more forms—condominiums, cooperatively-owned apartments, townhouses, second homes, mobile homes, and so on. You have a wide choice, particularly in the urban areas.

Some of the new forms of housing are adaptations of European methods. Some forms have private entrances and are otherwise designed for privacy. Often they have play yards for small children. And, each form of housing is available in a range of prices—rent or buy. So, the final choice in many instances will be a matter of personal preference, depending upon your own life style.

We satisfy our housing needs by renting or buying a: single family dwelling, duplex, townhouse, apartment, cooperatively-owned apartment, condominium, a second or country home (perhaps owned cooperatively by two or more families), or a mobile home.

Years ago the large house served a variety of needs. Often three adult generations lived in the same three-story house. Houses were that big, seemingly built for the purpose.

A household at that time might include one or two aged parents, a spinster sister or bachelor brother, a young married son or daughter and their still adolescent children. Each person had his or her private room or "nook" even though it might be a finished room in an unheated attic. A measure of privacy made the whole thing workable.

Today each adult generation lives apart, and the composition of its household changes as their children, in turn, grow up and leave. Consequently, housing requirements of a family change over time. We now need housing according to the stages of life—for single persons (young and old), for young married couples without children, for families with growing children, and for retired persons, couples, or singles.

Transportation has also been a factor in housing choices. Years ago we had fewer cars and walked or rode a streetcar to work. The place of work limited our choice. Nearness to street car lines dominated the housing advertisements.

Today, most families own two or more autos. We have more throughways and many of us commute much greater distances to our jobs.

With such a wide selection in housing available, you should give a great deal of prior thought and study to your own choice. Examine carefully what exactly is the life style of your family—husband, wife, children.

What are your priorities, individually and collectively? Consider the possible trade-offs between priorities. Are you really the outdoor type? Maybe you like home-grown vegetables—only if someone else does the planting and weeding.

Make a list of the things you like to do and how often. Perhaps your priorities aren't what you first thought they were.

Besides the kind of housing, you need to consider whether to own or to rent. Renting is more flexible if you move frequently. It is also a way of trying out a new location before you buy.

AUTHOR WARREN R. BAILEY is Deputy Director of the Farm Production Economics Division, Economic Research Service.

COAUTHOR ROBERT G. YECK is staff scientist, National Program Staff, Agricultural Research Service.

Renting frees you of most maintenance problems.

Ownership, however, has the economic advantage that interest paid on a home mortgage loan and real estate taxes are deductible expenses on Federal income taxes, whereas rent payments are not. Those two deductions could easily amount to $4,000 annually in the early years, and average $2,500 over the amortized life of the loan.

Another advantage of ownership in periods of steady price inflation is that your house increases in value—about 150 percent in the last 20 years. Thus, it is a hedge against inflation.

Generally, owning your own home is considered to be one of the first investments you should make.

Now let's take up characteristics of different kinds of housing.

APARTMENTS. The word apartment connotes having your own space for living apart. Most apartments today are fully integrated units providing facilities for cooking and eating meals, as well as sleeping and bathing. Laundry facilities are commonly shared with others.

Sometimes recreational facilities such as swimming pools and tennis courts are also included in the services that are available.

Apartments vary widely in size and cost, from a small one-room "efficiency" in a private home to spacious multi-room apartments with elevator service and doormen.

An apartment can provide short-term housing until you can afford something better or until an anticipated move to another city. You may prefer an apartment because it is convenient to public transportation, shopping, and the bright lights of downtown. Or, maybe you want to minimize the time spent on "keeping house," on maintenance, and so on.

A furnished apartment is traditionally the first housing for young singles and couples just getting started. All you need to provide is bedding and table linens, besides personal belongings, and perhaps a hi-fi and TV. Some furnished apartments, called "efficiencies," have wall "kitchens" behind folding doors and have in-a-door beds.

Furnished apartments are a good choice when starting on your own home. They require no major initial investment and allow for mobility in employment. Another advantage of a furnished apartment to a young couple is that it gives them a chance to better determine their furniture needs in relation to their new life as a couple before investing too deeply in furniture.

An unfurnished apartment is often the second stage in the progression of the housing ladder. It usually can save you money in rental but more importantly, it lets you have the furnishings as they best suit your desires. This can also be a step in building up your furniture for the time that you may move to your own home.

One should, however, be aware that the furnishings you obtain for an apartment may not be quite as suitable for a single unit dwelling.

It is not such a bad idea to utilize some "attic treasures" of friends and relatives.

DUPLEXES here are intended to mean units initially designed and built as two living units—not conversions. Duplexes generally are designed to provide the equivalent of single unit housing at substantially lower cost than a single unit home.

Each unit in a duplex is separately equipped with laundry and other appliances, and it provides its own heat—much like a townhouse.

Duplexes can be good income property to an owner with modest financial resources, as he lives in one unit and rents out the other.

Duplex living requires a compatibility between the two families. Noise can be more of a problem than in apartment houses.

TOWNHOUSES are self-contained units like conventional houses except they are built contiguously in rows—no space between—each having "side" walls in common with adjacent units, but having their own front and rear walls. Individuality is achieved by varying the front "set-back," height of roof line, and exterior finish and color.

Each unit has its private ground level front and rear entrances, its own laundry and other appliances, and provides its own heat. Some townhouses have garages, but generally there is off-street parking space used in common. They usually have very little "yard" space. Some complexes have community play yards for children.

Townhouses are owned individually and transfers are made directly between seller and buyer. Often one can be rented. Their major advantage is that they provide one of the lowest cost ways of owning a home.

Townhouses usually are built with three floor levels, which is a disadvantage to physically handicapped persons.

CONDOMINIUMS are apartment complexes in which the apartments are individually owned in fee simple—similar to townhouses—but there are "ground rules" and the overall complex is "managed" by a central administration. They may be "year-round" residences or recreational homes. In the latter case, owners may actually occupy their condominium apartment only a few weeks intermittently during the year. At other times, they may arrange with management to rent out their apartment to others. Under such circumstances, the condominium may qualify as rental property and provide some tax advantages to the owner.

HOUSES. Eventually most couples seek a single family house of their own. Greater space between houses usually results in more yard space for family recreation, more privacy, and a lower concentration of people in the community.

You can enjoy as much privacy as you want with fences, walls, hedges, and so on. Each member of the family can have his personal private room or hobby space.

You now more likely can have a workshop and tools, a greater choice in pets, and a garden. But all of this is not without some extra cost—not only in

initial outlay but also in operating and repair costs (including taxes).

Managing a house can take a lot of time. It also can interfere with your freedom to "go." Someone may have to look after the house when you travel. In an apartment, you can simply turn the key and leave.

MOBILE HOMES are designed for living, not for travel. They are transportable, but only by specialized motor trucks. Mobile homes are very useful for construction workers and others who need immediate housing near their job site. Student housing is another use.

Because of their mobility, mobile homes often are allowed greater flexibility in connection with building and zoning codes. This feature along with a different purchasing loan arrangement gives them definite short term economic advantages over permanent construction. As a result, mobile homes are used by a host of people who cannot afford anything else.

When anchored in a modern mobile home park, equipped with central coin laundries, toilets, and showers, mobile home living can be quite comfortable, though somewhat cramped. Some mobile homeowners have dogs, other pets, and flowers. They can have patio chairs and sit outside, weather permitting.

Often a strong feeling of comradeship arises among families in a mobile home park.

SECOND HOMES usually are associated with leisure time and outdoor recreation, usually out in the country, and usually near a lake (fishing, boating, water skiing), near woods and hiking trails, near horse stables and riding, or near a golf course. They are a retreat from your current way of life.

Second homes are especially attractive to an apartment dweller. Outdoor living space will be a feature that they often seek.

A second home in the country can vary from a temporary structure on rented land to a full-scale, year-round house.

Eventually, your second home may become a permanent retirement home.

In summary, your final choice in housing often is a matter of balancing personal preference in living against your current social and financial status. Today the old European custom of living in the village and going out daily to the farm tends to be one of living in the country and commuting to the city. What will be the next trend is anybody's guess, but you should make your choices according to your own needs as you see them now. The choice is yours.

Picking a Homesite: Soils Play a Big Role

YOUR HOMESITE must serve the needs of your family in many ways, special ways that only you can decide. Location, community services, privacy —all of these are important. But the physical aspects of the site, especially the soils, have a great impact on how well the site serves your needs. Don't overlook them.

Whether you are buying a home already built, or choosing a site to build on, there are certain items that your family will decide are essential. The process of making a list of your own special needs is certainly worthy of careful study. All members of the family should join in.

How about a family brain-storming session? Everyone should be free to make proposals. All proposals are listed, and no proposals are rejected until after the session is over.

Then after a day or so, go over the list thoroughly in a group session, discussing each item in depth. You will find that some of the proposals conflict. Some will cost too much. Hard decisions will need to be made as you assemble your final list.

Let's take a look at some of the things you will want to consider. First, the general location of your home—in relation to your employment and community services and facilities, police and fire protection, nearness to bus or rail lines or good highways, trash removal, local recreation facilities, schools, churches, shopping centers, sanitary sewers, storm drainage, electricity, gas, street lighting.

A great deal depends on your basic choice between country living, where you usually have privacy but must take care of many of your own facilities, or living in a developed community where these facilities are provided at a price.

In many areas, large lots are available only in the country. Then the question becomes: What facilities are we willing to give up in order to have a large lot? Important factors are size of your family and their hobbies, gardening, or play activities such as football and similar games. Number and kind of pets, number of cars owned, need for space for boats, trailers, or campers, and possibly also space for swimming pools or tennis courts may be important. Don't forget the work involved to maintain properly the lawn and shrubs on a large lot.

Noise level varies widely in different areas. Nearby highways, airports, or railroads may make some sites very undesirable to you. Smoke, fumes, and dust levels, in addition to noise, may be objectionable, and checking these items on Sunday morning may not give you an accurate picture of the situation on busy weekdays.

After thinking about the above items, you may know pretty well the general location for your homesite and how big the lot should be. Then the next question is: Should we buy an already existing home or have our own built? Relative costs may be different. Often a house a few years old may cost more than a similar one that you may build.

Don't overlook the cost of carpet, drapes, shrubs, trees, or lawn that the price of a new house may not include.

AUTHOR DONALD E. MC CORMACK is Assistant Director, Soil Survey Interpretations, Soil Conservation Service.

Also how long will it take to get the new house built? Often families having new homes built are disappointed when promised completion dates are not met. Get a firm commitment on the completion date.

Other points to check include the taxes; cost of insurance—it likely will be higher where no community water system exists; easements, covenants, or assessments on the property; and zoning of the property and surrounding area. If you want to buy a large lot with the possibility of subdividing it later, you may find that in some areas the zoning ordinance will not permit such subdivision.

Subdivision regulations, building codes, and sanitary ordinances may restrict use of the site and prohibit some of the very things you especially wanted. So check each of them carefully, and pick for further consideration only those areas that permit the uses you desire.

Now you are ready to pick *the* lot for your home. In addition to the above off-site, or general points, it is time to really get down to earth about this decision of yours. Consider the soil, for you and your home will depend upon it for a great many things, both physical and esthetic.

What are the qualities of the soil that you need to think about? Some of these qualities are often overlooked, probably because many of them are not easy for you to appraise for yourself.

Settling of foundation due to unstable soil is cause of severe damage to home.

The soil must support the foundation of your house. You have already checked the building codes and found that a given minimum footing width is required by law in your community.

For most and perhaps all soils in the community, the required footing width is adequate to support the weight of the house. In a distressing number of cases, however, there are soils so soft that the standard footing is inadequate. The result is settlement, usually uneven, with cracked basement floors, cracked basement walls, doors that no longer fit, and cracks along ceiling cornices or even down plastered walls. You need to check to be sure that the soil will support your home.

The soil must be stable enough to prevent high pressures on the walls, or slippage down-slope. Again, building codes require minimum strength of underground walls, and walls designed according to these codes are strong enough on most soils. Yet failures of basement walls are common on some soils where the standard walls are not strong enough.

Soils high in some kinds of clay have a tendency to expand considerably as they become wet. When such soils are placed along basement walls as backfilling is done, they are generally dry or moist, and when they become wet, large pressures are exerted against the basement wall.

In a new home in northeastern Ohio a section of basement wall about 20 feet long was pushed over onto the basement floor by extremely high soil pressures against it. The section of the house above this gaping hole settled about 3 inches, walls cracked, one door that had been closed splintered, and a very costly rebuilding job was required. The big rain came the day before the family was to move into its new home.

More common are cases where swelling pressure in soils pushes basement walls inward 1 to 3 inches, resulting in large cracks in these walls and some cracks in the house above that result from uneven settling. In one such case, a tall cabinet touched the wall about

107

3½ feet above the floor, but just above the floor the bottom of the cabinet was 3 inches away from the wall.

Some soils are so active on slopes that when they become saturated, they tend to slip down-slope. This slippage may be only fractions of an inch, or it may be several inches or more. Cracked walls and uneven settling result from mild slippage. In places where slippage is more severe, entire houses may be destroyed.

In southeastern Ohio, a home exploded after slippage broke the gas line entering the house. The housewife and her children had just left on a shopping trip.

Before final selection of a site for your home, make sure the soil is stable. You must depend on the soil as a solid support for your home.

If you plan to pave a carport floor, garage floor, or driveway in an area with cold winters, a soil that has high frost heaving will cause you some headaches. In such soils, thick layers of ice form below the soil surface. The ice pushes the surface and things resting on it upward. Garage doors that hang an inch above the floor in the summer may not close in the winter. Cracks develop in floors or driveways above these soils. When the soils thaw in the spring they get very soft and streets with inadequate paving may become very rough or even impassable.

If you'd like to have a basement, you certainly don't want moisture seeping into it from waterlogged soil next to the basement wall. Building codes in many parts of the country require drainage of footings in a specified manner, and grading around the house so that precipitation or water from downspouts can flow away from the house.

Such building codes result in good dry basements in many kinds of soil, but in most communities there are some soils for which this is not the case. In fact, there are some soils with such large quantities of subsurface water at shallow depths that it is next to impossible to provide drainage so that the basement will be dry.

The old cliche, "We had to drain five acres to get a dry basement," is literally true on some soils. If for some hapless reason a decision is made to build a house on such soils, the house really should not have a basement at all. This is especially true if it is necessary to depend upon a sump-pump to remove the water from the drains. Sump-pumps that run 23 hours and 59 minutes per day seem to have a tendency to break down, and if they do your basement will very likely be a mess.

Now, some soils are not quite this wet, but require footing drains both inside and outside the footing for adequate results—a dry basement.

On some soils it is very helpful to put the basement floor at a shallower depth than on well-drained soils. It is much easier to build a dry basement on some wet soils if the basement floor is placed only 2 or 3 feet below the existing soil surface instead of 4 to 6 feet as is often done.

Standard designs for storm sewers generally provide for an excellent job of handling surface runoff, but the sewers may not do their job if large volumes of subsurface water enter footing drains. There are some unfortunate examples where the storm drains back up into basements for this very reason.

So! How about the natural wetness condition of the soil? You and your house will be affected by it. Better find out.

Now you have checked out the soil as it will affect the house itself. Let's think about the lot. It wouldn't make much sense to have a stable foundation, a dry basement, and all the other requirements for the house and then place it on a lot that will not grow the grass, shrubs, or trees you want, will not dispose of the effluent if you have a septic tank, or will not support the play activities that you anticipate.

"Trouble with septic tanks causes more problems for homeowners than all other functional home problems put together," according to a health official in a rapidly growing area of a Northeastern State.

Above, excavation for basement in soil with high seasonal water table. Providing drainage for dry basement will be difficult. Left, home built on soil with high seasonal water table and low bearing capacity. Home was abandoned because of wetness and foundation breakup.

Below, cleanup work in flooded basement. A soil survey would have indicated soil wetness hazard.

109

Flood damage to a home.

"Not only are some practically unsolvable problems presented to the homeowner himself, but often unfiltered sewage makes its way into road ditches and streams, and as a result the whole environment in the community is affected. Odors, polluted surface water, and complaints to the zoning board, the health department, and elected officials, none of whom may be able to help—these problems result in a deteriorating community with large losses to many homeowners."

Yes, a tale of woe that you want no part of. So if you are considering a home in an area that is not served by sanitary public sewers, beware. Many soils are too impermeable or too waterlogged to properly dispose of the septic tank effluent.

Some soils are too permeable and allow the effluent to travel large distances without adequate filtration, polluting ground water. If your home will have both a well and a septic tank, and you have a very rapidly permeable soil, it would be a good idea to discuss this matter of filtration with a soil surveyor.

Several years ago we were considering purchase of a beautiful home on a 3-acre lot near Columbus, Ohio. It had both a well and a septic tank, and I knew that fractured bedrock was at a depth of 3 to 4 feet. The Division of Water tested a water sample from the well. The report returned "unsafe to drink without boiling!" Needless to say, we felt fortunate to know this before

buying the house, and we bought elsewhere.

Many communities require percolation tests before issuing permits for septic tanks. If these tests are performed during the wettest season of the year, they give a good indication of the capacity of the soil to absorb the effluent. But if the tests are performed during a drier part of the year, they cannot indicate the presence of a high water table and a waterlogged soil that can absorb *no* effluent during the wetter seasons.

There are many soils for which a percolation test in the late summer would indicate a sufficient percolation rate, but where the toilet will not flush properly for 3 months in late winter and early spring.

You will probably expect a great deal from your lawn. You visualize a lawn that is green and lush in the driest month, that is firm during wet periods, and that will support heavy foot traffic from children—yours and the neighbors'—in their football and other games.

Some soils are droughty and much watering is required. Some soils are soggy and wet during several months of the year. If you know the kind of soil on your lot, you can anticipate just how well the lawn will serve your needs.

Similar considerations apply to your shrubs and trees. Soil adaptability of various species varies widely. Some will grow well on dry, droughty soils but not on wet, heavy soils, and vice versa. Some grow well under both conditions.

The natural topsoil is a very valuable commodity to you as a homeowner, as are trees already growing on the lot. All too often we see building contractors destroy all of the trees and leave nothing but subsoil on the surface for your lawn and gardens.

Some homeowners spend years caring for small trees on lots when several trees that would have served their needs very well grew on the lot just before the house was built. Also, many hours of watering, seeding, weeding, and fertilizing often are required to have a good lawn when subsoil was left on the surface. But little effort would have been required for a beautiful lawn on the natural topsoil.

So, once you have selected a lot with the proper soil, hold grading to a minimum. When grading is necessary, stockpile the topsoil. Soil excavated from the basement can be spread, and after other grading and leveling is done, the topsoil can be put back on the surface. This will save you many hours of work, and often much frustration, in maintaining good lawns and gardens.

If everything checks out so far, and you decide to buy that homesite—alas, you may be awakened very early some rainy morning by the sound of rushing flood waters. Damage to a home that may result from flooding is often a major catastrophe, and utmost care should be taken to choose a site free of this hazard.

Less disastrous and probably more common problems occur if septic tanks and their absorption fields are located in low portions of a lot where ponding occurs; if the driveway crosses a low area that is sometimes ponded; or if gardens, shrubs, or trees are damaged by ponding. If a prospective lot is situated in a low part of the landscape, or in depressions on the upland, flooding or ponding may be a hazard. You will want to check thoroughly the possible occurrence of these hazards before choosing your homesite.

We have not discussed prices very much, but obviously they will have an important influence on the homesite that you can buy. The cost of a homesite where the soils are favorable is usually not very much more than where there are serious limitations.

You certainly will want to avoid the hazards we have discussed. If you don't check out possible soil problems, you are taking a needless gamble, perhaps with your entire lifesavings. Repairing damages due to soil-related failures can be very expensive.

You can find out about the soils on your prospective homesite from soil surveys. Soil surveyors of the U.S. De-

Soil surveyor at work with his soil auger and map board.

partment of Agriculture's Soil Conservation Service make detailed soil surveys of more than 40 million acres of this country each year. Published soil surveys are available for nearly 700 counties across the Nation, and unpublished data is available for many more areas.

Soil surveys provide information about all of the soil problems we have discussed. So instead of closing with a wish for "good luck" on your new homesite, we close with the hope that you will check to "make sure" it will serve your needs.

For further reading:

Bartelli, L. J., A. A. Klingebiel, and others. *Soil Surveys and Land Use Planning,* Soil Science Society of America and American Society of Agronomy, 1966.

Bender, William H. *Soils and Septic Tanks.* Agriculture Information Bulletin 349, U.S. Department of Agriculture, Washington, D.C. 20250, 1971.

Klingebiel, A. A. *Know the Soil You Build On,* Agriculture Information Bulletin 320, U.S. Department of Agriculture, Washington, D.C. 20250, 1967.

McCormack, D. E. *Use of Soil Surveys in the Identification of Floodplains*, The Ohio Journal of Science, Vol. 71, No. 6, 1971.

U.S. Soil Conservation Service. *Soil Conservation at Home*, Agriculture Information Bulletin 244, U.S. Department of Agriculture, Washington, D.C. 20250, 1962.

van der Voet, D. and A. A. Klingebiel. "Soil Problems on Homesites Can Cost You," *A Good Life for More People*, 1971 Yearbook of Agriculture, Superintendent of Documents, Washington, D.C. 20402, pp. 117–122.

Consider the Soil First, 71 frames; slide set, filmstrip, and record available. Tells how to use USDA soil surveys to avoid costly misuses of land for homebuilding, highways, subdivisions, or new town developments, 1971. Address inquiries to the U.S. Department of Agriculture, Office of Communication, Photo Library, Room 412A, Washington, D.C. 20250.

Financing a Home: Some of the Basics

IN THE COURSE OF YOUR lifetime, chances are you will buy a home. In fact, you will probably buy and sell several homes. Therefore, you should know something about financing.

Obtaining a mortgage at a reasonable rate of interest when you buy can save considerable money over the term of the mortgage.

When you sell, arranging for a value appraisal and a mortgage for the prospective buyer will give you an accurate estimate of what your home should sell for and save valuable time for both you and the buyer.

During the last four decades, homeownership has become available to the majority of Americans. Prior to 1930, the opportunities for homeownership were scarce.

Mortgage loans from private lenders in those days were based solely upon the property as security and did not consider the applicant's ability to repay the loan. The mortgage or short-term note was made for periods extending from 2 to 5 years at a specified interest rate.

The lender kept the option of demanding payment in full or renewing the note. If at maturity the lender did not choose to refinance the loan, the mortgagee had to find a new loan, pay off the indebtedness, or lose the property. Individual lenders were the principal source of loans until the disastrous effect of the depression on real estate and the subsequent pent-up demand for housing in the 1940's. Need for expansion and control of credit resulted in the establishment of institutional lending.

The economic depression of the early 1930's resulted in thousands of homeowners being threatened with foreclosure. To stabilize the real estate market, the Homeowners Loan Corporation was organized. Subsequently in 1934, the Federal Housing Administration came into existence.

FHA devised a mortgage whereby real estate loans could be made on a long-term basis rather than the customary 2 to 5 years. Such loans provided for regular monthly installments which included real estate taxes and insurance. To do this on a sound basis, a uniform system of real estate appraisal and credit analysis of the borrower was set up.

Quick acceptance by the public of institutional lending resulted in changes in private lender practices.

Money, like food, is a commodity and the price of money—expressed in interest rates—is determined by the law of supply and demand. When money is in short supply and the demand for it is brisk, interest rates rise. When money is ample and the demand is slight, interest rates decline. Generally speaking, the rates now vary between 7 and 8½ percent.

AUTHOR GEORGE J. SCHLADT is Director, Technical Services Division, Rural Housing, Farmers Home Administration.

In addition to interest rates there is a loan placement fee, commonly referred to as "points." Generally, this is paid for by the seller and included in the sales price of the house.

Many financial institutions are espousing "variable rate mortgages" which in theory would end the feast or famine cycles that have characterized home credit since 1966. Lenders believe that obtaining the going interest rate for mortgage money (that is, the rate determined by competition with all the other demands for money) would guarantee a steady supply of mortgage money and thus do away with "points." A borrower's interest on the mortgage would be adjusted at stated intervals—usually every 5 years—to assure him of an equitable long-term interest rate on his mortgage.

The table shows some typical monthly repayment schedules for varying sizes and lengths of self-amortizing mortgages, at various interest rates. Note that monthly installments do not include real estate taxes or fire insurance premiums, which are usually added onto the monthly mortgage payments rather than being left for separate payment by you.

MONTHLY MORTGAGE PAYMENTS

Amount of mortgage	Amount per month over 20 years		
	7%	7½%	8%
$10,000	$ 77.53	$ 80.56	$ 83.65
$15,000	116.30	120.84	125.47
$20,000	155.06	161.12	167.29
$25,000	193.83	201.40	209.12
$30,000	232.60	241.68	250.94
$40,000	310.12	322.24	334.58

Amount of mortgage	Amount per month over 30 years		
	7%	7½%	8%
$10,000	$ 66.54	$ 69.92	$ 73.38
$15,000	99.80	104.88	110.07
$20,000	133.07	139.84	146.76
$25,000	166.34	174.80	183.45
$30,000	199.60	209.76	220.14
$40,000	266.14	279.69	293.52

Various types of financing are available. The Federal Housing Administration, Veterans Administration, and Farmers Home Administration loans are all government insured, guaranteed, or direct financing. Advantages of this type of financing are twofold: a longer term, 20 to 30 years, and a fixed interest rate determined by law.

The Federal Housing Administration and the Veterans Administration generally serve urban areas. The Farmers Home Administration and the Federal Land Bank Association serve our rural areas.

For information, look up the numbers of these agencies in the phone book under U.S. Government listings. The Federal Housing Administration and the Veterans Administration will refer you to a lending institution which will help you to make your application and submit it to FHA or VA. The Farmers Home Administration and the Federal Land Bank Association will deal with you directly and aid you in filling out your application for a mortgage.

If you are able to buy your home with a large cash downpayment, it will pay you to shop around for the best financing available.

Generally speaking, a high downpayment will enable you to obtain a lower interest rate since security for the mortgage is based upon the value of the home and your ability to repay the loan. Thus, the more money you put down, the less risk for the lender.

Remember that mortgage lenders are in the business of making loans and will willingly grant you a mortgage provided they are satisfied with the risk based upon their review of your ability to repay the loan, and the value of the property.

You should, of course, investigate conventional financing sources—savings and loan associations, savings banks, life insurance companies, and commercial banks. They too are listed in the phone book. Dealing with conventional sources is much less formal and usually faster.

Conventional financing was offering very convenient rates and terms as this chapter was written. The availability of money and competition resulted in terms of 5 percent down with a 95 percent first mortgage. Loans could be obtained for 20 and 25 years. During early stages of the mortgage, however, there was apt to be a mortgage insurance premium to protect the lender.

No matter what type financing you decide on, the lending institution will have an appraisal made of the property, and will order a credit report on you and possibly a verification of employment. Cost of the appraisal is paid by you. Its purpose is to determine present market value of the home.

The appraiser will call in advance for an appointment to appraise a home. If you are the seller, it will pay you dividends to have the house and lot in as neat condition as possible. The appraiser must note the present condition of the property, major defects, and any requirements necessary to make the property marketable.

An appraisal is important in another respect. For instance, if the seller of the property is requesting $30,000 and the property is appraised for $25,000, the loan will be based upon the appraisal. Thus, if you wish to conclude the deal, you would have to come up with $5,000 cash in addition to the downpayment.

In this situation, it would pay to renegotiate your contract with the seller. If the seller will not reduce his price, it will be your decision whether to accept the increased downpayment or look for another home. But at least you should learn all the factors involved. You may wish to talk with the appraiser regarding the basis for his appraisal.

The mortgage company will require your attendance at a "closing" or settlement" of the loan. This is when you sign the papers for the new mortgage. Certain charges are the responsibility of the buyer or seller. At a minimum, the mortgage company will require prepayment of one year's taxes and insurance by the buyer of the property. Both the seller and purchaser should find out in advance from the mortgage company what charges they will be expected to pay for in cash at the time of "closing" or "settlement."

Disaster loans are a type of financing which hopefully you will never have to avail yourself of. They are available to homeowners or farmowners living in open country or towns with populations of not more than 10,000 that are rural in character.

Eligible buildings essentially are homes, farm buildings, or related facilities that have been damaged by a major disaster declared by the President or a natural disaster designated by the Secretary of Agriculture. Loans are repayable in up to 33 years.

Applications for this type of financing may be made at the county offices of the Farmers Home Administration within a year from the date of loss or damage.

The Small Business Administration has financial assistance in disaster areas for small businessmen and others who may be eligible. Information can be obtained from the Small Business Administration's offices in larger cities or the field offices set up when a disaster occurs in any particular area.

That Leisure-Time Spot in Shangri La: Charting Your Way To a Second Home

THAT CRUDE LITTLE CABIN in the pines, a stack of stovewood and wooden water bucket beside the door, was "fittin'" for Daniel Boone, but not for his countrymen today—however much they love the great outdoors.

They're taking to the woods, not to tame the wilderness but to be renewed by it. Escape is the goal, in peaceful revolt against urban miseries. The escape treatment usually includes a residence, rented or purchased, where the family can relax in an outdoor environment.

As many as 3 million families now have their own leisure-time residence in some remote Shangri La. Every year 200,000 more happily join them in this mass exodus from urban boredom.

Longer weekends and vacations, earlier retirements, and higher incomes make the "second home" dream possible, and more zest for boating, swimming, fishing, skiing, riding, hiking, and hunting hasten the reality.

But escape for most people does not mean roughing it. They want to bring along the flush toilets, hot water, smokeless cooking, washer-dryers, house heaters, television, and telephone.

And lo, new constraints have followed the nature pilgrim to his hideaway. Environmental standards have come, and none too soon. His very numbers make them imperative, to preserve the untrammeled nature that he invades.

Oddly enough, the urban amenities he brings along can help him preserve his favorite lake or stream, beach or mountain.

So join the leisure-time migration. The way is more complex than ever, but it promises excitement and fulfillment. Like climbing a cliff, take it one step at a time.

Be realistic, be cautious, be deliberate. The route can be trickier than that used for acquiring an urban home. But the pitfalls can be avoided. Keep in mind that the personal rewards can be among life's best.

You may even retire permanently to your leisure retreat—more than half of second-home buyers intend to.

As you choose your area, then your site, your house plan and builder, and seek your financing, it's advisable to check, investigate, and compare at every stage to protect your investment.

LOCATION. Consider the recreational interests of all the family. Mark on a map the likeliest areas, for scenery as well as activities. Estimate driving time to each, rather than mileage. Two to 4 hours is about the limit; for small tots, 2 hours can be plenty. That gorgeous lake may be only another hour away, but don't risk dreading the extra drive later on.

Tour the first area first; then the others, if necessary. Is the area fresh and clean? Are roads adequate all year? The one-season retreat often wins year-round favor. Study the area's basic ecological health. Is the river or creek polluted? Is the lake dying? Are land clearing and erosion excessive? Is industry encroaching? Is there a wildfire hazard to menace your development?

PUBLIC LANDS. Federal lands no longer are a ready source of sites. Unless you are a bonafide miner, forget about staking out a mining claim on public lands and building a cozy cabin while you pretend to find gold. The U.S. mining laws require legal proof of a valid claim before a land patent can be granted. Building occupancy of non-patented lands is illegal.

The U.S. Department of Agriculture's Forest Service has no plans for leasing additional private recreation sites on the National Forest System. A few unoccupied lots may be available in already established residential tracts in Forest Service regions at Ogden, Utah, and Portland, Oreg. The Interior Department's Bureau of Land Management has no lands available for residential occupancy, except for a few purchasable scattered small tracts in southern California.

Some firms advertising as agents with an "inside track" to help them acquire government land misrepresent the tracts and overstate what they can do for a client. They may exploit the myth of abandoned mining claims being available for purchase.

Reacting to reports of high pressure tactics, Congress 5 years ago began requiring that developers file a Statement of Record, and furnish the buyer with an approved Property Report before a contract is signed.

AUTHOR MERLIN BLAIS is Director, Promotion Department, Western Wood Products Association, Portland, Oreg.

Above and right, a mountain retreat intended to serve later as a retirement home. Exterior and interior walls are cedar. Below, a lakeshore cottage.

PRIVATE LANDS. Beware of enticing and colorful land sale advertisements in Sunday newspaper supplements. While many offerings may be legitimate, examples of fraudulence and misrepresentation are frequent. Don't invest in a site unless you have seen it. Disregard verbal promises of future tract developments and read the fine print in the contract.

If a developer is using interstate transportation or communications, including the mails, you are fully protected by the Interstate Land Sales Disclosure Act, administered by the Department of Housing and Urban Development. Check with that agency should you have any doubts about the honesty of statements in public advertisements or representations made in land sale contracts.

HOUSE SITE.—Are you seeking isolation? If so, you'll pay more for individual water, sewage, and lighting services. Check local newspaper ads, talk to realty agents about sites and prices. Inquire at farmhouses nearby.

Near beaches and streams, shun sites that are too low and subject to erosion. In mountains, avoid sites that are susceptible to slippage or snow and rock slides.

County officials can tell you about zoning regulations, title encumbrances, taxes, easements, building and sewer restrictions, pending road and other changes, schools, even soil and water conditions.

Double check promised access rights to beaches and other commonly-held recreational facilities. This may take you to State and county agencies, as well as to provisions in your sales contract.

Check the water potential: Is water piped in? What are the depth, flow and purity of neighboring wells? Are there any problems with septic tanks? Your drain field must be approved by local sanitation authorities.

Self-contained chemical or incinerating systems are not a complete substitute. Some local authorities require a full-size septic tank and field for backup service. In many areas building permits are not being issued until sewage disposal standards have been complied with.

A well can cost $1,500 or more; a septic system, $600 and up. How close is power service? A hookup beyond 200 feet or so costs extra.

Is there any police and fire protection? How prevalent are vandalism and thievery? How close is food and household shopping? Medical service? A telephone line?

A lawyer can help to dispel doubts about the title and liabilities, whether you're acquiring land or an existing house.

Don't overlook buying an older house, for it could be on a superior site and merely need remodeling. Frequently it costs less to remodel than to build a new house.

FINANCING. It's easier to get now, but can still be difficult to come by for an isolated site without utilities. Lenders look at resale value primarily.

In a well-planned tract development, a loan will not be much costlier than in a suburb. A surprising number of families keep recreation projects on a cash basis.

ISOLATION OR VILLAGE? If the maze of possible pitfalls has clouded your zest for isolation, consider settling into a planned development. The range of lot and house sizes and amenities is surprisingly wide, and prices might not be any higher than your lonesome aerie could eventually cost.

The properly planned village is "all systems go" on site, access and zoning, and usually offers community recreational facilities, such as pool, dock, courts, stables, or even a golf course. Site prices reflect the cost of these recreational facilities, but you might benefit from improved resale values.

Environmental demands today require that developments be kept natural looking. Homes often are built in clusters, leaving more land in undisturbed parks. This also should be a prime goal on an isolated lot. Preserve the natural beauty, especially the older trees and shrubs, and build with nat-

117

Above, cottage with wide overhangs, wraparound deck, and rough wood siding. Left, interior of another second home features native stone fireplace.

ural materials, such as wood and stone.

The condominium concept has spread across the country. Units are individually owned, but exterior and grounds upkeep and community facilities are handled by an owner association.

A further requirement makes condominium units available for rent at times not reserved by the owner. In some developments, rents are helping to pay off the mortgage, taxes, and rental expense. Prices are not low, as units and furnishings must be of good quality.

PLANNING YOUR HOME. A leisure home offers you opportunities for creating a freer, more exciting style and decor than you're used to in the city. And your ingenuity can show that being different need not cost more.

But really roughing it with primitive facilities is for the birds. Plan an equipped kitchen, two baths if feasible, water heater, and adequate heating. Figure heating capacity for year-round use. Insulate walls and overhead, and the floor—if open below.

Place your house to capture the best view, but also orient it to the sun. In cold climates, face any large windows to the south. Wide overhangs will shade windows in summer, and trees on the west side will reduce afternoon heat. Double-pane insulated glass pays off in rooms with high ceilings.

The floor plan should accommodate

your life style. Open layouts favor casual living. Numerous separate rooms assure more privacy. Plan rooms for double duty. A family room can be made convertible for guest use.

Locate one bath with shower close to the side or back entrance, to shortstop dirt and sand. Plan plenty of open deck space; the cost is relatively low, and it will be used constantly. Part of it can be screened in to furnish relief from insects.

Storage in quantity is essential, some of it designed for your sports interests. Plank floors best resist sand; tile and sheet flooring mops up more easily when muddy. Carpets are fine for bedrooms.

To plan a leisure home entirely without professional help isn't practical for most families. For custom tailored space and styling, hire an architect, one whose previous work pleases you. He's worth the extra cost.

Actually, most second homes result from a collaboration between the builder and owners, an adaptation of plans done by a designer for the builder, or readymade designs bought from a plan service.

Engage a builder who's been working in the area, as he knows available craftsmen and suppliers, is familiar with code requirements. But check him out through previous buyers, inspectors, and lenders.

Exterior styling and materials should blend with the scene, and be chosen for easy maintenance. The highly popular A-frame fits well among tall trees and on wooded hillsides; low-profile cottages are suited to open beaches and desert.

A crude box faced with the lowest-cost siding available may be an eyesore, and unfair to the neighbors. If need be, the family on a tight budget can launch its project with a shell house or small starter unit.

These units can put you under shelter quickly, perhaps for less than $5,000. But be sure you'll have the resources to complete the project reasonably soon. Plan carefully so later

Ever popular A-frame is recommended for wooded sites.

expansion won't require extensive moving of walls and plumbing.

PACKAGED HOUSING offers a persuasive alternative to on-site "stick building." This type of factory product is improving, and offers more diversified custom-like features. The packaged house is professionally designed, and uses good materials.

The factory-built unit can save you money, particularly at an isolated lot, because on-site hours are sharply reduced. However, shipping 300 miles or more may eat up the labor saving.

Packaged units are offered in various stages:

Modules complete even to furniture,

119

in boxes that can be linked together on site; mobiles, mounted on permanent wheel assemblies; panelized, shipped in flat sections including pre-assembled kitchen-bathroom cores; and precut bundles for assembly entirely on the site itself.

Be sure the factory-built unit meets code requirements; in many areas, some forms are not permitted. Site and foundations must be carefully prepared ahead of the unit's delivery—in most cases, this is a job for professionals.

Many of the half million mobile homes now produced annually are headed for vacation sites, as they are probably the least expensive way to obtain units with 400 to 1,100 square feet of floor space. Their boxy, metallic look can be softened by adding wood siding, and sunshades, arbors, screens, decks and benches, plus plantings.

READY-MADE PLANS and blueprints for leisure homes are available by mail in literally hundreds of designs and variations. Four or five major commercial plan services regularly describe their plan books in *Vacation Home* magazines, which can be found on the larger newsstands and in public libraries.

These books contain the basic floor plan and an artist's sketch of each design, plus forms to order working blueprints and material lists. Most plan books are offered at $1 to $3.50, and complete blueprints usually between $25 and $50 per dwelling.

Product brochures ranging in subject matter from fireplaces to fire alarms, heating systems to water heaters, plumbing to roofing, flooring to fencing, siding to septic tanks are offered free or for coins in leisure home magazines. One recent issue listed 233 such brochures.

Some building material associations and companies offer colorful design books, at $1 or less.

The Forest Service has worked up blueprints for low-cost home designs suitable for leisure homes. A copy of a booklet describing such plans and telling how to order them, titled "Designs for Low-Cost Wood Homes," may

This octagonal second home was built from plans created for Western Wood Products Association's The Second Home.

be obtained from the Superintendent of Documents, U.S. Government Printing Office, Washington, D.C. 20402, 25 cents.

Libraries vary greatly in the extent of their home planning files, but all recognize home planning as a major public interest.

Books may be listed under "Summer Homes" as well as "Vacation Homes." Check the "Reader's Guide to Periodical Literature" for current articles. Some librarians clip and file articles and are glad to get them out for you.

The U.S. Government Printing Office, Washington, D.C. 20402, offers a free listing of pertinent pamphlets, which can be ordered by its name, "Homes, PL-72, Sept. 1972."

Major sources of plan books (and stock blueprints) include:

Garlinghouse Company, P.O. Box 299, Topeka, Kans. 66601

Home Building Plan Service, 2235 N.E. Sandy Blvd., Portland, Oreg. 97232

Home Planners, Inc., 16310 Grand River Ave., Detroit, Mich. 48227

Master Plan Service, 89 E. Jericho Turnpike, Mineola, N.Y. 11501

National Plan Service, 1700 W. Hubbard St., Chicago, Ill. 60622

Association sources of design booklets include:

American Plywood Association, 1119 A St., Tacoma, Wash. 98402

California Redwood Association, 617 Montgomery St., San Francisco, Calif. 94111

Portland Cement Association, Old Orchard Rd., Skokie, Ill. 60076

Western Wood Products Association, Yeon Bldg., Portland, Oreg. 97204

For further reading:

U.S. Department of Agriculture. *Recreational Buildings and Facilities,* Agriculture Handbook 438, Superintendent of Documents, Washington, D.C. 20402, 70 cents.

Insurance Coverage For the Renter and The Homeowner

NATURAL AND MANMADE PERILS —fire, windstorms, theft, and liability suits, for example—bring about a heavy economic loss to the Nation each year. A fire breaks out in a home every 46 seconds, on the average, with damage annually, of over $700 million. In 1971 some 2 million burglaries resulted in property losses exceeding $700 million.

Much damage is caused by windstorms, and in 1971 nearly 900 of them were severe enough to be called tornadoes and five were classed as hurricanes. Property losses of all types from Hurricane Agnes in 1972 amounted to over $2.6 billion, one of the worst disasters in U.S. history.

We all hear about property losses but relatively few of us have first-hand experience with them. Each loss is unexpected and many people have the feeling "it won't happen to me."

The value and importance of your property can be quickly shown if you list your personal belongings, household goods, and home—if you own one—and add up how much it would cost for replacements if they were lost or damaged. Generally you accumulate property over the years and don't realize how much you have nor how it would be missed if it were gone. Inflation may have substantially increased replacement costs and any significant loss would hurt financially.

Many steps can be taken to prevent or reduce loss from fire, wind, theft and other perils, and some losses that may happen will not be large enough to be serious. For substantial losses, insurance is the best method of protection. By paying a relatively small, set payment —called a premium—to an insurance company, homeowners and tenants can protect themselves against the possibility of a large and unpredictable loss.

Property owners can insure themselves in several ways. They can build up their protection by buying insurance for most perils separately, or they can buy a package policy that protects against a dozen or more perils. Even with a package policy, additional insurance for special needs can be bought by paying an extra premium.

A policy is the document given to you by the insurance company to explain the protection and the conditions under which payments or indemnities will be made in event of loss.

When separate insurance coverages are bought, property owners usually start with a standard fire policy which insures the home and contents against fire and lightning. Then for an additional premium they may get extended coverage to include damage from wind, hail, smoke, explosion, riot, vehicles and aircraft.

Another policy—for burglary and

AUTHOR LAWRENCE A. JONES retired in 1973 as Assistant to the Chief, Agricultural Finance Branch, Economic Research Service.

theft protection—is available. Still another, called liability insurance, will protect against losses from lawsuits for injuries suffered by visitors or damage caused to the property of others.

Buying insurance through separate policies may be the best way for owners with specialized property or those facing certain definite perils. Also, in some localities package policies may not be readily available or may provide more costly protection than is needed or wanted. The value of some homes and their contents may be less than the minimum amounts of protection that must be bought in package policies. Probably separate insurance policies are used more for protection in rural areas than in urban communities.

The Federal Government has cooperated with the insurance industry in making several types of protection available. Flood insurance, for one, has long been generally impossible to obtain because of the potential catastrophic nature of this peril in certain areas. Now it is available at low cost through governmental cooperation in about 1,200 communities where there is danger of flooding. To be eligible for governmental participation, the community must pledge to set certain construction standards and to enforce land use measures in flood-prone areas.

In some cities and high-crime localities, homeowners and apartment dwellers have had difficulty in getting fire, theft, and vandalism insurance. To meet such needs, private insurers as a group with government cooperation have developed FAIR (Fair Access to Insurance Requirements) Plans. By 1972, there were more than 1 million FAIR policies providing $23 billion of insurance protection.

Property and liability insurance is generally regulated and supervised by States and not the Federal Government. The obligation of each State is to make certain that insurance companies do not overcharge or discriminate against customers and that companies remain in sound financial condition so as to be able to pay for losses.

If you feel you have been unfairly denied insurance protection or charged excessive premium rates, you may want to complain to the State supervisory official, usually called the commissioner of insurance and located in the capital city of your State.

Package policies which protect against losses from a variety of perils have been spreading rapidly since the mid-1950's. Familiar package policies are the homeowners, farmowners, and renters policies.

Such policies, as suggested earlier, are not always available, nor are they the best for everybody, but they do have advantages. You usually have only one policy and one premium to worry about and the wide variety of protection costs you less than if the same coverages were purchased in separate policies.

To buy a homeowners policy you must own and occupy a one- or two-family residence. The policy protects the house and additions to it such as an attached garage. It also insures other structures including toolsheds and detached garages; these latter are called appurtenant structures in the policy.

Buildings used for commercial purposes or that are rented to others (except garages) are not covered.

All household goods and personal property owned or used by the family are protected. Losses to personal belongings and other property are frequently covered whether they occur at home or away. An inventory of personal property, especially of more valuable items, is helpful in filing a claim in event of fire, theft, or other loss.

The homeowners policy specifies some exceptions and conditions under which indemnities for losses may not be paid. For example, pets are not covered and protection for jewelry and furs is usually limited to $500. Theft of credit cards may be excluded, as well as loss of boats and trailers when away from the insured premises.

Consult with your insurance agent to avoid any misunderstanding about coverage. The extra protection you need may be available by paying an additional premium.

Another coverage included in the homeowners policy is additional living expense. This pays for the increase in living expenses made necessary if the damage to the house is so severe it can not be occupied. It would cover costs of hotels, motels, and restaurant meals.

The *basic homeowner's policy* usually protects against 11 perils to property —fire and lightning, wind and hail, explosion, riot, aircraft, vehicles, smoke, vandalism, theft, breakage of glass, and loss of property removed from premises endangered by fire or other perils.

The *broad homeowners policy* covers seven additional perils—falling objects, weight of ice and snow, collapse of building, sudden and accidental damage to a steam or hot water heating system or water heater, accidental leakage within a plumbing, heating, or air conditioning system, freezing of these systems, and accidental injury from artifically generated currents to electrical appliances and wiring (excluding TV and radio tubes).

The *comprehensive homeowners policy* covers all perils except earthquake, landslide, floods of various kinds, backing up of sewers, seepage, war, and nuclear radiation.

In buying a homeowners policy the property owner decides the amount of coverage he wants on his dwelling. On this basis, the amounts on appurtenant structures, personal property, and additional living expense are automatically determined as 10 percent, 50 percent, and 20 percent, respectively, of the dwelling coverage. For example, if the dwelling is insured for $20,000 the coverage would be $2,000 on appurtenant structures, $10,000 on personal property, and $4,000 for additional living expenses.

A homeowners policy, besides paying for property losses from such perils as fire and wind, provides liability coverage for family members living in the home. Under the personal liability feature, you are protected against lawsuits from people who believe you, your family, or pets are responsible for their injuries or damage to their property. It covers accidents both on and away from the insured property.

For example, if your dog bites a neighbor or a visitor is hurt in a fall down your steps and you are sued, the insurance company will pay the legal costs and any damages assessed against you. The minimum personal liability protection offered in a homeowners policy is $25,000, but larger amounts can be purchased for an additional premium.

Medical payments to others also is a feature of homeowners insurance. Such payments are made for injuries to other people caused by you, your family, or pets. This feature is similar to personal liability except that it is designed mainly for minor injuries, and payments may be made regardless of who is at fault. Medical payments to any one person are limited to $500.

A farmowners package policy which provides basic protection comparable to the homeowners policy is available to owners of farms in many areas. Any protection needed on the farm service buildings, livestock, and machinery is added to coverages related to the dwelling.

A *tenants or renters policy* similar in many respects to a homeowners policy, is available for those who live in an apartment or rent a home. (In some cases, such a policy may go by the name of a homeowners policy). This insures contents of the home and personal possessions of the family against about the same perils and also provides personal liability protection and medical payments to others.

The cost of property and liability insurance to a homeowner or a renter depends on a variety of factors. The value of your property and the amount of protection you want is, of course, basic. Cost also varies with the number of perils protected against and differences in location and condition of property that may increase or decrease the chances of loss. Homes distant from fire departments or hydrants or those with faulty electrical wiring or heating systems would be relatively costly to insure.

Some insurance companies may charge more than others for the same protection but competition and State regulation generally tend to hold premium rate differences to a minimum.

Developing an insurance program at reasonable cost should begin with an appraisal of the perils faced. Consider the financial consequences of damages or losses. Study the various kinds of available insurance coverages and their costs. Select what matches as closely as possible your needs for protection.

Don't overinsure, as you won't be paid more than the replacement cost of any loss regardless of the insurance you carry. Talk with several reputable insurance agents for the lowest reasonable premium rates. Repairing hazardous conditions of wiring, roofs, and chimneys may be worthwhile in lower insurance costs.

Insurance where the property owner himself bears any losses up to the amount of a deductible will provide savings. Many policies already include a deductible of $50, but insurance with larger deductibles is available at cheaper rates.

Determining the value of your house or other property is often difficult, especially in times of rapid inflation or deflation. With respect to the dwelling, some help can be obtained by talking with neighbors and others about the going price of houses like yours. Real estate tax assessments are usually a specified percentage of market values and may be a guide.

The insurance agent, too, will have useful information on sales prices and construction costs. In fact, someone from the insurance company will probably inspect the property before the policy is approved so as to check on values and make sure no fire hazards or other conditions make it uninsurable.

What your insurance pays after a loss is spelled out in the policy, and it may not reach the exaggerated levels that you hear or read about. Most policies state that the company will pay "the actual cash value at the time of loss." This means that only the depreciated value is paid.

For example, if a 5-year old TV set is destroyed by fire, you should not expect to recover its original cost of $500, because it is not worth that much. Nor should you expect your insurance to give you the price of a brand new storm door to replace an old one that has been broken during a windstorm.

By paying an additional premium, however, you usually can get protection for the replacement cost rather than the depreciated value.

With a homeowners policy, you can receive full payment (except for deductible amounts) for any damage to the dwelling, up to the amount of the coverage, provided it is insured for at least 80 percent of its value. In periods of rising property values and building costs it is important to maintain this level of protection.

At the time you buy a homeowners policy you probably can get an endorsement that automatically increases the protection every 3 months or so.

At this point, the reader of this chapter will realize it does not tell him all he needs to know about insurance protection. Purpose of the chapter is to make the homeowner or renter more aware of his property risks, basic principles of insurance, and the main types of policies available. A little study before you talk to your insurance agent will help in building a sensible program of financial protection.

Legal Hurdles to Clear In Building, Buying, Or Owning a Home

This chapter covers legal problems involved in having a home built, buying an existing dwelling, settlement, and homeownership.

If you are having a home custom built or purchasing a house to be built in a planned subdivision, you must first select a site. If you are custom building the house, you need to acquire title to the site before construction, unless you are buying the site from the builder.

Prior to purchase of a site or house your attorney should check local zoning ordinances and building codes to find out if you can use the property for the purpose you intend. And you should determine whether, under the present zoning, the surrounding area will be compatible with your use of the property as a residence.

After deciding on the type of house, you and your attorney should sit down with the contractor and reach a written agreement as to the features of the house, costs, completion date, and the warranties.

If you have an architect, he should attend this meeting and be primarily responsible for drawing up plans and specifications. A split responsibility between builder and architect should be avoided, if possible.

When you are building a house and the builder gives you a contract to sign, do not sign until your attorney has reviewed it and made any changes needed to protect you.

Be sure that the contract, plans, and specifications (contract documents) set forth everything you and the builder agree should go into the house. These are the only documents which bind the builder. He is not legally obligated to include anything in the house not listed in the contract documents.

Any changes to the contract documents which you and the builder agree to should be written into the documents, and initialed by you and the builder. Your architect should review any change involving the structure or furnishings of the house itself; your attorney should review any other changes.

If you decide the best approach to obtaining a home for you and your family is to purchase an existing house, you should first decide whether to contract with a real estate broker or to try to find a house and deal directly with the seller or his broker.

In most cases it is a good idea to use a broker if you are moving into an unfamiliar town or community. The broker serves as a clearinghouse and a screening process for you. He will be able to save you considerable time and effort which you would expend looking at houses unsuitable for you and your family.

A good broker will also be able to give detailed information about the town, the neighborhood, schools, taxes, shopping, houses of worship, transportation, and other community facilities.

Even if you know the area where you wish to purchase a house, you would do well to check with several brokers to see what houses are listed with them. Generally a broker represents the seller and the seller has to pay him. This fee is often reflected in the price of the house.

When there is an exclusive contract with the seller, the seller may have to pay the brokerage fee even though you deal directly with him. But if there is no exclusive contract or the house is not listed with a broker, you may save money dealing directly with the seller, so long as you or someone you contract with is able to inspect the house and

AUTHOR JEROME G. OSLICK is an Attorney in the Community Development Division, Office of the General Counsel.

draw up the necessary papers such as an option or agreement of sale.

In this type of transaction, an inspection by an architect would be a wise investment.

Once you determine you want to buy a specific house, you make an offer. If the seller decides to accept the offer, the two of you negotiate terms of the contract of sale.

This contract, which is an agreement binding upon both parties, will state exactly what will be included in the purchase price. If you want the seller to leave a certain chandelier or mirror, this should be included in the contract.

The contract should state that it is conditional upon the house meeting all local building and health codes, a termite inspection being made, and free and clear title being obtainable. It also should be conditional on your being able to obtain financing for the purchase and provide adequate time for doing so.

Some contracts to purchase real estate provide that they not be recorded. Recording the contract may be a way of preventing the seller from selling the house to another purchaser. Whether to record the contract or not will be a matter of negotiation between you and the seller, subject to general practice in that area.

Assuming all has gone well in construction of your new house or that all the conditions set forth in the contract of sale for the existing house have been met, you are now ready for settlement—the closing of the real estate transaction. The closing represents the finalizing of the loan to finance the house or the purchase of the house. If you owned the site on which the house was built, a closing would have taken place at the time of purchase of the site.

You will want an attorney to represent you at the closing unless it is handled by a title insurance company. The mortgage lender may require that you use an attorney approved by him. You may also want your own attorney present at the closing.

At final acceptance of the house you should receive from the builder all guarantees and warranties which apply to the appliances, the equipment, and structural members (such as the roof) in the house.

The builder should also provide a warranty, which is usually in effect for a year, on the house itself as well as a certificate that he has paid all of his workers, subcontractors, or suppliers for work done on the house. He should also provide a waiver of lien from any worker, subcontractor, or supplier who has not yet been paid.

If you do not receive the certification and waiver, you may find that someone whom the builder has not paid will be able to file a lien against the house and require you to pay him under threat of a forced sale of the house. Thus, you should have your attorney review these items so that he is convinced you are reasonably protected against such liens.

Make sure the house includes everything the contract said it should include. You, or your architect, should inspect the house immediately before closing or final acceptance. Anything missing or not done properly should be brought to the attention of the seller or builder at the closing, or before if possible.

If agreement cannot be reached on how to rectify the errors, you may want to delay the closing until agreement is reached. It will be more difficult to get things done after closing, since the builder or seller will have been paid. Therefore, unless some of the purchase or construction money is held in escrow, which you should arrange for, you will not have much leverage to get the problem corrected after closing.

The deed is your proof of title to, or ownership of, the property. Usually title to a house is taken "in fee." This means you get absolute title to the property, subject only to existing recorded easements and liens and any encumbrances. The deed is signed ·by the seller and names you as the purchaser.

You may take title either in your own name, in which case your spouse may have certain legal rights to the property, or jointly with your spouse, either with or without a right of survivorship. The manner in which you take title will effect various tax, transfer, and inheritance consequences in the future and is a matter which you should decide in consultation with your attorney.

The deed should always be recorded to protect your ownership rights.

The promissory note is the instrument you sign in which you promise to repay the person or institution that lent you the money to purchase the house. This note will establish periodic (usually monthly) payments which you will have to meet to repay the loan. The note, or mortgage, may also require you to prepay to the lender an amount equal to the monthly real estate taxes and hazard insurance premiums on your house. The lender holds these amounts in escrow to be paid when the charges are due.

You should have a general idea of what the monthly cost will be before you contract to purchase the house. This, plus utilities, maintenance and upkeep expenses, is the monthly cost of homeownership.

The mortgage or deed of trust is the document you sign which in effect says that if you default on your obligations to the lender, he has the right to sell the house to recover the money you owe. Whether the document is a deed of trust or a mortgage will depend on the laws of your State. The lender will record the mortgage or deed of trust to protect himself against losing his security interest in the house.

The mortgage will encumber the property until it is satisfied, that is, until the note is paid off. It cannot be removed by a mere transfer of the property to another person.

You will probably want to take out a mortgage life insurance policy. One type of policy provides that, should you die, the mortgage will be paid by the insurance company, and your heirs will not be burdened with the costs of paying off the house. Another form of mortgage life insurance pays the proceeds to a named beneficiary who is free to use the money for any purpose.

Closing costs are sometimes called settlement costs. They are in addition to the price of the house. They may include costs such as mortgage service charges, transfer taxes, recording fees, title search and title insurance costs, and prepaid real estate taxes and insurance. Find out about them well in advance of the settlement.

Whether the buyer or seller pays these charges (other than the prepaid taxes and insurance which the buyer pays) varies from place to place and is subject to terms of the contract.

Title search is a check of the title records to make certain there are no overdue taxes, assessments, liens or other claims, or any outstanding restrictive covenants on file against the property you are buying. The search also will show the current ownership of the property—in other words, whether the seller has anything to sell.

Title insurance protects the lender and yourself, if you wish to purchase separate coverage, against defects in the title due to occurrences which are traceable to flaws in the legal title of previous owners, negligence of the examining attorney, and other causes as described in the title insurance policy.

Now that you own and have moved into your home, your legal problems as a homeowner have just begun. Some of the many problems you will face involve insurance, taxes and assessments, maintenance and repairs, and the possible refinancing of your home.

In addition to title insurance and mortgage insurance, the wise homeowner will carry a homeowners insurance policy. The lender may require you to carry a policy of this type. Such a policy will protect you from loss due to weather damage (with certain limitations involving floods and earthquakes), fire, other accidental occurrences, and theft. It will also protect you against liability to a person who is injured in your home or on your property.

These policies are available with various types and amounts of coverage.

The type and amount you choose will depend on your own needs.

As a homeowner you will be responsible for paying all real estate taxes and assessments levied against your property.

A real estate tax is a tax levied by the local or State government. It is based on a percentage of the assessed value of your property. The rate of tax normally is uniform for all single family residences throughout the taxing area.

If you believe that the assessed value of your house is too high, most jurisidictions provide a Board of Tax Appeals where you can appeal the assessment. If the board rules against you, you must pay the tax unless you decide to bring the case before a court.

A special assessment is a tax for a specific purpose, such as providing paved streets or new sewers. If your home is directly benefited by the improvement, you may have to pay your proportionate share of its cost.

Sometimes your home will be subject to a special assessment when you purchase it. If so, you should agree with the seller in the sale agreement as to who will pay the assessment.

After you have lived in your home for a while, certain items will have to be repaired or be replaced. Always, whether for maintenance or minor or major repairs, deal with a person with a good reputation in the area.

Do not sign repair contracts without carefully reading and understanding them. You should have your attorney review any documents you cannot understand, and many of the ones you think you do.

Before expanding or modifying your house you should check to see whether a building permit is required or whether a zoning ordinance restricts the type of project being undertaken.

Some repair contracts provide for taking a lien on your home. This type of provision could mean, at worst, loss of your home and, at best, considerable anxiety if you miss a payment on your repair bill.

Sometime during your homeownership you may find you need to borrow a relatively large sum of money, for which the lender will require some form of security. You may wish to make major repairs to your home, add a room, perhaps send a child to college.

This can be accomplished by pledging your equity in your home as security. The lender will take a second mortgage or second trust on your home. The conditions of such security are usually the same as those of a first mortgage or deed of trust, except that the interest rate will probably be higher, depending on market conditions, since the second security has a lesser priority than the first.

The best advice for dealing with any of the problems discussed in this chapter and any other legal concerns of the purchaser and owner of a home is to seek the advice of a reputable attorney on whom you can rely.

Developing a Plan For a House to Fit Family Needs

THE KEY in planning your house is to choose and develop ideas that will meet present and future needs of yourself and your family. From the plan, you will be able to visualize the important relationship of the various areas of the house and to convey to others your ultimate ideas of housing needs. In its completed form, the plan will serve as the basis for financial arrangements, the securing of building permits, and finally the building of your house— whether contracted or self-help.

Space requirements will be determined by your family's size, day to day living, and possessions. Living units should be planned to have enough space for furniture or equipment. To try this out, test your preliminary floor plan with furniture drawn to scale.

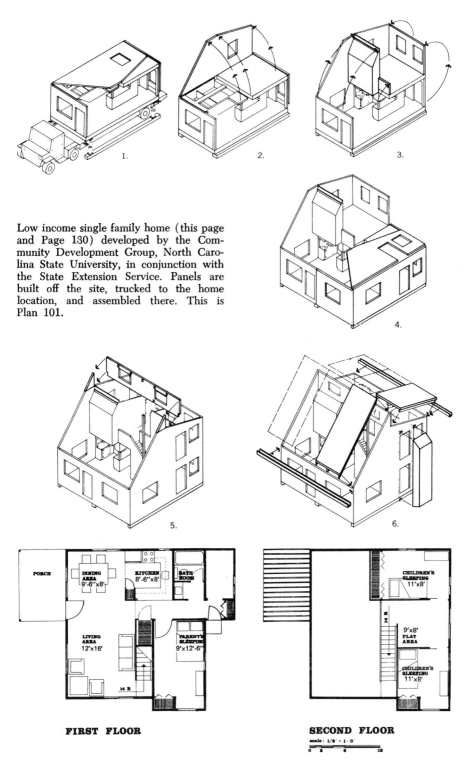

Low income single family home (this page and Page 130) developed by the Community Development Group, North Carolina State University, in conjunction with the State Extension Service. Panels are built off the site, trucked to the home location, and assembled there. This is Plan 101.

FIRST FLOOR

PORCH

DINING AREA
9'-6"x8'

KITCHEN
8'-6"x8'

BATH ROOM

LIVING AREA
12'x16'

PARENTS SLEEPING
9'x12'-6"

14 R

SECOND FLOOR

scale: 1/8" · 1'-0"

0   2   6   12

CHILDREN'S SLEEPING
11'x8'

14 R

9'x8'
PLAY AREA

CHILDREN'S SLEEPING
11'x8'

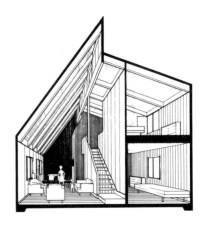

Exterior and cutaway of home depicted on page 129.

Your idea may start with an existing plan that you have developed, with the making of slight changes. By considering revisions at the planning stage on paper carefully, it is simple to check whether the changes are workable before you get into actual construction.

The size and shape of rooms in relationship to each other influence how well your housing unit will function. But room size does not always show the amount of usable space. Doors, windows, and closet openings can be so poorly located that usable space in the room is reduced to a minimum. Choose a plan that permits flexibility regarding use of space.

In studying a plan, pay particular attention to circulation. The hallway should provide access to all rooms, including the bedrooms and bath. In some plans, the hall leads from either front or rear entrances to the center of activities. Use the hallway where necessary, but keep use of it to a minimum.

Allow adequate space for sleeping and for other related activities, such as

AUTHOR W. RUSSELL PARKER is Architect, Cooperative Farm Building Plan Exchange & Rural Housing, Agricultural Research Service.

dressing, personal care, study, or reading. Required space should be provided for clothes storage and housekeeping in the bedroom area.

The larger bedroom or primary bedroom in your plan should be a room approximately 11 ft., 6 in. by 13 to 15 ft., in order to accommodate twin beds. Secondary bedrooms can be smaller as they will have a single or a double bed taking far less space. The larger bedroom should have at least one uninterrupted wall space of about 10 feet for arranging beds and other furniture.

Except when you have a minimum plan, your bedroom area should be large enough to permit several alternate arrangements of furniture.

In looking over your plan of the bedroom area, you might ask yourself the following question:

• Are the bedrooms convenient to the bath?

• Can you reach the bath without passing through another bedroom?

• Are the bedrooms in a quiet zone, away from activity areas such as busy streets, playgrounds, or the recreation room?

• Are bedroom closets being used as noise barriers between rooms?

The bath should be planned based on

BATHROOM ARRANGEMENTS

FAMILY BATHROOMS	MINIMUM BATHROOMS

PLUMBING PIPES IN ONE WALL

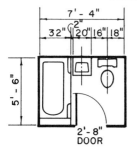

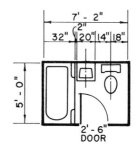

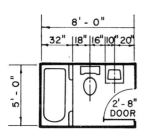

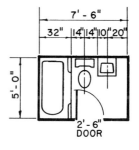

PLUMBING PIPES IN TWO WALLS

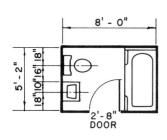

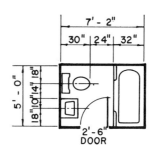

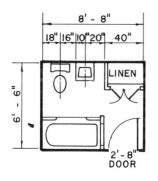

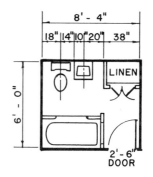

your family needs, and if there is only one in your plans make sure it is easily accessible from all rooms. The entrance should not be visible from rooms where guests are being entertained in order to preserve privacy. A good location for the bath is close to the kitchen and the service entrance, for use by the mother and children during the day.

If there is an additional bath in the plan, consider a walk-in shower instead of another tub-shower for those who find it difficult getting in and out of a bathtub.

Even in the minimum bathroom, leave adequate floor space around the fixtures for comfort and accessibility.

Provide adequate linen storage outside the bathroom for towels and for face cloths.

The kitchen is the most expensive room in the house so take time to perfect a good arrangement that will be attractive, efficient, and permanent. Remember that the sink, wall cabinets, and range are difficult to move. Usually the location of the windows and of doors to the exterior or adjacent rooms will limit you to the choice of one of five basic kitchen arrangements as illustrated in this chapter.

An L-shaped kitchen fits well on two walls and provides a good location for dining or even the laundry equipment on the opposite wall. There is less walking distance between the work counters than in a straight line arrangement that is used where only one sizable wall is available.

The U-shaped kitchen is usually compact, step saving, and out of the traffic flow. Special planning is needed to make full use of the corner storage in the base and wall cabinets with drawers and shelves opening from the adjoining room, or in special lazy-susan cabinet doors.

Often in a combination of rooms such as kitchen-dining or kitchen family rooms, the broken-U arrangement fits very well with the complete uses of all available space.

If you pick a parallel-wall kitchen arrangement, provide at least the recom-

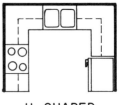

U · SHAPED KITCHEN

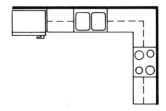

L · SHAPED KITCHEN

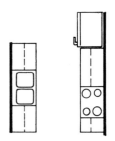

PARALLEL WALL KITCHEN

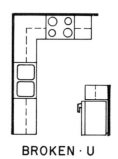

BROKEN · U KITCHEN

STRAIGHT LINE KITCHEN

132

mended width of 4 ft. 6 in. between facing equipment, the space that is needed for two people to work and pass each other. If possible, avoid placing the refrigerator or oven so the door opens across a frequently used doorway.

Base cabinets are usually 24 in. deep and 36 in. high and have a 4 in. high toe space at the floor. If wall cabinets are hung about 15 in. above the counter, you may be surprised to find you can reach the top shelves. Most wall cabinets are hung too high, requiring a chair or stepladder to reach the top shelves.

The kitchen should be the control center of your house. When it is near the service entrance, fewer steps have to be taken with heavy loads. The kitchen should have a clear passage to the front door and should be close to the bedrooms and bath. It is also desirable if the driveway can be viewed from the kitchen window so as to be able to observe activity in that area and the children at play.

The living room needs to contain enough space for general family living activities, such as entertaining, reading, writing, listening to music, watching, relaxing, and children's play, unless provided for elsewhere in the house.

In the living area, provide adequate floor space for convenient grouping of furniture with separation of traffic ways from centers of activity. The following furniture might be accommodated in the living area:

—A couch, 3'-0" x 6'-10"
—Two easy chairs, 2'-6" x 3'-0"
—A desk, 1'-8" x 3'-6"
—A desk chair, 1'-6" x 1'-6"
—A television set, 1'-4" to 2'-8"
—A table, 1'-6" x 2'-6"

The space you allot to dining will be based on the number of persons to be served and the proper circulation. Your dining area may be combined with the living room or kitchen.

Figuring individual eating space on the table should be based on a frontage of 24 in. and an area of approximately 2 sq. ft. Provide additional table space to accommodate the serving dishes.

Desirable room for seating should have a clear 42 in. all around the dining table. The following minimum clearance from the edge of the table should be provided: 42 in. for serving from behind chair, 24 in. for passage only, 48 in. from the table to base cabinet (in the kitchen).

The ideal situation would be to employ the services of an architect to help develop a plan for you, but this is not always economically feasible.

Most individuals look over stock plans, choosing one that will satisfy the family needs. Seldom is such a plan accepted without at least minor revisions.

Several stock plans are available from the U.S. Department of Agriculture.

The Extension Service distributes complete working drawings. They may be obtained through your county extension agent or the extension agricultural engineer at most State land-grant colleges. There is usually a small charge.

The Farmers Home Administration distributes plans through its field offices that were developed as guides to potential borrowers. They have been popular and meet the agency's loan requirements.

The Forest Service has published a number of plans to fill the demand for housing for low-income families. All the houses are frame construction with wood used throughout. Very complete construction prints of these drawings, with specifications, are for sale by the U.S. Government Printing Office.

A booklet describing these plans and telling how to order them, titled "Designs for Low-Cost Wood Homes," may be obtained from the Superintendent of Documents, U.S. Government Printing Office, Washington, D.C. 20402. It costs 25 cents.

In the final analysis of the design and planning of your living unit, be sure you provide for the essential needs of people for space, light, food, water, sleep, safety, sanitation, comfort, companionship, and periods of quietness. Adequate housing quality should be provided, yet costs must be kept at a minimum by efficient use of space.

490-100 O - 73 - 10

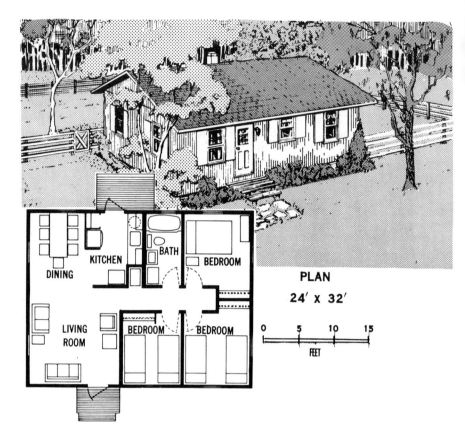

PLAN

24' X 32'

0   5   10   15

FEET

3-Bedroom House
Cooperative Farm Building Plan Exchange
Plan 7185
Forest Service Plan FPL-1

This plan is for a low-cost wood house.

The floor plan is 24 by 32 feet and contains 768 square feet of living area. Despite its relatively small size, the house has three bedrooms, affording desirable privacy for a family with three to five children. All the rooms are conveniently arranged, so there is little wasted space.

This house is set on a treated wood post foundation and has a crawl space underneath. Thus, it can be constructed on a sloping site without costly grading and masonry work. Most of the materials used may be obtained from local lumberyards or small local mills.

Shutters on the windows are optional and may be added if the desired effect is needed and can be afforded.

Exterior siding panels and trim can be finished with long-lasting stain obtainable in many pleasing colors. Wide overhangs at the cornice and gable ends provide a good appearance as well as excellent protection for the sidewalls. Insulation in walls, floor, and ceiling reduces the heating cost and keeps the house cooler during the hot summer months.

This house plan was developed to provide a good livable home at a cost acceptable to low-income families and is shown without extras.

An outside storage closet can be built on the rear porch for additional storage space. Plans for larger front and rear porches are included. A small, paved area near the rear porch can be used for outdoor eating.

3-Bedroom Farmhouse
Cooperative Farm Building Plan Exchange
Plan 7165

Exterior appearance of this house is conventional and in good taste. It is a style that hopefully will retain its charm throughout the years.

Vertical boards and battens on the main house and horizontal siding on the storage area behind the carport have a comfortable familiarity. Shutters on the front carry through the traditional style.

The pleasing exterior is matched by convenience of the inside planning. The sleeping zone has three moderate-size bedrooms and two baths arranged compactly and set apart for quietness. The dining-activity area provides space for informal family activities. The living room offers a place for quiet conversation or reading.

There is easy access to the work area from the carport. Storage for chore clothes is convenient to the kitchen entrance. Bathrooms, bedrooms, living room, and dining area can be reached from the back entrance without having to go through the kitchen work area. The family bathroom is located off the hallway where it is accessible from all areas of the house.

Grouping the two baths and heater room is economical. The baths are on the same wet wall; the hot water heater is close to the bathrooms, where hot water is used frequently but in small amounts.

The following storage facilities are conveniently located:

—Adequate clothes closet in each bedroom

—Linen storage near bedrooms and bath

—Coat closet at front entrance

—Hooks for chore clothes near kitchen entrance

—Pantry storage and freezer near kitchen

135

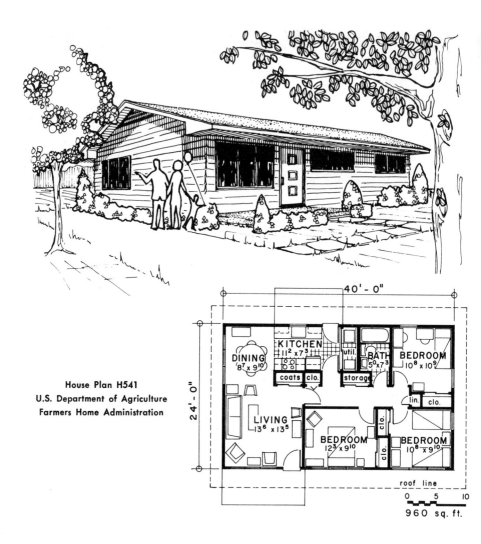

House Plan H541
U.S. Department of Agriculture
Farmers Home Administration

40' - 0"

24' - 0"

KITCHEN
11² x 7³

DINING
8⁷ x 9¹⁰

util.

BATH
5⁰ x 7³

BEDROOM
10⁸ x 10⁹

coats clo.

storage

LIVING
13⁶ x 13⁵

BEDROOM
12³ x 9¹⁰

clo.

clo.

lin. clo.

BEDROOM
10⁸ x 9¹⁰

roof line

0   5   10

960 sq. ft.

This three-bedroom frame construction house which has proven popular has many commendable features.

The main entrance leads directly into the center of the house, and the family entrance is through the kitchen from the patio out back. Children can enter the house from the back and go to the bath or bedroom area without passing through the living room. The bath is easily accessible from all rooms in the house and linen is stored in a closet off the hall.

From the kitchen, the housewife can control all the entrances. The three

bedrooms and closets are adequate in size. Due to the relationship of the bath, utility room, and kitchen, short runs of piping will be necessary which should make an efficient and effective plumbing layout.

For further reading:

U.S. Department of Agriculture. *Plumbing for the Home and Farmstead,* Farmers Bulletin 2213, Washington, D.C. 20250, 1971.

————. *Planning Bathrooms for Today's Homes,* Home and Garden Bulletin 99, Washington, D.C. 20250, 1967.

Pick a Good Builder
And Live Happily
For Ever After

From early childhood, we are conditioned by rhyme, story, and song to the importance of strong, sturdy construction. This requirement has been drummed into our consciousness from the tragedy of the two little pigs who built their homes of sticks and straw to the storming of an impregnable castle when knights were bold and fortresses were meant to withstand everything short of the atomic bomb.

As we mature and take on the responsibilities of job and family, we are often beset with the task of producing our own home, or castle. This is an awesome task. It is frequently the largest single investment we will ever make. The task becomes even more formidable if we are to produce this home—this congenial abiding place, this symbol of domesticity and love—from scratch.

Again in our minds, the lesson of the three little pigs crops up and we are bent on finding the builder who will build our house to withstand the ravages of use and time. Thus begins the search for the man or team of men who can transform our house plans and dreams into full-scale, three-dimensional ideal space for living.

Assuming you have already purchased and paid for your lot and have acquired or had produced for you the plans and specifications of your dream home, the next step is obviously the engaging of a building contractor to produce it.

Perhaps you have had a previous successful experience with a building contracting firm in your community, or have friends or acquaintances who have recently completed their homes and have been pleased with the contractor's results. If this is the case, the search for

your builder may be of short duration. You may wish to enter into direct negotiations with this good builder and get the project underway.

But that is not the usual case. Ordinarily, in small residential work, a selected list of bidders is made up consisting of qualified and experienced contractors, and they are invited to submit, for your consideration, a lump sum bid for which they will complete the work.

The list of bidders should consist of about five firms—never less than three—and should be contractors whom you would be willing to have build your house. Selection of contractors to make up this list may be difficult if you are new in the community or have had no contact with the building industry.

In the event you have engaged complete architectural services for your home, your architect is in a position to recommend builders who have undertaken similar projects from his office and who are reliable, reputable and good builders. If this is not the case, however, you will have to rely on recommendations from friends and others who have recently had something built for themselves.

A good means of locating a builder for your house is to contact the building organizations in your community. Members are bound by a code of ethics and building qualifications for membership. Most reputable contractors will be active in these organizations.

Sometimes you will find a special section in the Yellow Pages of your telephone book listing officers and members of the organizations. Many of these homebuilders associations are affiliates of the National Association of Homebuilders (NAHB); it and the Associated General Contractors of America (AGC) are probably the most widely known nationally of the building organizations.

An alternative method of building is to act as contractor yourself. This, however, is not recommended unless you

AUTHOR RICHARD H. SLATER is an architect in the Technical Services Division, Farmers Home Administration.

are experienced in the building trades and familiar with building costs.

You must be absolutely certain of costs and have the time and talent to contract for and to coordinate all the trades involved in the building—such as excavation, concrete placing and finishing, carpentry, masonry, plumbing, electrical, heating and air conditioning, roofing, cabinet work, tile setting, floor finishing, and all the others. Furthermore, unless you intend to pay cash for the house, you may find it difficult to locate a lending agency willing to allow you to undertake this work.

Contractors from the invited list of builders should be informed at the same time that the plans for your home are ready for their estimates, and all bids should be opened at the same time—preferably in the presence of the bidders.

Generally, 10 days to 2 weeks is sufficient time for the contractors to gather the necessary subbids and materials and labor takeoff that comprise their bids. However, the scope and complexity of the design will determine the amount of time the bidders will require to finalize their estimates, or bid. If the plan is one that is widely in use in the area, undoubtedly less time will be required.

The bid opening is an exciting and suspenseful happening. More than a giant stride toward your new home, it determines whom you will select to do the work and whether the contract cost is one that you and your banker can live with.

More often than not, it becomes necessary to make minor changes or to accept alternate plan details or materials to bring the project into the realm of reality. This is usually a heartbreaking and frustrating exercise, but quickly forgotten after construction commences.

Once the final details of building plan, construction time, and cost are worked out with your builder and have received the nod from your lending agency, a contract should be prepared between you and the contractor which sets forth in detail the conditions of

your agreement. At this point, it may be well for you to contact your lawyer to draw up the contract.

Specific items which should be included in the agreement are: date of the agreement; names of the parties of the contract; description of the work—a reference to the drawings and the specifications and the location of the project; time of commencement and completion of the building; the contract sum; the method of progress payments—when, percentage of payment withheld, and amount to be paid when the house is substantially complete; final payment; any miscellaneous provisions; and your signature and that of the contractor, with witnesses in both cases.

The American Institute of Architects (AIA) has for several years produced a number of helpful documents related to building and contracts. These forms, which are widely used, undergo constant revisions in order to perfect them and to reflect changes occurring in the building industry.

The forms are available to anyone who wishes to use them and can be secured from the American Institute of Architects, 1735 New York Avenue, N. W., Washington, D. C. 20006. There is a small charge for them. Therefore, you should obtain a current price list from the A.I.A. before ordering.

AIA Document A107, Standard Form of Agreement Between Owner and Contractor, Short Form Agreement for Small Construction Contracts, contains an abridged section of General Conditions which sets forth sufficiently the elements of the conduct of the work.

It includes such items as subcontracts, payments, protection of persons and property, various insurances required during construction, changes in the work, correction of the work, and methods of terminating the contract if necessary. This contract is especially intended for residential and other small construction.

Other AIA documents relating to residential buildings which are useful in planning and in the conduct of construction are: Land Survey Requisition, AIA Document G601; Change Order, AIA Document G701; Certificate of Substantial Completion, AIA Document G704; Certificate of Insurance, AIA Document G705; and Contractors Affidavit of Release of Liens, AIA Document G706A.

Besides these documents, AIA produces a handbook with useful information for those who are contemplating building. Chapter reprints are available at a nominal cost. The chapters that contain especially helpful information are: chapter 13, General Conditions of the Contract for Construction; chapter 16, Selection of Contractors; and chapter 17, Owner-Contractor and Contractor-Subcontractor Agreements.

One of the greatest pitfalls you can unwittingly fall into with an unscrupulous or careless builder is the mechanic's lien. This lien on real property is created by statute in all States in favor of persons supplying labor or materials for a building for the value of the labor or materials supplied by them.

Clear title to the property cannot be obtained until the claim for the labor or materials is settled. It is important, therefore, to receive a sworn, or notarized, document from your contractor that all labor and materials used in your home are paid for.

In case of inclement weather or other reasons, it may be impossible to complete all of the work on your dwelling at a specified time. This may include such things as walks and drives, certain difficult-to-get pieces of equipment, landscaping or other items.

However, the house may be substantially completed and otherwise be ready for you to move in. When this happens, it is not unusual to withhold the cost of these items plus a small percentage and set up an escrow account to be released at a specified time when the work is completed to your satisfaction. That enables you to move in and to make a final payment less the escrow fund to the contractor. Most home financing agencies are amenable to such an arrangement.

When you make final settlement with your builder, do not forget to obtain from him all guarantees, warranties, operating instructions, and other descriptive material concerning equipment placed in the house. This would include material and warranties on such things as roofing, water heater, cooking range, refrigerator, dishwasher, disposer, heating and cooling equipment, and any other equipment or materials guarantees that apply. These should be stored in a safe place, where they are available for easy reference.

Usually gas and electric companies will send a service representative to explain the operation and maintenance of the various items of equipment to get you off to a good start. You should become thoroughly familiar with the operation and maintenance of your heating and cooling system.

Building can be frustrating and fun. It is a great experience. As you sit back in your armchair before a roaring blaze in the fireplace of your comfortable new home with the winter winds howling outside, reflect upon this adventure and give thanks that the fireplace is not smoking because you picked a good designer and builder.

Many Constraints Will Affect Your Plans for the Site and House

IDEALLY, HOUSE PLANS and site plans should be developed together and complement each other. All too often they clash. Hillsides are bulldozed level to build ranch houses where two or three step hillside houses should have been built. We see split level houses on prairie lots, requiring construction of unnatural earth mounds around one house corner so that sliding glass patio doors do not open 6 feet above grade.

Most site planning problems have alternative solutions. Usually there is not a clear cut "right" or "wrong" answer. The task of the designer is to find out what the alternatives are and what the consequences of their selection will be.

In starting his job the site designer should first determine the restraints which apply to his site. More often than not, he will find these restraints are of a natural or a legal nature. Sometimes they will be a combination of the two.

Natural constraints are those imposed by the characteristics and features of the site. Steep slopes, generally those over 12 percent, are difficult to walk on, and to mow and maintain lawns on. They are subject to severe soil erosion and can be difficult to use for on-site sewage disposal systems.

Some steep slopes have been known to creep or slide down hill, taking the house with them.

In northern latitudes, slopes which slant down toward the north, commonly called north slopes, will retain ice and snow longer on sidewalks and driveways than will south slopes.

A garden on a south slope will generally permit "green thumbs" to start work earlier in the spring and to continue longer in the fall than will one placed on a northern slope.

The prevailing wind direction should influence both house and site design. Most localities have seasonal changes in prevailing winds. Strong fall, winter, and spring winds from the northwest suggest that a patio be located on the south, southeast, or east side of the house—thereby allowing the house to provide some shelter for the patio in the spring and fall.

If that is not possible, then a patio might require erection of some type of wall to serve as a windbreak. In this case an attached garage placed in the

northwest corner of the house will cut down on the heating bill, not require as large a home heating system, and reduce drafts in the house on cold winter nights.

Soil conditions affect both the house and the site design.

Soils that shrink and swell a great deal with changes in their moisture content will cause sidewalks to crack and heave up.

High water table soils can result in wet basements and soggy yards, to say nothing of failing septic systems and tracked-in mud.

A soil that is excessively drained will make it difficult to maintain a lawn. It will require a lot of sprinkling and if local water rates are high, this can be expensive. In some communities water shortages have resulted in bans on lawn sprinkling.

Soils that are shallow to rock can provide picturesque and unique yard settings while at the same time being difficult to build on. Today's house requires a great many utility and energy services. Many of these enter the house from underground sources. Blasting and digging through rock in order to install a utility service can be costly and troublesome.

Legal restraints or limitations influencing the siting of residences and their accessory buildings may be local, State or Federal in origin.

Local laws such as zoning ordinances, building codes, housing codes, health ordinances, sanitation codes, flood plain regulations, and deed restrictions all have to be considered. For the most part, these controls are enacted, administered, and enforced by municipalities, townships, or counties.

Frequently, the individual States have set minimum standards for construction, water supply, waste disposal, highway access, flood plain use, etc., which can also influence the siting of a building on a parcel of land.

In some cases Federal departments or agencies have minimum standards which have to be complied with if the Federal Government is providing direct

---

AUTHOR JOHN QUAY is an architect with the McHenry County Regional Planning Commission, Woodstock, Ill.

financial assistance or if there is a federally guaranteed mortgage on the property.

Practical experience has shown that where local ordinances exist, are reasonably current as to their requirements, and are enforced—then a project which complies with them in all probability will also comply with State and Federal regulations. However, do not automatically assume that this is so.

Zoning ordinances frequently establish front, side, and rear yard setback requirements as well as limitations on the permitted height of buildings and other structures.

Setback requirements establish the minimum distances back from a street property line to the principal or main structure, the distance in from both side lot lines that must be maintained clear of building, and the distance in from the rear of a lot that must be maintained free of buildings.

The height limitation for both principal and accessory structures is sometimes set forth as a specific number of feet and inches and at other times as a number of stories. In some cases they are combined. For example, the ordinance might permit a three-story structure in a residential zoning district so long as its maximum height does not exceed 35 feet.

Some ordinances set forth side yards as percentages of the width of the front of a lot, others set forth a specific number of feet and some will use a formula combining both percentages and specific minimums.

Setback and height restrictions, which are often referred to as bulk regulations, and the techniques of determining them were simple when most urban building took place on rectangular lots created within a gridiron street pattern.

Contemporary subdivision designs often do not conform to a grid street pattern and today many lots are not rectangular. Consequently, complicated formulas for calculating setbacks and height regulations have sometimes been incorporated into zoning restrictions. Yard setbacks actually define the build-able area within a lot—or, if you will—a lot within a lot.

Another restriction often found in zoning ordinances deals with the type and height of fences, hedges, gardens, and free standing walls. These restrictions are important when dealing with site design problems because they influence such things as the location, type and size of patios, gardens, play areas, service entrances, driveways, etc.

Building codes generally will involve the structural design, performance standards, and specifications for the construction of buildings. Often the codes deal with establishing minimum floor elevations and the finished grading of the building site. They play an important role in site design by setting forth requirements for exterior building materials, window and door sizes as well as type of foundation, roof drainage, lot grading and standards for free standing and attached garages, carports, breezeways, etc.

For example, a code requiring that the exterior of all building walls be built of masonry materials would influence selection of materials to be used in constructing an attached patio. This requirement would have architectual consequences and in all probability influence the patio's total cost.

As in the case of zoning ordinances, before starting to develop a site design you should familiarize yourself with the applicable building code and determine which parts of it will influence the project.

Housing codes usually set forth minimum design standards for various types of dwellings, and minimum maintenance standards which must be met. Some overlap and deal with standards normally found in building codes. They may also overlap health and sanitary regulations.

In general their primary purpose is to establish minimum overall liveability and maintenance standards which apply to both the interior and exterior parts of the dwelling as well as the lot.

Health and sanitation codes influence site design to a much greater degree than most people realize. This is especially true in areas where private or on-site wells are used for water supply and where septic systems are used for sanitary waste disposal.

The codes usually establish minimum distances which must separate these two utilities, and set design standards and materials specifications for both wells and septic systems. Distance requirements apply not only to the individual lot being considered, but also relate to facilities on neighboring lots.

In subdivisions where the designers have not considered location for well and septic facilities, it is quite common to find that some lots will not meet the sanitation requirements. This frequently occurs in older subdivisions platted before establishment of modern day health and sanitation standards.

A number of different soils are found in the United States and each has distinct capabilities for assimilating the effluent from septic systems. Because of soil conditions it is not uncommon for the septic system to require more square footage of lot area than the principal structure.

Such a large number of variables enter into the proper design and operation of septic systems that it is almost impossible to establish any hard and fast rules concerning them. Just a few of the factors that must be considered when designing and siting a septic system are the number of people using it, slope of the land, soil porosity, depth to bed rock, the local rainfall patterns, nearness to lakes, creeks, or drainage ditches, existing and proposed trees and shrubs, historical flooding, and ground water table.

It is not considered good practice to have driveways, parking areas, or accessory buildings located over septic tanks, lines, or fields.

Some types of trees and shrubs will die if their root zones are continually saturated with the effluent from septic systems. Other species will thrive in locations where septic effluent is available—often they grow so profusely that within a couple of years their roots will penetrate the tile field and completely fill the line, causing the system to fail.

If an on-site septic system is to be used for waste disposal, determining all the detailed requirements governing design, installation, and maintenance of the system is a *must* first step.

Local and State flood plain regulations often play a major role in site design. Even if your chosen site is not on a lake, river, or stream, you should investigate the local flooding history. Many a beautiful lot purchased during a dry season has become a dreadful nightmare during a wet period.

Local flooding conditions can develop in just about all types of terrain. However, areas where the landscape is relatively flat or nearly level can be the most difficult to evaluate from a flooding standpoint. In these areas relatively small amounts of rainfall can cause **streams and rivers to overtop their banks and spread water out for miles on all sides.**

The amount of flood plain data that is available to, and recognized by, local authorities will vary. In some cases good reliable data is readily available while in others the pickings are rather meager.

The local soil and water conservation district and the local office of the U. S. Geological Survey are two agencies which can often provide information concerning the type and the severity of local flooding and can advise you whether your site will be affected by it.

However, these agencies do not conduct individual lot surveys. If they indicate that your property might have a flooding problem, you serve your own best interest by securing the professional services of someone intimately familiar with local conditions. Have him determine just where the flood plain is in relation to your property.

Keep in mind that you may construct your house so it does not suffer directly due to flooding, but in this day and age of underground services, it is possible to have electrical, gas, telephone, sewer, and water services interrupted as a result of flooding.

Low lying roads which serve as access roads may also become impassable or washed out. If this happens, your home is isolated from both regular and emergency services as well as communication with the rest of the community.

The first step in dealing with a site design problem is to investigate all restrictions enforced by all governmental and financial institutions which are relevant or relate to the project.

Bear in mind, though, that requirements can vary considerably from one jurisdiction to another within the same general locality. Just because you are familiar with county requirements does not mean you can assume they will be the same in a municipality within the county. This is especially true in suburbia where often the lot next door is in another political jurisdiction which has completely different regulations.

The second step is to make a complete evaluation of the natural features and their limitations.

Site plans and house plans should be developed simultaneously. All major features of a house plan should be reviewed in light of the impact on the site plan, and vice versa.

Cheap Construction Costs a Bundle, So Look Carefully Before You Buy

JOHNNY AND SALLY could talk of nothing else but the little three-bedroom cottage. They had seen the for sale sign that day in the older neighborhood built after World War II by an out-of-town contractor. He came along and began underbidding all of the long established builders in our town.

You remember that contractor, don't you? Most people wondered at the time how he could charge less and still provide attractive houses with all kinds of shrubs and flowering trees.

At a barbecue supper in our backyard, many of our friends were commenting that Johnny and Sally should buy the place because it sure looked like a dream house. The young couple were all excited but their enthusiasm cooled a bit when they learned that the house had been on the market for 6 months. I thought this a good time to suggest they see the inside of the house and check the structure itself.

I noted that in purchasing an automobile they would inquire about engine performance, brakes, gas mileage, safety features, warranty, and many other details. This same common sense approach should be used in buying or building a house.

Too many times the way a house is built is of little concern to a potential buyer. The attractiveness of the front exterior becomes the chief concern, and aside from that almost anybody's construction standards will do. High standards of construction, and how the floor plan design functions for the family, are hardly ever considered.

Standards of construction are set for your protection by the local, county, or State building codes and also perhaps by the government lending agency that insures or guarantees the housing loan. Plans and specifications for the house are generally drawn to provide design and construction according to these standards or codes.

Unfortunately, many families pay little attention to the established construction standards. Any standards will do as long as they can get the house in the shortest possible time and at the least cost. The most costly purchase of a lifetime is treated as though it were an insignificant article on a bargain counter.

Little wonder, then, that there is a class of builders with low prices as

AUTHOR EARL R. BELL is architectural engineer, Rural Housing, Farmers Home Administration.

their principal stock in trade—with construction standards of questionable merit.

It is not my intention to imply that lavish spending is needed to insure a satisfactory house. Economies can and should be practiced in house building. The legitimate contractor knows them.

Find out who the contractor was for your choice of house and inquire as to his reputation before going deeply into considering buying or building a house.

But back to my young friends. They asked me to assist them with an inspection of the house.

The next evening, as we drove to the house, I emphasized that no one, **even a professional building inspector,** is infallible. Oversights by builders and inspectors can occur, but obvious faults in construction many times can be found with careful observations and an understanding of materials and structural systems.

When in doubt, the lay person should seek professional assistance. If there is a charge, it may pay for itself many times.

Johnny commented that he was already picturing himself toasting his shins before the open fire in the cozy living room. As for me, I did not picture him that way because I had noticed as we parked in the driveway that the fireplace chimney did not appear to be high enough above the roof to provide an adequate draw in the flue. I could imagine Johnny opening windows and doors to let the smoke out of the house. Trees surrounding the house had grown so tall that they would more than likely cause this problem.

The flue would have to be increased in height to about 2 feet above the roof ridge and an open cap provided to prevent possible back drafts in the fireplace.

Let us see what we found as we inspected the house—the information might be enlightening to the homebuilder and to the neophyte in house buying as well.

We started on the outside, checking the foundation, walls, eaves, and roof-ing as we walked around. The foundation was not the required minimum of 8 inches from the finish grade to the top of the foundation. Adequate slope was not provided either. There should have been about 6 inches fall in 10 feet distance from the house.

We found a one and one-half inch vertical crack in the foundation wall 8 inches from the right front corner. This might mean the corner had settled. We saw many little hair line cracks caused by concrete shrinkage during the initial curing process, but they have little significance to the life of the structure.

Insufficient slope away from the house and foundation footings that were probably either too small, made of a poor concrete mix, or were not properly reinforced with steel rods caused the crack. If settling was the problem, then it would probably settle more and the crack would grow larger and spread to the gypsum wall board inside the house if it had not already done so.

I pointed out that the grading slope was insufficient all around the house and the downspouts would need to be extended and splash blocks added.

As we came back up the front walk, I noticed that the walk sloped towards the house and rain water had to run somewhere. We found that it had run under the front stoop footings, which were too shallow, and out next to the foundation behind shrubbery that had overgrown and hid a large crack between the house and the stoop.

The concrete stoop was not properly attached to the house foundation. Freezing and thawing actions in the wintertime were gradually moving the stoop down and away from the house.

We entered the main door with a bump of Johnny's shoulder because the door was sticking at the top. This meant that the footings were settling and the door no longer fit the now out-of-square opening. This would have to be corrected. When inside, I looked up and there it was, the crack I expected in the wallboard above the corner of the door. It would soon start moving across the ceiling.

We went directly to the basement. We began descending the stair to the basement but I had to duck down uncomfortably low because the stairway head room was less than six feet. The minimum service or basement stairway head room standard is 6 feet 4 inches. Another head-banging error costly to correct.

There in that right front corner we found a streak of daylight coming through the foundation crack and evidence that water had entered many times, indicating that costly footing and foundation repair and reinforcement would be required immediately.

The center supporting beam had wooden posts the correct distance apart. But the posts were set in the concrete and would have to be cut off at the bottom above the floor line about 4 inches and supported on a short concrete post to prevent further decay of the wood. There was an uneven quarter inch crack in the basement floor that indicated further skimping in the concrete mixes and probably that no steel reinforcing had been provided.

Sally had noticed some squeaking floors in the living room and dining room. We checked the floor joists and found that the joist span was over 14 feet under the living room, and the 2 x 8 joists were supposed to be 2 x 10 for the species of wood used.

This, and the fact that the wood cross bracing or bridging was never nailed tightly between the joists, had allowed the joists to sag only slightly. But it was enough to loosen the nails holding the strip flooring, which causes squeaks between the tongue and groove of the flooring boards.

As we came back upstairs, we passed the rear door. I opened it and tried to slam it shut. It bounced open. The latch would not catch without first lifting the door and being certain the latch caught. This was another indication that the poor footings were settling on yet another part of the house.

Now Johnny and Sally began questioning, on their own, some of the signs of cheap construction they found. And they decided that buying this house was not such a good idea. I noted that any prospective buyer should bear in mind that the history of a house is written not alone on the first purchase price but on future maintenance costs as well. Fifty dollars saved today by cheapening the construction of a house may return a repair bill five times that amount in a short time.

Needless to say, Johnny and Sally never did buy the house.

I had been a builder once and I am against shoddy and unworkmanlike construction because it makes a lot of unsuspecting house buyers like this young couple lose confidence in the building industry. That is why I want you to understand and recognize good construction and obtain permanent satisfaction in the house you buy or build.

In discussing "good construction," I want to talk mainly in terms of how to judge an older house. But you can apply just about anything I say to construction of a new house that you may expect to build.

Today's houses are no different from century-old homes in that they all have foundations, floors, walls, doors, windows, and roofs. And they have always been intended for much the same purposes—to comfortably shelter a family. How well and how economically the house does this depends on the attention paid to the construction by the builder.

Oversights by even efficient builders and inspectors can be expected. If you have the services of an architect or competent designer for an individual house, inspections will be made by them to determine compliance with the plans and specifications and to obtain satisfactory workmanship. On small individual houses without these services, the owner will have to do the inspecting himself.

In addition to what Johnny and Sally found, if you discover other faults in a house, do not buy it unless the faults can be economically corrected and the cost of correcting will be reflected in the price you pay.

Problems that are more complex or that cannot be answered by comparison with a published standard or code may require the services of an architect or other professional housing person.

Specific technical questions to help prevent the high cost of cheap construction can be referred to such organizations as the National Association of Home Builders, the American Institute of Architects, or the National Association of Building Manufacturers, all in Washington, D.C., or any of their local offices in larger cities.

When you are building a new house, using a contractor, be certain you have complete and accurate Contract Documents. The Contract Documents will include the Plans, the Specification and the Construction Contract.

Proper execution of these documents is necessary to help reduce any chance of misunderstanding as to the intent of the construction proposed. Many costly law suits have been avoided with good Contract Documents and they will help you obtain the house you are paying for.

A Builder's Warranty is generally provided by the contractor on a house for up to 1 year. If a warranty is provided, be certain you follow the instructions closely and report any deficiencies you uncover to the contractor immediately, in writing. You will surely want to do this as soon as you find the problem or at least within the last month of the term of the warranty.

In the case of a manufactured house, the manufacturing company will provide the builder-dealer with a certificate which certifies that the house has been built in substantial conformity with the plans and specifications, any attached modifications, and local, county, and State codes or regulations. You should get a copy of this signed certificate along with the Builder's Warranty.

If you have questions or problems, discuss them with your local lending agency to get advice on proper procedures to follow.

Further technical assistance is available at your public library and in the housing industry's many magazines. You may also wish to have your own copy of the Department of Housing and Urban Development's *Minimum Property Standards for One and Two Living Units*, No. 300 (price $2.50), and the U.S. Department of Agriculture Handbook No. 73, *Wood Frame House Construction* (price $2.25), which show good construction in detail. The latter publication is in so much detail that it will not only tell you how many nails of what size to put in each joint but it almost tells you to yell "Ouch!" if you hit your thumb.

You can order a copy of these publications from the Superintendent of Documents, Government Printing Office Washington, D.C. 20402. Be sure to enclose a check or a money order with you letter.

Close observations of the housing structure and your interest in seeing that you get what you pay for will help all of us reduce the high cost of cheap construction.

Well Water Supplies: Getting the Best From Your Own System

Fifty million people in the United States depend upon individual water supplies. If you asked them, nearly every owner would say his was the best for miles around. This happens because each one has grown accustomed to the taste of his particular well water and has come to prefer that taste to all others.

Unlike 50 million Frenchmen, some of these well owners are wrong. Surveys show about two-thirds of the private supplies have some serious defect. Waterborne diseases (typhoid fever, dysentery, amebiasis, hepatitis) continue to occur sporadically.

The owner of an individual water supply has to be more knowledgeable about sanitation and well construction than his city friend who depends on a municipality for such service. Fortunately, it is possible to prevent the risk of waterborne disease with proper attention to location and construction.

Sometimes water sources are contaminated, but such sources should be avoided or sealed off in the drilling process. We do not recommend the treatment of such sources for individual water systems.

Water systems should be disinfected after completion or after major repairs. The best disinfectant is a chlorine solution. A suitable chlorine solution—not unlike liquid bleach—can be prepared from one ounce of hypochlorite containing 70 percent available chlorine for about 50 gallons of water. Enough solution is added to fill the well volume and it should stand for a period of at least 24 hours.

The well should be pumped until the system is free of chlorine before the water system is placed in use. A sample of water should be analyzed and found safe for human consumption. Your health department can advise you on how to arrange for this testing.

Public water supplies are treated for safety and then continuously chlorinated as an additional precaution against accidental contamination of the system.

Individual systems are usually not equipped with mechanical chlorinators and it is not recommended that they should be. The source should be safe and free of contamination as proven by bacteriological analysis. If it's unsafe, it should be corrected or abandoned.

Treatment of an unsafe source is not recommended. The system is too small and the possibility of equipment failure too great to rely on any treatment processes for safety. If you have a system which cannot be made safe and free from bacteriological contamination, see your available environmental health service immediately and obtain specific advice to solve the problem.

Entrance of surface contaminants into well water is not an accident. Three factors must exist: (1) the contaminant source; (2) a contaminant transmission path terminating in the well or ground water; and (3) a transporting medium to move the contaminant.

Knowing these three factors, the rural resident can consider questions such as: Are there obvious contaminant sources near the well? Does the well structure provide an adequate barrier to contaminants? Is the space between the drill hole and the casing adequately sealed with cement grout? Does the well site have excellent drainage? Is the upper casing terminal adequately protected from surface flooding and storm blown debris?

A common path for surface contamination to find its way down to the ground water source is along the outside of the well casing. In the process of installing the well, natural clay barriers are disturbed by the penetration of the pipe. Vibration compacts the earth away from the pipe and the drilling process breaks and cracks rock immediately adjacent to the well casing. It is relatively easy to seal off this path during well construction. A grout made up of neat cement and water is most commonly used as a sealant.

The well driller has the experience and equipment best suited for placement of the grout, which is most effectively introduced from the bottom to seal the annular space around the well casing.

Remember that the best construction may fail with age. Watch for signs of water quality changes and regard them as indications of possible failures of sanitary protection.

AUTHOR JOHN H. POMEROY is a Sanitary Engineer, Rural Housing, Technical Services Division, Farmers Home Administration.

COAUTHOR ELMER JONES is Agricultural Engineer, Farmstead Water Systems Research, Agricultural Research Service.

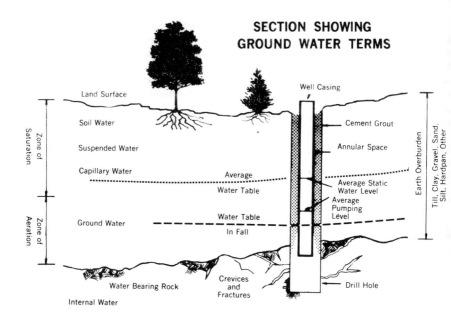

SECTION SHOWING GROUND WATER TERMS

Of almost equal importance to the rural resident as the sanitary quality of water is the quality of service. Many new rural homes have poor water service because water source requirements have been confused with the service requirements.

This can be illustrated by comparing the water supply requirements of one person with the service requirements of a bathtub. The average water requirement per person is 50 gallons per day or 2.08 gallons per hour. At this rate, it would take about 12 hours to fill a bathtub to bathing level. Nearly everyone would call this poor service.

Several other factors besides design flow rate are important for excellent water service in the home. Among these are the effect of competition (using more than one fixture at a time). Simultaneous uses of water might include sprinkling, clothes washing, bathing, or flushing a toilet. This instant demand would range from 12 to 15 gallons per minute.

With excellent service, the competition for water is never noticed. The two activities most affected by lack of good service are the scheduling of laundry periods and the postponing of bathing during peak periods.

While peak demand in the home is quite high, average domestic water requirements per day are quite low normally less than 360 gallons per day

Where water supplies are adequate and costs are reasonable, water use for lawn and garden greatly exceeds domestic use.

An inch of water on a half acre of lawn and garden requires about 15,000 gallons of water.

For a home applying that much water weekly, this would average about 2,000 gallons per day or seven times the domestic requirements. However if watering is postponed in hopes of rain until many plants are showing signs of stress, a heavy extended watering program could result in the use of over 6,000 gallons in one day.

In planning the individual water system, both the peak minute and peak day requirements are important. If adequate water of good quality is available at reasonable depth, a direct pumping water system sized to meet peak demand from the source will be most economical—ignoring the value of water in storage for fire protection and other emergencies.

A simple direct pumping system consists of the well, a pump controlled by a pressure switch, a pressure tank, and the distribution system. A pressure switch setting of 35-55 pounds per square inch is recommended for these systems. It will provide adequate pressure for lawn sprinkling, "first aid" fire protection, and for modern automatic laundry equipment.

The pressure tank is sometimes called a hydropneumatic tank. It contains a small volume of water and a larger volume of compressed air which expands and contracts depending on the water pressure. The compressed air supplies energy to deliver the water to household faucets and fixtures without the necessity of pump starts for every small demand for water.

For many rural homes, intermediate storage systems will be needed to provide good to excellent service. Intermediate storage is atmospheric storage (free water surface at atmospheric pressure), located between the source of supply and the distribution pump, carefully planned and constructed to preserve water quality.

Intermediate storage tanks may be steel or fiberglass tanks constructed for potable water storage or they may be made of reinforced concrete. The cost for effective storage capacity will be much less than the cost in pressure tanks where only a small percentage of the space is available for storing and delivering water to the system. The pressure tank's biggest function is to prevent the pump from recycling too frequently.

The intermediate storage tank is in effect the source of supply of the distribution system. It is filled at a low and prolonged rate from a well which may be of low yield. The well pump may have a low capacity as compared to the delivery pump and pressure tank drawing water from the intermediate storage.

With more storage, system reliability is increased and water is available at the surface for emergencies and fire protection. Intermediate storage may be the most economical system where water must be pumped from great depths.

Reliable but low producing wells can give excellent service if water can be stored during the period of low demand to be available for the short periods of high demand. Such a system may consist of a one-third horsepower submersible pump delivering 2 to 5 gallons per minute with a minimum pumping cycle of 10 to 30 minutes.

The intermediate storage tank size may vary from one to several days' requirements. But an excellent system might have a 3,000- or 4,000-gallon capacity and a three-fourths horsepower shallow well jet pump capable of delivering 25 gallons per minute at 35 pounds per square inch. The storage tank drain may be fitted as a hydrant meeting suction hose requirements of the local firefighting equipment.

Mineral content of water is important. A high content may soon clog home humidifier systems. Hot water heating systems are made less efficient by minerals that form hard scales and sludges. On the other hand, too "soft" a water or one with too low a mineral content will taste flat. Minerals give the water taste.

In hard water areas, it may be desirable to install a water softener. When the hardness exceeds about 150 milligrams per liter (8 or 9 grains per gallon) one might consider the benefits of softening. A hardness of about 80 milligrams per liter seems ideal. A very soft water is likely to corrode pipes and tanks.

People have a wide tolerance for different degrees of hardness and the general use of detergents has made hard water less objectionable. Detergents do not precipitate the minerals and no curd or film is formed as in the case of soap and hard water.

We mentioned that hot water systems are affected by hard water, and this is more noticeable the hotter the water. It is best to hold temperatures down to as low a range as will satisfactorily serve. One hundred and forty degrees Fahrenheit is hot enough for most home requirements and the water heater will be far more efficient and waste less energy.

The cost of heating water is much greater than the cost of the water. Making efficient use of hot water is important to the family and to the national energy situation. In many homes, insulating the hot water lines would result in significant savings.

In new home construction, locating the water heater centrally to minimize hot water pipe lengths should be considered. A great deal of energy is wasted when hot water faucets run for a time before hot water is delivered to the tub or fixture. In some houses where major distances separate the bedroom-bathroom group from the kitchen-laundry area, two water heaters and less piping might result in savings.

An excessive amount of iron and/or manganese may cause staining of water fixtures or of clothes washed in such water. Again treatment is relatively simple. Some minerals may be difficult to remove, however, and occasionally removal is so difficult as not to be economically worthwhile.

When softening or removing iron by oxidation and filtration, exercise care in disposing of backwash from the filter equipment so that the waste will not pollute water-bearing strata.

This precaution also should be taken when softening or removing iron by filters which require rejuvenation. Backwash from the filter equipment should be discharged as storm water at some distance from the well.

Suppose a new home site is contemplated. An important question is "Does this site permit development of a safe and adequate water supply available on a year-round basis?"

Frequently, an otherwise acceptable housing site will be found impractical because a potable water source is lacking or would prove too expensive to develop and operate. This often occurs where crystalline nonwater-bearing rock comes near the surface, and soil above the rock has little or no permeability. A home buyer in such a situation may spend thousands of dollars on dry holes without developing an adequate source of water.

Some sites may have a ground water source subject to contamination or to pollution because the water-bearing strata has insufficient natural protection. Sometimes water is available but of poor chemical quality not suitable for drinking or other domestic uses without overly expensive treatment.

A home site should not be selected unless evidence indicates that obtaining a safe and adequate water supply will not be difficult. The home buyer can usually obtain sufficient information to make a judgment about a site from the nearby residents, local well drillers, the State geologist, the State department of natural resources, the engineering section of the State and local health department, the U.S. Geological Survey (ground water bulletins), or the Water Resource Commission.

It is best to drill and test the well before proceeding with other major expense so as to avoid unpleasant surprises.

A good supply has a naturally safe source rather than one which requires treatment.

In addition to safety, the water supply should be clear and palatable, containing no significant amount of objectionable chemicals. Drinking water standards recommended by the State health department or those of the Federal Government should be followed.

In some areas, it may be common to provide water softening or iron removal or treatment to reduce corrosiveness of the water supply.

Beware of areas where well flows are known to fluctuate seasonally. This may mean insufficient natural protection exists, and it may forewarn of water shortage under drought conditions.

If the well is properly located, sufficiently deep, properly grouted and sealed, there will be little possibility of contamination. If rock is near the surface, construction and grouting and proper depth of casing must be carefully planned and executed in addition to providing the proper isolation distance from any sewage disposal system. Farm yards, pigpens, and chicken enclosures should not be in the immediate vicinity of the well.

An excellent guide for well location and construction is *Water Supply Sources for the Farmstead and Rural Home*. (Write for FB 2244, Superintendent of Documents, Government Printing Office, Washington, D.C. 20402, 15 cents.) In addition, most States have published similar bulletins. For additional information, see your local health department or environmental protection agency.

Where a new supply is planned, the home buyer will need to determine that a safe, adequate, and palatable water supply can be developed at the desired location. The owner should have several estimates and analyze the bids carefully. Points he needs to check include:

How far will the well be from sources of contamination?

Will a detailed well log be made available?

What diameter well will be installed?

Will a flow test of 4 or more hours be made in order to determine the well's sustainable yield?

What type and minimum length of casing is proposed? What amount of casing will extend above ground? How deep will the casing be sealed into rock?

Will any undesirable formations be sealed off?

To what depth will cement grouting extend?

What type of pump and pump capacity will be provided or recommended?

How will the well be capped on completion? Will any abandoned well hole be sealed?

Will the well be pumped until clear?

Will the water supply system be tested and free from coliform bacteria?

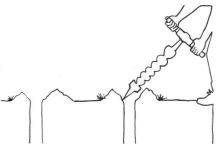

Does the well driller carry statutory compensation and liability insurance?

Are former customers satisfied?

Local conditions vary throughout the country. Except for a few areas of creviced limestone and sink holes or areas of fractured rock under a very shallow mantle of soil, it is not difficult to have a safe well from a bacteriological standpoint. State and local health authorities can warn you of any other problems typical to the area.

In a few places, fluorides may be too high. Some areas have high concentrations of nitrates. Excessive iron and manganese or hardness are common local problems. High chloride content or salt water intrusion are problems in certain areas. Tests for these chemicals are not too costly but are usually not requested unless the problem is known to be common to the area.

In developing a water supply, remember that avoidance of a poor source of supply is many times better than trying to provide remedial treatment.

If you have gone to the trouble to test your well, searched for possible paths of contamination and removed them, designed the system for adequate flows so that there is no competition for water between fixtures and water uses which occur simultaneously, provided for irrigation and "first aid" fire protection—if you have done these things, you may have the best individual water supply for miles around.

For further reading:

U.S. Department of Agriculture. *Simple Plumbing Repairs for the Home and Farmstead,* Farmers Bulletin 2202, Washington, D.C. 20250, 1972.

Individual Systems
For Sewage Disposal

A CITY DWELLER is accustomed to public sewers and tends to get wasteful of water. For instance, he might flush one cigarette butt down the toilet—wasting 5 gallons of water to do so. His rural counterpart has learned to be far more careful and disposes of such things in the trash and not as sewage. He has learned the hard way that too much waste of water inside will result in septic tank effluent bubbling onto the lawn outside.

This chapter is limited to a discussion of individual sewage disposal systems.

More than 99 percent of sewage is water. Although less than 1 percent of sewage is the organic disposable part, that part can be most objectionable and difficult of disposal. But all sewage—the entire 100 percent—should be regarded as dangerous!

Sewage contains all the bacteria and viruses common to the household. In the event of sickness in the family, these germs also are found in the sewage. So it is important that an individual sewage disposal system function properly.

Sewage discharging on the surface results in a nuisance due to odors and appearance of the surfacing septic effluent. Then too, some disease organisms may be present in the effluents that seep from an improperly operating disposal field.

Community or public sewage systems free the neighborhood of this problem and should be utilized when possible.

An individual sewage disposal system should only be used where ade-

quate land for the absorption of effluent is available. The subsurface soil characteristics should favor absorption without endangering the ground water, nearby wells, or neighbors. The usual household sewage disposal system consists of a septic tank and an absorption system for disposal of septic tank effluent.

The septic tank is a simple holding compartment of about 750 to 1,000 gallons capacity. This includes capacity for garbage grinders and automatic washers. Some codes don't provide for the use of these appliances, and the tank size required would be 50 percent smaller.

Flow through the tank is slow and sluggish and for long periods no flow may occur. In the tank, heavier solids settle. Lighter fats and greases rise to the surface and form a partly submerged floating scum. The outlet of the tank is designed to prevent passage of the floating scum and settled sludge. Liquid leaving the tank flows from a depth which traps the scum and sludge in the tank. This is usually accomplished by a baffle or submerged pipe outlet.

Within the tank, the trapped materials undergo strong forces of putrification and decomposition as the result of bacteria which are found naturally in the sewage. So it is unnecessary to add any compounds or ingredients for this purpose.

Eventually, the tank has to be cleaned to prevent the bypass of sludge or scum which would clog the soil absorption part of the system. How often? Three-to 5-year intervals should be sufficient, but this can only be learned through the particular family's experience. A new system should be cleaned after about one year and experience will then dictate the proper interval.

To measure the accumulation of sludge, lower a stick to the bottom of the tank. Adhering sludge will reveal the sludge depth.

The tank does not need to be cleaned until sludge is within 8 or 10 inches of the bottom of the outlet pipe. Most tanks have a tee for an outlet pipe and

AUTHOR JOHN H. POMEROY is a Sanitary Engineer, Rural Housing, Technical Services Division, Farmers Home Administration.

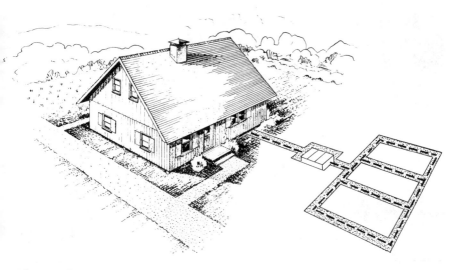

A home and its septic tank system.

it is possible to lower the testing stick down through the tee to avoid it being smeared with surface scum. A nail in the stick will help locate the bottom end of the tee or outlet pipe.

Nearly every vicinity has septic tank cleaners who specialize in cleaning tanks. It is best to negotiate the price in advance of the job. Unscrupulous persons have been known to charge by volume and then recirculate liquid or add water to "clean" the tank. The tank does not need to be flushed or hosed down but rather emptied.

SECTION OF A CONCRETE SEPTIC TANK

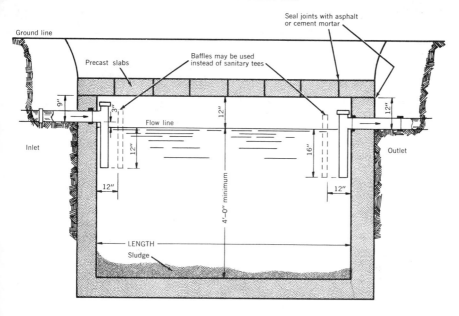

Checking the grade of the field line during installation of a septic tank system.

Liquid leaving the tank outlet is known as effluent and still contains much of the original organic mineral and bacterial content. At best, the septic tank retains only one-third of such material. The two-thirds remaining is greyish in appearance and consists of particles too small to settle out in the septic tank.

Sanitary disposal of this septic tank effluent is the biggest task of the system. Usually, the effluent is discharged to a subsurface soil absorption trench, bed, or pit. The absorption system retains for further decomposition the particles of organic matter and other solids passing the septic tank and permits the liquid portion of the effluent with its dissolved solids to percolate away into the subsoil.

154

As long as this percolation takes place faster than the household adds sewage to the system all is well. When it doesn't, effluent appears on the surface creating a nuisance and a health hazard.

Absorption systems of all types begin to fail the day they are put in use. A mat or crust of decaying organic slimes, precipitated minerals, and 'bacteria coats the bottom of the absorption system. This makes it less permeable to the passage of liquid. The coating begins to extend up the sides of the absorption system as creeping failure begins.

If the subsoil is sufficiently porous and if the clogging mat formation does not become too dense and thick to pass liquid, the absorption system may have a useful life expectancy of several years.

The mat formation can be kept less dense and impermeable by an intermittent flow of sewage. The mat or crust becomes most dense and results in clogging the soil when it is continually wet. Much of the original absorption capacity would return if it were possible to let the mat dry out.

Some soil absorption systems fail prematurely because of poor construction. Heavy equipment can compact the soil, reducing its pore space and permeability. Mechanical diggers or shovels can smear the trench or pit wall and bottom with clay particles—effectively reducing its ability to transmit water.

If the system is left uncovered in a rain, small particles of silt and clay may be washed in to clog it.

When backfilling a trench or absorption bed, a barrier of decomposable paper or straw should cover the stone until the fill material has a chance to stabilize. Without such a barrier, the silt and clay particles in the fill will wash down into the stone and clog it.

On locating and constructing the disposal system, surface water should be diverted so that rainfall will not flood out the system.

Some systems fail prematurely because the site was poorly selected. Many subsoils are not sufficiently permeable to transmit and absorb large volumes of effluent. At other locations, a seasonally high water table may occur and defeat the absorption system —forcing effluent to the surface during every wet season.

It may surprise you, but the volume of effluent discharged to the absorption system exceeds by several times the rainfall the same area may receive. In addition, the sewage discharge is more or less constant as compared to rainfall which comes intermittently with frequent drying out periods between the rainy periods. It is not really too surprising that absorption systems fail. Reducing the volume of water is the easiest way to prolong a system's life.

Check the footing drain sump and the sump for the laundry tray if you have one. Is ground water entering the plumbing system and being pumped to the sewerage system for disposal? No rain water should find its way to the system.

Are the water closets flushed only when necessary and not used as ash trays or disposal units for facial tissue?

Avoid running water to waste just waiting for warm water or cool water to appear at the faucet. The shortest possible runs of pipe and/or insulated pipe will help. Discourage those in the family who let water run from habit when it serves no good purpose.

Leaky faucets and fixtures can waste gallons of water per day. Keep them in repair. Bath water can be reduced without any loss in hygiene. Do not overfill the tub or run the shower unnecessarily strong. A needle point spray may help.

Use the water you must, but do not waste it. Try to space the use of water through the week instead of doing all the laundry on one day.

When shaving, it is wasteful to run water throughout the shaving period. Use it to clean the razor and rinse your face.

Educate the children and company to water thrift. Water thrift postpones absorption system failure.

When failure does occur, you have

a chance to evaluate the system and your use of it. First, make sure the absorption system *has* failed. Stoppage can occur between the house and the system due to an obstruction in the sewer. Diapers, toys, children's shoes, and tree roots are common offenders along with broken or collapsed sewer pipe.

If the absorption system is at fault, effluent usually appears on the surface near the system's low end.

When the system was built, it may have been the minimum cost setup acceptable to the authorities and the building industry.

Let us say you have not been wasting water to the system needlessly. If you had 4 or 5 years of trouble-free service before the first failure, that's not too bad. The prorated cost isn't exorbitant and you have every assurance you can rebuild the system at less than its first cost. Replacing or rebuilding the absorption part of the system should make it as good as new.

Keep the original absorption system dry, and in a matter of months it will return to serviceability should you want to use it again. Switching from one system to the other after long rest periods will prolong the life of both systems.

At this time you may wish to add a sewage lift pump to the system. Install it in a sump after the septic tank. The submersible pump is set to discharge effluent to the absorption system as a concentrated dose rather than as a more continuous trickle throughout the day. The pump should discharge about 50 gallons at a pumping. This intermittence has been found to increase the daily volume which can be disposed of through the absorption system into the soil.

If you have cleaned the septic tank routinely, cleaning at the time of failure is not necessary. The failure is in the absorption system. Cleaning the tank will give only a few days of relief.

If you are wasting water, cut down drastically. Send the laundry out or take it to a laundromat until you have installed your new absorption system. Don't waste money on septic tank additives—additives are not known to add to the life of the system, and the bacteria needed by the system are naturally found in the sewage.

Failure after the first year or two of use is bad news unless you have been wasting a lot of water to the system. If the absorption system fails despite precautions and no construction defect is apparent, you need some expert advice beyond that possible in this article.

If you have lots of friends in the neighborhood with similar problems, begin to work together to develop a central sewerage system. The county office of the Farmers Home Administration may have some helpful ideas on how to go about this and on how to finance such a system.

Suppose you are in an isolated location and suffer premature failure. Then you have some research to do before you proceed. First, verify that the subsurface soil characteristics were responsible for the premature failure. The Soil Conservation Service may be able to advise as to the soil types and their absorption characteristics in your area.

Percolation testing may be in order. If the soil percolates slowly or not at all, or if you have high water table problems or encounter rock at shallow depths, the conventional system of disposal was an error in the first place.

Visit or write for help to the local and State authorities having jurisdiction over sewage disposal or water pollution control. They are in the best position to advise you and guide you to the proper solution considering the circumstances at your location.

To summarize, be very careful in the use of water if your home is served by an individual sewage disposal system of conventional design. It probably was not designed for the wasteful use of water in the first place. When you have to replace the absorption system, do it in such a way that the original system is salvageable and can be used again at a future date after a long rest and drying out period.

156

Water Problems On the Homesite

As a homebuilder, buyer, or owner, you need to be concerned about water and the problems it may create. To recognize the various problems, you should understand:

• How rainfall and the resulting runoff may affect your homesite. How runoff can cause flooding, erosion, and deposition of silt

• How a high water table or lack of drainage can impair the development of your homesite

• And, finally, how these problems can be avoided or resolved.

If you understand the problems and can recognize the causes, you can avoid them when you purchase your lot. You can correct or avoid them in the planning and development of your homesite. Or, if you are plagued with a water problem on your present homesite, you can make the needed corrections.

When rain falls on the ground, part of it soaks into the ground and the rest runs off. The type of soil influences the amount of water that soaks in. A soil that consists mostly of sand or gravel soaks up most of the rainfall, while a tight, sticky clay soil soaks up very little.

Another factor affecting the amount of water entering the soil is the kind of cover. An impervious cover, such as concrete, causes almost 100 percent of the rain to run off. A clay soil with no cover causes more water to run off than that same soil with a heavy grass covering.

If you are concerned about the amount of water you might expect to pass onto and through your homesite, you need to determine the types of soil and watershed cover in the area that contributes water to your lot. Condition of the ditches and channels in which the water travels, and whether they are debris clogged, are factors in how fast this water will move from one location to another.

The usual procedure when an area is converted from woodland or farmland into homesites is to restrict the small ditches and channels that collect water by filling or by installing culverts that are undersized.

Changing the cover of the land from cropland or woodland to one with a large percentage of asphalt or concrete and rooftops results in little of the rainfall soaking into the ground and more running off over the surface.

A determination of how much water can be expected to flow to or past your lot depends on the soil and the cover on that soil, and it depends on the amount of land area that contributes water to your lot. The steepness of the land in the watershed above your lot must also be considered. It is obvious that a large watershed with steep slopes requires more capacity to carry the water than a small watershed with flat slopes.

When the watershed above your lot is large and steep, a larger channel through your lot is needed in order to carry this water. If the channel is unimproved, that is, not modified by man but in its natural state, the water can be expected to overflow usually about once every year or two and, on some occasions, to get very deep outside the channel.

Cries of Flood! Flood! have scared many homeowners. On several occasions homeowners have found, too late, their home was in a flood plain. Often the process of development has obscured visible signs of past flooding

AUTHOR NEIL F. BOGNER is Assistant Director, Engineering Division, Soil Conservation Service (SCS).

COAUTHOR ROBERT M. PASLEY is Head, Central Technical Unit, SCS.

COAUTHOR WILLIAM P. WELDON is State Conservation Engineer, SCS, College Park, Md.

Hurricane Agnes causes flooding of the first floor of a home on a flood plain.

or created situations that cause flooding problems that did not exist before.

Before selecting your homesite, it is well to consult with local residents about the possibility of a particular site being flooded.

Sediment, the byproduct of erosion, creates problems on your lot and in locations far removed from it. Sediment deposits on your lawn, driveways, and sidewalks are problems that are obvious and are a direct cost to you.

Sediment deposits on your neighbor's lawn, on the streets, in storm drains, and ultimately in ponds, streams, lakes, or estuaries are a less obvious expense to you. However, as a taxpayer, they also are costly to you. Of equal seriousness is the damage this sediment does to the environment. Sediment deposits are unsightly, muddied streams lose much of their appeal, and marine life is damaged or destroyed.

The duration of flow and quantity of water that you determine must be handled on your homesite are an indication of the principal water-related problem you face as a homeowner. This is soil erosion. Erosion on your homesite results in an unsightly lot and can be very costly since it is often responsible for serious foundation and stability problems.

The rate and amount of erosion on the homesite is determined by soil type,

cover, surface slope, and the rainfall patterns.

Soils vary greatly in their erosion characteristics. Generally, soils that contain a high percentage of sand are more readily eroded than heavy clay soils. Bare ground is more readily eroded than if it is protected by grass or trees.

While paved areas do not erode, neither do they permit rainwater to enter the soil. Since water cannot enter the soil, it must travel over the surface causing greater flows, more erosion, and perhaps flooding.

The homeowner who has steeply sloping land soon finds that erosion damage can be very severe unless the area is protected.

Soil erosion during construction of a housing development, or a commercial or industrial development, is magnified many times (up to 500 times) over the rates from agricultural lands. The resulting sediment when deposited on flood plains, in streams, rivers, lakes, and estuaries becomes a major handicap to the development, maintenance, or restoration of these resources. The loss of fish and fish habitat may be irretrieveable.

The best control for erosion is vegetation. Establishing a quick, temporary vegetative cover during construction reduces the sediment problem and keeps your topsoil in place. If the season is

such that a quick cover of vegetation cannot be established, then a mulch can be spread to prevent the erosion.

Other practices are required to supplement the establishment of vegetation. Diversions and waterways, or structures of metal, concrete, or rock are frequently used to control erosion in places where water collects. If a development above your lot is producing large quantities of silt, you—or hopefully, the developer—should install a basin or settling area to collect debris and sediment. These can usually be installed in the channel or by excavating a basin in or alongside the stream.

Subsurface water problems are frequently hard to identify until a prolonged wet season occurs. Then wet basements, inoperative septic fields, drowned out trees, lawn, and shrubs, and standing water make it all too clear that a real problem exists.

When selecting a lot, study the area carefully to determine if a high water table exists, if seeps or springs are present, if the soil is slowly permeable, or if rock is at a shallow depth that would prevent drainage. A soil survey of the area is of great help in identifying these limitations. A check of adjacent road cuts or utility excavations frequently gives an indication of potential problems.

A free draining site with a ready out-

Top, this type of erosion and the resulting tons of sediment can be avoided by prompt seeding or mulching of disturbed areas and by careful planning during construction. Above, mulch is anchored by boards set as baffles across the slope to spread runoff water and give further protection.

let usually requires only grading to keep water from downspouts and paved surfaces from collecting along the foundation. A drain around the footings of the basement is cheap insurance against a wet basement—if an outlet can be ob-

159

Above, a diversion terrace and drainage inlet coupled with established lawns help control water problems on this newly developed area. Top, channel tile (coping tile) used to carry surface water from behind homes to the street.

tained for the drain. Sites with low wet areas or seeps can often be improved by using subsurface drains.

High water table areas where outlets are difficult to obtain should be avoided for homesites. In some areas where the lot has unusual value as a homesite—

offering a desirable view of coast or estuary areas—the high water table can be overcome by filling to raise the house and service area above the water table. Special care is needed in designing and installing foundations in these areas.

Seeps and springs can be either collected and removed by a subsurface drain or developed into controlled pools or streams that with proper plantings can add greatly to the property's esthetic value.

Drainage problems around your existing home are usually more expensive to correct than those on a site under construction. Measures to correct water problems on an existing site are the same as those discussed for a new site, except that installation is frequently much more difficult. Downspout water often needs to be carefully collected and carried away from the foundation.

Grading around the homesite is another important factor to consider. Correct grading involves eliminating all areas where water could pond. This can be done by sloping the yard away from the foundation and collecting water from low spots in surface waterways.

Seeding an eroding area or shaping your lawn to drain away from your house are simple, easy chores.

Installing a drain around your house foundation, collecting surface waters and carrying them to a storm sewer, or determining the size of channel needed to pass the increased flows that result from a newly developed area upstream from your lot are neither simple nor easy. In such cases, you need help.

Some of the sources for assistance and information are: Engineering firms, contractors, city, county, and State engineers, State natural resources agencies, the Extension Service, soil and water conservation districts, and the Soil Conservation Service.

For further reading:

U.S. Department of Agriculture, *First Aid for Flooded Homes and Farms*, Agriculture Handbook No. 38, Superintendent of Documents, Washington, D.C. 20402, 20 cents.

Don't Blow A Fuse!
Tips on Electricity

ELECTRIC ENERGY perhaps contributes more to the convenience and high standard of living in the home than any other one item. But if the electrical system is not properly designed, installed, and maintained, it can be a safety and fire hazard as well as a great source of irritation to the homeowner.

Are you planning to build a house, or to purchase or remodel a house, which includes a rewiring job? Have someone from the electric power supplier assist in design of the wiring system, and hire an electrician to install the wiring. Some knowledge of electric systems will be of help when you contract for the installation, and aid you in future maintenance.

To meet all your needs for electric power, install enough lighting and general purpose outlets and circuits. There should be sufficient special purpose circuits to handle those larger appliances which are generally operated in the same location. A rule of thumb is to have lighting branch circuits with a total capacity of 3 watts per square

foot of building area. There should be one 15- or 20-ampere branch circuit for each eight to 10 convenience outlets or duplex receptacles in the house.

The National Electrical Code, a recognized authority, has given guidelines as to needs and safe practices in electrical systems. The code requirements in your own locality may differ in some details. These are minimum requirements for safety and do not necessarily cover adequacy of the wiring for convenience.

Now let's check the wiring system for adequacy. Convenience outlets or duplex receptacles should be spaced at most 12 feet apart, so that no point on the wall measured along the floor line will be more than 6 feet from an outlet. Any wall space more than 2 feet wide also needs an outlet.

Outlets in the kitchen, laundry, pantry, dining room, and breakfast room should be equally divided between two or more 20-amp branch circuits.

Some homeowners have each kitchen outlet installed on an individual circuit. This increases the cost of installation, but the extra load-handling capability is worth the difference.

Under provisions of the National Electrical Code, all outlets are to be grounded. Grounded type outlets permit the connection of parallel-blade two-wire cords and plugs used on appliances, as well as three-wire plugs or cords which are attached to devices which must be grounded.

Weatherproof outlets are desirable on the driveway side of the house and on the opposite side, about 4 feet above the ground. Additional weatherproof outlets may be needed in outside walls of the house or on patios or porches to serve the many appliances used in outdoor living.

All circuits serving outside outlets must be protected by ground-fault interrupter equipment that automatically disconnects the circuit in case something goes wrong with the wiring or

---

AUTHOR **WILLIAM T. COX** is an Agricultural Engineer, Extension Service.

161

This kitchen features an entire ceiling of indirect light. Tubes are recessed slightly in the false beams so they can't be seen. Honeycomb material diffuses the light. Additional lighting is above the sink.

the appliance which would cause an accidental shock.

Install convenience outlets in the wall 18 inches above the floor in bedrooms, living room, and dining room, no more than 12 feet apart. Additional outlets take care of furniture arrangements.

Have one wall outlet in the dining room above table height to connect portable cooking or warming appliances from the table. Put kitchen and work area receptacle outlets 8 inches above the worktable level.

Clock outlets in kitchen and workshop areas can be connected to lighting circuits but not controlled by the wall switch.

Center the outlets for ceiling lights in bedrooms, dens, kitchens, dining and living rooms, halls, passageways, and stairways. Lights in bathrooms are placed above mirrored cabinets and overhead in shower stalls.

Work areas in kitchen, laundries, and home workshops need lighting outlets directly over task areas. Overhead lighting is also recommended in basements and recreation rooms.

Outlets for lights are desirable over or alongside each outside entryway to the house and for flood lights around the dwelling.

Outlets for the switch control of lights are placed in the wall about 48 inches above the floor at the latch side of entrances.

You can install dimmers in place of off-on switches to control the amount of light for different moods or effects.

Three-way and four-way switches are needed to control lights from two or more locations. These may be at entry points to the living room, dining room, kitchen, at the top and bottom of stairways, and inside and outside entrances to the basement and recreation room. A switch control for outside floodlighting outlets may be desired in the master bedroom.

Time clock switches for inside and outside lights will turn lights on and off at pre-set times. This will allow you to return home to a lighted house. It will also discourage burglars while you are away. Photo electric cells do a similar job of turning lights on at dusk and off at dawn.

Lighting outlets may also be controlled by low voltage switching systems which are currently available. In these, the actual switching is done by a relay operated by a 24-volt circuit and controlled by low-voltage switches. Any number of switches to control the same light outlet can be easily and inexpensively added to the circuit. In addition, the use of master switches allows control of many lighting outlets from several different locations.

At least one receptacle outlet for floor or table lamps in the living room should be controlled by a switch, especially when ceiling outlets are not used.

Here, as well as in the bedrooms, silent-type or mercury switches may be desired. Most low-voltage switching systems are silent.

Bathrooms may require an outlet for a heater. The frame of electric heaters must be grounded for safety. Receptacles for electric shavers, toothbrushes, makeup lights, etc., may be incorporated in the lighting fixture over the mirror.

In the kitchen and the workshop, individual circuits for each receptacle provide minimum interruption in the use of appliances. Circuits of 20 amp at 120 volts are a minimum requirement here. They include outlets for irons, automatic washers, garbage disposals, dishwasher, roaster, refrigerator, food freezer, and the like.

Individual power circuits of 240 volts are needed for such major appliances as electric ranges, table top cooking unit, wall oven, clothes dryer, space heater, and large air conditioning equipment.

Thought should be given to the proper selection of wire sizes for circuits throughout the home. General purpose circuits and lighting circuits should be number 12 copper wire or larger. In some old installations, number 14 wire was used for these circuits. The wire sizes are increased whenever heavier loads or larger appliances or equipment are expected.

Protective devices built into home electric systems for safety and convenience are of two approved types, circuit breakers and fuses. Both give acceptable protection for the wiring system.

Use only the proper size fuse or circuit breaker to protect the wire in the circuits; generally a 15-amp fuse or circuit breaker with number 14 wire, and a 20-amp fuse or circuit breaker with number 12 wire.

The procedure used to restore interrupted service varies. A blown fuse must be replaced with a new one of the same capacity. Circuit breaker resetting requires operation of a toggle, or switchlike handle, to restore the circuit connection.

Replacing a fuse or resetting the circuit breaker should be done only after the cause of interruption has been removed.

Circuit breakers or fuses may be installed in a cabinet whose exterior trim and covers are flush with the walls in which they are placed. The interior of this cabinet should be covered with a plate so only the top of the fuses or the circuit breaker handle portions are exposed and all wiring connections are concealed.

The main service entrance of wires and load center in most homes is in the utility area of the home nearest the point of entry of the electric service. Never locate these in a cabinet or closet where they are not readily visible or accessible.

Most homes today require a capacity of between 100 and 200 amperes.

When much of the heavy electrical load is some distance from the main service center, a subcenter is extended with a second distribution panel in order to shorten the length of the circuit conductors.

In the choice and planning of main disconnect and load center equipment, branch circuits of 120 and 240 volts must be provided to care for the needs of installed circuits. At least two 120-volt and one 240-volt circuit spaces should be allowed for future circuits.

The cabinet door of each load center has a table of numbered circuits. Your electrician should list on this table exactly which area or individual appliance is served by each circuit.

Finally, require your electrician to have his work checked and inspected for safety. An authorized inspector can furnish you with a copy of the Certificate of Approval.

Examples of methods used to calculate required circuits, feeders, and main entrances may be found in the National Electrical Code, a copy of which may be purchased from your State fire insurance writing bureau which is most likely in your State capitol, or obtained from the National Fire Protection Association, 60 Batterymarch Street, Boston, Mass. 02110 for $3.50.

Other helpful guides may be obtained from the National Electrical Manufacturers Association, 155 E. 44th Street, New York, N.Y. 10017, or from the Residential Group, Electric Energy Association, 90 Park Avenue, New York, N.Y. 10010.

State universities and your power supplier generally have pamphets.

Foundation Facts, Basement Basics

A FOUNDATION SERVES several purposes. It supports the weight of the house and other vertical loads such as snow. It stabilizes the house against horizontal forces such as wind. It is a retaining wall which supports the earth fill around the house. And often it is a basement or cellar wall which may need to be a barrier to moisture, heat loss, or sound transmission.

The most common foundation is the continuous wall which may be built of stone, clay tile, block, brick, or concrete. Recently, treated wood, metal, and other materials have been used.

CONTINUOUS WALL FOUNDATION

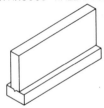

Continuous walls are used to support heavy loads or to enclose a crawl space or basement. If enclosure of space is the main objective, then the wall may be built of lighter, more porous insulating materials which will reduce heat loss and sound transmission.

A step foundation is a continuous wall of variable height. It is used on steep grades or for houses with partial basements.

The pier foundation is a series of piers which support the house. They are generally masonry but sometimes

AUTHOR JERRY O. NEWMAN is an Agricultural Engineer, Rural Housing, Agricultural Research Service.

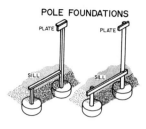

POLE FOUNDATIONS

they are made of other materials. The pole or post foundation is a special kind of pier foundation built of pressure-treated wood. It is often used on steep terrain where there is considerable variation in the height of the piers and where a regular masonry pier might bend and break.

Beams placed between the piers of a pier foundation support the house.

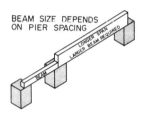

BEAM SIZE DEPENDS ON PIER SPACING

The size of such a beam depends on the load it must carry and the distance between piers. The space between piers is generally enclosed with curtain walls which carry no load and whose main purpose is to enclose the space and act as a barrier to wind, heat, moisture, and sometimes, animals.

GRADE BEAM

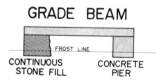

CONTINUOUS STONE FILL — FROST LINE — CONCRETE PIER

A grade beam foundation is a pressure-treated wood or reinforced concrete beam which is submerged to a depth of about 8 inches below grade. It may be supported on a stone fill or on underground piers which extend into the ground below the frost line.

The grade beam is especially useful in dry climates or well drained soils where the house can be built close to the ground.

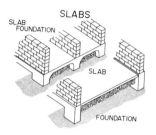

SLABS

The slab foundation is a special foundation which floats on top of the soil and also serves as the floor of the house. The slab is thickened under all of the walls to support their heavy loads.

All slab floors are not slab foundations; many are simply concrete floors. A separate foundation supports the wall loads.

Every foundation must support the weight of the house and its contents. This load can vary considerably depending on the type of construction, the kind of furniture, and the special uses the house is subjected to. In colder climates, the foundation must carry the ice and snow which may accumulate on the roof. If the foundation loads are heavy, reinforced concrete will provide the strongest wall. Wider masonry walls will carry heavier loads than narrow ones.

WHAT IS A . . .

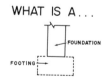

Some houses are so heavy that the foundation must be widened at the bottom to keep them from sinking into the soil. The widened bottom on the foundation is called a footing. Its size depends on the kind of soil under it. Soil strengths vary from 1,000 to

12,000 pounds per square foot. In general, footings are designed for 1,000 pounds per square foot, but if you know your soil type you may design smaller footings.

FOOTING THICKNESS

THICKNESS = 1 1/2 X THE LARGEST PROJECTION

Thickness of the footing depends on how far it protrudes beyond the foundation wall. The rule is that the thickness should be 1½ times as great as the largest projection.

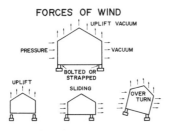

FORCES OF WIND

Since wind may lift or slide houses off their foundations, houses must be securely fastened to the foundation.

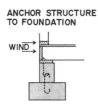

ANCHOR STRUCTURE TO FOUNDATION

For masonry walls the fastening device should be extended through the foundation to the footing. In all cases there should be a continuous tie extending as far into the soil as practical.

Foundations acting as retaining walls must be designed to prevent overturning or breakage. Breakage may be prevented by reinforcing or by making the wall thicker. Overturning may be prevented by making the wall thicker,

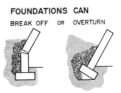

FOUNDATIONS CAN
BREAK OFF   OR   OVERTURN

tying the wall to anchors in the soil, or counter-balancing the wall.

PREVENT WALL OVERTURN

WIDE HEAVY WALL

PREVENT WALL BREAKING

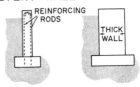

PREVENT WALL OVERTURN

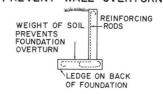

Other jobs of a foundation wall are to insulate and to moisture proof. Basements have been traditionally used as cellars to store foods and supplies, especially in the colder climates. But in recent years, with less need for long term food storage, houses are being built without basements or with basements to be used as family living areas and/or game rooms. If you are going to use your basement as a living area, you will want a dry basement which can be kept at a desired temperature.

The temperature can generally be maintained by installing a proper size heating system. But if you are going to heat economically, the foundation or basement wall must be of reasonably tight construction to prevent warm air from escaping through cracks. Most people will also want a well insulated wall to achieve maximum economy, and comfort.

SLAB FLOOR INSULATION

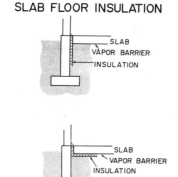

Since concrete is a good heat conductor, you must take special care when concrete slabs are installed close to the soil surface. A sheet of rigid insulation may be installed vertically down the inside of the foundation wall, or between the floor slab and the foundation wall and then horizontally under the slab.

Moisture in basement air is particularly troublesome in wet climates. Hot and relatively dry air from outside enters the basement where its temperature is reduced by several degrees. As air cools, it can't hold as much moisture; thus cooling the air causes it to become quite humid. If such humid air comes in contact with an even cooler surface such as the wall or the floor of the basement, it will become so humid that it will deposit some of its moisture

upon the cold surface. This is called sweating.

Sweating creates an atmosphere conducive to the growth of mold and/or fungi and can be quite objectionable. This problem generally goes away in the winter months when the outside air is colder than the inside air. However, there are exceptions. One example is moisture being produced in the house by extensive boiling of water or by frequent use of hot showers. Another is moisture from the soil soaking through the basement wall and evaporating into the air.

High humidity can be dealt with. Dehumidifiers will remove several quarts of moisture per day from the air. But for dehumidification to be economical and effective, the atmosphere must be closed. Doors and windows should be kept shut. Any outside air getting into the basement will bring more moisture in and cause the dehumidifier to have that much more work to do.

Another way to deal with moisture is to eliminate cold surfaces in the basement or house. This can be done through insulation. Floors may be covered with felt paper and tile, walls may be insulated and finished.

If you insulate the wall or floor, you must provide a vapor barrier to prevent moisture in the air from flowing through the insulation to the cold surfaces where it will condense under the insulation. A plastic film, some paints, and several other materials can be vapor barriers.

One common example of moisture passing through insulation is the condensation of moisture under a carpet on a basement floor. Many people must take basement carpets up during the summer months to avoid such condensation.

In winter, ventilation can remove excess moisture from the basement or crawl space. Ventilation becomes extremely important if moisture is being produced there. But ventilation brings in cold air and exhausts warm air, so excessive ventilation will carry off a good deal of heat.

Ventilation should be used when the problem can't be handled by insulation, or when periods of high moisture production are of short duration. It is especially effective when the crawl space is not heated.

Ventilation will carry moisture being evaporated from the warm soil out of the crawl space. This keeps it from condensing on the timbers, which causes mold to grow and results in rotting of the timbers. Make sure your unheated crawl space is well vented in winter.

Heating the crawl space and insulating the foundation wall can eliminate the need for vents, and probably reduce total heat loss from the house. In this way, air from the living area can be used to ventilate the crawl space, and moisture carried out of the soil will humidify the dry air in the living area.

Another problem is moisture which flows out of the soil into the basement in liquid form either though the wall or the floor. The smart builder will give the foundation every possible advantage against ground or surface moisture by:
• Providing the house with gutters and down spouts to carry roof moisture away from the foundation wall.
• Sloping the grade away from the house on all sides.
• Using swales or open drainage to carry off surface water
• Back filling behind the foundation wall with porous fill, and providing drain tile at the base of the footing below the basement floor level to drain moisture away from the house.

SURFACE WATER REMOVAL

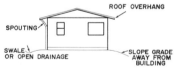

Parging (plastering) the outside of the foundation wall with a rich cement paste will prevent moisture which comes in contact with the wall from soaking into or through it. Water proof paints and coating should also be used over the parging to increase moisture resistance.

MOISTURE PROOF FOUNDATION WALL

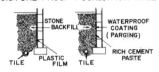

If you have surface moisture leaking through your basement wall, the most effective solution is to dig down on the outside of the wall and install a drain field below the basement floor. Then parge and paint the wall and backfill with a coarse aggregate, such as cinders, gravel, sand, or stone. If the drain field can't be emptied by gravity, install a sump pump to carry the moisture away from the bottom of the foundation wall.

Since this solution is expensive, most homeowners will look for an alternate method.

If soil moisture will flow down along the outside of the basement wall and under the house, such moisture may be removed by breaking a hole about 2 feet square and 1 to 2 feet deep in the basement floor and using a gravity drain or a sump pump to carry the moisture away.

Several patching and plastering materials have been developed for sealing cracks on the inside of basement walls. Most are ineffective. Those that are good will stop the flow in one place, but the moisture will simply back up and find a new flow path.

If you can be satisfied with a wet wall, some systems have been developed to keep the floor dry. They collect the water at the base of the wall and carry it to a drain or sump.

Using this same collection system, one can reduce the wall moisture by drilling a series of holes near the base of the wall just above the collection system. This causes the moisture to flow through the wall at a lower level.

MOISTURE CONTROL

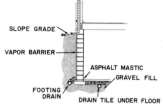

SLOPE GRADE
VAPOR BARRIER
ASPHALT MASTIC
GRAVEL FILL
FOOTING DRAIN
DRAIN TILE UNDER FLOOR

MOISTURE CONTROL METHODS UNDER SLAB

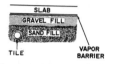

SLAB
GRAVEL FILL
SAND FILL
TILE
VAPOR BARRIER

Floor slabs can be protected from moisture by a gravel fill and drain tile below the floor level. A plastic vapor barrier placed over the gravel fill and under the concrete floor is another aid in keeping soil moisture from flowing through the floor into the basement.

A foundation or basement wall is often called upon to be a decorative surface, equipped with all the conveniences found in other walls.

Basement walls can be insulated and finished in several different ways. If you decide to use rigid insulation, you can attach ½ inch to 2 inches of foam plastic or other materials to the wall with a recommended adhesive. Preferably, the rigid insulation should be a vapor barrier or should have a vapor barrier attached to it. Some rigid foam panels have a plastic treated paper surface which stops water vapor.

After insulation is installed, panel board or other wall finishes can be attached to the insulation with a good grade panel adhesive. Adhesive can likewise be used to attach baseboard and moldings. Electrical outlets may be surface mounted or wires may be counter sunk into the insulation.

Another way is to use furring strips on your basement wall, and then attach a panel board to the strips.

If you are going to attach the strips

to the wall with masonry nails, don't use furring thicker than ¾ inch or nominal 1 inch lumber. Thicker strips are too rigid to conform to the shape of the wall. Too often when driving the last nail you will loosen the other nails which had been securely fastened. If you want thicker furring, use two or three layers of ¾ inch strips.

With furring strips, electric wires can easily be strung from outlet to outlet and the lower cost bat type insulation may be used. A 4-mil polyethylene vapor barrier may be placed over the entire wall. The panel of wall board or other material can then be attached to the furring by conventional methods such as gluing or nailing.

If you are building or buying a house, take a little extra care and save yourself the enormous problems which are common to poorly installed basements and foundations.

When purchasing a house, check the foundation carefully. Look for sloping or unlevel floors; this can indicate the foundation has settled, timbers have rotted and/or moved, or that the floor was not level at the time of construction. You may find small cracks in most foundation walls which you can tolerate, but large cracks occur only if there is excessive foundation movement or settling.

Moisture problems are generally seasonal or intermittent. Therefore, consider the season and the current weather when examining the house. Look for moisture lines on the walls, or for dark or dry mold spots on timbers. Check timbers for soft spots, especially close to the wall and/or floor. Make sure the grade slopes away from the house and drainage is good.

When you are building, remember that if the builder follows the recommended installation procedures, chances of having a wet basement are remote. So insist on recommended installation. Find out if there are soil problems which can cause foundation headaches, and seek advice on handling such problems from your State extension engineer or other consultant.

Basements can add economy to your house. First, they are relatively low in cost. Basements are cooled by the soil in summer, thus reducing the need for air conditioning. In winter they are warmed by the soil, reducing the heat needed to keep them comfortable.

For environmental economy, solve the moisture problem, insulate adequately, and live in your basement in all weather. Keep the upstairs just for show.

Preventing Moisture Damage in Houses

Homeowners can use simple procedures that control movement of water through wood construction materials to prevent moisture problems like decay, warping, paint peeling, or window condensation.

Decay is caused by small plants called fungi. Like all living things, fungi need water, almost always more than is present in the air. When wood in a house or other structure becomes damp, the ever present fungus spores come to life and use the wood as food. Drying will send the plants into dormancy until the next period of wetness. Some fungi, those causing what is erroneously termed "dry rot," are able to transport water over some distance and can work in what appears to be dry wood.

Warping, another common moisture problem, can occur because one side of a board gains or loses more moisture than the other. Since moisture causes wood cells and fibers to expand, the wettest cells and fibers expand the most and twist the board out of shape.

Moist wood is also more pliable than dry wood, and wet beams or planks supporting a weight will bend more

readily. Subsequent drying will lock the wood into its warped shape.

Paint blistering may be caused by temperature changes, water, or other factors. Water in or coming through boards may collect under the relatively impervious paint layer and raise a blister. The blister may crack and cause peeling or may subside and leave a rough spot.

Many of the water sources and problems are easy to spot and correct. For example, condensation of water vapor is almost always a problem in colder climates. One of the best places to look for condensation in a house is on the windows.

Movement of water is controlled by vapor pressure, which, in turn, is controlled by temperature if all other factors are equal. Warm air can hold more moisture as vapor than can cool air. During periods of cold outdoor temperatures, the windows in a house are always colder than the air inside the house. Consequently, when the air touches the window glass, it is cooled and promptly loses some of its moisture which condenses on the glass.

Now, since all gases move from areas of high concentration to areas of low concentration, water vapor moves toward the relatively drier air near the window. It also condenses when it touches the glass and the process repeats.

The amount of condensation is determined by temperature difference and amount of water in the air. The colder the window and the wetter the air, the faster condensation proceeds.

If the air is very moist, its dewpoint, the temperature at which condensation occurs, will be higher. Hence mirrors at room temperature become clouded in a steamy bathroom.

The process of water vapor moving from warmer to colder locations can also take place in walls that allow material to move through them. Here, the movement is much slower. In the winter time the moisture moves from the warm, inner side of the wall to the cold, outer side.

AUTHOR H. O. FLEISCHER is Director of the Forest Products Laboratory, U.S. Forest Service, Madison, Wis.

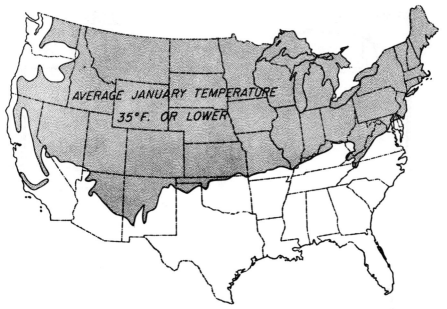

AVERAGE JANUARY TEMPERATURE
35°F. OR LOWER

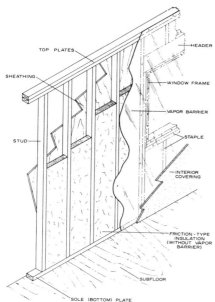

TOP PLATES

SHEATHING

STUD

HEADER

WINDOW FRAME

VAPOR BARRIER

STAPLE

INTERIOR COVERING

FRICTION-TYPE INSULATION (WITHOUT VAPOR BARRIER)

SUBFLOOR

SOLE (BOTTOM) PLATE

Winter condensation problems generally occur if the average temperature for January is 35°F. or lower, as indicated in map above. Vapor barriers help protect homes in such areas from decay and other moisture headaches. Left, installing vapor barrier over friction-type insulation, a process called enveloping.

Internal sources providing water vapor are humidifiers, unvented gas heaters, showers and baths, cooking and laundry activities, plants, and just plain breathing. This vapor moves through the air and walls until it reaches a surface cool enough for condensation to take place.

One important way to prevent vapor movement through walls is to install vapor barriers. These barriers are usually plastic or metal foil sheets that can be part of the insulation or wallboard. Asphalt roll roofing can serve as a vapor barrier in some cases. Some paints or other finishes serve as barriers but are more subject to cracking or other wear stresses.

Vapor barriers must be placed as near as possible to the warm or inner side of any insulation. This will slow down the water vapor moving through walls and retard its reaching surfaces cold enough for condensation. Plastic sheets are stapled to the inside edge of wall studs and wallboard placed on top. Insulation with attached vapor barriers usually has tabs that overlap and are stapled to the inside edge of the studs. Wallboard with a foil or plastic backing is fastened in place with the foil or plastic facing the studs.

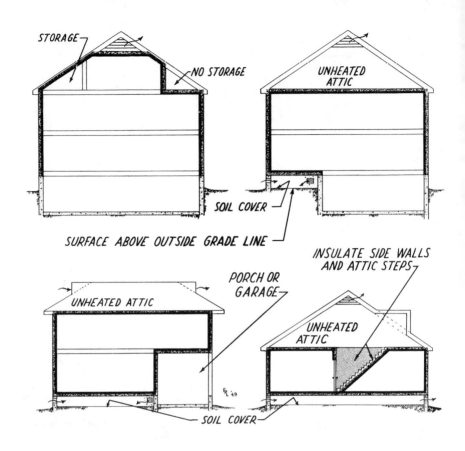

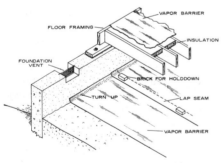

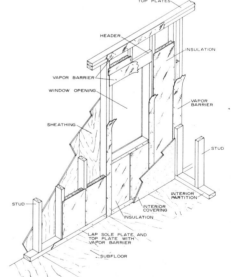

Top, dark black lines show where insulation and vapor barriers should be installed. Below, vapor barriers for both floor and ground cover in crawl space. Right, installing blanket insulation with vapor barrier attached in exterior walls. Additional vapor barrier film should be placed over joints not covered by the insulation.

In cool climates vapor barriers are needed in all exterior walls and in the ceiling separating living areas from an unheated attic. To retard entry of water vapor from the subsoil, barriers under concrete basement floors and on the outside of basement walls are helpful. Basement walls are sometimes coated with a waterproof substance on the inside also.

A very important place for vapor barriers is in the crawl spaces under houses without basements. Besides a barrier in the floor, a layer of roll roofing or plastic, lapped and held in place with weights, should cover the ground. External vents help any water vapor trapped between the two barriers to escape. If the crawl space is heated, external vents are eliminated and the barrier in the floor is not essential.

Vapor barriers should be free of holes and come as close to window and door openings as possible. Any gaps, such as those frequently found around electrical outlet or switch boxes, allow considerable moisture to enter the wall cavity. Caulk around all openings to seal the edges of the vapor barrier.

Excessive air conditioning during the summer will lead to the reverse of the situations described occurring in winter. Water vapor will move toward the cooler inner walls from a warm humid exterior and soak insulation as it condenses at the vapor barrier kept cool by air conditioning. In humid climates or on humid days, air cooling should be kept to a minimum and a dehumidifier used instead in homes with vapor barriers.

Condensation on windows is a problem that cannot be eliminated by vapor barriers. However, installation of storm windows will cause the inner window to be warmer and less likely to act as a condensation point. Reducing water vapor in the house by keeping humidifiers turned low and by placing exhaust fans in bathroom, laundry, and cooking areas will also help to keep windows free of water in cold periods. Heat ducts that open beneath windows and open drapes aid air circulation at the window surface and help evaporate any water that does collect.

A little condensation will usually form on windows even with precautions being taken, and rain water may collect at the glass-wood joints and between the various moving parts of the window.

It is advisable to purchase windows whose wood pieces have been treated with a toxic, water-repellent substance (sometimes called a water-repellent preservative) which will retard fungal growth. If windows are showing mild decay or staining from water and fungal activity, scraping, drying, and treatment with a water-repellant or sealer before revarnishing may alleviate the condition.

Although external water sources can bother windows, they are rarely a problem on well designed and maintained houses. A good overhang will help keep much rain off the house walls. Well designed and properly operating gutters will also stop rain water from running down the sides of a house or splashing up from the ground. Good gutters will keep rain from leaking into joints of the overhang and keep the roof boards dry.

Another roof problem, the ice dam that may form during cold weather, is a major source of water damage. Ice dams form when heat escaping through ceiling insulation warms the roof and melts snow. Water runs down the roof to overhangs or gutters, which are not warmed by the escaping heat, and freezes into a ridge called an ice dam. The dam gets larger and larger as the process continues until water may be backed up under the shingles and drip through the roof boards into the attic.

One way to prevent this damage is through better ceiling insulation and ventilation of the attic. Louvered outlet vents near the roof peak and screened inlet vents in the underside of the overhang, aid air flow and keep the attic at the same temperature as the outside air. This prevents roof warming. Extra insulation on the ceiling is needed to prevent heat loss in attics that are well vented.

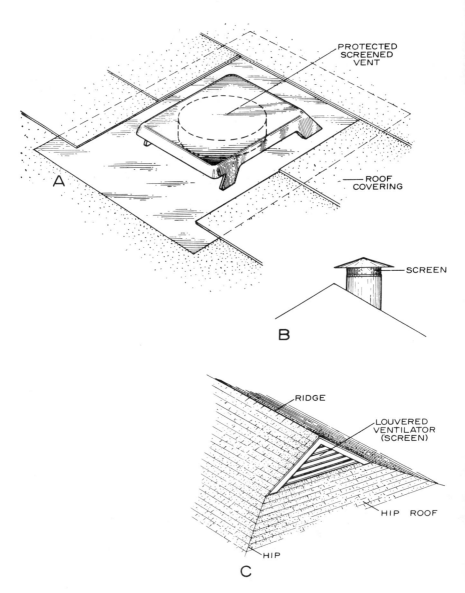

PROTECTED
SCREENED
VENT

ROOF
COVERING

A

SCREEN

B

RIDGE

LOUVERED
VENTILATOR
(SCREEN)

HIP ROOF

HIP

C

Above, ridge outlet ventilators. A, low silhouette type. B, pipe ventilator type. C, modified hip ventilator. Right, inlet ventilator in frieze, for open cornice.

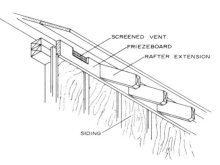

SCREENED VENT

FRIEZEBOARD

RAFTER EXTENSION

SIDING

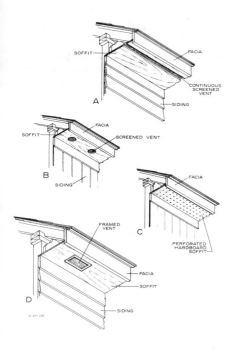

Top, inlet ventilators in soffits. A, continuous vent. B, round vents. C, perforated. D, single ventilator. Below, gable outlet ventilators. A, triangular gable and ventilator. B, rectangular gable and ventilator. C, soffit ventilators.

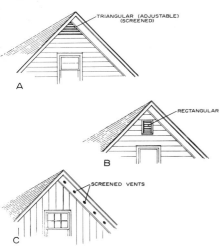

Alternatives or supplements to venting are wide, waterproof flashing along the roof edge and the use of electro-thermal melters. A 3-foot wide strip of 45-pound roll roofing laid under the shingles at the roof's edge may prevent water from entering the attic unless a large ice dam backs water more than 3 feet up the roof. An electro-thermal wire can be strung along the roof edge or at other problem areas to melt the ice dams and prevent water backup.

Signs of a moisture problem are often easy to spot.

Indicating excess moisture are discoloration or staining of both inside and outside walls; warping; paint blisters that contain water; decay; or water beads forming on windows, roof supports (especially in the overhang), or joists in the crawl space or basement. Periodic checks should be made of problem areas such as. attics; crawl spaces; north walls; or walls outside bathroom, kitchen, and laundry areas.

Problems may be corrected without tearing everything apart and rebuilding. External walls can be scraped, allowed to dry, and repainted. If the water source is internal, inside walls can be painted with a relatively impervious paint and the outside walls painted with a more porous paint.

Humidity inside the house can be reduced by installing vents in areas where considerable moisture is produced. Vapor barriers can be installed in crawl spaces and in attics if the insulation can be removed temporarily. Inexpensive vents can be installed in attics and crawl spaces. If the basement is a problem area in the spring, a dehumidifier can be used.

Sections of roof or wall that show extensive water damage or decay should be replaced since they are proven routes of water entry and are even more susceptible to water movement in their reduced condition. The money spent on preventing or repairing moisture damage may save much larger sums incurred through premature deterioration of the building.

For further reading:

U.S. Department of Agriculture. *How to Prevent and Remove Mildew—Home Methods*, Home and Garden Bulletin 68, Washington, D.C. 20250, 1971.

Selection of Exterior Siding, Paint, or Stains for the Home

For most people the task of repainting the house on the weekend is not their idea of a fun weekend. However, this job may need to be done frequently if the homeowner did not carefully select both the siding and the protective covering.

This chapter will discuss selection of various exterior siding materials with respect to composition, appearance, application, maintenance, and approximate cost.

Painting the exterior of the house still provides the predominant protective coating, since most homeowners can use a paint brush or roller. The common fault of most weekend painters is to buy "bargain" paint that's on sale and then have to repaint the house each year. When you go to the store to purchase paint, I would recommend a good quality paint.

You have two choices basically in the selection of exterior paint. These are exterior water-thinned (commonly called latex) or solvent-thinned (commonly called alkyd base) paints.

Exterior latex paint in the past several years has developed to the point that it now accounts for a significant portion of the house painting market. There are a number of reasons for this —the cleanability of latex (both during and after painting) is quite simple by using plain tap water, total drying time is only 2 to 3 hours, and drying to a dust-free surface takes about 30 minutes.

Before you paint your house, you should do several things to ensure a good job. First, check the house exterior for chalking. If you run your hand over the siding and you get a deposit of fine, white dust, this is chalk. Chalking means that the paint is deteriorating to the point the paint job must be redone.

To remove chalk, use a mild detergent and a stiff brush or heavy cloth. Once the house is washed, it needs to be rinsed thoroughly and then checked for additional chalking. If chalking is still present, a primer coat is required.

While removing the chalk, check for mildew. Mildew will show up as dirty patches that did not come clean with the mild detergent solution. Usually a strong chlorine bleach solution with just a little detergent added will get rid of mildew.

If the mildew is persistent, you might try adding triosodium phosphate and some household ammonia to the solution. Be sure to wear protective clothing when using these solutions and then be sure to wash the solution off the house when you have finished.

Other age-old paint problems to be checked are blistering, peeling, and flaking. For such areas you need to scrape the paint off, sand the area, and then wipe it clean. This procedure would be used for nail heads that are staining through the old paint.

Finally, these scraped and sanded areas must be spot primed with either latex primer (if you are not down to bare wood) or regular primer if you are down to bare wood. DO NOT use a blowtorch to burn off the old paint.

On spots where peeling is excessive, be sure to check for leaks that have allowed moisture to get behind the siding. A good practice is to seal all cracks around doors, windows, cracks in the siding, and areas around the foundation wall. Give particular attention to joints in the guttering.

Now, how do you paint your house? First, use a good quality nylon brush for latex paint. You will need a bucket for water, or solvent if using solvent-

AUTHOR LELLAND L. GALLUP is an Extension Specialist in Housing, Department of Design and Environmental Analysis, Cornell University, Ithaca, N.Y.

Western cedar bevel siding is stained driftwood gray, trim a darker shade.

thinned paint and several pieces of cloth for clean-up, possibly a stepladder, and some ground cloths to cover the shrubbery and grass.

After you have prepared the house for painting, you should begin painting at the top and work your way down the house. Also, you should follow the sun around your house so you will be painting in the shade. This will result in a more satisfactory paint job because the paint will not dry out too rapidly.

Before dealing with prefinished siding materials, let's discuss the use of semi-transparent stain. For most rough sawn or weathered siding, a penetrating stain will give better results than paint. Pigmented penetrating stains are much more durable than the clear finishes. Stains penetrate and lightly color the wood, obscure or tone down the grain pattern, and leave little or no apparent surface film.

However, once the stain has penetrated, the wood is protected. Bear in mind, though that a second coat of stain would be advisable in about 6 to 8 months after the first application. There will be some checking of the siding with application of the first coat; the second coat will fill the checks with stain. Again, when you purchase stain be sure to buy a quality product and the results will be much more satisfactory.

Moving now to the actual siding materials—you have choices between wood, plywood, aluminum, masonry, hardboard, and vinyl.

Regarding wood and wood products, your decision-making process does not stop with the selection of wood, plywood, or hard board. You are confronted with the possibilities of unfinished or untreated, preprimed or prefinished, smooth or textured surface, contemporary or traditional pattern, and horizontal or vertical treatments.

Rather than describe in detail all facets of the differences mentioned, let me outline a decision-making process in the selection of siding materials,

177

since the actual selection should be based on individual taste and design requirements.

First, your siding material should harmonize with the surroundings. As an example, a rough sawn texture might look better in a wooded area than a slick, bright finish.

Next consider the maintenance factor. If the siding material you select for the location you have will be subjected to severe weather conditions, care should be given to selecting siding with a low maintenance factor.

Another aspect is cost of the material desired. If the material supplier has the particular siding you desire in ready stock, it will generally be cheaper than if it has to be a special order. Some of the newer designs in siding tend to run higher in cost than standard stock items.

Still another consideration is the application. Check your local area for contractors who are familiar with application techniques of the siding material you desire. If the contractors are hesitant about the newer products this does not necessarily mean they will not do a satisfactory job, but it would cost more since it will require more labor time for the application.

If you desire wood or wood products for your siding material, I would strongly recommend either a preprimed or prefinished one if possible. Preprimed materials are excellent because they have built-in protection during the construction phase. They can be easily painted, and generally you have fewer problems with them.

Prefinished products, on the other hand, once installed require only the routine maintenance you would ordinarily give any siding material. One caution however—be sure to check the possibility of repainting should you ever desire to do so. Check for the problems encountered in preparing the surface of prefinished materials.

Finally, whether you are building or remodeling, remember that the siding material becomes a structural member of the house. Treat it as such. Siding is not like the window treatments inside the house that you can change almost at will. Changing materials, color, or design of the exterior of the house is a costly item and extreme care should be given in the decision made.

Now let's turn to aluminum and vinyl siding. While not the same product, they do have similar working characteristics. Both materials can provide either a vertical or horizontal appearance; they can be applied over old siding or over sheathing; they are either smooth or textured; they can be purchased with or without insulation backing, and both are lightweight.

However, aluminum has some problems in that it does dent and it should not come in contact with concrete. Vinyl has the characteristics of being somewhat noisy (in hailstorms, for instance); and to change the color is difficult.

Conversely, aluminum and vinyl siding materials have some very desirable characteristics. They will not peel, blister, rot, rust, or corrode. They do not support fire readily. Neither material is attractive to termites. They also tend to cost less than other sidings.

The final category is masonry. Basically, you have three options—stone, brick, or stucco. Each has its own design characteristics.

Generally, masonry materials are the most expensive because cost of the materials is higher and the labor time is increased. In fact, in some areas it is difficult to find a stonemason or other tradesman who can apply stucco properly; and when you do, his fee is rather high.

Masonry siding is virtually maintenance free if the initial application is done properly. As an example: if your house has a brick exterior and this work was completed during cold winter months, there is a good possibility you will have problems with the mortar joints in only a few years. In other words, any concrete work should be done under almost ideal conditions, whether it is placing a concrete floor or applying native stone.

Generally, native stone work is left the natural color of the stone itself. Stucco can be tinted any color to give the desired appearance. Brick can be left natural or painted. If you know you are going to paint the brick, you could use a less expensive brick to begin with.

A caution on painting brick: Once you have painted the brick you have made a lifetime decision.

A few final thoughts on selecting exterior siding materials. I would recommend you go to your local material supplier (lumber dealer or hardware store) and seek his advice. Get the product literature from such companies as Masonite Corporation, Bird Vinyl Siding, Evans, Abitibi, American Plywood Association, Alcoa, U.S. Plywood Association, Southern Forest Products, or U.S. Steel to know what products are available and then use this information to make any needed comparisons.

For further reading:

U.S. Department of Agriculture, *Exterior Painting,* Home and Garden Bulletin No. 155, Superintendent of Documents, U.S. Government Printing Office, Washington, D.C. 20402—Price 10 cents.

Do's and Don'ts For Shade Trees

Y OU HAVE MOVED into a new home, and begin discussing with your husband or wife the need for several shade trees. Perhaps you would like to plant and care for the trees yourself, but you really don't know much about which of the wide variety of trees is best for your property. You should take into consideration the following factors before buying and planting the trees.

Keep in mind the mature height and spread of the tree. Shade trees ideally should be sturdy, long-living species that grow relatively fast and produce the size and shape desired. If yours is a one-story house on a small lot, you should plant small trees. For example, the following can be recommended for small properties:

SMALL SHADE TREES RECOMMENDED

Trident maple (*Acer buergerianum*)
Hornbeam maple (*Acer carpinifolium*)
Fullmoon maple (*Acer japonicum*)
Manchurian maple (*Acer mandshuricum*)
Nikko maple (*Acer nikoense*)
European hornbeam (*Carpinus betulus* 'Globosa')
American hornbeam (*Carpinus caroliniana*)
Eastern redbud (*Cercis canadensis*)
Flowering dogwood (*Cornus florida*)
Russian-olive (*Elaeagnus angustifolia*)
Balkan ash (*Fraxinus holotricha*)
Flowering ash (*Fraxinus ornus*)
Golden-rain-tree (*Koelreuteria paniculata*)
Saucer magnolia (x *Magnolia soulangeana*)
Sourwood (*Oxydendrum arboreum*)
Chinese elm (*Ulmus parvifolia*)

On the other hand, if you have space for a larger tree, you might desire one of the following:

LARGE SHADE TREES RECOMMENDED

European beech (*Fagus sylvatica*)
Sugar maple (*Acer saccharum*)
Littleleaf linden (*Tilia cordata*)
Red maple (*Acer rubrum*)
Northern red oak (*Quercus borealis*)
Tuliptree (*Liriodendron tulipifera*)
Pin Oak (*Quercus palustris*)

AUTHOR A. M. TOWNSEND is Research Geneticist, Shade Tree and Ornamental Plants Laboratory, Agricultural Research Service, Delaware, Ohio.

COAUTHOR CHARLES L. WILSON is Research Leader of the laboratory.

179

White Oak (*Quercus alba*)
Cucumbertree (*Magnolia acuminata*)

Consider the planting site and its soil type, compaction, and drainage. Select only those trees which will be hardy enough to survive summer heat as well as winter cold. Many species when planted north of their adapted range are killed by early fall or late spring frosts. U.S. Agriculture Handbook 425, *Shade Trees for the Home,* gives the adaptive range of shade tree species.

Depending on the location of the seed sources, most species are quite variable in their response to cold. A red maple seedling from Florida, for example, will not survive when grown in Ohio. Seed collected from plants growing near the northern-most limits of their range is likely to give rise to seedlings that will prove hardier than will seedlings grown from milder parts of the range.

For wet soils, plant one of the species which is naturally adapted to such conditions:

RECOMMENDED
SHADE TREES
FOR WET SOILS

Red maple (*Acer rubrum*)
Sweetgum (*Liquidambar styraciflua*)
Black tupelo (*Nyssa sylvatica*)
Swamp white oak (*Quercus bicolor*)
Sweetbay (*Magnolia virginiana*)

In contrast to the above, many species will grow well on dry, sterile soils:

RECOMMENDED
SHADE TREES
FOR DRY SOILS
AND THE CITY

Dahurian birch (*Betula davurica*)
Velvet ash (*Fraxinus velutina*)
Golden-rain-tree (*Koelreuteria paniculata*)
Seedless green ash (*Fraxinus pennsylvanica*)
California black oak (*Quercus kelloggii*)
Japanese pagodatree (*Sophora japonica*)
Sassafras (*Sassafras albidum*)
Sawtooth oak (*Quercus acutissima*)

The above species are not only adaptable but quite attractive. For example, the Dahurian birch (***Betula davurica***) which does well even on gravelly sites, has curling, reddish brown bark, and shows beautiful yellow autumn foliage. The Japanese pagodatree (*Sophora japonica*) blossoms in late summer with large pyramidal clusters of yellowish, pealike flowers. As with all of the species listed above, the pagodatree grows quite well even under severe city conditions.

Beware of trees with undesirable characteristics or with unusual pest susceptibility:

NOT RECOMMENDED
SHADE TREES

Silver maple (*Acer saccharinum*)
Horsechestnut (*Aesculus hippocastanum*)
Siberian elm (*Ulmus pumila*)
White mulberry (*Morus alba*)
Tree-of-heaven (*Ailanthus altissima*)
Weeping willow (*Salix babylonica*)
Poplar (*Populus species*)
Ginkgo (female) (*Ginkgo biloba*)
American elm (*Ulmus americana*)

Trees such as the female ginkgo and mulberry produce unpleasant, messy fruit. Other species (such as silver maple, Siberian elm) have brittle wood with v-shaped crotches which make them subject to storm damage. The poplars, willows, and silver maple clog sewers and heave sidewalks. The American elm is susceptible to Dutch elm disease.

Select those trees which are relatively disease and insect free in your area. The following species are the most likely to be pest free under reasonably good growing conditions:

SHADE TREES
RELATIVELY FREE
OF INSECT OR
DISEASE PESTS

American hornbeam (*Carpinus caroliniana*)
Katsuratree (*Cercidiphyllum japonicum*)

Cornelian-cherry (*Cornus mas*)
Golden-rain-tree (*Koelreuteria paniculata*)
Scotch laburnum (*Laburnum alpinum*)
Sweetgum (*Liquidambar styraciflua*)
Hophornbeam (*Ostrya virginiana*)
Amur corktree (*Phellodendron amurense*)
Japanese pagodatree (*Sophora japonica*)
American yellowwood (*Cladrastis lutea*)
Maidenhair tree-male (*Ginkgo biloba*)

Plant at least a few shade trees which display unusual esthetic features, such as foliage and bark color, large flowers, and presence of attractive fruit. Literally hundreds of unique varieties or cultivars are available. Although your local nurseryman may not have a particular tree in stock, he will be glad to order it for you from another nursery.

RECOMMENDED SHADE TREES WITH COLORED LEAVES THROUGH TWO OR MORE SEASONS

Name	Foliage color
Russian-olive (*Elaeagnus angustifolia*)	gray
Silver linden (*Tilia tomentosa*)	gray
Purple-leaf sycamore maple (*Acer pseudoplatanus* 'Purpureum')	purple
Weeping purple beech (*Fagus sylvatica* 'Purpureo-pendula')	purple
Fullmoon maple (*Acer* japonicum 'Aureum')	yellow
Golden oak (*Quercus robur* 'Concordia')	yellow
Japanese maple (*Acer palmatum* 'Atropurpureum')	red
Norway maple (*Acer platanoides* 'Crimson King')	red

Many homeowners are aware of trees which show a conspicuous autumn color. Some trees, however, can be used for their colored foliage throughout the spring and summer.

Remember that the bark of many trees can be quite conspicuous, especially on deciduous trees in the winter. The birches, cherries, and beeches are all valued primarily because of their bark. An accompanying list names some of the shade trees which show an interesting bark.

SHADE TREES WITH UNUSUAL BARK

Name	Bark Characteristic
Paperbark maple (*Acer griseum*)	cinnamon-brown, peels off
American hornbeam (*Carpinus caroliniana*)	gray, "muscled" trunk
Chinese paper birch (*Betula albo-sinensis*)	bright orange, peels off longitudinally
Red bark cherry (*Prunus serrula*)	brilliant glossy red
Striped maple (*Acer pensylvanicum*)	green and white stripes
Amur corktree (*Phellodendron amurense*)	mature bark corky
Russian-olive (*Elaeagnus angustifolia*)	brown, shreds off longitudinally

Before you make a final purchase of a tree, seek professional advice. Nurserymen, arborists, and landscape horticulturists can offer valuable advice on selecting the tree most suited for a given location and purpose, when and how to plant, and how to prune the newly planted tree. Also, they are familiar with the growth rates of trees, relative sizes and shapes at maturity, and the requirements for best growth.

Now let's turn to the protection of existing trees. Contractor, spare that bulldozer! If you are lucky enough to have a naturally wooded setting for your house, it will take extreme care to maintain it following construction. Details on protecting shade trees during home construction can be found in USDA Home and Garden Bulletin No. 104, *Protecting Shade Trees During Home Construction.*

While you are enjoying the excitement of the groundbreaking for your new house and thinking about how you will decorate it inside, heavy equipment may be causing irreversible damage to your landscape outside. You may have failed to realize that the sturdy-looking trees that attracted you to your lot have a very delicate relationship with the soil and humus around them. Soil and humus are essential for the uptake and retention of water and nutrients. The compaction and scalping of soil around trees by heavy equipment, and the placing of fill dirt near trees, results in tree decline and often death. The effects of such treatment may not be realized until 1 or 2 years after construction when trees show early signs of decline and death. Removal of such trees is distressing and costly.

The functional root system of most trees is in the top 2 to 3 inches of soil. The small feeder rootlets have a delicate relationship with soil particles that allows the uptake of water and nutrients.

Compaction of soil around trees destroys air spaces between soil particles and deprives roots of essential oxygen. Excavation destroys and wounds roots. Wounded roots provide entrance ways for root rotting fungi which may progressively destroy the root system after your house is built.

Cuts and fills on your lot may profoundly influence water movement and moisture levels in the soil. A tree that has enjoyed near optimum moisture conditions for the past 100 years may suddenly be in a drought situation, or

another tree may become flooded. It is important to realize that excavation some distance from your trees may influence them through changes in drainage patterns.

All of these possible difficulties need to be anticipated in the early planning of your house. They should influence the placement of your house on the lot and your instructions to the contractor.

Protection of newly planted trees is another matter.

After you have selected and planted new trees, you have the job of maintaining and protecting them.

The most frequent cause of death to newly established shade trees is the lack of ample water. There is a critical period following transplanting before an adequate root system is established to maintain the plant. During this period, ample water must be provided to allow maximum efficiency for those roots that are functional.

The soil around each tree should be saturated deeply but not flooded. The number of times you water will depend on rainfall and the soil conditions. For

Shade trees enhance an apartment house.

the first two months following planting it may be necessary to water twice a week. Soil around the root system should be kept moist. A mulch around the tree consisting of organic material (coarse peat moss, pine bark, tan bark, ground corncobs, or peanut hulls) will help prevent water loss through evaporation.

Even after your plants are well established it will be necessary to water them during periods of drought. In arid regions, permanent irrigation systems are recommended.

In newly established yards it is a good practice to fertilize your plants every year until they are well established. Liquid premixed fertilizers are available at garden centers. They are advantageous in that they are available immediately to the plant and no fertilizer residue is left to burn the plant roots or grass. Follow the directions on the label in applying these fertilizers.

Established trees should also be fertilized at least once every three years. The fertilizer should be applied to the area around the tree that is shaded by the branches. Measure the area to be fertilized and determine its size in square feet.

Nitrogen, in the form of ammonium nitrate or urea, is the nutrient most needed by trees. Nitrogen fertilizers can be applied to the soil surface at the rate of 6 pounds per 1,000 square feet. A spreader commonly used to apply lawn fertilizers can be used. Fertilizers are most effective when applied in the fall or spring.

Fertilizers containing phosphorus or potassium should not be used in surface applications to trees. They should be applied only if a soil analysis shows it is necessary. If needed, application can be made in dry holes 12-15 inches deep made with a crowbar at 2-foot intervals in parallel lines 2 feet apart in the area shaded by the tree. The following quantity of fertilizer should be placed in each hole, depending on the proportion of nitrogen to phosphorus to potassium (for example, 10-10-10 or 12-12-12):

Nitrogen-phosphorus-potassium	Amount per hole
10-10-10	1/2 cup
12-12-12	1/3 cup

Your plants may show various symptoms of decline such as diebacks, wilting, yellowing, streaking, spotting, etc. Many times the symptoms result from insect and disease attack or perhaps adverse environmental conditions. Diagnosis of such problems and recommendations for their treatment generally require an expert.

Don't use chemical sprays until you know you have the right compound and that you are applying it properly. Some chemicals can cause severe injury to your plants as well as to those of your neighbors. Always read the label on chemicals that you use to control diseases and insects, and store these compounds in a safe place which is away from children.

It is obvious that a beautiful landscape does not just happen, but requires careful planning and maintenance on your part. As with all endeavors that require effort, there are rewards. Also, you are not left without friends who can give you good advice. Among these are your county agricultural agent, city park superintendent or arborist, State horticulturist or State experiment station horticulturist, or local nurseryman. These people are more familiar with your local growing conditions and can give more specific answers to your problems.

For further reading:

Landscape for Living, the 1972 Yearbook of Agriculture, Superintendent of Documents, Government Printing Office, Washington, D.C. 20402, $3.50.

U.S. Department of Agriculture. *Protecting Shade Trees During Home Construction*, Home and Garden Bulletin 104, Washington, D.C. 20250, 1971.

U.S. Agricultural Research Service. *Shade Trees For the Home*, Agriculture Handbook 425, Superintendent of Documents, Washington, D.C. 20402, 1972, 75 cents.

A Quick Rundown On Pools, Decks, Patios and Fences

Leisure time is becoming more and more abundant, thus making your home not only your castle, but your playground. To gain more enjoyment from your open space, give careful thought to developing your personal recreation facilities.

The subject of pools, decks, patios, and fences, as a part of your recreational facilities, will be discussed as a complete unit, although each can be thought of or constructed as separate and individual projects.

The building of a fence, patio, deck or a pool is a significant investment; therefore as a homeowner, you must do a competent job of planning. Professional aid is recommended for at least the final phases of the plan so that an integrated picture of the design factors and cost will be available.

During the thinking stages of the improvement, make a plot plan of your property to scale, with the exact dimensions and locations of your house and other permanent objects. After accurately measuring and plotting existing structures, trees, plants, etc., you have probably found that there is not as much space available as you had anticipated. With tracing paper over your plot, you can now try out your ideas.

Next, take your ideas and plans to the local governmental building inspector and have him advise you of regulations and ordinances that will affect your proposed improvement.

The first and most significant phase of implementing your plan will be the pool. This has to be first because heavy equipment must have access to your property and you do not want it moving through or over the other improvements.

Size and depth of the pool will be dictated by your geographical location, area size, ordinances, soil conditions, and cost.

Do you want the pool deep enough for diving? Probably only 10 percent of the pool use will be for diving, but if you include it you must have a depth commensurate with diving heights. The deeper you go the more expensive it becomes. Depth has an effect on the extent of reinforcing in the structure. It will also affect the size of the pump needed to circulate water through the filtration media.

Shape of the pool will affect its use. If you have small, active children, it might be advisable to have straight, or broadly sweeping curves to the walls that afford fewer sharp edges to catch an unwary child.

Left, porch deck of 2x4 Douglas fir, on edge. Above, deck and screens help create pleasant outdoor area for a mobile home.

Above, patio screened from view of houses on high side of street by trellis roof of western red cedar sunshade over plants. Right, raised patio with exposed aggregate deck and mosaic tile pool coping. Below right, different effects of exposed aggregate on a flat patio and fence that allows good shadow effect.

Pool construction material can be wide and varied . . . from glass fiber and aluminum that can be moved in, completely formed, to inlaid tile that has been conceived by a master designer with elaborate and colorful designs.

Construction of a pool is only the initial cash outlay. Once the construction is completed, upkeep maintenance will be continuous. Water must be warmed in most areas of the country. The pool water must be continually circulated through filtration media to keep clean, and chemicals must be added to purify the water.

Except in unusual circumstances, most of the excavated soil should be removed from the property and only the top soil saved. This soil can be used to grade away from the pool. Subsoil should be used only under the pool decking. The remaining soil should be carried away because the excavated material would ordinarily not be suitable for plants.

Decking around the pool must be graded away from the pool so that dirty water cannot flow into the pool. Be-

AUTHOR GEORGE A. PRICE is Assistant Professor, Park Administration, California State Polytechnic University, Pomona, Calif.

cause of the chemicals in the water it is best if this water is kept out of the garden, and carried away in the sewer.

The deck need not be just a slab of concrete. It can be poured in sections, with exposed aggregates in different

185

Above, western wood screen separates entry sidewalk from driveway. Right, this privacy screen takes to a slope. Snow fencing fills the framed sections.

sizes, colors, and designs. An unusual idea is to draw into the concrete, depicting historical highlights of your family. To do this, make small paper cutouts, lay on freshly poured concrete and copy the picture. By the use of concrete coloring and aggregates, interesting variations can be created.

A patio is defined as "the court of the house." The patio should be designed so it relates to the house and the other features. You might consider a raised patio that would break up the flat lines of the pool surface and deck. Redwood decking laid on 4 inches by 4 inches offers a fast drying area by the wet pool side. Patio furnishings can be constructed or purchased to complement the decking.

If you decide on a concrete patio, color and exposed aggregate can add greatly to the beauty of the area. If the area is raised, allow a small apron around the edge so lawns can be maintained with a minimum of clipping.

After all construction has been completed and you no longer need to enter

186

Wire mesh on lower part of fence allows free circulation of air, yet keeps out animal intruders. Panels are of hardboard.

the area with large equipment, you are ready to install a fence. Fences have been used by man since he settled down from the nomadic and hunting life. Fences are used to make you feel secure, to afford privacy, wind protection, or to prohibit trespassing.

Assure yourself that your fence is constructed on your property, for some of the greatest feuds of history resulted from a fence which was built over the line.

Your fence can be designed for more than one type of construction material and for variable heights. Fences built to protect against prevailing winds can be constructed of materials which will not shut out the sun.

The fence next to the pool must be specifically treated to withstand the water that will be splashed out of the pool against the base of the fence.

Because fences are a horizontal protrusion that will be very visual to you and your neighbors, it is sometimes well to discuss and cooperate on border fences.

Planning the extensive improvements described in this chapter should prove tremendously interesting and complex. As indicated earlier, professional help is recommended for the more technical aspects of your plan.

Despite the inconvenience of having your yard slightly disrupted and the additional cost, any one of these improvements will provide many hours of relaxation, fun, and fellowship with family and friends. The improvement will give a most worthwhile addition to your property value, and your style of living.

Outdoor Lighting Has Many Roles

IN TIMES PAST outdoor lights were incandescent lamps with a porcelain reflector used sparsely in urban or small towns and on poles or buildings around the farm or home.

Today there are many types of outdoor lamps and the use of lighting has risen greatly. Our present society gives more emphasis to beautification, security, safety, and convenience in outdoor lighting. Work or leisure activities and shopping during night hours have vastly increased.

We now are somewhat accustomed to the glare and poor distribution of lighting outdoors. In urban and suburban areas, lamps with little or poor shielding glare at us from parking lots and roadways. In rural areas unshielded lamps can be seen for miles like a beacon, but as you approach the source the glare becomes very apparent and annoying.

Shielded fixtures which reduce glare and control light are more expensive and less efficient. However, better fixtures enhance our surroundings, providing the needed light without annoyance. Many existing roadway and home yard lighting fixtures can be shielded to reduce glare or stop light from shining in unwanted directions.

Outdoor local or spot lighting is usually based on esthetics or ability to see rather than calculations of illumination levels.

With a portable incandescent lampholder and an extension cord, you can try various sizes of incandescent lamps in different locations. This will give you an idea of how the permanently installed lighting will appear.

For lighting larger areas you can get help from electric power supplier representatives, electrical contractors, and manufacturers of lamps and fixtures.

Electric wiring for outside lighting must be weatherproof in accordance with the National Electric Code and local regulatory agencies.

Incandescent lamps or fixtures are simple and inexpensive for outside the home. The "gooseneck" fixture, a porcelain reflector fastened to a pipe curved like a goose neck, is still in use mounted to the vertical side of buildings or poles.

At present, new installations use a floodlight holder for incandescent lamps with built in reflectors (PAR). Some types completely shield the lamp, permitting use of indoor lamps. Others shield only the lamp base, and outdoor or weatherproof lamps must be used.

Although not as efficient as other types of higher wattage lamps, incandescent lamps are used where the lamps are turned off and on frequently or where color rendition is important.

Outdoor incandescent lamps are available in colors for decoration emphasis, to limit insect attraction, or for effects upon vegetation. Blue, green, yellow, amber, pink, and red lamps can be used separately or in combination. Reflector lamps (PAR 38) in colors are normally 150, 100, and 75 watt sizes.

Regular pear-shaped lamps in colors are available in standard sizes—40, 60, 75, 100, and 150.

Tungsten-halogen are incandescent lamps with improved maintenance of light and longer life and are used in larger wattage floodlights. Tungsten-halogen is normally a tubular lamp with electric contacts at each end, although some are available in reflector types with regular screw bases.

Fluorescent lamps can be used for outdoor lighting provided that: (1) a weatherproof fixture is used; (2) the lamps are enclosed with a transparent cover for temperatures below 50°F.; and (3) special ballasts or fixtures are used for operation at below freezing temperatures.

A fluorescent lamp's light output efficiency at indoor temperatures is normally two to three times that of an incandescent. For outdoor temperatures of freezing or below, without enclosed fixtures, the efficiency is only slightly more than incandescent lamps.

Most outdoor fluorescent fixtures are either 4 or 8 feet in length, using two or more 4-foot or 8-foot lamps. Gasoline service stations and other small commercial establishments use them to supplement outdoor flood lights, replacing incandescent floodlighting where extra illumination is needed.

Gold or yellow fluorescents are used to reduce insect attraction, yet provide about three-fourths the visibility of white lamps.

High intensity discharge lamps (HID) are used for floodlighting larger areas such as roadways, parking lots, yards. All three types—mercury, metal halide, or high-pressure sodium—require an electrical ballast which is different for each type and size (wattage) of lamp. The fixture (luminaire) shell or housing may be the same for equivalent wattages of lamp used, but the internal electrical components differ.

High-pressure sodium has an intense yellow color. Metal halide lamps have a white or slightly greenish color. Mercury lamps are blue white or greenish white. Mercury lamps are available in color variations from blue to almost white and in a size variation from 50 to 1,500 watts. Metal halide sizes are 400 to 1,000 watts; high-pressure sodium 250, 400, and 1,000 watts.

For a rough comparison, the lumen output is about equal for these lamps —one 250-watt high-pressure sodium, one 400-watt metal halide, three 250-watt mercury, three 500-watt incandescent, and ten 40-watt fluorescents. Metal halide or combinations of metal halide and high-pressure sodium are used for architectural floodlighting.

AUTHOR LOWELL CAMPBELL is an Agricultural Engineer, Northeastern Region, Agricultural Research Service, Beltsville, Md.

COAUTHOR HENRY M. CATHEY is Chief and Research Horticulturist, Ornamentals Laboratory, Northeastern Region.

Choosing Light Sources for General Lighting	LUMEN OUTPUT PER LAMP	EFFICACY	LIFE EXPECT- ANCY	COLOR ACCEPT- ABILITY	DEGREE OF LIGHT CONTROL	MAINTE- NANCE OF LUMEN OUTPUT
INCANDESCENT	FAIR	LOW	LOW	HIGH	HIGH	GOOD
TUNGSTEN HALOGEN	FAIR	LOW	LOW	HIGH	HIGH	HIGH
MERCURY	GOOD	FAIR	HIGH	LOW	GOOD	GOOD
PHOSPHOR MERCURY	GOOD	FAIR	HIGH	FAIR TO GOOD	FAIR	FAIR
METAL HALIDE	HIGH	GOOD	FAIR	GOOD TO HIGH	GOOD	FAIR
HIGH-PRESSURE SODIUM	HIGH	HIGH	FAIR	FAIR	GOOD	GOOD
40-WATT FLUORESCENT	LOW	GOOD	GOOD	GOOD TO HIGH	LOW	GOOD
HIGH-OUTPUT FLUORESCENT	FAIR	GOOD	GOOD	GOOD TO HIGH	LOW	GOOD
1,500-MA FLUORESCENT	GOOD	GOOD	FAIR	GOOD TO HIGH	LOW	FAIR

As HID lamps require about 5 minutes to start, they are not suitable for the frequent "on-off" situations.

Mercury luminaires, usually 175 watt, known as "dusk to dawn" have been widely used for rural yard or security lights. Operated by a photo electric control, the unit is similar to street lights, operating automatically from dusk to dawn.

Fifty- and 75-watt mercury lamps are used in post lanterns in yards or by driveways operated either by switch, time clock or photo electric control with underground wiring from the nearby residence or building.

Low voltage outdoor lighting consists of 6- or 12-volt lamps operated from an isolation transformer which converts 120-volt normal power to 12 volts. The lamps are usually 25 and 50 watt incandescent.

The total number of lamps that can be operated depends on capacity of the transformer, normally about six 50-watt lamps. This low voltage lighting is usually a supplement to regular lighting for decoration or display.

Gaslights illuminate by direct burning of gas in an enclosed mantle. The light output of a simple mantle lamp is similar to a 40-watt incandescent lamp. Normally gaslights operate continuously day and night.

Additional equipment for automatic lighting at dusk and turn off at dawn is relatively expensive.

Torches burning kerosene or similar fuels are decorative and portable for occasional outdoor use in patios and gardens. For frequent use or unattended operation, camping lanterns are preferred because of convenience and safety of operation. Open torches should be kept remote from combustible materials.

AVERAGE LUMENS PER LAMP

Incandescent, standard

Watts	Lumens
15	125
25	225
40	430
60	810
100	1,600
150	2,500
200	3,500
300	5,490

Incandescent, tungsten-halogen

Watts	Lumens
400	7,500
500	10,000
1,000	21,000
1,500	31,000

Incandescent, reflectorized PAR-38

Watts	Total Lumens°
75	680
100	colors only
150	1,600
250	2,900

°More than half the lumens are in the beam. Beam spread is 30° for spot lamps, 60° for flood lamps.

Fluorescent

Lamp Watts	Length, inches	Lumens
15	18	660
20	24	1,000
40	48	2,600
110	48	5,400
210	96	12,400

Mercury, clear

Lamp Watts	Lumens
40	1,200
75	2,800
100	3,800
175	7,500
250	11,600
400	21,000
700	39,000
1,000	57,000

Metal Halide

Lamp Watts	Lumens
175	12,000
400	34,000
1,000	95,000

High-Pressure Sodium

Lamp Watts	Lumens
250	25,500
400	47,000
1,000	130,000

Night flying insects (except mosquitoes) are attracted to blue or ultraviolet (blacklight) lamps. Insect traps use ultraviolet lamps, sometimes in combination with chemicals, to trap insects. Yellow incandescent lamps provide three-fourths the visibility of white lamps with insect attraction held to a minimum.

Of the HID lamps, high-pressure sodium attracts the least insects. Metal halide lamps attract more, and mercury lamps the most. Outdoor lamps should be placed so insects which collect around them will not fall on walks or around doorways.

Swimming pools can be lighted by overhead or underwater lights (sometimes in combination). Underwater lights installed in the side of the pool below water level require safety inspections at least once each year. Underwater fixtures deteriorate rapidly and require frequent renewal of gaskets and other parts or replacement of the entire fixture.

Satisfactory lighting for pools can be obtained from floodlights on 20-foot poles located 20 feet from the pool edge. Electric wiring to lamps must include a separate grounding conductor and be more than 10 feet from the edge of the pool. Ground-fault interrupters (GFI) are usually required by regulatory codes for any wiring around pools.

An illumination level of 10 foot-candles (lumens per square foot) is recommended at the pool surface. Sixty lumens of light sources per square foot will be required to produce about 10 foot-candles at the pool surface, using underwater lamps. For floodlights, 35 to 50 lumens of light sources per square foot will be required to provide 10 foot-candles. It is critical for safety to see clearly at night to the bottom.

A lumen is the unit of light quantity

produced by a light source. One lumen per square foot equals one foot-candle.

Green plants require light for normal growth and development. They have evolved under the presence of daily illumination from the sun. The amount, duration, and quality of sunlight varies enormously through the 12 months of the year.

Plants have become adapted to widely varying lighting situations. Some thrive only with thousands of foot-candles of light in tropical regions, others are adapted to seasonal changes of light duration and amount. Most plants, however, may be grown with a basic day of 8 to 10 hours of sunlight to accomplish the requirements for photosynthesis. All greenhouses do is provide a covering to maintain minimum night temperature and an exposure to available sunlight.

We have learned in recent years—from the late 1920's—to manipulate the growth and development of plants by using artificial light, generally from an incandescent-filament source. We can change flowering time and delay the onset of dormancy of many plants; this is the basis for a number of recent advances in the controlled growth of ornamental plants.

Incandescent street lamps provide low light levels—usually much less than 1 foot-candle at plant level. In recent years, however, lighting requirements for increased security and visibility purposes have been increased to more than one foot-candle. For example a 400-watt HID (high-pressure sodium) street light on a 30-foot pole gives about one foot-candle 20 to 30 feet horizontally on the ground. The light level increases as one moves closer to the light source.

After 8-hour day in greenhouse, these red maple seedlings were kept under varying light conditions for ensuing 16 hours. One at the far left was kept in darkness. Others, second from left to right, were exposed to one foot-candle of (1) incandescent filament, (2) mercury, and (3) HID-high pressure sodium lighting.

Woody plants above were left in darkness for 16 hours following 8-hour day in greenhouse. Plants below were exposed to one foot-candle of high pressure sodium lighting for 16 hours after 8-hour day in greenhouse. Left to right, rhododendron, Norway maple, golden rain tree, birch, and littleleaf linden.

Research studies at the Agricultural Research Center shows that some trees, shrubs, and flowering annuals are responsive to this small amount of light all night, provided the night temperature is above 65°F.

Greenhouse tests under controlled conditions indicate that light from the new HID lamps can delay the onset of dormancy of some woody plants and may make them vulnerable to sudden drops in temperature.

Flowering of plants in nearby greenhouses may also be altered. Chrysanthemum buds form but they never develop normal flowers; the flowering of poinsettias was inhibited indefinitely by one foot-candle of illumination from HPS lamps.

When you install security lighting, consider the effects on the growth of your plants. Since plants vary greatly in sensitivity and night temperatures can be erratic, the fixtures should have shields to direct the light on pedestrians and traffic and away from plants.

We have become accustomed to the way plants look under sunlight and incandescent-filament lamps. These light sources emphasize the yellow-green parts of the plants and dull the reds and blues.

Color-improved lamps are preferred for most visual lighting effects. They bring out the reds and blues of plants and add to the intensity of the greens. Putting on filters to make the light some specific color—red, blue, green—greatly reduces plant visibility, distorts the natural colors, and creates something of a carnival atmosphere.

Ponds for Suburban Or Rural Homesites

Have you ever dreamed of your own private pond away from the crowd? Your own fishing hole? Your own beach? Your own water wonderland with all the pleasures that go with it?

Your dream may not be as far fetched as you think. Many suitable sites for ponds are available close to suburban and rural homesites. On a good site, a pond can be constructed at very reasonable cost, many for as little as $1,500 to $2,000. Perhaps you should take a look at your own situation.

Ponds serve many useful purposes. They can provide water for lawns, home gardens, small orchards, and livestock, for home fire protection. A well-managed and stocked pond can produce a dependable supply of fish for sport and food. You can swim and boat. What's more, ponds attract birds, waterfowl, and other wild species, and add to the area's natural beauty.

There are two general types of ponds, the embankment type and the excavated type. In the first, water is impounded behind an earth embankment or dam constructed across a watercourse. This type is suitable if the slope of the ground ranges from gentle to steep and if the watercourse is deep enough to provide water storage to a depth of 6 feet or more.

An excavated pond is built by digging a pit below the surrounding ground level. Such a pond is usually built in nearly level areas where there would be little advantage in building a dam.

Many sites lend themselves to a combination of a dam and excavation.

Most ponds depend for their water on runoff from the watershed above the site. Some may be supplied by springs. Many excavated ponds are supplied by an underground water table.

Size of the watershed furnishing water to the pond is important. If the area is too large, excess runoff may create erosion problems and make it difficult to bypass the extra water after the pond fills. If the watershed is too small, the runoff may be too small to fill the pond and offset water loss due to seepage and evaporation.

In many situations, excess water from a watershed that is too large can be diverted from the pond. Similarly, needed extra water may be diverted into a watershed that is too small.

The size of watershed required can range from a very few acres in the eastern humid region of the United States to many acres in the arid West and Southwest.

AUTHOR R. C. BARNES, JR., is an Agricultural Engineer with the Soil Conservation Service in Washington, D.C.

COAUTHOR J. J. COYLE is an Agricultural Engineer with SCS in Fort Worth, Tex.

Pond at top is lined with Bentonite. Other ponds are spring-fed and used in part for fire protection.

Conditions in the watershed determine the quality of water available for the pond. Ideal is a good cover of grass or woods, which controls erosion and yields runoff water relatively free of silt and other pollutants. Also desirable is a combination of good cover on pasture and woodland, and cultivated land properly treated with conservation measures to control erosion.

Beware of actively eroding, unprotected watersheds as they can fill your pond with silt in a short time. Likewise, approach with caution watersheds that have severe sources of pollution such as concentrated animal or poultry production, processing plants, and uncontrolled urban expansion.

Soils at the pond site are important from several viewpoints. First, will they hold water? Clays, silty clays, and in some cases sandy clays are satisfactory. Sand, gravel, or sand-gravel mixtures are generally unsuitable as the seepage rate is too high.

If the only sites available are those with excess seepage, you may still be able to have a pond as there are many

194

sealants that can be used to reduce seepage rates. These include chemical dispersants, expansive clays, and flexible membranes of plastic or rubber. The dispersants similar to some detergents, actually run the soil particles together. The expansive clays, such as bentonite, expand and fill the soil voids. The flexible membranes, of course, are impermeable. Sealing will, of course, increase construction cost.

Other points to consider are: Is the soil OK as a foundation for the dam? Is it suitable for use in constructing the dam? Will it provide an erosion-resistant emergency spillway?

Many States have laws controlling use of water and the design and construction of ponds. Some States may require that plans be approved and a construction permit obtained from a State agency before work starts. If yours is one of these States, you should contact your State water agency for minimum requirements and procedures.

Several components of a pond bear consideration. The dam must be proportioned so it will be safe and easily maintained. The top should be wide enough to provide adequate bulk and stability, accommodate construction equipment, and provide a suitable travelway.

A top width of 10 to 12 feet is considered adequate for the average small pond. The sides must slope gradually enough to prevent earth slides and to permit mowing and recreational activities such as fishing. Permissible slopes depend on the soil but ordinarily a 3-foot horizontal to 1-foot vertical on both sides of the dam provides a good combination.

Embankment-type ponds require one or more spillways for discharging water after the pond fills. The common arrangement is a grass-covered earth spillway around the end of the dam and a pipe spillway installed through the dam. The grassed spillway takes care of large infrequent flows that could damage the dam.

The pipe spillway handles small flows from springs and snowmelt and maintains the permanent water level below the earth spillway. Equipped with a suitable valve, the pipe spillway can be used to drain the pond for maintenance.

If the pond is to supply water for livestock, a small-diameter pipe with a float valve should be installed through the dam to a watering trough below the dam. Livestock should be excluded from the pond by a fence to prevent polluting the water and creating other problems.

If the pond is to be used for fire protection, a non-freezing dry hydrant with access to fire trucks is needed or an alternate pump, motor, and hose can be installed.

Other features such as boat docks and sand beaches may be added.

Design, plans, and specifications for a pond involve such things as preparing engineering surveys, estimating water runoff, determining soil suitability, estimating spillway size, setting elevations for spillways and top of dam, preparing drawings, and prescribing construction methods. Consequently you will want to secure the assistance of a qualified engineer or technician. This kind of assistance is available from private engineers and through your local soil and water conservation district.

The pond should be constructed in accordance with the plans and specifications developed. Many failures have occurred as a result of cutting corners in an attempt to save a little on construction costs.

While you will want some assistance from an engineer or technician during construction, you should become familiar with the plans and specifications yourself. This will help you determine if construction is going as planned.

The area to be occupied by the dam and the area where the earth will be obtained should be stripped of topsoil, vegetation, roots, stumps, and other material not suitable for placing in the dam. The topsoil may be stockpiled and spread back on the completed dam and emergency spillway

Farm pond yields a 12-inch bass.

to aid in establishing and maintaining a good grass cover.

Trees, brush, and shrubs in the area to be covered by water should be removed and disposed of.

The plan may call for a cutoff trench lengthwise of the dam foundation. If so, it is important that it be excavated to the depth, length, and shape shown on the plans. Failure to do so could result in an unsatisfactory pond due to seepage under the dam.

The cutoff trench should be backfilled and compacted in layers as specified. Compaction can be obtained by using a sheeps-foot roller or by proper routing of construction equipment over the entire area of each layer. The soil should have sufficient moisture for good compaction. Extremely dry soil cannot be compacted to desired density without adding water.

After the cutoff trench is backfilled, the trench for the pipe spillway should be prepared, and the pipe, cutoff collars, and riser installed as shown on the plans. If a water pipe is to be placed through the dam to supply a watering trough, it should be placed at this time. Fill material should be tamped around the pipe by hand or

mechanical tamper. Construction of the dam would then continue as described for the cutoff trench.

Deepening the edges of the shoreline during construction can make a better pond. This will eliminate shallow water areas, help control water weeds, aid in mosquito control, and provide a pleasant bank from which to fish. Edges of the shoreline should be excavated to a slope of 3 feet horizontal to 1 vertical, out to a depth of 3 feet.

The pond will probably be used for boating and swimming regardless of the intended main purpose. For this reason all trees, stumps, and brush should be removed as well as all rubbish, discarded machinery, and old fences.

Sharp dropoffs and deep holes in the swimming area should be eliminated by grading and filling.

Mark with float lines the area suitable for swimming. Put warning signs at danger points. Lifesaving devices such as ring buoys, ropes, planks, and long poles should be placed at strategic points. If ice skating is expected, put long planks or ladders near the skating area to use for rescues. Check with local and State safety authorities as to safety and insurance requirements.

The completed dam, earth spillway, and other areas above the proposed water area that were denuded during construction should be smoothed, fertilized, and seeded or sodded to grass or other vegetation suited to your locality. A good vegetative cover protects these exposed areas from erosion, gives a more attractive appearance, and cuts maintenance costs.

Suitable shrubs may be incorporated in the landscape plan for added scenic beauty and to provide bird and wildlife food and cover. Trees should not be planted on the dam, as their roots can penetrate the fill and cause problems.

Good maintenance is as vital as good design and construction. Examine the pond after each rain. Reseed bare areas and erosion rills and mulch with straw. Fertilize grass and mow regularly. The pipe spillway, valves, and watering trough should be maintained free of debris at all times.

Inspect your pond frequently and make repairs as needed. In this way you will avoid the big repair jobs that result from neglect.

For information on technical assistance, pond design, stocking and management of fish, and planting of grass and other vegetation adapted to your area, consult your local soil and water conservation district office, your county Extension office, or the local office of the Soil Conservation Service.

Vegetable Gardens: A Happy Escape, Especially If the Harvest Is Good

Vegetable gardening is the relaxing art and science of turning a love for growing plants into a productive activity.

A combination of attributes make it a national hobby with both young and old. For an ever-increasing number of individuals, seed catalogs and the thoughts of spring gardening provide a happy escape from the winter doldrums.

Vegetable gardeners unanimously agree that many home-grown vegetables picked at their peak of maturity have quality seldom found in vegetables purchased from commercial markets. From spring through late fall, a well-planned and maintained garden can provide a supply of fresh vegetables, thus increasing the nutritional value of the family diet. Freezers make it possible to preserve some of the surplus vegetables to be enjoyed at a later date, while other vegetables can be stored for a few months in a cool area. Not to be overlooked is the finger-

tip convenience of having vegetables in the back yard; this in itself justifies home gardening for many individuals. In addition, vegetable gardening provides exercise and recreation for both urban and suburban families.

Although the initial dollar investment for gardening may be nominal, one cannot escape the fact that gardening requires manual labor and time. Many of the gardening tasks must be performed at times that are most inconvenient. Neglecting jobs that should be performed on a regular basis may result in failure and a negative feeling towards gardening.

Do not allow spring enthusiasm to dictate more than you can handle. A small, well-maintained garden is more enjoyable and profitable than a large neglected one. The garden usually expands proportionately to the positive experiences and with the sense of "pride of accomplishment".

Vegetables thrive in full sunlight and need at least 5 or 6 hours of sun during the middle of the day. Excessive shading results in rank, spindly plants and poor yields. If possible, the garden should be reasonably near the house so the gardener can work in it at odd moments.

Soils for vegetables should be friable (easily crumbled) and porous for quick water drainage, deep crop root penetration, and good aeration. A deep, fine, sandy loam or silt loam is best.

Usually the home owner has little choice in the soil type he can select. Fortunately, many vegetables can be grown on relatively poor soils if the soils are properly conditioned.

An area consisting of "fill dirt" is difficult to reclaim for a vegetable garden. A filled area usually contains a high percentage of bottom subsoil (clay), stones, and debris. The fertility is usually very poor. It requires time,

---

AUTHOR LEONARD D. TOPOLESKI is an Associate Professor in the Department of Vegetable Crops, Cornell University, Ithaca, N.Y.

fertilizer, and a considerable amount of energy to make a fill soil productive.

Low and wet spots should also be avoided. If water remains in puddles on the soil surface for several hours after a moderate shower, the site should not be used for vegetables. Very few vegetables can tolerate "wet feet" for long periods.

Some heavy soils can be used for vegetables if improved by adding organic matter and lime, but they are difficult to handle and must not be worked when they are too wet.

Sandy soils are quite satisfactory for vegetables in years with average rainfall, but supplemental irrigation may be necessary in dry periods. Adding organic matter to these soils will improve their structure and value.

Vegetables are frequently classified according to their ability to survive frosts.

Hardy or cool-season crops will survive medium to heavy frosts. Seed from this group can be planted as soon as the soil can be prepared in the spring or in mid-summer for a late fall crop.

Semi-hardy vegetables will survive a light frost. Seed will germinate at relatively low temperatures, and can be planted 2 to 3 weeks before the last frost date.

Tender or warm season crops are injured or killed by frost, and their seeds seldom germinate in cold soil.

The home gardener should choose those vegetables which the family likes best.

Certain vegetables, such as celery, are difficult to grow. Celery from the grocery store is usually as good or of better quality than home grown.

The more perishable vegetables such as sweet corn, peas, snap beans, broccoli, and asparagus should receive first consideration in the home garden. These vegetables, when freshly harvested, have a flavor seldom found in grocery store produce.

Space is another consideration. A small space will provide vegetables for many meals if it is planted with crops such as tomatoes, snap beans, summer squash, broccoli, and cabbage. Corn, peas, winter squash, and melons require more space in relation to the amount they produce.

The inexperienced gardener should grow few crops and select those that are easy to grow. Corn, snap beans, peas, tomatoes, radish, and squash are good for beginners. Broccoli, cabbage, cucumbers, and melons require more attention because of the need for disease and insect control. Care must be taken in seeding the small-seeded crops such as beets and carrots in order to obtain good germination.

The garden can be planted at one time, or in a succession of plantings. One planting will give a long harvest of tomatoes, peppers, summer squash, beets, carrots, broccoli, and cucumbers.

Sweet corn is a one harvest crop. Planting varieties with a spread of maturity or several different plantings of the same variety is necessary to obtain a steady supply of corn when it is at the peak of quality.

Crops such as summer squash, broccoli, and cucumber must be harvested as they mature in order for the plants to continue bearing.

On the other hand, a single planting of some crops will produce for only a short time even if more than one variety is used. Radishes, head lettuce, and peas are in this category.

Sweet corn should be picked fresh and cooked immediately for best flavor.

198

Bolting—flower and seed stalk development induced by high temperatures—is common with spinach, radish, and lettuce. Note seed stalk development in variety in background. Summer bibb in the foreground is resistant to bolting.

An intermediate group in which two or three plantings may be needed to ensure a long season includes cabbage, snap beans, and leaf lettuce.

If the family is going on an extended vacation, crops that have a short harvest period should be omitted or else planted to mature before or after the vacation.

It is especially convenient to grow garden vegetables that are frequently used in cooking or in salads, such as tomatoes, peppers, parsley, and chives.

A paper plan of the garden drawn to scale which lists the crops to be grown with the number of rows, the distance between rows, and the planting dates for each vegetable will be an asset at planting time. By keeping the following points in mind, the gardener can work effectively:

• Group the crops according to height to prevent shading

• Garden rows can be faced either east and west or north and south. If they run east and west, plant the tall growing crops on the north side of the garden so they do not shade the small ones

• If the garden is on a hillside, run the rows across the slope—not up and down it. This helps to hold water and reduce erosion

• Group together the small-growing, quick-maturing crops

• Productivity of a small garden may be increased by succession planting.

Remove the refuse from early maturing crops and make a second application of fertilizer before the second planting. Practice crop rotation if possible.

Seed quality varies but seed laws protect the gardener fairly well against poor seed and misrepresentation. The kind, variety, percentage of germination, and date of testing are marked on every package offered for sale.

A general guide to the quantities of seed to buy is given in the table with this chapter. Buy enough seed at one time to last through the entire season.

Saving seed from the garden is a poor practice. Many of the best varieties are hybrids that will not breed true to type.

There is also a risk of carrying disease with the seed.

Selection of vegetable varieties is a difficult problem. Seed catalogs are colorful and profusely illustrated; the written description of each variety convinces the gardener that he must include it in his garden. Since it is impossible to grow every variety, the following rules will simplify your selection:

Buy vegetable seeds and transplant by variety name. The time of maturity, quality, and disease resistance differ so much among varieties that success or failure in your garden may be determined by the choice of variety.

Since the best means of disease control in the home garden is using disease- and insect-resistant varieties, these varieties should be bought whenever possible.

Purchase your seed and transplants from a reputable firm.

Try new varieties on a limited scale until they prove to be better than the ones you have been growing.

Every gardener needs a hoe, an iron rake, a spading fork, and a spade or round-pointed shovel. For large gardens, a good wheel hoe or hand cultivator and a small garden tractor multiply a gardener's efficiency.

It is important to know the pH of your garden soil. A pH test may be needed if the garden is in a new location.

A soil with a pH of 7.0 is neutral, while one with a pH of 7.1 or above is alkaline or sweet. A pH reading below 7.0 is acid or sour. Most vegetables grow best on a slightly acid soil where the pH is between 6.0 and 6.8.

Lime should be applied to the garden when a test has indicated the soil is too acid, that is, below 6.0.

Commercial fertilizers are applied to increase the nitrogen, phosphorus, and potash content of the soil. A 5-10-10 fertilizer contains 5 percent nitrogen, 10 percent phosphoric acid, and 10 percent potash.

A 5-10-5, 5-10-10 or similar analysis fertilizer should be used at the rate of 4 to 5 pounds to each 100 square feet of garden area. On soils that have been well fertilized for many years, 1 to 2 pounds of fertilizer may be adequate, especially if the pH is in the 6.0 to 6.8 range.

Organic matter increases the water-holding capacity of sandy soils and makes them more workable. It makes heavy soils more tillable, reduces soil compaction, increases ability of the soil to take up water rapidly, and improves drainage.

Incorporating organic matter also improves soil aeration and tends to enable soils to warm up earlier in the spring.

Besides furnishing organic matter, farm manure can supply the bulk of the fertilizer elements (nitrogen, phosphoric acid, and potash) if it is supplemented with 1 to 1½ pounds of superphosphate to each bushel of manure per 50 to 75 square feet of garden area. Unless the manure is well rotted, it should be applied before plowing or spading and then turned under.

Poultry, sheep, and goat manure should be used at the rate of no more than 1 bushel to 100 square feet of garden.

Compost is a good source of organic matter for the home garden. A compost pile can be made with leaves, weeds, straw, waste hay, and any waste vegetable matter other than diseased parts of vegetables.

Pile these materials together as they accumulate, keeping the lighter ones, such as leaves, from blowing away by throwing a little soil over the pile. Add 1 cup of agricultural lime and 1 cup of a complete fertilizer with each bushel of compost to hasten decay. It is not necessary to include special bacteria or fertilizers.

Each spring start a new pile. Turn the old one over several times during the year to ensure even decay; it will be ready to apply to the garden before spring plowing the second year. Leaf compost can, however, be used for a mulch the first spring after the pile is built or it can be put directly on the garden and turned under the first year.

Compost makes good potting or plant growing soil for use during the winter.

Rows are designed for convenience in planting, cultivating, and harvesting. If they are too closely spaced, competition between plants for water, plant nutrients, and sunlight and weed control is intensified and harvesting becomes difficult.

Suitable row spacings are given in the table with this chapter. Standard 3- and 6-foot row spacings are the most convenient if small power tools are used.

Seeds should be sown a little thicker than the plants will finally stand, to allow for those that fail to grow or that may be killed when they are very young. Space the seed uniformly. Heavy seeding wastes seed and time in thinning the plants.

A general rule is to plant shallowly in early spring, especially on heavy soils. In warmer weather and on lighter soils deeper seeding is usually advisable.

Cover large seeds such as corn, peas, and beans with one to two inches of soil. Cover small seeds such as carrots and lettuce with ¼- to ½-inch of soil. When covering the seed, provide good contact between the soil and seed by gently firming the soil over the seed.

In hot, dry weather when the soil around the seed dries out quickly, frequent light watering to keep the surface soil moist will help germination. Remove surplus plants before they can compete with those that are to remain. The total yield is likely to be much greater if thinning is done early than if it is done only by removing vegetables that are large enough to eat.

Here are some transplanting tips. Water plants in flats or market-packs an hour or more before transplanting them. Keep a block of soil around the roots and set out the plants as soon as they have been removed from the container.

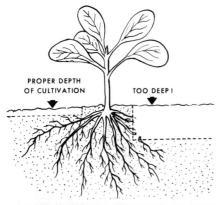

Top, deep cultivation destroys necessary plant roots. Bottom, warm season crops and especially the vine crops benefit from black plastic mulch and hot-tents.

Holes for the plants should be dug slightly larger than the blocks of soil around the roots. The plants should be set slightly deeper than they were in the original containers.

After partially filling the hole with soil and firming it around the roots, pour a cup of water or transplanting solution into the hole around each plant. Finish filling the hole with loose soil.

Weeds can be the gardener's worst enemy. They compete for moisture and nutrients, and they can harbor insects and diseases. They shade the plants and interfere with air circulation.

Since tall weeds can retard evaporation of dew and rain from foliage, they can increase the incidence of diseases during periods of excess rainfall.

Weeds can be controlled by a combination of hand weeding, cultivation, and mulching. Shallow cultivation is less injurious to crop roots than deep cultivation, and is just as efficient in controlling weeds. A wheel hoe with weed knives is one of the most efficient and useful tools for the home garden. A hoe is the next best hand tool for weed control.

Weed growth can be effectively controlled by using either organic mulches or black plastic (polyethylene). Mulches also tend to conserve soil moisture, prevent erosion, and eliminate root damage caused by deep cultivation or hoeing. They also keep the fruits of such crops as tomatoes, cucumbers, and melons clean.

Organic mulches are especially desirable on light sandy soils and with cool-season crops. Straw, old hay or grass, leaves, sawdust, and wood shavings are the most common organic mulches.

Black or very dark polyethylene plastics have proved effective in hastening maturity as well as in controlling weeds.

Using black plastic mulch with cucumbers, pickles, melons, and squash in many instances has resulted in a three-fold increase in yields. Black plastic frequently increases the yield of the warm-season crops such as peppers, eggplant, and tomatoes, and may increase the yield of all early planted crops.

Because mulches reduce heat radiation from the soil, increasing the chance of frost damage on a cool night, the gardener should apply mulches after the soil has become warm and *after all danger of frost is past.* With black plastic, it is important that the soil be well supplied with water from either a good soaking rain or an irrigation a few days before the plastic is laid.

Additional water during periods of drought (no soaking rain for 10 to 14 days) may improve the quality and yields of summer vegetables. Moisture is more likely to be a limiting factor on sandy or shallow soils than on heavy or deep soils.

From seeding until harvest, diseases and insects may cause some losses to vegetables. Home gardeners may be disappointed in their attempts to control diseases if they rely only on spraying or dusting after diseases appear. Successful control requires a 7 to 10 day dusting or spraying schedule. Many dual home-garden mixtures are available.

Pesticides are poisonous to humans and wildlife. Read the precautions and follow the directions on the label.

Even the best cared for garden has its problems. Some are inconsequential; often they cannot be attributed to gardening mistakes. An occasional plant may suffer an abnormality or even die from an unknown cause.

Adverse weather such as excessively high or low temperatures, too much or too little rain, and high winds can cause poor growth, blossom drop, and plant damage.

In many instances, poor soil conditions—including improper fertilization, soil compaction, inadequate drainage, poor texture or structure, and undesirable pH—are responsible for inadequate growth.

Poor location of the garden, exces-sive shading or competition from near-by trees, insects, diseases, root pruning caused by deep cultivation, and careless use of herbicides, insecticides, and fungicides are frequently the cause of abnormal plants.

Sometimes soil testing shows the reason for poor growth. Perhaps the trouble is simply a lack of adequate fertilizer. A shortage of an essential plant nutrient is likely to reduce the yield of any crop before the deficiency causes visible symptoms.

Gardeners growing tomatoes, peppers, or eggplant are occasionally confronted with the problem of poor or no fruit set. Poor setting of fruit and blossom drop can be caused by periods of cold weather with nights below 55°F., abnormally hot weather, warm nights above 75°F., low soil moisture, and excessive shading.

Have you considered growing a dishpan full of radishes or a plastic pailful of tomatoes? Recent developments allow urban and suburban gardeners to grow vegetables in a soilless mix. This method of growing plants which uses various assorted containers filled with artificial or synthetic soil is known as patio gardening, mini gardening, container gardening, pillow pak, and sausage culture.

The synthetic soil or mix is a combination of sphagnum peat moss, horticultural vermiculite, lime, and fertilizer. It can be purchased as a prepared mixture or the gardener can prepare his own. The mix is lightweight and free of weeds and disease.

To prepare a bushel of mix, simply combine ½ bushel of #2 size horticultural vermiculite, ½ bushel of peat moss, 5 tablespoons of ground limestone, 2 tablespoons of powdered superphosphate and 8 tablespoons of 6-12-6 or 5-10-5 fertilizer.

Thoroughly mix the materials on a clean surface or in a container. Add water until the mixture is wet. If it is very difficult to wet, add a small amount of detergent to the water.

Containers in which plants can be grown are limited only by the imagi-

Top, dwarf cherry tomato plants are ideal for container gardening. Plastic bags filled with artificial soil make excellent mini-gardening containers. Above, salad-type tomato plant in a 10-inch plastic pot with artificial soil.

nation. Frequently used containers include heavy duty plastic bags, plastic pans or pails, bushel baskets, and large flower pots. For the more adventurous gardener, a rectangular bin can be constructed from 1″ x 12″ lumber.

Successful mini gardening depends in part upon the selection of crops. Where possible, dwarf varieties should be grown. Do not overcrowd the plants. A dwarf tomato, or small varieties of pepper, or an eggplant can be grown in a plastic water pail or wastepaper basket.

Root crops such as radishes and onions do well in a dishpan or bushel basket. Vine crops such as cucumbers should be grown in bushels or tubs and placed in an area where they can "run" or be trellised to the side of a building.

The long season crops such as peppers, cucumbers, and eggplant will need supplemental feeding during the course of the growing season. This is easily accomplished with the water soluble fertilizers available in most garden centers.

When using plastic containers, make several holes in the bottom to allow for drainage.

For those who do not have adequate space or time but enjoy the quality of fresh vegetables and outdoor activities, patronizing a "pick your own" vegetable operation is an enjoyable alternative.

Vegetables and fruits commonly grown for "pick your own" operations include peas, tomatoes, corn, snap beans, strawberries, blueberries, cherries, and apples. Other crops may also be available in your area.

Because unit prices are considerably lower than at roadside stands and markets, this is an economical method of obtaining quantity and quality for canning and freezing.

Many of the operations allow the entire family to pick.

Preserving of excess vegetables through canning and freezing provides a means of enjoying home-grown produce all year.

Overproduction of vegetables from the average home garden is not likely to be a problem. However, a large garden usually produces more than the family can consume, sell, or distribute to neighbors, and the gardener is confronted with the problem of surplus vegetables.

The initial investment for canning and processing equipment is considerable. It is recommended that the inexperienced housewife consult with the local county home economist before launching a full-scale home vegetable preservation program.

203

If canning and freezing are a traditional family activity, the following points may be helpful.

Can or freeze only high quality vegetables. The quality of vegetables cannot be improved by processing. Under or overmature vegetables should not be preserved.

Process the vegetables as soon as possible after harvesting. Peak quality may be lost in a 2- to 3-hour period. If it is inconvenient to process soon after harvesting, place the vegetables in a refrigerator or in cold water.

Freshly harvested and immediately frozen asparagus, lima beans, and broccoli retain quality very close to that of the freshly harvested vegetable. Tomatoes, the vine crops, root crops, and the leafy vegetables—with the exception of spinach—do not freeze well. Cauliflower, brussels sprouts, snap beans, peas, corn (off the cob), are also excellent for freezing.

In regions of the country subject to early killing frosts, certain vegetables can be harvested prematurely or at maturity and stored fresh for future consumption.

Partially ripened tomato fruit will develop good color and flavor most rapidly if allowed to ripen at 70°-75°F. Large, solid green tomatoes can be picked and slowly ripened in a cool (60°F.), moist, dark place over several weeks. Sunlight is not necessary.

Muskmelons harvested at fullslip will continue to ripen satisfactorily after being removed from the vine if they are held at room temperature. In contrast, watermelons will not continue to ripen if harvested prematurely.

Winter squash and pumpkins should be harvested before heavy frost. Frost-injured fruit do not store. Cut the stem from the vine and store fruit where it is dry and the temperature can be kept at 55°-60°F. or slightly above.

Cabbage, mature dry onions, and potatoes store well in a ventilated, dark room where the temperature is near 45°F.

Root crops can be kept for several months if they are stored in an outdoor pit covered with boards and sod. It is essential to maintain a high humidity and temperatures just above freezing.

Many home gardeners use the home basement for vegetable storage, but usually this is undesirable because it is a bit too warm and too dry. Yet many of the above crops can be held for 2 to 3 months if placed in cool areas.

Within a given community, many individuals are well-versed in home gardening. Gardeners are usually willing to discuss techniques and relate their experiences. The neighbor who has an outstanding garden probably did not develop it in one season.

The county cooperative extension agent is an invaluable source of information. Seed catalogs contain a wealth of information and are easily obtained by writing to seed companies.

Excellent resources are also available through men's and women's garden clubs, botanical gardens, arboretums, the State land-grant universities, and the U.S. Department of Agriculture.

For further reading:

U.S. Department of Agriculture. *Minigardens for Vegetables*, Home and Garden Bulletin 163, Washington, D.C. 20250, 1970.

———. *Home Canning of Fruits and Vegetables*, Home and Garden Bulletin 8, Superintendent of Documents, Washington, D.C. 20402, 1972, 20 cents.

———. *Insects and Diseases of Vegetables in the Home Garden*, Home and Garden Bulletin 46, Superintendent of Documents, Washington, D.C. 20402, 1971, 40 cents.

———. *Selecting Fertilizers for Lawns and Gardens*, Home and Garden Bulletin 89, Washington, D.C. 20250, 1971.

———. *Storing Vegetables and Fruits in Basements, Cellars, Out Buildings and Pits*, Home and Garden Bulletin 119, 1970, Superintendent of Documents, Washington, D.C. 20402, 15 cents.

———. *Gardening on the Contour*, Home and Garden Bulletin 179, Washington, D.C. 20250, 1970.

———. *Mulches for Your Garden*, Home and Garden Bulletin 185, Washington, D.C. 20250, 1971.

————. *How Much Fertilizer Shall I Use?*, Leaflet 307, Superintendent of Documents, Washington, D.C. 20402, 1958, 5 cents.

————. *Sprinkler Irrigation*, Leaflet 476, Washington, D.C. 20250, 1970.

————. *Muskmelons for the Garden*, Leaflet 509, Superintendent of Documents, Washington, D.C. 20402, 1968, 5 cents.

————. *Rhubarb Production—Outdoors and In*, Leaflet 555, Washington, D.C. 20250, 1972.

————. *Greenhouse Framing for Plastic Covering*, Misc. Bulletin M1114, Superintendent of Documents, Washington, D.C. 20402, 1969, 5 cents.

————. *Aphids on Leafy Vegetables— How to Control Them*, Farmers Bulletin 2148, Washington, D.C. 20250, 1969.

————. *Growing Vegetables in the Home Garden*, Home and Garden Bulletin 202, Superintendent of Documents, Washington, D.C. 20402, 1972, 70 cents.

Sound Advice For Controlling Home Noise

APPLICATION OF NOISE control techniques requires some knowledge of the nature of noise. Noise is unwanted sound. Sound is the hearing sensation originated by vibrating bodies and borne as an elastic disturbance through the air.

Airborne sound is associated with a measurable pressure variation in the air, usually measured in decibels (db).

Tone, or pitch, of sound is a function of the frequency of vibration of the originating source in hertz (cycles per second).

Human hearing ranges from a pitch of 25 hertz to about 18,000 hertz depending upon the decibel level. At low frequencies, decibel level must be comparatively high for the tone to be heard. Tones about 500 hertz can be heard even though decibel levels are very low. Low frequency, high-pressure sound waves may be perceived by sense of touch as well as hearing. The human

aging process causes loss of hearing sensitivity in the upper frequency region of the hearing curve.

Annoyance level of a noise is related to decibel level and frequency with pitches near and above 2,000 hertz being more psychologically annoying. Sudden high pressure sounds are associated with an abrupt mechanical failure or other calamitous occurrence. They have a startling effect that is not desirable.

If sound waves are allowed to bounce off surrounding hard surfaces (or reverberate), then noise originated by a single vibrating source is perceived by the listener as coming from a multitude of directions.

Reverberation causes some degree of psychological disorientation and is not desirable.

A complete absence of background sound in our surroundings is as undesirable as noise. Human hearing is conditioned from birth to some background sound and a complete lack of such sensation may aggravate symptoms of insecurity or anxiety. Subconsciously everyone listens for sounds to assure that pump, furnace, or refrigerator is still functioning.

Noise may originate from within or outside of a dwelling. The most common source of outside noise is land or air traffic although manufacturing plants may contribute. Common sources of inside noise are musical instruments, household appliances, plumbing fixtures, human traffic, and loud speech.

Transmission of noise in dwellings is generally classified as airborne, or structure-borne. Airborne noise is a wave phenomenon caused by alternate compression and decompression originated by the action of a vibrating body. It can best be visualized as the wave action caused by dropping a stone in still water.

Structure-borne noise is caused by

AUTHOR B. CARL HAYNES, JR., is Acting Research Leader, Housing and Environmental Engineering, Athens (Ga.) area, Agricultural Research Service.

sympathetic vibration of a solid in intimate contact with a vibrating body. When a vibrating body is brought into contact with structural framing it causes the framing to vibrate.

An example is a poorly balanced, improperly shock-mounted, compressor motor, mounted directly to floor joists. Poor balance causes the motor to vibrate and the vibration is directly transmitted to structural framing through the floor joists. The mechanical energy is then transmitted through the building.

Unlike airborne sound, vibrations may be transmitted rapidly, over long distances, with very little attenuation (loss in power).

Impact noise may be either airborne or structure-borne. It is caused by striking a solid object. Examples of impact noise are a hammer blow, walking in hard shoes, or dropping solid objects on a bare floor. Most impact noise originates within the dwelling.

Noise starts with vibrations and always ends with air pressure waves. To develop methods of reducing noise in dwellings it is well to consider the maximum path noise may take while understanding that this path may be short circuited at several stages.

Consider a vibrating source, a tuning fork, to be in intimate mechanical contact with a structural member. The structural member is in turn directly connected to a large surface sounding board (wall panel) which is free to pulsate. Pulsation of the sounding board alternately compresses and decompresses the surrounding air.

Pressure waves induced in the surrounding air may also reverberate off an adjacent smooth hard-surfaced and rigid wall. It is also possible that these reflected air pressure waves then strike a second large surface sounding board and start it vibrating.

Ears may sense as noise the air pressure waves directly from the tuning fork, those from the front surface of the vibrating wall panels, those that are reflected from the hard-surfaced wall or those from the rear surface of the vibrating panel.

Since all of the vibrating elements may possess inherently different natural frequencies of vibration, the final tone sensed by the ear may be different from the tone originated by the tuning fork. If one of the vibrating sounding boards has a natural frequency of vibration identical to its driving vibrator (is resonant), very little power input (amplitude of vibration) is required to maintain a high decibel output.

The most effective method of noise control is to reduce the amplitude, or eliminate vibration, of the original source. Planning for this technique should begin with home site selection. In selecting a site the prospective home builder ought to avoid:

• Congested areas
• Depressions in the natural topography
• Major traffic artery intersections
• Crest of hilly traffic arteries
• Airport proximity and air traffic patterns
• Sites in a prevailing down-wind position from noisy areas

Care should be exercised in selecting mechanical equipment. Some manufacturers now include noise ratings in their specifications; many more will in the future. If noise ratings are not available to compare, it is to the home builder's advantage to shop, listen, and beware. In some instances it may be necessary to subjugate noise reduction to other operating characteristics.

Careful design of home heating systems and plumbing systems will also help to reduce noise from inside sources.

Plumbing noises can be reduced by using slightly larger pipe sizes, air compression standpipes above frequently used faucets or valves, and pressure-reducing valves.

Heating and air conditioning blower noise can be reduced by keeping blower speeds and air velocity to a minimum.

Besides minimizing amplitude of vibration of the noise source, vibration should be isolated from the building structure. This is done by the use of soft, compressible, vibration absorption material which has a low natural resonant frequency. It should be placed between a vibrating source and any structural member.

Rubber, some plastics, canvas, and steel springs are commonly used to absorb vibration.

Several types of vibration absorbers may often be found on new appliances and equipment. They isolate vibrating mechanisms from the frame and thus reduce structure-borne vibration when installed in a dwelling.

Design of vibration mounts is critical. They must have a natural resonant frequency that is not excited by the frequency of vibration of the supported mass. Failure to observe this precaution may result in increasing amplitude of vibration and eventual destruction of the vibration mount.

Where mounts restrain, or support the weight of, the vibrating mechanism it is important that positive mechanical restraint be provided in event of failure of the cushioning material.

Amplitude of vibration can be further reduced by mounting the vibrating equipment on a concrete slab at least three to five times the weight of the

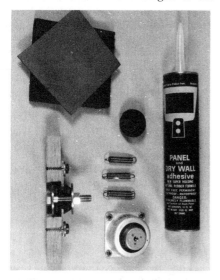

Rubber, springs, shock mounts and adhesive mastic are commonly used vibration absorption materials. The grommet mount shown in cross section may be used either as a support or hanger.

equipment. The slab should be placed on vibration isolation pads to reduce vibration transmission to the building structure.

Sheet metal heating ducts are often a source of noise or a transmission medium for vibration or airborne noise. Flat sides of duct work should be crimped to reduce expansion and contraction noise associated with heating and cooling of the metal. Short sections of flexible ducting (such as canvas) should be inserted in the supply and return air duct to reduce vibration transmission from the furnace to the duct work. Commercially available acoustical lining may be applied to these ducts to absorb sound that would otherwise be airborne through the duct.

Back-to-back heating outlet grilles in adjoining rooms should be avoided. For maximum reduction of room to room noise, a flexible section and acoustical lining should precede each outlet grille. Where outlet grilles pass through the wall, rubber padding should be used to isolate them from the structure.

Similar precautions should be taken to prevent transmission of vibration through piping. Where piping goes through a structural member or wall, the opening should be padded with rubber and sealed to prevent airborne noises through the opening. Piping and ducting should be supported by rubber or felt padded hangers.

The greater the mass of building material used, the less noise will be transmitted through a wall. Rigid building materials also reduce noise, since such materials are less able to act as sounding boards. Usually materials are dictated by architectural styling and not acoustical characteristics. Acoustical properties must be obtained by good design and building methods.

House plans should be examined and modifications made to reduce the number and area of walls, ceilings, and floors common to noisy and quiet areas. Bedrooms can often be separated from the highest noise areas by an intermediate or intermittent noise area such as study, bath, or closet.

Walls between adjacent quiet and noisy areas should be designed to reduce air and structure borne vibration. High mass walls, such as concrete block, are effective.

Masonry walls of concrete block should be plastered to fill pores and cracks in mortar even though furring strips and interior paneling are to be applied.

An excellent material for this purpose, called "Surface Bonding", was developed by Agricultural Research Service personnel in recent years. If applied to both sides of a block wall, "Surface Bonding" eliminates the use of mortar, waterproofs, and effectively blocks airborne noise penetration through cracks with a single application.

Wooden stud walls are effective if one finished surface is isolated from the other. Isolation is obtained by using staggered stud construction with alternate studs supporting the opposite wall surfaces. A fiber insulating batt should be fastened between studs attached to one wall surface.

An alternate method, requiring less material, utilizes slotted wooden studs formed by a vertical saw cut extending to within four inches of top and bottom of each stud. Insulating batts should be placed between studs.

Interior plumbing walls should utilize double-stud construction.

Adhesives should be used to attach wood veneer paneling and other wallboards to stud frames. The adhesive

not only increases rigidity but also acts as a vibration absorption material.

Felt underlays should be used under flooring to reduce air- and structure-borne vibration. All peripheral crack areas around room walls and window frames should be caulked with a commercial acoustical sealant to exclude airborne noise. Doors should fit tightly and bedroom and bath doors should be of solid core construction with gaskets and drop closures.

One of the more effective drop closures consists of a spring retracted felt strip mounted in the bottom edge of the door. When the door is closed, a lever actuator causes the felt strip to drop and completely seal the crack between door bottom and floor.

Acoustical tile ceilings will aid in absorbing noise within a room. Tile should be mounted with a mastic adhesive or suspended from ceiling joists in a vibration absorbing frame. If construction is two story, fiber insulating batts should be placed over the acoustical tile in the ceiling of the lower story to reduce impact noise from above.

Interior decorations such as carpets, draperies, and furniture also absorb airborne sound. Carpeting with underlay is effective in reducing impact noise. Research studies concluded in 1968 by Agricultural Research Service personnel delineate the effectiveness of various types of carpeting and draperies in reducing airborne sound.

For further reading:

Beranek, L. L., editor. *Noise Reduction*, McGraw-Hill, New York, 1960.

Harris, C. M., editor. *Handbook of Noise Control*, McGraw-Hill, New York, 1957.

Peterson, A. P. G., and Gross, E. E., Jr. *Handbook of Noise Measurement*, General Radio Company, West Concord, Mass., 1967.

Simons, J. W., J. J. Mize, and B. C. Haynes, Jr. *Acoustical Properties of Carpets and Draperies*, RB-38, University of Georgia, College of Agriculture, Experiment Station, Athens, Ga., 1968.

Simons, J. W., and Haynes, B. C., Jr. *Surface Bonding of Concrete Block*, AIB-343, Superintendent of Documents, Washington, D.C. 20402, 1970—Price 15 cents.

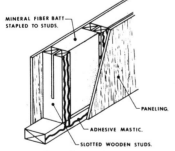

MINERAL FIBER BATT STAPLED TO STUDS.

PANELING.

ADHESIVE MASTIC.

SLOTTED WOODEN STUDS.

Use of slotted studs in frame construction reduces their vibration transmission. Mastic helps isolate paneling from vibrating studs. Fiber batts absorb air borne noise between wall surfaces.

Interior Wall Guide: Paneling, Masonry And Sheet Rock

IF YOU ARE BUILDING a new home or remodeling the home you now live in, sooner or later you will have to select the interior wall covering.

Basically you have a choice among three types of walls: 1) sheet rock, 2) paneling, or 3) masonry. I will discuss each of these different types of walls and the options available to you so that your interior walls can have a distinctive and attractive appearance and still stay within a specific budget.

Sheet rock is currently the leading material being applied to interior walls. There are several reasons for this. First, it is relatively inexpensive, as a 4- by 8-foot sheet will cost approximately $2. The total installed cost would be slightly higher since you have to tape and apply sheet rock compound to the edges (joints).

Then, too, sheet rock is not difficult to apply. The average handyman can hang sheet rock because it can be cut with a handsaw, razor blade knife, or pocket knife. Finally, sheet rock can be easily repaired with little if any signs of the repair showing.

There is one additional cost factor to sheet rock. Another surface coating must be applied as sheet rock is not a finished material.

The options for surface coatings include paint, paneling, and wallpaper.

In regard to paint, you can use either a water-thinned (commonly called latex) or a solvent-thinned (commonly called oil-based) paint. You have the choice of either a flat, semi-gloss, or high gloss, and wide selection of color. You can apply a sand-textured finish. You can also wallpaper or plaster over the paint at a later date if you so desire.

Even though the solvent-thinned paints are much improved, they are still more difficult to apply than the latex paints.

Buy quality in paints. Sometimes you can purchase "bargain" paint that is not worth the effort of putting it on the wall. Basically, you need to read the label on the paint can and this will tell you the quality of the ingredients.

For better quality latex paint, at least 50 percent of the pigment binder should be latex solids. The main ingredient in the pigment should be titanium dioxide, the ingredient that provides covering up or hiding ability, with the ingredients specified by weight and *not* by volume.

Here are some tips for painting either an old wall or one newly constructed.

Latex paints can be applied over sheet rock or plaster walls once the walls are dry. But keep in mind that taped joints of sheet rock are basically a wet material and like a plastered wall should "cure" for about 2 weeks before the surface coating is applied.

Another precaution comes from the paint can label, and this gives the number of square feet one gallon will cover. If the label indicates that the gallon will cover 450 square feet, then do not exceed this. If you do, the result will be unsatisfactory. In fact, you might see weak spots in the paint film even though the guarantee states the paint will cover in one coat. For truly satisfactory results, apply two coats of latex paint.

For painting, you need two brushes: a 3-inch brush for trimming around doors and windows, and a 1-inch brush (tapered) for trimming around the baseboard.

A roller and roller cover are helpful. The roller should be the type to which a longer handle can be attached for use on either the ceiling or top portions of the wall. The roller cover selected should have a medium nap and be recommended for the paint used.

Some additional items you need to

AUTHOR LELLAND L. GALLUP is an Extension Specialist in Housing, Department of Design and Environmental Analysis, Cornell University, Ithaca, N.Y.

GUIDE FOR SELECTING PAINT

	Aluminum paint	Casein	Cement base paint	Emulsion paint (including latex)	Enamel	Flat paint	Floor paint or enamel	Floor varnish	Interior varnish	Metal primer	Rubber base paint (not latex)	Sealer or undercoater	Semigloss paint	Shellac	Stain	Wax (emulsion)	Wax (liquid or paste)	Wood sealer
Floors:																		
Asphalt tile																	X•	
Concrete																X•	X•	
Linoleum							X								X	X	X	
Vinyl and rubber							X	X								X	X	
Wood							X•	X•									X	
Masonry:																		
Old	X	X	X	X	X•	X•					X	X	X•					
New			X	X	X•	X•					X	X	X•					
Metal:																		
Heating ducts	X				X•	X•				X	X		X•					
Radiators	X				X•	X•				X	X		X•					
Stairs:																		
Treads							X	X						X	X			
Risers					X•	X•			X		X		X•	X	X			
Walls and ceilings:																		
Kitchen and bathroom				X	X•						X	X	X•					
Plaster		X		X		X•					X	X	X•					
Wallboard		X		X		X•					X	X	X•					
Wood paneling				X•		X•			X									
Wood trim				X•	X•	X•			X		X	X	X•	X	X		X	X
Windows:																		
Aluminum	X				X•	X•					X	X	X•					
Steel	X				X•	X•					X	X	X•					
Wood sill					X•				X				X					

Black dot (X•) indicates that a primer or sealer may be necessary before the finishing coat (unless the surface has been previously finished).

have on hand when working with latex paints are a bucket and water for spot cleaning and final cleanup, a sponge or heavy cloth for cleaning the walls before painting, and several small cloths for spot cleaning.

Next, let's turn to wall paneling and the options you have in both selection and application.

You can apply paneling directly to framing materials of the house or you may apply it over the sheet rock.

Top, rough-sawn, channel pattern western cedar wall paneling, repeated for cabinet front and doors. Family room formerly was basement storage area with unfinished concrete walls. Above, V-groove western red cedar boards applied diagonally on wall facing stone fireplace.

Personally, I would recommend that most plywood, pressed wood, or hardboard paneling be applied over sheet rock because there is more strength behind the panel. If it is applied directly to the framing member (the stud wall), you have over 14 inches of unsupported space behind the panel and this could cause problems. However, solid board paneling, which is generally more expensive, can effectively be applied directly to the stud wall without serious problems.

Most paneling used today is plywood or pressed wood. Plywood makes the best paneling for use in the home. Pressed wood paneling should be reserved for commercial use. However, this rule is not followed in many parts of the country.

All interior paneling comes in a variety of thicknesses, panel sizes, colors, textures, and prices. Generally the true plywood panel, if it is good quality, will cost more than pressed wood paneling. The price differential will range anywhere from $3 to $20 for a 4- by 8-foot sheet.

It is safe to assume that the higher the price you pay the better the quality will be.

Pressed wood and hardboard paneling can be used effectively in the home. These two types have more variety of color and texture. In either you can get a wood veneer, vinyl coating, vinyl clad, smooth finish, textured finish, or leather finish.

One major caution: what you see is not always what you get. The difference between true wood and wood-grained is that a simulated wood grain is photographically reproduced either directly on the panel or printed on paper or vinyl film laminated to the panel. Sometimes the panels are embossed to not only simulate the appearance of wood but to actually feel like wood.

Generally the more expensive paneling (either solid wood or true wood veneer) is used in dining areas, the study, or the home office. Hardboard or pressed wood paneling with the guaranteed washable finish would be used in kitchens, baths, or recreation rooms.

Tools required to apply most paneling are a handsaw or a portable power saw with a veneer blade, hammer, nail set, calking gun, and several tubes of panel adhesive. With these tools almost anyone can apply paneling. One good trick for the hesitant handyman is to visit a construction site where a craftsman is putting up paneling and simply observe, pick up some of his techniques, and then go home and do it yourself.

Most major manufacturers of paneling have available the matching molding necessary to trim the corners and panel edges. Be sure to check with the supplier to insure these items are in stock prior to purchasing the paneling. Also get from the supplier the installation instructions for the particular paneling you have purchased so you can apply the paneling according to the manufacturer's recommendations, thereby satisfying the guarantee.

Masonry walls are becoming popular again. You see solid brick walls in homes, concrete block, and even some concrete walls either painted or covered with stucco. While a masonry wall can be quite distinctive and add to the architectural design, consider these factors:

• While there are a number of different sizes to choose from in brick, remember that each brick weighs about 5 pounds and thus a brick wall adds greatly to the structural problems of the house.

• A concrete block wall will weigh about 8 pounds per block, and stucco will add 6 to 8 pounds of weight per square foot to the house. Native stone will vary in weight depending upon the type of stone used, but for a guideline consider it the same as concrete block.

• For the average person, laying concrete block or brick is no easy task. I would recommend employing a tradesman to lay brick or concrete block, or to plaster a wall. This could very likely be the best money you will spend in the building or remodeling process.

A wall covering you can apply yourself with little trouble is wallpaper. You will have to choose between paper, vinyls, foils, burlap, felt, grass cloth, cotton, linen, and silk. You will also need to determine how much paper you need, how you apply it, how to match the pattern (if at all), and tools and equipment required.

For the amount of wallpaper required simply measure the space you are going to paper, select the type of wallpaper you want, and then have the local supplier assist you in estimating how much paper you will need.

It is a good practice to purchase more paper than you will require to compensate for any errors in measuring or mistakes you might make in application. Generally the supplier will take back uncut rolls of paper, but it is difficult to get paper from the same "dye lot" if you have to reorder.

Paper hanging tools are inexpensive and easy to use.

The tools required are a gallon bucket to mix the paste in, a smooth 4- by 8-foot work surface, pasting brush, smoothing brush, trim knife, seam roller, sponge, and a 6- to 8-inch straight edge. The trim knife can be sharp single-edge razor blades, the straight edge, a 6-inch-wide putty knife, and the sponge anything that would clean the surface of the paper once the job is finished.

Before I discuss the types of paper available, I would recommend you visit a home under construction, one where a professional paperhanger is working, and observe his technique. You can pick up some helpful hints on things to do and things to avoid, for your own job.

The most popular paper on the market today is vinyl. This is popular because most people can apply it with little difficulty. The edges are butted together and not lapped, it does not stretch, it is durable when handled wet, and extremely tough after it is applied, it is completely washable, and the patterns are endless.

One major concern is whether to purchase prepasted paper or mix your own paste. This depends largely on the amount of work you have to do.

Let's assume you are going to hang paper which requires you to mix your own paste. Depending upon the type of paper, either a wheat germ paste or a vinyl paste will do the job.

Each carton of paste that you purchase will have mixing instructions on the carton.

The advantage of prepasted paper is that you omit some intermediate steps in getting the paper on the walls, such as the requirement of mixing the right consistency of paste and the requirement of having a large smooth work surface. However, it may be less expensive if you mix your own paste for large areas.

If you use lightweight vinyls, either the prepasted or mix-your-own type would be equally satisfactory.

For the heavy vinyls, use a heavy vinyl paste.

Part of your decision on weight of the paper should be based on the surface the paper is being applied to. I recommend that you talk with your local supplier and follow his recommendations.

Buy from reputable firms since there will be some guarantee of quality.

For further reading:

U.S. Department of Agriculture, *Interior Painting in Homes and Around the Farm,* Home and Garden Bulletin No. 184, Superintendent of Documents, Washington, D.C. 20402—Price 10 cents.

Options Available In Air Conditioning, Heating a House

WE WISH TO control the climate within our living space for our comfort and well being. Comfort is attained by a body heat balance. That is, the combined energy losses by radiation, convection, and evaporation must balance the energy generated due to metabolism.

We try to adjust the energy lost by the body to agree with the energy generated by the body at that particular time. The amount lost depends in general upon the type and coverage of clothing, air temperature, air movement, and humidity; skin temperature and evaporation; and the temperature of the surroundings.

For the most part, surrounding temperatures mean the inside surface temperature of the walls, ceiling and floors. It is easy to tell that the windows are especially critical areas. When standing close to a window on a cold day, it is not only cold to touch, but unless one is heavily clothed, you feel a cold sensation as the body is radiating energy to the much colder window surface. Also a thin film of cold air is usually sliding down the inside surface of the window. This phenomenon is especially noticeable on the longer floor to ceiling windows and glass patio doors.

Many variations and options are available in designing a home and selecting a heating and cooling system to provide "climate control" which, in turn, provides various degrees of comfort. Options you select will vary somewhat with the geographical location. The amount of comfort will, of course, also depend on how much you spend.

Central heating or complete house heating systems are capable of providing the comfort most Americans want. They are a good investment in all but the lowest cost houses and in warm climates. Thermostats make their operation almost automatic. The type with ducts distributes heated air to all rooms and is capable of providing a fairly uniform temperature if the system is properly installed in a well built house.

Furnaces for central warm-air systems using gas, oil, and electric resistance heaters or heat pumps with electric resistance boosters heat quickly. This is a desirable feature for heating on chilly fall and spring mornings.

A basement is the best place for a furnace, especially coal fired furnaces. These are used where coal is cheap but they are apt to be dusty or messy.

Electric furnaces need no chimney and require no maintenance other than fan, motor, and filters. A larger service entrance may be required for electric heat, usually 200 amperes.

Installed costs of heating systems vary somewhat according to the type of fuel, but there may be more variation in cost between a good and poor duct system. The duct system should be large enough to handle a large volume of air at low velocity. This will help insure quieter operation, and permit a lower air temperature in the ducts.

High air temperature from the furnace has an increased drying effect which is undesirable in most parts of the country. Addition of a humidifier will be found desirable if the heating system causes a low humidity and too much drying.

AUTHOR M. CONNER AHRENS is Program Analyst for the Northeastern Region, Agricultural Research Service, Beltsville, Md. He was formerly with the Agricultural Engineering Research Division.

Placement of supply and return registers is important as well as their size. Many systems have one return register, usually located in a hallway, but returns in individual rooms help balance the system and allow for more adequate circulation in each room.

The outer walls, windows, and doors are usually cold and often drafty. This leads to two schools of thought concerning location of registers in the room.

With warm-air supply registers on the inner walls and return registers on the outer walls, the cold air from outer walls and windows is drawn to the return. Also, warm air is drawn across the room to the outer walls where the return registers are located.

With warm-air supply registers on the outer walls and return registers on the inside walls, the warm air mixes immediately with the cold air from the walls and windows if they are placed correctly.

Both of these methods prevent massing of cold air on the floor.

In any event, consideration should be given to location of registers so as not to interfere with draperies.

Baseboard heating is usually provided by a central hot water furnace or by electric resistance heaters in the baseboard. These are installed on the outside walls and provide a uniform, desirable type of heat as they tend to warm the cold outer walls. Also, there are no drafts from furnace fans. On the other hand, the initial cost of a baseboard system plus central air conditioning may be more than a warm-air system with air conditioning.

The baseboard systems eliminate ducts which may interfere with plans to finish ceilings of rooms below.

Heat pumps provide warm air heating. They cool like a conventional air conditioning system. While heating, they operate as if you turned a window air conditioner around so the warm air is discharged inside and cold air outside. In practice, this is done by valves whereby the refrigerant direction of flow is changed.

Heat pumps have been available in three types: (1) Window units for individual rooms, (2) split system, much like central system air conditioning equipment, and (3) package, self-contained units like an enlarged window unit.

The split system and the package units are for central systems.

The heat pump extracts heat energy from the colder or lower temperature air and delivers it to the higher temperature side. It pumps heat energy from a lower temperature to a higher temperature, and thus the name "heat pump."

While heating, it delivers to the house the heat energy it has extracted from the outside plus most of the electrical energy supplied the compressor motor. If the outside temperature is about 20°F. or above, the heat pump can deliver in heat energy about 2 times (more above 20°) the electrical energy required to operate it.

In areas where heating is the biggest requirement, the heat pump size should be selected so it will just be capable of heating the house with an outside temperature about 20° or 30°F. When the temperature falls below 20° or 30°F, booster heaters (electrical resistance) come on to help.

Many heat pumps are used in the South, where cooling is the major requirement. In this case the size is determined by the cooling requirement. They can also be used in moderate northerly climates.

Heating and cooling loads should be estimated by an experienced person. Utility companies usually have someone who will do this for you. Oversized cooling equipment can result in inadequate dehumidification. The wrong size heating equipment can result in poor efficiency.

Electric heating is also provided by compact unit heaters, usually wall mounted with fan and individual thermostat. These are especially adaptable to rooms with limited installation space and where the operation of a fan in the room is not undesirable. The bathroom and utility room are examples.

Ceiling cable installations provide a high percent of radiant heat. They give an even heat, and will warm the floor except where the radiation is interrupted such as under a table. Addition of a baseboard heater is usually recommended under large windows in rooms with ceiling heat.

This type of heat adds comfort to houses built on slabs, and to basement recreation rooms. Electric heat has the additional advantage of individual room control.

Infrared heat lamps can provide additional comfort by providing instant warmth. The three sizes—125, 250, and 375 watts—will fit a standard light bulb socket. A heat resistant or porcelain socket should be used because of the heat generated. The type with the red colored thermally stable glass should be used where there is any danger of water or other cold liquid coming in contact with the lamp while it is hot.

Heat lamps can be installed in bathroom ceilings for added warmth on chilly days. A recessed fixture with porcelain socket is available for this. An additional benefit is that they give a high level of illumination. They also will provide worker comfort in places such as utility rooms and basements or other areas you do not wish to heat.

Cooling your house can involve a great many considerations. If practical, orient the long axis East and West. South windows can then be protected with wide eaves or overhang. Avoid large glass areas in east and west walls; they are hard to protect against the sun.

If you do not plan to have mechanical air conditioning, make certain of good cross ventilation. Arrange shrubs and trees to provide shade without limiting breezes. Use deciduous trees (which lose their leaves) and let in the sunshine during the winter.

Awnings or louvered bar screens may be used over windows if it is not feasible to have trees or overhang.

Window or attic fans may be used where nighttime temperatures drop sufficiently to cool the house.

One air change in the house each minute is generally needed. Use a 36-inch-diameter attic fan for a house with about 7,500 cubic feet of volume, and a 42-inch fan for 11,000 cubic feet of volume. In the Northern States and along the west coast, about two-thirds as much air is needed.

Air conditioning by central system mechanical refrigeration provides the most uniform comfort. It both cools and dehumidifies the air. In some instances a dehumidifier may also be needed to help reduce the humidity—particularly in basements during periods when air cooling isn't needed.

With mechanical refrigeration, you can keep the house closed, and even leave storm windows on the year around. Leaving the storm windows on reduces the air conditioning load, helps seal out infiltrating air, and reduces weather exposure to the regular windows, minimizing maintenance.

Besides, with the house closed, less dust and pollen enter. The aged, those with heart ailments, babies, and persons affected by dust and pollen often are helped. Less noise from the outside may be an additional benefit.

Room air conditioners mounted in windows are generally less expensive than central systems, but provide less uniform temperatures. They are noisier than well-designed central systems and shut out some light from windows where they are installed.

On the positive side, the house can be air conditioned initially with room air conditioners and additional units added as funds permit. Also, the amount of cooling in various rooms with window units can be varied.

Conditioners of small capacity operate on 115 volts, but larger ones require 208 or 230 volts. Therefore, you may need additional wiring.

Central air conditioning units can be installed in many hot air systems and thus use the same ducts for distributing cool air through the house. Insulation of ducts from cooling coils is recommended. All ducts in the attic or crawl space must be insulated to prevent condensation and conserve on refrigeration needs.

Hot air systems with small delivery ducts, such as 3-inch diameter, are not fully satisfactory for air conditioning. The higher air velocities required for cooling need more power and create undesirable noise.

New forced air cooling systems may be installed in the basement, hung from the ceiling in central halls where the ceiling heights permit, or placed in the attic. The cooling coils are frequently placed in the attic and the cooled air is distributed to ceiling outlets when air conditioning an existing house with baseboard heat.

Many modern warm-air furnaces will accept the cooling coils of an air conditioning system. This facilitates the installation of air conditioning in existing homes.

Do-it-yourself air conditioning equipment is available for homes with warm-air central heating systems having furnaces that will accept the cooling coils. Some wiring, plumbing, and handyman expertise is essential for making this installation.

It is important that the correct size equipment be installed to obtain optimum humidity modification.

In dry climates, including the western half of Texas and most other areas of the Southwest, evaporative type coolers are used. These are also referred to as "wetted pad," "pad and fan," and "swamp" type coolers. They are satisfactory for many people.

Evaporative coolers draw outside air through wetted pads. The air picks up moisture, increases in relative humidity, and decreases in temperature. This cooled air is then discharged into the house and exhausted, usually through a window opened on the opposite side of the room or house.

Evaporative coolers usually provide 20 to 40 air changes per hour. From 5 to 10 gallons of water per hour are used for a house of average size. They are less expensive than mechanical refrigeration.

Reports indicate that evaporative coolers are only effective when the outside temperature is 90°F. or above simultaneously with wet-bulb temperatures of 75°F. and below. (Wet bulb is the 100 percent saturation temperature, or the lowest temperature which water evaporation will produce in that air).

For more precise information, check with the Weather Bureau on the number of hours per year in your area when the temperature (dry-bulb) is 90°F. or above simultaneously with wet-bulb temperatures of 75°F. and below. Compare this total with the total number of hours during the year when cooling is desirable. This will give you an idea of the percent of time that an evaporative cooler would be effective.

Experience indicates that most people find evaporative coolers quite adequate if weather data indicate effective cooling 90 percent of the time as figured above.

In areas of 80 percent effectiveness, the refrigerant type of air conditioning is preferred, but the evaporative type is a good investment if the former is too costly.

In areas of less than 80 percent effectiveness, the evaporative cooler is not recommended but is much preferred to none at all.

Operation and maintenance tips for your heating and cooling equipment are helpful. Central system, warm air equipment probably requires the most maintenance.

Especially if you do not have a service contract, some scheduled service is desirable. It may save a few expensive service calls.

It is helpful to obtain operation and maintenance information from the manufacturer. Different types of motors need different service. In any event, they should be inspected once or twice a year. The dust should be cleaned off. If there are oil openings, a few drops of motor oil (non-detergent) is usually in order if the motor has been in service for some time and specific information is not available.

Too much oil can be harmful. It is messy and collects dust. Accumulations of dust interfere with normal motor operation and can cause overheating.

Fan belts should be inspected for wear and tension, although the mounting is usually such that the motor weight provides constant tension. Fan bearings should be checked for wear. Some require oiling, if they have become worn; it is usually difficult to maintain oil in them.

Servicing the air filter is probably the most important and most frequent maintenance requirement. Dust restricts air flow—thus system efficiency is reduced. Most systems have disposable filters although washable filters are available. These are also called rough or mechanical filters.

Tests have shown that mechanical filters having an adhesive (not necessarily sticky) coating for the particles to adhere to are more efficient. Some may be fairly effective on ragweed pollen. Efficiency depends upon the adhesive used and the velocity of air through the filter (the higher the velocity the lower the efficiency).

Electrostatic filters are available in both the portable type and for installation in central systems. It is estimated that 140,000 were installed in residences in 1972. Although more costly to install, they are in general more efficient. They must be cleaned quite often, but are available with an automatic cleaning (washing) feature.

Tests have shown that electrostatic filters can efficiently remove some bacteria from air. Trade information recognizes the ability of these filters to remove smoke particles from the air.

A properly installed mechanical air conditioner will provide acceptable temperature control. The humidity, however, is not controlled. It is only reduced when the air conditioner operates. The more the air conditioner operates the more dehumidification the house receives. Obviously, the design and size selection of the air conditioner are important as they affect the amount of dehumidification you will receive.

Fortunately, some of the things you do to effect improved climate control will not only improve comfort but they will reduce heating costs and help national conservation of energy. These include attic and wall insulation, as well as insulation of the floors of houses without basements.

Windows and doors should receive special attention. Those that open need weatherstripping. In most climates, storm doors and windows should be a must. Insulating glass will cut the heat loss through picture windows and glass patio doors in half.

Wood window sash has been recommended over metal because of its insulating properties. In comparative studies, it has been reported that wood rates as a far better insulator than metal.

Loose windows without weatherstripping or storm windows was comparable to having holes in the wall the size of three building blocks.

In severe climates, triple-glazing is recommended. Storm windows can serve as one layer of glazing.

In addition to increased comfort and reduced heat loss, double and triple glazing will usually prevent condensation. This not only helps maintain higher humidity on cold dry days, but reduces interior paint deterioration on windows and sills.

Adequate insulation is not only an important factor in attaining desirable comfort and climate control, it also saves in operating costs. Installation of smaller size heating and cooling equipment is possible, the cost of monthly operation is less, and an important natural resource (energy) is saved during the life of the house.

Variations in the climate, the cost of insulation, the cost of heating and cooling equipment, the cost of borrowing money, and the local energy rates are important.

As an example of optimum insulation for electric heating, calculations made in 1963 show the most economical

thickness of attic insulation to be 9 inches. This is for moderate climates of 3,500 (Mid-Atlantic) degree days, 1.5 cents per kilowatt-hour, and other practical considerations. When energy costs 2 cents per kilowatt-hour, the most economical thickness increases to 10 inches.

For the more extreme weather conditions of 8,000 (Northern States) degree days, the two cases cited above become 13 and 14 inches of ceiling insulation.

Remodeling a Home: What's Involved

THE EXTENSIVE REMODELING of a home requires careful planning. Ask yourself these questions:

Is the house worth remodeling?

What structural changes or improvements will I have to make?

What kind of plan can I work out?

Will I have to add on?

Will the wiring, plumbing, and heating have to be changed?

What will it look like when the job is completed?

Can I live in the house when the work is being done?

What will it cost?

These and other questions should be carefully studied before remodeling so you know what's involved when tackling a major project.

A structurally sound house is usually worth remodeling—someone knowledgeable on house construction could help to determine its structural condition and suggest what needs to be done to restore deteriorated or damaged parts.

Older houses often may have problems associated with one or more of the following:

FOOTING AND FOUNDATION—The footing transfers the weight of the entire building to the soil. If it fails or if the soil does not adequately support the house, structural damage may result.

The foundation wall rests on the footing and extends the weight of the building from above to the footing. The footing is normally several feet below ground level. In northern areas basements are common, with the foundation wall extending 5 to 6 feet below grade to the footing, thus providing walls for the basement. Foundation failures are often due to inadequate footings or to lateral pressure from surrounding soil.

Repairing or replacing the footing or foundation is expensive and will usually require the advice, the estimate, and the help of a professional. A foundation that has settled will usually damage the house itself and require repairs to the house.

Is there a water problem in the basement? Correcting such a problem generally is difficult and expensive. The most positive solution is to intercept the entering water before it reaches the foundation wall and divert it away. In an existing house it is not often easy or very feasible to excavate around the foundation and install tile to intercept and divert the water away.

If extensive remodeling of the basement structure is needed, can the basement be made more useful and will it fit the remodeling plan?

POSTS AND COLUMNS—Footings and posts supporting the floor system are often inadequate and should be checked to see if rotting or settling has taken place. It is advisable to repair or replace these if they have failed or settled and level the floor system before doing any remodeling.

Supports around stairways and chimneys are always a good place to look first for a settled floor system.

FLOOR FRAMING—In the basement, check the size and spacing of the floor joists and on the main floor check for a shaky floor. If the dishes rattle in the cupboards the floor will need reinforcing. Can this be done easily?

Ceiling joists or the upstairs floor joists should also be checked for firmness. A ceiling that has sagged or a shaky floor upstairs may be hard to reinforce.

Badly cracked plaster will require repairs and may indicate settling somewhere. Often all the plaster may have to be removed and replaced with new plaster or a wallboard of some type.

Look for doors that bind—this usually means settling which may be hard to correct.

In old houses, the windows should be checked for weather stripping, fit, and rot. If they have to be replaced, check to see if replacements will fit the existing openings. If a different size is installed or if the window must be moved, labor costs for installing and finishing around the new opening can be high.

INSULATION—Older houses may lack insulation. If the plaster has to come off, this is the best time to install insulation in the outside walls. Be sure to protect the insulation with a vapor barrier and make sure it fits properly. Blown in insulation is most often used when the interior wall materials can't be removed.

ROOF STRUCTURE—The roof structure protects the house and its contents from the weather. With time there is almost certain to be a problem with leaks around the chimney, next to dormers, in valleys or at the drip edge.

A systematic program of roof repair and maintenance will usually mean a sound roof structure. Repairs to a roof structure that has failed may require a great deal of labor.

CHIMNEY—The chimney may need repairs or replacement.

A chimney flue is often missing in older houses.

A chimney that shows cracks, or creosote stains, or lacks a flue, may actually be a hazard and should be replaced. Certain prefab chimneys may work as a replacement.

New masonry chimneys usually mean framing new openings through the floor and roof structure, and may require a new footing below the basement floor.

AUTHOR THEODORE J. BREVIK is Professor and Extension Agricultural Engineer, University of Wisconsin, Madison.

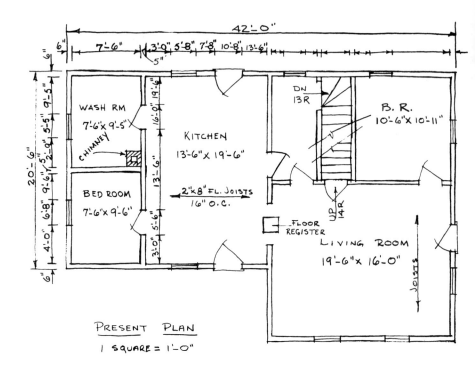

PRESENT PLAN

1 SQUARE = 1'-0"

A properly installed chimney is one that has a flue and is framed in so it is structurally free of the house frame.

On the outside, take a close look at the drainage, the gutters and downspouts, the foundation, the porches, the siding, the windows, the roof overhang, and the roof itself. Repairs and replacement of any of these will be an important part of a total remodeling project.

Assuming that the house is sound and that any structural changes or improvements are reasonable, a next step in remodeling is to develop your plan.

First, draw the present floor plan. This can be done on graph paper or more precisely on a drawing board.

Once drawn, don't erase lines on the original drawing! Use overlays of tracing paper or onion skin paper to explore various plan possibilities. If you are not satisfied with one possibility—try another. Using this process, different solutions can be compared. Sometimes combining one idea with another can result in an acceptable plan.

Remember that any plan usually means compromises. Judgments and compromises will have to be made to arrive at a plan acceptable to you.

In developing your plan, remember that walls have thickness. They are usually about 6 inches thick, but check the actual size. In planning, it is often forgotten that wall thicknesses can consume 2 feet or more of a typical house's total length.

To arrive at a desirable plan you may want to move walls or actually take some out. Because of this, it is important to know the direction of the floor joists and the ceiling joists.

In most houses one of the center walls is a bearing wall and its removal will require the substitution of a beam. This can be costly and if not done properly may weaken the entire structure. Determine which is the bearing wall and try not to change it too much in your remodeling plans.

If a suitable plan can be worked out without moving walls, the expense of

220

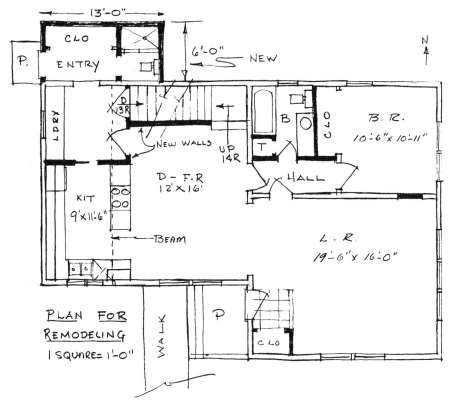

PLAN FOR REMODELING

1 SQUARE = 1'-0"

remodeling will be considerably reduced—particularly if this is done with hired labor. Doing it yourself will involve mostly materials cost.

Stairways in older houses—particularly the one leading to the basement—are often too steep or in need of extensive repair. A good stairway to the basement or to the second floor requires a floor opening of 3 to 3½ feet wide and 9 to 10 feet long. A comfortable stair step measures 7½ inches high and 9½ to 10 inches long.

Many remodeling plans are possible. To arrive at an acceptable solution, try various arrangements and then settle on the one that comes closest to meeting your needs and desires. Avoid, if possible, too many costly structural changes. The final plan should be drawn to scale on a drawing board.

Older houses often have a charm or an exterior design that is attractive and belongs to the period in which

they were built. Additions or exterior changes may alter all of this and the end result may be a house that is less attractive than before.

If the original house is attractive, it may be desirable to avoid too many exterior changes and to design any addition along the same lines as the original. Moving windows, removing porches, changing the siding, changing styles and sizes of doors and windows, will alter the house's appearance.

Most people find it hard to visualize what a house will be like after remodeling. One good approach is to check other houses that have been remodeled to see how they look. A good job will be attractive and easy to recognize. To record good ideas, use a camera as you look around.

Remodeling will almost always involve changes in the plumbing, wiring, and heating. These changes must be carefully planned and checked with any codes that may apply in your community. Beyond this it is often desirable—and good planning—to replace or update the utilities to meet present day standards.

Extensive changes require careful planning and may be costly. Be sure any changes planned in the utilities are part of the total remodeling plan and included in the final cost estimates.

The neighborhood where you live will be a factor in deciding if you should or should not remodel. Is the neighborhood changing from residential to some other use? If so, it may not be a good idea to remodel extensively. The value of residential property may be on the decline and an investment in extensive remodeling may be difficult to recover if you were to sell.

Included in your decision should be such factors as access to schools, churches, parks, shopping, transportation, and places of employment. If your neighborhood is attractive, well maintained, relatively free from noise, heavy traffic and the like, the decision to remodel may be a sound one.

Determining the cost of remodeling may be the most difficult problem of all. In most cases, remodeling will usually exceed the expected costs. Remodeling will almost always cost more than doing the same thing if you were to build new, so it is most important that complete plans be developed before undertaking major remodeling.

Be sure, too, to get accurate cost estimates. There have been many cases where the cost of remodeling exceeded the estimates. Plans, specifications, and complete details are very important if the final cost estimates are to come close to the actual cost of doing the remodeling.

It has often been said that if you spend more than two-thirds the cost of a new house, the cost of remodeling may be hard to justify.

For further reading:

Rosenberg, Charlotte L. "Which Home Improvements Will Pay Off?", *Medical Economics*, September 25, 1972, pp. 146–153.

Taking the Work Out of Housework

You can greatly simplify housework. Carefully analyze the house plan when selecting a house or planning to have one built. Select furnishings that will require a minimum of maintenance. Use effective cleaning supplies and equipment. Develop efficient cleaning methods.

It helps to approach the task with a positive attitude, too.

A well-planned home should function efficiently, be esthetically pleasing, and yet stay within the economic resources of the occupants.

Base your decisions about family housing on the family's needs, values, and resources. Size of the family, the ages and sex of family members, and their interests and activities now and in the future should be carefully weighed in determining the number and size of rooms needed.

Circulation through the house should be direct, convenient, and logical. Entryways are the control centers for circulation throughout the house. Family members or guests should be able to reach other areas of the house without interfering with activities in any room.

Consider the traffic flow at the outside entrance, too. Much of the family traffic will be from this entrance to various parts of the house. Direct access to a cleanup area is desirable, especially in the farm home or beach house. Removal of dirt as near the entrance as possible will reduce the amount of cleaning later needed throughout the house.

Adequate storage for coats, boots, and other outdoor wear near the entrance will reduce the amount of traffic through the house and provide for better care of garments. When rods

Top, unit like this built on a blank wall encourages kids to keep toys and books picked up. Below, well planned closet features clothing rods within reach of youngster. Left, medicine cabinet on bathroom end wall extends from counter top to ceiling.

or hooks are within their reach, children can get and return their coats, thus eliminating much of the picking up after them.

Adequate storage areas throughout the house are essential for efficient organization of personal and family possessions. Well planned storage areas provide for items to be stored in the area where they are used.

Highest priority in the planning of storage space should be given to the items needed most frequently. Items used less frequently may be stored at less convenient locations. Have storage areas for the frequently needed items readily visible and in easy reach of those most likely to be using them.

Fortunately, storage facilities can be greatly improved in most homes by using the existing storage space more efficiently. Carefully evaluate items requiring storage space before expending time, energy, and money to provide additional space and facilities.

Flexibility is the key word to keep in mind as storage areas are being

Top, drawers built into child's bed can store blankets or toys. Bookcase may be used for toys now and books later. Above, pull-out trays give easy access in kitchen.

224

developed. Space requirements may differ with new interests and activities of family members and with changes in products in the marketplace.

In small homes, where every inch of space is important, built-in storage areas can use the space to better advantage and reduce the number of furniture pieces required, thus creating a feeling of more space. Adjustable shelves, turntables, and drawer dividers all improve the efficiency of cabinets. You can secure these features in quality cabinets today, or you may add some of them to improve your existing cabinets.

Meal preparation and cleanup can be greatly simplified if the kitchen is convenient. Design the kitchen work area small enough to save steps, but large enough to provide the necessary work and storage space.

When you devote too much space to work centers, efficiency is lost. Too little space means preparation and cleanup in cramped quarters. Inadequate work space usually results in inadequate storage space.

Efficiently organized work centers permit you to proceed from one center to the next without retracing steps. Each center should include the utensils and supplies needed to perform the task relating to the appliance in that center.

Careful selection of portable appliances can speed up food preparation and reduce the energy required to perform frequent tasks. Cleanup after meals will be greatly simplified by use of a garbage disposal, automatic dishwasher, and trash compactor. The dining area where most family meals are served should be adjacent to the food preparation areas for the greatest convenience.

Next to meal preparation, the cleaning, pressing, and mending of family clothing and household linens requires the greatest effort by homemakers.

Time and energy required to launder the family's clothing and household linens can be reduced to a minimum when care required is one of the criteria considered in purchases. Easy care fabrics and today's laundry appliances can greatly reduce the time involved in keeping the family's clothing and household linens in good condition.

Plan your laundry center, preferably a complete clothes care center, in a central location in your home. Include adequate space for storing and sorting items to be laundered. A laundry chute in multi-storied homes would be advantageous.

A sink next to the washer will save you steps in pretreating garments or doing hand laundry. Plan cabinet space to keep laundry supplies above or near the washer. Provide room for folding and hanging items as you remove them from the dryer.

Allow space for using and storing the iron and ironing board.

Mending can be easily done either before or after laundering if you have the sewing machine and mending supplies in this area, too.

Arrange equipment, work surfaces, and storage areas so work may progress in a logical sequence. Good lighting is essential.

Provide adequate storage for your household cleaning supplies and equipment at a central location so they are readily available for use. Store cleaning supplies out of reach of small children.

Housing with snug fitting doors and windows will reduce the amount of dirt and dust coming into the house. Air conditioning with filter systems will aid in meeting this goal. Clean mats at the entrances will help remove dirt from shoes or boots, thus reducing the amount of dirt tracked in. Mats placed inside the doors on rainy days will further reduce the need for cleaning later.

Select durable and easy-care floor surface materials for areas of the house with heavy traffic or where soiling is

AUTHOR GLENDA L. PIFER is Housing Specialist, Home Economics, Extension Service.

more apt to occur. Study characteristics of various floor coverings before making a purchase.

Hard surface floor coverings with pattern and color all the way through show wear less and last longer than those with only a surface pattern or color. Other characteristics to be considered are personal or family preference and cost.

A certain amount of routine cleaning is inevitable. It becomes less drudgery when you develop a workable plan of attack and a positive attitude.

Appropriate cleaning action is determined by the type of soil to be removed and the surface on which the soil is located.

Routine cleaning becomes more complicated when several different types of floor surface materials have been selected which require different cleaning methods, supplies, and equipment. Keep in mind that all surfaces require some care. The amount will depend upon the surface involved, its location in the house, and the frequency and way in which the area is used.

Floor surfaces should be cleaned

Top left, restaurant utensil rack and butcher's meat hooks provide storage for pots and pans. Other items are stored on pegs and shelves. Top right, double pantry for kitchen needs. Above, kitchen clean-up center planned with efficiency in mind.

regularly to prevent damage, for sanitation, and for appearance. Hard surfaces may be scratched when grit and other objects are walked on. Carpet fibers are cut when grit becomes embedded.

A vacuum cleaner will take up more dust and grit than a dust mop or broom. A central vacuum system may make removal of dust and grit easier

Top, lacquer, varnish, or wood wax finish aids cleaning of paneling on walls and ceiling. Above, homemaker attaches hose to central vacuum cleaning system.

since there is less equipment to get ready to use and then to put away. If you don't have a central system installed, be sure to have convenient placement of electrical outlets for attaching your vacuum cleaner.

Good suction, plus brushing and beating action from a vacuum cleaner are essential for good care of carpet and rugs. Suction alone is adequate for cleaning smooth surface floor coverings and for above-the-floor cleaning.

Spots should be removed from carpets and rugs promptly to avoid the possibility of permanent spotting or other damage.

Spots and the all-over film that accumulates upon a hard surface floor covering may be removed by washing with a solution of detergent water or a commercial product. Be sure the product can be used safely on the surface you wish to clean, and follow the manufacturer's directions.

Some floor surfaces will be easier to maintain if wax is applied after the floor has been thoroughly cleaned and dried. Be sure to get a wax that is recommended for the kind of floor covering you have.

Carpets and rugs need to be cleaned from time to time either by a dry cleaning method or by shampooing. In shampooing be extremely careful not to get the backing wet. Many people prefer to have this job done by a reliable professional.

Walls account for a large amount of surface area. They may be easy or difficult to maintain depending upon the materials used, the finish or covering applied, and the amount of use or contact.

Pick wall materials or finishes that will resist dirt or stains and withstand some type of cleaning. Wood, brick, glass, and ceramic tile are examples of extremely durable wall surfaces. Materials one usually thinks of as typical floor coverings such as carpeting or vinyls can serve as durable and relatively easy-to-maintain wall coverings.

Wallpaper and painted surfaces are more common wall coverings. These finishes are less expensive and less durable, yet relatively easy to replace.

Wall surfaces are more apt to become soiled around light switch plates, the range area, or in children's play areas. You can remove soil from these or other such areas if the wallpaper is capable of being washed or cleaned with a dough type cleaner. Painted surfaces may be washed or a small area repainted without showing. A thin coat of clear wax will protect a paneled surface from becoming scratched or otherwise damaged and will make cleaning easier.

Sharing home care responsibilities with all members of the family helps get tasks done, provides a chance for family members to work together, and teaches children how to care for a home and to assume responsibility. Allow children some choices in the tasks they perform and give them recognition for jobs well done. Change tasks from time to time and be sure they are appropriate for the age, size, and maturity of each child.

228

Barrier-Free Housing For the Handicapped

SPECIAL CONCERN is needed to make a house barrier-free for handicapped individuals. While many measurements based on averages are given in this chapter, the measurements which are most basic are those of the particular disabled individual—which allow him or her to function effectively.

Function has long been a primary consideration in family housing. However, it becomes even more important when planning homes for the wheelchair-confined, persons using walkers or crutches, or individuals with stiffness of joints, impaired coordination, and lessened energy.

Every physically handicapped person, whether disabled by accident, disease or old age, can be benefited by adjustments in housing. And any of us may become disabled!

Physical handicaps come in various types and degrees for individuals of all ages and of both sexes, so planning housing for the disabled becomes an individual affair. Housing designed for an individual's special needs, whether temporary or permanent, makes a difference in the personal development and happiness not only of the individual with the physical limitation but also for his or her family.

A person's self-concept has a direct relationship to his ability to "do" for himself. Functional housing, barrier-free, makes possible many capabilities for independent living.

During the past 25 years, research has been conducted in rehabilitation centers, colleges and schools of home economics, and by architects in a variety of settings. It focused on ways in which individuals can be independent in daily living activities. Yet many individuals, unfortunately, continue to live in environments with architectural bar-

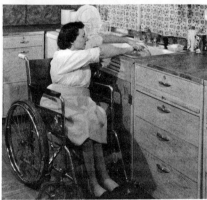

Top, when homemaker in a wheelchair can get to her work counter, she is able to continue with household responsibilities. Above, counter level is too high, and the closed undersink front creates a barrier.

riers which limit their capacity to live independently.

Housing should be adjusted to the needs of individuals whether they are disabled or not. Requirements for the physically disabled often become the "best" and safest arrangement for all persons.

Studies have produced basic measurements from which housing can be planned. For instance, the standard wheelchair decreases a person's height by one-third, and doubles his width. A path at least 3 feet wide is needed for travel in a straight line. Almost 5 feet of straight travel are needed before negotiating a turn and 25 square feet (at least 5 feet by 5 feet) of clear area are needed for a turnabout.

For the wheelchair-confined, the underside of work surfaces should be a clear 30 inches from the floor. Width of the knee space should be at least 28 inches. Usually 30 inches are allowed for seating space at work surface or table.

Most wheelchair users can negotiate hallways 4 feet wide (4½ feet is recommended), and straight line travel through a doorway which is 2 feet 8 inches if the door opens 180° (otherwise, 2 feet 10 inches is recommended). A 90° wheelchair turn through a doorway requires a 36-inch doorway and a 42-inch hallway.

The average height for a woman is 5 feet 4½ inches. She will have a reach from floor to upward extended wrist of 6 feet when standing but only 4 feet 3 inches when sitting in a wheelchair using a forward vertical reach.

A relatively new concept in wheelchairs is now on the market. This chair is on a platform measuring 18 inches by 35 inches. Motorized wheels and a steering-handle are included. Dimensions for barrier-free housing would be quite different for this wheelchair.

An individual on crutches who is 5 feet 6 inches tall requires an average of 31 inches between crutch tips in a normal gait. An individual who is 6 feet tall requires slightly over 32 inches between crutch tips.

Because relatively few individuals are of the so-called average size and because of the assortment of kinds and sizes of wheelchairs, individual measurements may be entirely different from the average.

AUTHOR LOIS O. SCHWAB is an Associate Professor in the Department of Education and Family Resources, College of Home Economics, University of Nebraska–Lincoln.

229

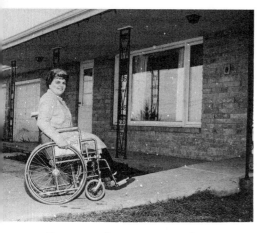

Ramp can be attractive and inviting as entrance to a home.

This chapter carries guidelines in the form of a checklist based on research for two of the main types of problems faced by the physically disabled (the *wheelchair-confined* and the *ambulatory* with crutches, cane, or walker) for various aspects of the physical structure of the house. A checklist also is furnished for analyzing the home in terms of needs of the visually impaired.

Houses are built for persons. They must be functional and barrier-free for all—including individuals with physical disabilities.

CHECKLIST FOR ANALYZING THE HOME FOR THE WHEELCHAIR-CONFINED AND THE AMBULATORY WITH MOBILITY PROBLEMS

Wheel-chair	Ambula-tory	Carport or Garage
———	———	Is the carport/garage at least 13 feet wide?
———	———	Is there a covered entrance from carport to house?
———		Is the entrance to the house from carport/garage ramped with no more than a 5° slope?

° Ambulatory refers to the physically limited, having to use crutches, cane, or walker.

Wheel-chair	Ambula-tory	Entrance
———	———	Is at least one outside entrance ramped (no steeper than 1 foot rise for every 12 feet length) or at ground level?
———	———	Are thresholds flush with floor or less than ½ inch higher than the floor?
———		Does doorway have a clear, unobstructed opening at least 32 inches wide?
———	———	If ramp is longer than 20 feet, is there a 5 foot landing every 20 feet?
———	———	If there are steps in the walks, are there also ramps to bypass the steps?
———	———	Is the ramp at least 4 feet wide?
———	———	Are handrails mounted on at least one side of the ramp?
———	———	Are the handrails 32 inches from the floor of the ramp?
———	———	Is there a landing of at least 5 feet by 5 feet adjacent to the door? The landing should also extend at least 1 foot beyond each side of the door.
———		Is the doorknob 36 inches above ground level?
———	———	Are lever-type handles or ones equally easy to use installed?
———	———	Is there a kickplate on the door?
———	———	Is the entrance sheltered by an overhung roof?
———	———	Are halls wide enough for wheelchair passage and maneuvering (42-inch minimum suggested)?
	———	Do handrails extend beyond top and bottom step? Handrails should not extend beyond top or project into traffic areas and doorways.
	———	Do steps have rounded nosing with sloping risers?

Wheel-chair	Ambula-tory	Entrance
	———	Are step risers no greater than 7 inches high (6 inches recommended)?
	———	Are step risers no less than 10 inches wide (11 inches including nosing area)?
———		Is there an elevator (cab 4 feet wide by 6 feet in depth) to bypass stairs, if the wheelchair-confined should have use of other floors? Note: Location of all functional areas on one level may be preferable.

Allow ample footing on steps. This should be no less than 10 inches.

Wheel-chair	Ambula-tory	Floors
———	———	Do floors have a nonslip surface (new surface finishes provide alternatives)?
———	———	If floors are carpeted, are they easy to maneuver over (deep shag carpeting is often difficult)?
———	———	Have small scatter rugs been eliminated?

Wheel-chair	Ambula-tory	Lights, Switches, and Controls
———		Are switches horizontally aligned with door handles at 36 inches from floor?
———		Are electric outlets not lower than 2 feet, preferably 3 feet above floor?
———	———	Are there master switches in kitchen, living room, and bedroom?

Wheel-chair	Ambula-tory	Lights, Switches, and Controls
———	———	Is a telephone available (no higher than 48 inches) near center of house?

Wheel-chair	Ambula-tory	Doors and Windows
———	———	Do doorways have a clear, unobstructed opening at least 32 inches wide?
———	———	Are lever-type handles or ones equally easy to use installed on all inside doors?
———	———	Are thresholds flush with floor or less than ½ inch high?
———	———	Are opening and ventilating mechanisms accessible and easy to operate, such as push-bar or gear-type handles? (These should be operable with one hand by the ambulatory).
———		Do all windows have panes which begin no higher than 36 inches above floor level?
———		Are drapery pulls or controls for window covering easily accessible?

Wheel-chair	Ambula-tory	Bathroom
———		Is there room for a wheelchair to make a 180° turn, i.e., a minimum of 4 feet 3 inches, if turn is necessary for use of lavatory, toilet, or tub?
———	———	° Is toilet equipped with grab bars on both sides, 26-33 inches from floor depending on measurements of individuals?
———	———	Is toilet seat a good height for the person with the disability? (19 inch height is often preferred over standard 15-inch).

231

Wheel-chair	Ambula-tory	Bathroom
———	———	Is a bathroom close to the bedroom of the person with the disability?
———	———	Is the lavatory mounted so that person can be seated to utilize it? (This may be at 28-34 inches from floor depending on the chair and individual measurements. Some ambulatory may not wish to be seated, so the lavatory should be raised to 36 inches from floor).
———		Are soap dishes, towel rack, and toothbrush holder no higher than 40 inches from the floor?
———	———	Is it possible to unlock bathroom door from either side?
———	———	Is there a pushbutton near tub and toilet for activating an audio and visual alarm unit located outside housing unit?
———	———	Are mirror and medicine closet low enough for use from seated position?

Wheel-chair	Ambula-tory	Tub
———		*Is there a handrail (grab bar) securely mounted at either the foot or head end of the tub which can easily and safely be reached for getting in and out of tub?
———	———	*Is there a handrail mounted parallel to the length of the tub to safely facilitate sitting or rising?
———	———	Does the bottom of the tub have an abrasive anti-slip surface?
———		Does tub have a substantial bench at one end for sitting to bathe and at an appropriate height for wheelchair transfer?

Wheel-chair	Ambula-tory	Tub
———	———	Are water and temperature controls (preferably a mixing faucet with non-scald temperature control) accessible from bathing position?

Wheel-chair	Ambula-tory	Shower
———	———	Does shower stall doorway have at least 32 inches of clear opening?
———	———	Is shower stall floor level with room floor without an obstructing riser or curb?
———		Does shower stall floor have an anti-slip surface? (Tile floor should be unglazed).
	———	*Is there a handrail on at least one side of the shower stall when facing the shower head and also near the stall entrance to facilitate going in and out?
———	———	Is there a seat in the shower stall? (Seat should have a smooth, easily cleaned surface).
———	———	Is the shower equipped with a mixing faucet with non-scalding temperature control valve? (Hose-type, detachable, handheld shower head recommended).

* Grab bars should be capable of supporting 250 pounds, of nonslip finish, allow for 3-4 inches between bar and wall, and devoid of sharp corners, with ends returning to wall. Towel bars should be of grab bar quality and strength for safety because they may be accidentally used as grab bars.

		Bedroom
———		Is there a 3-foot clearance for wheelchair approach to bed?
———		Is mattress level with wheelchair seat for easier transfer?
———	———	Are telephone (or outlet for plug-in phone) and light switch within easy reach of bed?

Wheel-chair	Ambula-tory	*Bedroom*	Wheel-chair	Ambula-tory	*Kitchen*
———		Does closet have sliding or out-swinging doors and one rod no higher than 48 inches?	———	———	Does the kitchen include appropriate energy-saving equipment, that is:
———	———	Is there a pushbutton near head of bed for activating an audio and visual alarm unit located outside dwelling?			——— dishwasher
					——— electric disposal
					——— oven (or portable combination oven-broiler)
		Note: At least one bedroom should be large enough for twin beds as these are often preferred by couples.			——— electric mixer
					——— refrigerator with some freezer space, self defrosting
———	———	Is dressing table 30-32 inches high with desk-type opening of at least 28 inches?			——— range surface units
———	———	Is storage space adequate for different items at general place of use?	———		Is sink at appropriate height, i.e., 29-33 inches from floor, depending on wheelchair and individual measurements?
		——— Outerwear coats and hats	———		Does sink have desk-type opening at least 28 inches wide with insulation of hot water pipes and bowl?
		——— Suits, dresses, etc.	———		Is oven low enough for homemaker using it to remove dishes from it easily?
		——— Undergarments as slips, bras, shorts	———		Does kitchen have a minimum of 5 feet for turns between counters and walls?
		——— Bath linens			
		——— Bed linens	———	———	Are there places to set dishes when taking them from oven, range units, and refrigerator? (Each space should be at least 15 inches wide).
		——— Cleaning equipment and supplies			
			———	———	Is there reachable storage near place of first use for most used items?
		Kitchen	———		Is the refrigerator (and its freezer compartment) accessible, with easily opened doors?
———	———	Are there sit-down centers, especially a mix center? (Many ambulatory find it easier to sit down to work at any job that takes more than a few minutes).	———		Is the mix center 27-32 inches high or appropriate to the individual's measurements?

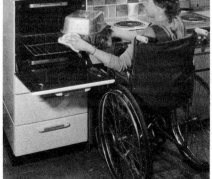

Bottom-hinged oven door can lead to an arm burn. Side-hinged door is preferable.

233

Wheel-chair	Ambula-tory	Kitchen
—		Does the mixing center have a desk-type counter with 28 inches wide opening for knees?
—	—	Is there a pullout work surface of 24-29 inches from floor?
—		Are range surface units available to individual, preferably in an arrangement so he does not have to reach over burners?
—		Is a toe space 9 inches high and 6 inches deep provided under each base cabinet?
—	—	Is the refrigerator as near as possible to the sink and mix center?
—	—	Is wheeled table available for transporting food and dishes to and from dining area?
—		Are faucets and all controls side-mounted rather than rear-mounted?

Note: Due to difficulty of reach, base cabinet space may need to be minimal. Individual range of movement will be the primary consideration in planning.

Wheel-chair	Ambula-tory	Laundry
—	—	Is the laundry area conveniently located on main floor at a point where there is the most laundry?
—		Are washer and dryer of front-loading types?
—		Are washer and dryer of top-loading types?
—	—	Is there a sit-down table for sorting and/or folding laundry?
—	—	Is there an adjustable, substantial, easy-to-handle ironing board?
—	—	Are there provisions for hanging ironed clothes and placing flat linens?
	—	Is there a comfortable chair for sit-down ironing (appropriate to individual measurements)?
	—	If outside lines are used for drying, is the area easily accessible from house?
—	—	Is a laundry cart available for carrying laundry?
—	—	Is there a convenient storage space for supplies?

Bottom-hinged door gets in the way.

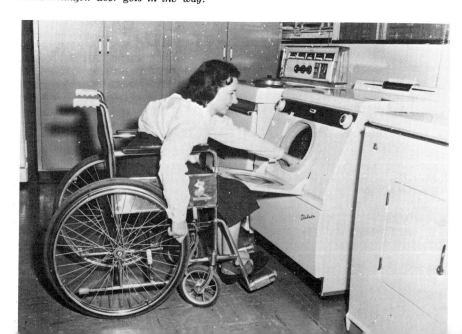

———— Are raised number or letters used on entrance doors (especially in apartment dwellings)?

Note: These numbers should be at side of door near handle 5 feet above floor.

———— Have all hanging objects under 6 feet 2 inches (depending on height of the blind person) been eliminated?

———— Is there a minimum of low tables, stools, etc., near major traffic-ways?

———— Are sliding doors used on closets and where possible to eliminate walking into an edge of a partially open door?

Door handles leading to a potentially dangerous area should be treated with knurling or special adhesive.

———— Are handles treated with knurling (or a special adhesive) on doors which lead directly to steps or other potentially dangerous area?

———— Are all push button controls identifiable by touch (such as *off* and *on* switches for lights)?

———— Are all control dials marked or shaped so fingers can feel location of dial and be able to interpret setting? (In some cases, click stops may be substituted).

———— range

———— oven

———— mixer faucets

———— Is storage adequate so that items can be stored separately (or like items on like) upon adjustable shelves—not piled high?

———— Are faucets in lavatories always arranged so the hot water faucet is on the left and the cold water faucet on the right of the user of the sink?

For further reading:

Goldsmith, Selwyn. *Designing for the Disabled, A Manual of Technical Information,* Royal Institute of British Architects, London, 1967.

Making Buildings and Facilities Accessible to, and Usable by the Physically Handicapped, American Standards Association, New York, 1961.

Making Facilities Accessible to the Physically Handicapped, Performance Criteria, State University of New York Construction Fund, Albany, N.Y., 1967.

May, Elizabeth E., Neva R. Waggoner, and Eleanor M. Boettke. *Homemaking for the Handicapped,* Dodd, Mead and Company, New York, 1966.

Rusk, Howard A., and others. *A Functional Home for Easier Living for the Physically Disabled, the Cardiac and the Elderly,* Institute of Physical Medicine and Rehabilitation, New York, 1959.

U.S. Department of the Interior. *Housing for the Physically Impaired, A Guide for Planning and Design,* Washington, D.C., 1968.

Women's Committee, President's Committee on Employment of the Handicapped, *Homemaker Rehabilitation,* A Selected Bibliography, Washington, D.C. 20210, 1972.

Household Insect Pests, and Ways To Control Them

Many species of insects can temporarily invade or live continuously in our homes. Most of us consider even a single insect to be a pest when we find it in the house. The first thought is to get rid of it. Then questions come to mind about what it is, where it came from, whether there are more around, what damage they may cause, and how to eliminate or prevent an infestation. This chapter will discuss some of those questions and tell you where to get the answers to others.

The actual importance of insects as household pests varies tremendously, according to the kind involved and the numbers present. A number are nothing more than a nuisance or an annoyance. Some people, however, detest or fear insects to the extent that their mere presence is a major disaster. A few kinds of insects will sting or bite, while others can carry diseases. The reference to diseases is not made to scare you, because none of the house flies, cockroaches, mosquitos, or fleas you see may have had a chance to become infected with disease germs. But the potential does exist.

Some species of insects get into our dry food products. The fact that an insect or two has been in such food is not esthetically acceptable to most people. After the insects have lived and multiplied in the product for a time it can become contaminated or consumed to the extent that it is no longer suitable for food. Considerable quantities of food are thus ruined in kitchen cupboards and pantries.

AUTHOR LYMAN S. HENDERSON is a staff scientist on the National Program Staff, Agricultural Research Service.

Still other insects feed on wool, and damage clothing and fabrics. Then there is a group of insects that lives on wood. They can attack the timbers in a home and damage, weaken, or even destroy a structure if not controlled. Some will also attack wooden furniture.

As a result of all this, insects cause a loss of hundreds of millions of dollars every year to our homes, food, and personal belongings. It is well worth the expenditure of some time and effort to reduce these losses.

Those who have not studied insects are amazed over the number of kinds that can be found in or around homes, and wonder where they come from. Insects are the most abundant animals on earth and several hundred thousand different kinds exist just in the United States. They usually live out in nature, in the yard and the surrounding areas of fields, pastures, and forests.

It is not surprising that some insects should stray into the house occasionally through an open window or door. Many kinds are attracted to lights and some are small enough to squeeze through the cracks around doors or screen frames. Others can even get through the mesh of ordinary screens. There is no reason to be concerned about most such insects. They will not harm anythings in the house, cannot live long indoors, and some are actually beneficial in nature.

You will often find dead insects on the windowsills and around the baseboards where they perished trying to get back outdoors. Many of these will be midges, gnats, and small leafhoppers or beetles. Of the larger beetles and moths attracted to lights, an occasional one will get into the house. The moths, sometimes called "millers," are not the kinds that attack woolens or live in our dry foods.

Other insect pests invade our homes under various conditions. In this article the term insect is used in its broad sense to include some closely related species that are not true insects.

When conditions outside get excessively hot, dry, or wet, some pests will crawl into houses. Or heavy populations may build up, and the insects are on the move in search of a new food supply. Others just wander in.

Few houses are constructed tightly enough to avoid cracks or small openings where these insects can enter. They are most troublesome in basements, the ground floors of garden-type apartment complexes, or houses on slab construction. The pests may include millipedes, centipedes, crickets, earwigs, ground beetles, or some kinds of ants and spiders. Most of these pests are harmless except for annoyance, and they soon die indoors.

Exceptions to the harmless invaders are scorpions and one or two kinds of poisonous spiders. They occur mostly in the Southern States. Fleas and biting mites can invade homes from bird or rodent nests around or in the structure. Permanent relief will depend upon eliminating the bird nests or the rodents. The use of sprays will give temporary relief from insects in the house at the time, as with other kinds of invading insects.

Other obnoxious invaders include several kinds of mosquitoes, and some other small biting flies, occasionally called gnats, midges, or punkies. Some temporary protective sprays against mosquitoes can be applied around patios, yards, or picnic areas. The best approach is a community, county, or State mosquito control program.

Stinging insects of the wasp group may also get into the house once in a while. Bees, wasps, hornets, and yellowjackets may nest under the eaves or porch ceilings, in shrubs, or in the lawn around the house. Insecticides can be applied to kill out the nests. Such treatments can be made most safely at dusk or after dark, when the insects have become quiet.

Still another group of insects invades houses in the fall when seeking a protected place to spend their winter period of hibernation. These include clover mites, boxelder bugs, cluster flies, face flies, and some of the wasps. They usually get into attics or the space between outer and inner walls of the structure near a door or window.

A few may wander into the interior of the house while they are looking for hibernation quarters. They are more of a nuisance in the spring when they become active and numbers of them become confused, entering rooms rather than finding their way outdoors where they wish to be.

Up till now, most of the discussion has been about the numerous outdoor insects that can incidentally or accidentally invade your home and become temporary residents. A more important group of 50 or more kinds of insects are true household pests. They can live and multiply continuously inside our homes.

Originally these insects were all inhabitants of nature outdoors, and some still are. But as man has gradually become more civilized over the centuries, some insects have become domesticated along with him.

It is easy to believe that as early man began to make pallets and sleep in caves, bedbugs were ready to move in with him from the nests of bats, birds, or animals in the caves. As those men began to bring seeds and nuts into their caves for a reserve food supply, they brought in the insects that were feeding on them. Other insects that lived on the seeds that rodents brought into their burrows also found man's stored-up food supplies.

As man began to build permanent shelters and warm them with fires, other insects such as cockroaches moved in with him.

There are interesting accounts of the problems with household-type insects in the ancient sailing vessels that were at sea for weeks at a time without touching a port. "Weavels" fouled or destroyed food. Bedbugs and lice infested the sailors' bunks and clothing. Cockroaches became abundant.

What we have done in our modern homes is to create a set of conditions so favorable that some insects would rather live with us than outside in the rigors of nature.

Insects are quite adaptable and seem to be so ingenious that they have no trouble in finding and becoming accustomed to the comfort of our homes. We provide a temperature that is mild, favorable, and rather constant. Plenty of food is always available to meet their varied dietary needs, which may include our own food, some of our possessions, our blood or that of our pets, or structural timbers of our homes.

The so-called household insects are universally distributed and abundant in numbers. There are many places from which they can fly, crawl, or be introduced with the things we bring into our homes.

Cockroaches are among the most obnoxious pests to many people. Five species inhabit homes. About 50 others live in the United States and some may be attracted to lights or be brought in with firewood, but most of them cannot develop in the house.

Cockroaches are easy to control in most homes. Thorough sanitation and good housekeeping are highly important, to remove available food supplies. Insecticides can then wipe out an infestation.

Under some conditions there may be a continuing problem of cockroaches entering a home from the outside or from adjacent apartments or premises. To counter this problem, first try to close up all the openings you can through which they enter. Then apply a surface spray to the typical hiding places for cockroaches. This will kill them as they come in and prevent them from becoming established or multiplying in your home.

Occasionally cockroaches will crawl into prepackaged items or cartons in the back room of a food store or in a warehouse. They can be just waiting for a free ride into your home, so check such things if there is reason to question your source of supply.

Another common way in which cockroaches are brought into homes is when used furniture, TV sets, refrigerators, or kitchen ranges are moved in from an infested house.

Several kinds of ants may be troublesome household pests. They may march in lines to your kitchen from nests outside the house. Other kinds will build their nests within the walls or partitions of the house. Try to find the nest and treat it with an insecticide. Close up openings and cracks through which ants enter. Apply a surface spray to entrance cracks and places where the ants crawl. Keep food where they cannot get into it.

About a dozen kinds of beetles or moths infest dry foods. They are often called weevils but most of them are not true weevils. They may be in flour, meal, breakfast cereals, crackers, spices, macaroni, spaghetti, prepared mixes, nut meats, dried fruits, even in dry pet food or birdseed.

Many people blame the manufacturer of these products for the infestation. It is most likely to have occurred after the product left the processing or packaging plant. There is a complex system of shipments and storage points before these foods get to your home. Insects are lurking at many places to invade the packages.

Cross infestation of products often occurs right in the home cupboard, especially when partially used bags or boxes of products are put at the back of a shelf and may stay there for weeks or months.

Fabric insect pests are not as serious a problem now that we have so many synthetic fibers which are resistant to insect attack.

There are still substantial numbers of wool suits, sweaters, skirts, and carpets, however, which can suffer expensive damage from carpet beetles or from clothes moths.

A heavy request continues for the USDA Home and Garden Bulletin No. 113, *Protecting Woolens Against Clothes Moths and Carpet Beetles*. It describes the preventive and control measures to be carried out.

There is an erroneous belief that fabrics of mixed wool and synthetic fibers will not be damaged. The insects will selectively feed on the wool thread

Firebrat.

and can make lacework out of such a fabric. The fabric insects also feed on fur and feathers. They do not attack cotton goods, but silverfish and cockroaches will, probably because of the added starch. The latter insects also feed on rayon, apparently attracted by the sizing.

Silverfish like cool, damp places such as basements. Firebrats are similar in appearance but prefer warm places such as attics in summer and furnace rooms in winter. Both hide during the day and move about at night. You are likely to find them in a bathtub. They did not come out of the drain but were trapped in the tub. They eat foods high in protein, sugar, or starch, and feed on paper coated with sizing, glue, or paste. They are easily controlled with sprays or dusts.

House flies and blow flies are troublesome in some locations or at certain times of the year. A primary defense is proper care of garbage and the elimination of decaying organic matter that attracts the flies or on which they can develop. Good screens help keep flies out of the house and fly sprays will kill those that get in despite all else you do.

House spiders are a nuisance largely because of their webbing. They can be picked up along with their webs by the hose attachments of a vacuum cleaner, or are easily killed with sprays.

Ordinary house spiders are not dangerous. It would be a good idea to obtain literature on the black widow and brown recluse spiders so you can recognize them and know what to do if you find or are bitten by one. Both are poisonous and can invade houses from the outdoors.

Bedbugs are not the common and feared pests they were a few years ago. Yet they can still show up in mansions, ordinary houses, or dives. Several insecticides will effectively control them.

Pets have become an integral part of many families. There is always the possibility of them getting ticks or fleas, some of which can become established in the home or lawn. The fleas will also bite humans, but the brown dog tick that lives in the house feeds only on dogs.

The structure of the home can be attacked by subterranean termites, dry wood termites, powder post beetles, wood borers, carpenter ants, or carpenter bees. Some of the powder post beetles also attack wooden furniture. Various preventive or remedial construction features or insecticide treatments can help. You should obtain bulletins describing these. You may find you need to call in a pest control operator who specializes in such work.

The discussion till now has given some background and indicated the more common and most important household insect pests. In a few cases the importance of preventive measures has been stressed. The same thought applies to most kinds of infestation. Closing up small openings in buildings has been mentioned, and calking compound is useful for this purpose. Screens on windows and doors must be installed so the frames fit tightly. The screen loses part of its effectiveness if there are even small gaps around the frame where insects can squeeze through. And the screening is of little value if not maintained to repair punc-, tures, rips, and tears.

Sanitation and good housekeeping are key preventive measures against many pests, often outside the house as well as inside. This helps to eliminate harborages for unwanted pests and reduces the amount of food material available to attract insects or support a growing population. It takes only a few words to tell you about cleanliness, but do not let that mislead you as to how large a part it plays in avoiding infestations.

Several kinds of insecticides or their combinations can be used safely and effectively in the home. These materials are sold under a wide variety of brand names.

Some insecticides are only effective against certain insects and are of little value or useless against others. Insecticides are formulated in different ways for particular types of applications. Being confronted by an array of these insecticides on the store counter can be puzzling, even confusing.

Fortunately, the labeling of insecticides is controlled by a law. It is administered by the Environmental Protection Agency, which only approves for home use the materials that are effective and safe. The label must state the kind of insecticides present as the active ingredient.

Many of the insecticides have long, complex technical names. A slight difference in some part of the name may indicate a completely different kind of chemical, or it may only be another way of designating the same chemical. Most labels also give you the common name of the insecticide, by which it is more easily recognized.

The label must also tell what kinds of insects it is to be used against, give at least basic instructions for use, and describe any precautions that are to be exercised in handling or applying the insecticide.

Therefore an excellent guideline is to "READ THE LABEL."

It is most important to know the kind of insect to be controlled in order to select the right insecticide to be effective, and to know how and where to make the application. There are several ways to find the identity of an insect you may not recognize. Some people may not realize that the larva, or immature stage, of a fly, beetle, or moth looks nothing like the adult stage. The larvae are sometimes called maggots, "worms," or caterpillars.

You can take or send insects to your county agricultural agent, State extension entomologist, or the department of entomology at your State university for identification. From those same places you can also find out what insecticide is best to use for that kind of insect.

Many states have excellent bulletins on household insect pests and how to control them. In some instances there are separate bulletins on individual kinds of pests. Such bulletins are also available from the U.S. Department of Agriculture.

Some people do not wish to take the time or trouble to deal with an insect infestation. Others may encounter a situation where an infestation is deep seated, persistent, or difficult to control. In those cases the best thing to do is to call in a professional pest control operator.

Many reputable firms have experienced, trained personnel and the right kinds of equipment and insecticides to do an effective job. For effective prevention or control of some pests it is necessary to spray or dust underneath, outside, or around the house. In such cases the experience and equipment of the professional operator will be helpful, or even essential.

Mention has been made of the formulation of insecticides in different ways for different applications. Space sprays are for use against flies, mosquitos, or other flying insects. You can apply them with a small hand sprayer that breaks up the liquid into a mist of small particles that float in the air for a time. Coarser particles that you can see settle down rapidly, but smaller particles may remain suspended 20 or 30 minutes longer.

240

A space spray is not very effective against crawling insects. It kills the flying insects exposed at the time of spraying, so it is only a temporary measure. For permanent relief you must eliminate the source where the insects develop or prevent them from getting into the house.

Aerosols are commonly used for space treatments because of the convenience and ease of application. They are dispensed by simply pushing a button on a pressurized container. Aerosol particles are finer than those from most handsprayers, so they stay in the air a longer time.

Surface sprays, sometimes called residual sprays, are used against crawling insects. The objective is to leave a thin deposit of insecticide that remains effective for several weeks, perhaps months. As insects crawl over the deposit they absorb some of it and are killed.

It is not necessary or desirable to treat large expanses of walls or floors with surface sprays. Limit the application to cracks and crevices, behind and underneath objects—in other words the places where these insects live or hide.

Apply just enough spray to moisten the surfaces, not so much that it runs or drips off. You can use a hand sprayer that delivers coarse, wetting particles. Fine particles as used from a space spray will mostly drift away where they do no good. You may also use a small paint brush to make a more careful application of surface sprays, especially around kitchen cabinets and shelves.

Pressurized containers are available for applying surface sprays. They have a lower pressure and a larger nozzle opening than the aerosol dispensers so they release coarser, moistening particles. Many of them are designated as a "Roach and Ant Spray". If you read the label, you will find that some may also be used against other crawling insects.

Insecticidal dusts are useful for treating inaccessible places. With a special applicator you can puff the dust through small openings and into wall

voids or into the spaces at the bases of kitchen cabinets.

Baits are sometimes used against cockroaches, house flies, ants, silverfish, crickets, or earwigs. Some baits are sold commercially and you will find formulas for preparing others.

You may be disappointed that I have not told you more about the different insects and how to control them. Those details are available in bulletins or books.

Through experience with the public, I have learned the reactions and questions asked by people who encounter a serious problem with household pests, especially for the first time. Therefore part of the discussion was to give you information that is not in official bulletins. Along with that is enough general and background information to help you understand the situation when household insects trouble you. You have also been told where to get the further information and aid you need.

I hope your preventive and control efforts are succesful!

For further reading:

U.S. Department of Agriculture, *Ants in the Home and Garden,* Home and Garden Bulletin No. 28, Superintendent of Documents, U.S. Government Printing Office, Washington, D.C. 20402—Price 10 cents.

———, *Protecting Woolens Against Clothes Moths and Carpet Beetles,* Home and Garden Bulletin No. 113, Superintendent of Documents, U.S. Government Printing Office, Washington, D.C. 20402—Price 20 cents.

Some Background On Rats and Mice

Rₐₜₛ, ᴍɪᴄᴇ, and some other animals become nuisances and occasionally serious problems. They prefer the same kinds of shelter comforts and foods that man enjoys—and if nothing is done to prevent it, they will be more than happy to move in with man at every opportunity.

Rats and mice are a source of annoyance and cause considerable damage in nearly every locality where food, clothing, or manufactured goods are processed or stored. They also transmit many types of diseases to humans and domestic livestock.

It is impossible to calculate the economic loss to the U.S. public as a result of the activities of these rodent pests. Losses of food products through contamination far exceed what they actually consume.

In addition to economic losses, it must be recognized that rat and mouse infested areas are symptoms of poor environmental planning or conditions. Our greatest concern should be to correct environmental conditions where humans coexist with these creatures.

Removal of available cover, food, and water is usually the first step in controlling rodents, followed by appropriate control methods to reduce the existing population. The only exceptions are dumps, or disease suppression efforts where population reductions should normally be effected before the environment is disturbed in order to avoid population dispersal.

To make an area less attractive to rodents, stored materials should be placed on racks 12 to 18 inches off the

ᴀᴜᴛʜᴏʀ ᴏʀᴠɪs ᴄ. ɢᴜsᴛᴀᴅ is Staff Specialist, Division of Wildlife Services, Department of the Interior.

ground, and other forms of protective cover removed. Food materials should be stored in containers or places where they are inaccessible to rats and mice.

Although mice can get along without water, rats need it every day. Therefore, removal or control of available water can be a very important factor in controlling rat populations.

Eliminating conditions favorable to these rodents must also be accomplished on adjacent areas besides the specific problem areas in order to discourage reinfestation.

To prevent reinfestation, buildings must be made as rat and mouseproof as possible. Cement, hardware cloth of ¼ inch mesh, and sheet metal of 26 gage or heavier are good materials to use.

All possible routes of entry must be effectively blocked. If rats and mice might possibly enter a building beneath the foundation, a curtain wall in the shape of an "L" (2 feet deep and extending 1 foot out) should be installed. Rats will tunnel down 3 to 4 feet, but will rarely cut around a footing of this type. Mice need only a dime-sized hole to gain entrance to a building.

Killing rats and mice without correcting environmental conditions generally accomplishes very little. People must be taught to recognize conditions which foster rats and mice, to know the signs and consequences of their presence, and how to implement the needed preventive measures—on a community basis. They should be encouraged to follow the basic principles of sanitation including proper handling, storage, and disposal of food supplies, refuse, and waste. Only then will eradication efforts give lasting results.

Rodenticides are usually the most economic, effective, and thus the most commonly used methods to reduce rat and mouse numbers. Precautions must be taken in handling rodenticides to avoid contaminating food materials and to protect humans, as well as pets and other animals, against accidental poisoning.

Although rats and mice will devour

Fundamentals of Rodent Proofing

1. Close openings over 1/2 inch in diameter to prevent access by rats, and over 1/4 inch in diameter for mice.

2. Cover all edges subject to gnawing with sheet metal or hardware cloth.

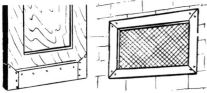

3. Concrete floors and shallow foundations should be constructed with a curtain wall around the outer edge extending 36 inches into the ground, or in an "L" shape 24 inches into the ground with a 12 inch lip extending outward.

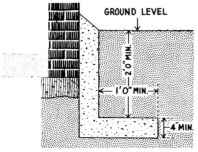

4. Extend rodent proofing to a height of 36 inches above the highest probable level of stored or piled materials.

5. Concrete foundations should be at least 12 inches above the ground level to discourage and prevent the gnawing of holes.

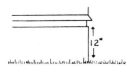

6. Sheet metal, 12 inches high, should be smoothly inserted on all corners above floor or ground level to prevent climbing.

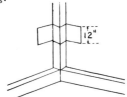

7. Check holes around pipes. Force heavy hardware cloth piece into opening, then fill with concrete. Where pipes enter wood wall, fit sheet metal around pipe.

8. Install devices to keep doors closed.

9. Keep floor drains tightly fastened to stop entry from sewers.

Recommended Materials

1. Concrete - 2 inches thick if made of precast reinforced concrete plates fastened together or at least 3-3/4 inches thick if not reinforced. Determine the proper cement mixture before undertaking concrete work.

2. Galvanized sheet metal - 24 gauge or heavier except that perforated sheet metal or grilles should be 14 gauge.

3. Brick - (regular size) 3-3/4 inches thick with joints filled with mortar.

4. Hardware cloth - 19 gauge 1/2 x 1/2 inch mesh to exclude rats, 24 gauge 1/4 x 1/4 inch to exclude mice and rats.

5. Aluminum - 22 gauge for frames and flashings, 20 gauge for kickplates, and 18 gauge for guards.

almost any kind of food available—and are often associated with filth—their bait materials should be kept fresh and clean, and should be of a quality as good or better than their regular food source.

These rodents seek as much shelter and protection as possible in their movements, and baits placed in, under, and around shelters are far more likely to be found and consumed than those exposed in the open. Proper placement

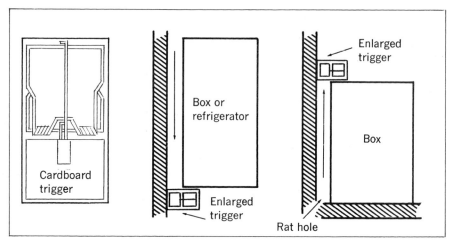

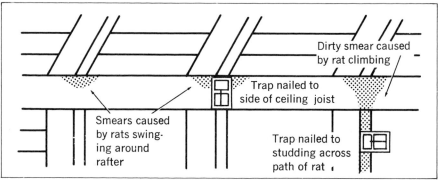

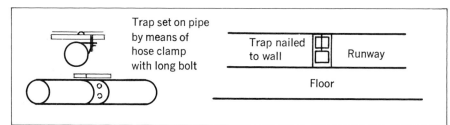

Suggestions for Setting Rat Traps

is also necessary from the standpoint of safety for the protection of children, as well as pets and other non-target species.

Entire buildings can be sealed and fumigated with poison gases. This has the advantage of destroying fleas, mites, and other parasites, as well as the rats and mice—a factor of consider-

able importance in controlling the spread of some diseases.

Poison gases are dangerous, however, and are usually employed in specific situations by experienced, professional exterminators. In view of the hazards, complications, and relatively high costs, this technique is not commonly employed.

In trapping, proper placement of the trap is the key to success. Good rat and mouse attractant baits—such as bacon strips, a piece of fresh fish, or bacon-scented oatmeal—greatly improve trapping efficiency. However, it is not always necessary to bait traps.

The trigger surface of an ordinary snap trap may be enlarged to increase effectiveness by attaching a piece of cardboard or tin to the original trigger treadle. Obstacles or barriers properly placed are effective in routing rats and mice over the trap treadle to further increase the trap's efficiency. Traps can also be nailed to walls, attached to pipes, etc., to intercept regular travel routes.

Many other animals besides rats and mice may become a nuisance at some times and under some circumstances—bats, squirrels, skunks, raccoons, and snakes are examples.

Presence of these animals may also be discouraged through the removal of available sources of food, water, and shelter.

Techniques to use in accomplishing effective environmental alteration to discourage the presence of various animals may vary considerably, however, because of the different habits and characteristics of each animal species. Each technique must be as humane as practical, and must be carefully employed in a manner which will minimize the impact of its use on non-target species and the environment.

Information leaflets for most types of animal species which occasionally become pests are available through your local extension offices and other Federal, State, or county offices responsible for wildlife management.

Assistance may also be obtained from commercial pest control operators. Check the yellow pages in your telephone directory for reputable firms.

If you plan to handle a problem situation yourself, be sure to check local and State laws and ordinances concerning the status of the animal species and the registration of the control agent you plan to use.

Extras That Make A House a Home

No one would argue with the adage that it takes a lot of living to make a house a home. But in today's pressurized age of speed and mobility, accented by thickly populated areas, it takes even more to make a house a home. I like to call these things the amenities of gracious living—those "extras" that transform a place to eat and sleep into a place to live and enjoy—that make a house more than just a shelter.

For instance, "extras" can increase your feeling of space in the place where you live. You can blend the inside of your dwelling with the world outside, bring into your dwelling only the light from outside, or create inside your dwelling miniature living worlds. How do you do it?

Use large areas of glass. Where views are pleasing, make a whole wall out of glass or use sliding glass doors which can also give physical access to the outdoors.

Use mini-gardens to accent and lend interest to small or monotonous outside areas.

Install sky lights to heighten and illuminate space.

Make patio gardens, perhaps with bird feeders for year-round enjoyment.

Raise ceilings of small rooms to create illusion of greater space.

Create flower pot or roof top gardens in apartment buildings where land is nonexistent but sky is plentiful.

Use translucent glass or glass bricks to admit light but keep out undesirable views that transparent glass would reveal.

AUTHOR BARBARA GRIFFIN works with housing in the Agricultural Engineering Department of the Clemson University (S.C.) Cooperative Extension Service.

490-100 O - 73 - 17

Place large mirrors to reflect and deepen space, or cover an entire wall with mirrors.

Use a terrarium or aquarium to make a miniature life of land and water when there is nothing to blend from outside.

Extras can make space more flexible, comfortable and useful. The space in a home needs to serve many purposes. At one time or another you will want a place to study or relax, play or work on your favorite hobby. Incorporate some extras that will allow you to use space in a number of different ways.

Feature a fireplace to give a warm cozy atmosphere for relaxing. Choose a fireplace that meets your preferences.

Should you choose to build of brick or stone, consider using the brick or stone over the entire wall, thereby creating the illusion of more space and beauty. Or install a well-chosen compact fireplace being manufactured in a variety of forms today.

In choosing the manufactured type, take care in meeting recommendations for fireproofing adjoining walls. Perfectly safe prefabricated fireplaces can be attached to walls with built-in flues or they can be free standing with flues installed through roofs.

Whether you choose the expensive permanent wall fireplace or add the prefabricated accent, a damper must be included. A fireplace is roughly equal to an open window in terms of heat loss, and a damper lessens this effect. The cozy warmth of an open hearth can be yours for as little as $200 or as much as $2,000 or more.

Use folding doors or walls to change a large recreation room into several small hobby or study nooks.

Use a walk-in storage room or a basement corner for a photography buff's dark room.

Run a small heat duct from your heating system to your pet's shelter outdoors. This will keep him a member of the family without adding his presence inside the house.

Build storage walls—ceiling to floor— wherever you want "special use" areas. The den collection of small games,

Top, panels admit light to entry area while maintaining privacy by blocking view into house. Above, mirrors visually double space.

records and tapes, flower containers, newspapers, and magazines must be dealt with sometime. Full height built-in storage walls can serve much the same purpose as fireplace walls. They can separate rooms as well as provide storage.

Gadgetry extras can add ease to living and change the mood and atmosphere of your dwelling. The gadgetry extras you need are determined by your life style and pocketbook.

If the game room or hobby room is far from the kitchen, if children's rooms are separated from parents' rooms, if there are several levels in the house or if elderly people are family

246

Above, wall of stone maintains "wholeness" of space. Left, divisions are good, and attractive storage is provided.

and TV equipment into your walls when you build, thus eliminating dangling and unsightly wires.

Create ways to change the atmosphere in your home. Your mood changes from time to time. Lighting is one effective way of controlling change. Dimmer switches built into the lighting system allow you to change the effect of a room whenever you want to.

Make life easier with automatic switches. Automatic switches can turn on closet lights for you when you are burdened with an armload of coats from arriving guests. Photo-electric cells and remote controls can raise the garage doors and turn on the path lights to welcome you when you come home late at night.

Soundproof your study—and perhaps the children's study, too. Sometimes you need an atmosphere of quiet to get work done, or to enjoy your solitude. Soundproofing at the time of construction is fairly inexpensive.

Install a charcoal grill or a special small appliance center in the kitchen for oft-repeated tasks.

Make life more comfortable with a humidifier and de-humidifier, an air cleaner in the heating and cooling system, exhaust fans over ranges and in bathrooms.

members, consider installing an intercom system.

If music and news are part of your interests, build in a stereo system to satisfy the music lover and keep the housewife company. Combine it with an intercom system.

Put antenna wires running to radio

Hallways separate the noise of the late TV movie from others who want to sleep.

Build a half-wall instead of a full one. Ornamentally screen the top portion or plant it so you can peep into the next room rather than be plunged into an activity for which you are unprepared.

No matter what type dwelling you live in, you can make it more livable and enjoyable by considering the extras mentioned here. Increase the feeling of space. Make the space you have more flexible and usable. Expand your conveniences with gadgetry. Help yourself make transitional adjustments from one situation to another. All with little extras.

Install a system that allows you to open and close draperies with the touch of a button.

Finally, there are extras that cause areas in a dwelling to flow together easily and gently, and help us make transitions from one situation to another.

Use porches and patios to provide a pause between outside and inside environments. Sometimes you need more than a door to separate the two.

Plan an entry into the house. A moment between the car and the party going on in the living room eases the change.

The mud room allows the gardener or baseball player to clean up a little before speaking to grandmother.

Any dwelling, any place you choose to live is at best the end result of a long series of compromises. But in order to make the best choices, list the things you want in your home in the order of their importance to you. Determine their importance by describing in your own words the atmosphere you want to live in everyday. Then select those "extras" or amenities which can best provide that atmosphere for you. Make your house a home.

The Mobile Home—Creative Solution To a Challenge

DURING THE DECADE of the sixties the mobile home came into its own and now monopolizes the moderate cost home ownership market. The conditions that fostered establishment of the mobile home as a full-fledged legitimate member of the American housing scene were primarily population growth and inflation. The key, however, is the ability of people to respond creatively to challenging conditions.

As the 1960's wore on, we increasingly felt the pressure of an often underestimated but relentless demographic fact: the baby boom of the post World War II era.

Children born during that period began to marry and come into the housing market in the middle sixties and since. The pressure of population on the housing market appears in those segments of the population's age structure that are expanding most rapidly.

The pressure was especially severe in terms of small, moderate-cost dwelling units, since newly married couples do not need large dwellings and cannot for the most part afford expensive housing.

Parallel with the population growth was one of the most troublesome inflationary periods we have experienced in modern times. The effects were especially severe in housing, since the population trends were inflationary as well; demand rose very rapidly.

Efforts to control the inflation placed additional burdens on the conventional housing market, since a tight money policy that was instituted severely reduced the supply of mortgage money. Mortgage money was placed in more profitable areas. The result was declining production of conventional housing.

Thus, several factors joined together to set the stage for the mobile home boom: (1) rapidly rising numbers of small families with limited incomes, (2) rapidly inflating costs of conventional housing, (3) declining supplies of mortgage money for conventional mortgage finance, and (4) declining conventional housing production.

What was needed was a small, moderately priced type of housing which could be quickly expanded and purchased with financing other than conventional mortgage money.

Mobile homes were a solution. They sell, on the average for considerably less than conventional homes. Often less than $8,000, with perhaps $1,000 to $1,500 down and financed with consumer finance methods that produced higher yields to the lender and involved shorter terms than conventional mortgage investment.

The "factories" in which mobile homes were and are built are essentially roofs and walls to keep the weather from interrupting work on the production line. Large investments in buildings and machinery were simply not necessary for establishing a mobile home plant.

The price was right, the financing readily available, and expansion of production was easy. The result was a growth to over half a million units in 1972.

Despite the rapid expansion of production and the ready acceptance on the part of consumers, there was resistance of housing experts to the mobile home. For example, it was not until 1970 that the production of mobile homes was recorded as housing production by the U.S. Department of Housing and Urban Development.

The average American also thought of the mobile home and the trailer parks as housing for transients who did not fit into their community. Zoning ordinances, housing, building, and

AUTHOR EARL W. MORRIS is an Associate Professor in the Department of Family Environment, Iowa State University, Ames.

health codes often either specifically prohibited mobile homes and mobile home parks or treated them as a member of the nuisance class along with glue factories and slaughter houses.

A typical example is a city in upstate New York that had in its city ordinances a "mobile home ordinance" which, in considerable detail, set up standards for mobile home parks within the city. Elsewhere in the same set of statutes was an absolute prohibition of mobile home parks in the city. This exclusion was subsequently declared illegal by the courts, and an excellent mobile home park is now under construction in the newly established mobile home park zone included in the now revised zoning ordinance.

Such revisions in the law are evidence that a real change—perhaps even a revolution in American housing—has been accomplished. The source is the ingenuity and adaptability of the families of our nation and the mobile home manufacturers (often small builders and former carpenters) who, far from the limelight, prevented the housing crisis of the late sixties from becoming a disaster.

The mobile home revolution, if we dare to call it that, was accomplished by (1) families with limited resources faced with a conventional housing market that was unable to serve them, and (2) manufacturers with modest resources, no striking technological developments, and a labor force with only modest training and skills.

Rather than hold onto old housing prejudices, the families saw a chance to buy housing within their means that provided some of the important aspects of the American dream in housing.

The kind of housing thought desirable by most American families, regardless of income level or social class, is surprisingly uniform. Most people when they dream about what they themselves and others should be able to live in, think of the following:
• A single-family owned home on a good sized lot
• A good school district

• Neighbors like themselves
• At least three bedrooms
• A full set of furnishings and equipment
• High quality streets that are safe to walk at night
• Convenience to employment opportunities

Such housing often sells new these days in excess of $40,000 with $6,000 down and at least $250 per month in mortgage payments.

Many families cannot afford such housing. Compromises must be made. For a large number of families, the mobile home has offered, within their price range, most of the crucial items from the foregoing list. Perhaps most important of them is the single family wned home. There is no doubt that one's own home is a very important possession to American families.

Also of extreme importance to American families has been residence in a neighborhood of people who are readily recognizable as friendly, trustworthy people. This has depended upon a certain amount of homogeneity in terms of ethnic background, social class background, and life style.

Moderate-sized mobile home parks can offer very much that kind of atmosphere with a highly structured means of maintaining it, including the park owner who carefully selects tenants and controls the behavior of those he accepts. The result tends to provide desirable levels of social interaction, mutual aid, and social control.

The structure of the park tends to foster a fellow feeling within the park.

In a very real sense the mobile home park is a community.

Basic reasons for consumer satisfaction with the mobile home during recent years are its moderate cost and the convenience of care and maintenance. In addition, purchase and finance are rapid and convenient. Trends in mobile homes, however, are consistently in the direction of larger and more expensive homes.

In 1955 the difference between the travel trailer and mobile home became

Mobile home scenes.

clear with introduction of the 10-foot-wide model. In the sixties the 12-foot model was introduced and finally the 14-foot-wide mobile home began to appear. Lengths grew from 30 or 40 feet in the fifties to as much as 70 feet at the present time for the 14-foot single wide home.

A number of kinds of expansion or slide out sections were developed. Some expanded horizontally to enlarge the living room or other rooms, and others expanded vertically to raise ceiling heights. Carports, cabanas, patios, and storage sheds multiplied to provide additional living or storage space and visual appeal.

Double wides have become a substantial portion of the mobile home market, where two 12-foot wide homes are joined side by side to form a unit 24 feet by 40 or more feet in length, providing as much floor space as many smaller conventional homes. Triple wides offer as much space as many new conventional homes but generally without basement or attic space. Such multiple width homes may often be classified as prefabricated homes.

We mentioned above that the mobile home represents for moderate income people the nearest thing to conventional housing they can afford. Mobile home manufacturers and the mobile home consuming public, however, gradually are moving back to conventional dwelling types. The difference between the double wide placed on a lot owned by the homeowner often will be nearly indistinguishable from the inexpensive smaller conventionally built home with aluminum siding and pitched roof.

Purchase and financing of the truly mobile homes is very similar to the purchase of automobiles. Financing through Federal Housing Administration and Veterans Administration mortgages are permitted on some of the more permanent types of mobile homes. Any assessment of the mobile home must take into account the system of sales, financing, and resale.

The first mobile home a family is likely to buy will be a smaller, lower priced one, especially if they are a recently married couple. They will need a down payment of $1,000 to $1,500 depending on the size and quality of the home, presumably a 12- by 50- to 60-foot home. Payments on the home would run for 5 years.

Somewhere in the range of 2 or 3 years after the original purchase, the couple may have children and decide they need a larger home. As is the situation with automobiles, equity in the older home is usually enough to cover the down payment on the new and the only change may be in a slightly larger monthly payment for a new mobile home with new furniture.

Although many, perhaps most, people who live in mobile homes do so because they fit their pocketbook and family size, an important factor for many people is the reduced amount of maintenance and yard work that the mobile home represents compared with the conventional home.

In addition, many people simply like the close social relations, the identification with their park and the people in it, and in general what might be referred to as a mobile home life style. That life style does not include a great deal of mobility since mobile home owners do not move any more often than other people of similar age and family size.

Families with moderate incomes and relatively small families will find in the mobile home the only *new* housing within their purchasing range. Of course there are older homes that may be purchased in the mobile home price range. Such housing, however, is not likely to have a full set of new furniture and appliances as does the mobile home.

(Unfurnished mobile homes are available, but in general the furniture tends to be a bargain since it may not add nearly as much to the price of the mobile home as it would cost if purchased separately from a retail furniture store).

In general, the monthly outlay for a mobile home including the park rent is quite comparable with rental of a new apartment. Both rental and mobile home purchase tend to require smaller monthly outlays than the purchase of equivalent conventional detached dwellings. Mobile homes, however, do tend to depreciate in value whereas there sometimes is a capital gain appreciation value in conventional homeownership.

It should be recognized that a mobile home is usually less expensive because it provides less than the conventional home does. It tends to be smaller, more lightly built, and does not provide opportunity for investment in land and buildings that might increase in value. One analysis, however, has shown that the money invested by conventional homeowners in their house and land would have brought a greater return if they had lived in a mobile home and invested the savings elsewhere.

If you are interested in the purchase of a mobile home, there are three things you should do: (1) find out about the reputation and reliability of your dealer by talking to people who have bought homes from him, (2) find out about the reputation and reliability of the park owner and park manager by talking to people who have lived in the park, (3) go to your library or book store and obtain a reference book like *All About Mobile Homes* by John L. Scherer, published by Fawcett in paperback.

New Developments In Home Building

Nᴇᴡ ᴄᴏɴsᴛʀᴜᴄᴛɪᴏɴ methods and materials are rapidly replacing many of the time-honored ways of building. Labor costs are now too high, particularly in urban areas, to rely solely on building housing on-site stick by stick and brick by brick.

Using large size panels generally reduces labor costs. Material costs can be kept down by using items stocked locally. House plans must be designed to use standard lengths and sizes of materials. These guidelines should be kept in mind in selecting plans and when considering the use of new methods and materials. Just a few of the relatively new materials and methods can be discussed in this chapter.

Many low-income families can afford adequate housing only by doing much of the building themselves. Some of the new methods suitable for semi-skilled or unskilled workers also tend to reduce contractor costs.

One amazingly simple way of building concrete block walls is known as the surface bonding method. It is equally adapted to self-help and contractor-built structures.

You need an accurately leveled concrete footing or slab floor on grade to support the walls. Bed and level the first course of blocks in rich mortar. Leveling and plumbing the first course is very important.

Stack the remaining courses dry without mortar. Some blocks are not square and the faces are not always parallel. Plumb and level individual blocks by inserting small pieces of galvanized sheet metal or brick veneer ties between the blocks. Work to a mason's line stretched from corner to corner to get the wall straight. Fasten the wood plate on top of the wall at intervals by means of steel rods running through the block cores to the foundation.

When stacking is completed, trowel a thin coat of cement-base surface bonding mix on both sides of the wall. Chopped glass fiber filament in the mix provides reinforcing so that the coating need be only 1/16 inch thick.

A surface bonded wall is much stronger than a conventional one with

ᴀᴜᴛʜᴏʀ ᴊᴏsᴇᴘʜ ᴡ. sɪᴍᴏɴs retired in 1973 as Research Leader, Housing and Environmental Engineering, Athens (Ga.) Area, Agricultural Research Service.

Left, using mason's line assures straight wall in stacking blocks. Top, plumbing and leveling blocks. Above, surface bonding is applied to block wall with trowel. Holding tray (hawk) of mix against the wall with hand prevents excessive spillage.

mortar joints, and is highly waterproof. You can add mineral coloring to the mix to eliminate painting for a number of years. Use white cement in the mix. Pastel colors do not splotch and fade like dark colors.

If some insulation is needed, you can fill the cores of the blocks with pellet insulation. In cold climates attach furring strips to the wall and insulate between the strips. A prefinished ply-wood attached to the furring strips makes an attractive and durable interior finish.

Preservative-treated poles and posts have been used for many years in farm service buildings and warehouses. Pole construction has gained in popularity in recent years, especially on hillside sites or otherwise rugged terrain.

Although this type of construction is well adapted to low-cost, self-help

Panelized house construction.

housing, it is often used in expensive, custom-built homes.

Lumber, poles, and posts are now available which are treated with preservative salts. This treatment leaves the wood clean and non-staining to hands and clothing. It also allows the wood to be painted or stained.

Pole foundation for otherwise traditional house.

Now wood frame foundations can replace conventional masonry footings and walls. They avoid the difficulty and expense of pouring concrete footings and foundations, especially in winter weather.

This type of foundation lends itself to self-help home builders as well as contractors. The walls are easily insulated and covered with interior wall paneling for attractive living space.

Prefabricated roof trusses, wall and floor panels, and preassembled, weather stripped doors and windows are available in many localities. Even prefabricated brick veneer panels are being manufactured in some areas. They require power lifts to set them in place.

Use of these various prebuilt components save much on-site labor. They enable a builder to "close-in" a house quickly so that work can be done inside during bad weather. Cost savings are more likely in urban areas with high labor costs than in rural areas.

If you are going to use some prefabricated components, plan your house dimensions for the standard sizes available. Otherwise you will lose the advantages of using prebuilt or precut components.

Rough-sawn and special rough-textured surfaces have become popular and are attractive in both wood siding and plywood. Finish these surfaces with durable penetrating type stains. Stains may be obtained in a clear natural finish or in a variety of colors. A water-repellent preservative formulation is best. Stains are easy to apply, economical, and do not peel.

Vinyl siding is a new material suitable for either new construction or remodeling. It should have a reasonably long life and does not require painting. The type with fiberboard backing is more rigid and worth the extra cost.

Aluminum siding, and overhang and trim panels, have a baked-on enamel finish which should be quite durable. The aluminum siding dents more easily than wood or vinyl siding.

Steel guttering and downspouts are now available with a special galvanized coating which permits immediate painting without treatment. This coating appears to have eliminated much of the problem of peeling paint associated with ordinary galvanized steel.

Aluminum guttering and downspouts with baked-on enamel finish may now be purchased. The slip-fit joints require caulking every few years. Full-length aluminum guttering formed on the job without joints is available in some localities. This eliminates the problem of caulking numerous joints. Expansion joints may be needed on long lengths of guttering.

Finishing the interior of a house is much easier today than some years ago. A wide range of paneling materials is available. Those with a vinyl surface are much easier to clean and are especially desirable in kitchen, bath, and utility rooms. Special nails with heads colored to match are available for some materials.

Prefinished plywood is available in both light and dark woods.

Choose the lighter woods for small rooms and those with limited lighting.

Resilient tile, sheet vinyl, and carpeting are fast replacing hardwood as practical floor coverings for modern homes. Generally they are less expensive and may require less care.

For the subfloor, most builders use a sheathing-grade plywood covered with an underlayment grade of plywood or particle board. Special grade plywood can serve as a single layer floor. Use underlayment grades made with exterior glue where excessive moisture conditions exist such as in bathrooms and utility rooms, or over damp crawl spaces.

Using prefabricated, prefinished kitchen cabinets and bathroom vanities saves much time. They are generally less expensive in the long run than if built on the job by skilled workmen. Make sure your house plan will permit use of standard size cabinets.

Plastic water and waste piping is becoming popular for do-it-yourself installations. It is easy to cut and join. Use a special cleaner on the joints before the cement is applied.

After joints are cemented and put together they cannot be taken apart. To avoid costly mistakes you should make a complete temporary lay-out before cementing the joints.

Getting the proper slope on waste lines is one of the most difficult steps. Double check this in order to be certain all lines will drain properly, especially if lines are installed under a concrete slab floor on grade.

Glass fiber tub and shower combinations can be quickly installed. The wall and end enclosure are sometimes made integrally with the tub. This avoids the necessity of tiling walls around the tub or otherwise providing a waterproof wall covering. Since the enclosures are often seamless, leakage at joints and the need for repointing joints are eliminated.

Tub and shower combination of glass fiber reinforced plastic.

Do not use abrasive cleaners and be careful not to scratch the surfaces. Roughened surfaces are hard to clean.

Completely prefabricated bathrooms are available in certain areas. The bathrooms are lowered into place on a prepared foundation, using a crane. Adjoining walls can be preframed or constructed after the bathroom is in place.

The only additional on-site work consists of connecting water and waste lines and making electrical connections.

Prefabricated bathrooms provide an easy method of adding a bath onto an existing house. The initial cost may seem high. Compare the in-place cost with that of a conventional bathroom.

In determining whether to use the newer materials and methods, you must decide how you are going to get your house built. Today the labor cost on a contractor-built house may run 60 percent or more of the total cost. To get maximum savings you must plan to do much of the construction yourself.

Consider several questions before you decide to do all the construction work on a house. Do you have a lot of spare time to work on a house, or will your job permit you to do construction work only a few hours at night and on week-ends? How much can your family help? Have you had any experience in building? Do you have any power tools to reduce labor or can you rent or borrow the most essential ones?

If you are inexperienced and have limited spare time, plan on at least 15 to 18 months to complete the job.

You may be able to build the main part of the house and subcontract those features for which you have neither equipment nor experience. Contracting the plumbing and wiring may be necessary to meet building codes. Pouring and finishing a concrete slab floor on grade requires a certain amount of skill, extra help, and some equipment. These are all expensive parts of the building process. Although you won't save as much on the total cost by contracting part of the work, you can reduce the construction time. If this work is done by reliable contractors you can be more assured of getting a loan to cover the building costs.

As other new materials and methods become available, you must decide whether they are better and less expensive than time-tried ones and whether they will last for many years. This is not easy to judge. Get all the information you can and take time to study manufacturers' claims. If possible, inspect installations in your area before you make your decision. Better be safe than sorry.

For further reading:

American Wood Preservers Institute, "FHA Pole House Construction," 1651 Old Meadow Road, McLean, Va. 22101.

Anderson, L. O. *Wood-Frame House Construction,* Agriculture Handbook 73, U.S. Department of Agriculture, Washington, D.C. 20250, revised 1970.

———. *Low-Cost Wood Homes for Rural America—Construction Manual,* Agricultural Handbook 364, U.S. Department of Agriculture, Washington, D.C. 20250, 1969.

The Carpet and Rug Institute. "Carpets & Rugs—The Now Way to Choose Them," Dalton, Ga. 30720.

Good Housekeeping, "Preventing the Most Common Problems With Resilient Floorings," November 1972, p. 234.

Haynes, B. C., Jr., and J. W. Simons. *Surface Bonding of Concrete Block Walls as Related to Structural Properties,* Research Bulletin 110, University of Georgia College of Agriculture Experiment Station, Athens, Ga. 30602, 1972.

———. *Surface Bonding of Concrete Block Walls Without Mortar Joints,* Agriculture Information Bulletin 343, U.S. Department of Agriculture, Washington, D.C. 20250, 1970.

The Hoover Home Institute, "Carpets and Rugs," The Hoover Company, North Canton, Ohio.

House and Garden, "Carpet Takeover and the Rug Boom," Vol. 141, March 1972, pp. 86–91.

Mechanics Illustrated, "Consumer's Guide to Vinyl Floor Coverings," Vol. 68, February 1972, p. 98.

NAHB Research Foundation, Inc., "Manual of Lumber- and Plywood-Saving Techniques for Residential Light-Frame Construction," P. O. Box 1627, Rockville, Md. 20850, 1971.

National Forest Products Association, "The All-Weather Wood Foundation—Design and Construction Requirements," Technical Report 7, 1619 Massachusetts Ave., NW., Washington, D.C. 20036.

Parents Magazine, "There Are Nine Major Kinds of Resilient Floorings," Vol. 47, August 1972, pp. 76–77.

Plastics Pipe Institute, "Standards for Plastic Piping," TR-5, 250 Park Avenue, New York, N.Y. 10017.

———. "ABS Plastic Piping Installation Procedures" TR-12, 250 Park Avenue, New York, N.Y. 10017.

———. "PVC Plastic Piping Design and Installation," TR-13, 250 Park Avenue, New York, N.Y. 10017.

U.S. Department of Agriculture. "Forest Products Laboratory Natural Finish," Forest Products Laboratory, FPL-046, Madison, Wis., 1970.

Pressure-Treated Wood Foundations

Homes are now being built with foundations of pressure-treated wood walls instead of masonry block or concrete. Builders and homeowners select treated wood foundations because they want the advantages of a warm, comfortable, and more attractive house. They want a house that can be built faster in all types of weather and at less expense.

AUTHOR GERALD A. KOENIGSHOF is Branch Chief, Forest Products Requirements, Forest Service.

Top and above left, building lot is excavated, then gravel or crushed stone is placed in the excavation. Left, pressure-treated wood basement foundation is set on gravel in excavation. Above, crawlspace foundation is set on crushed stone in trench.

House foundations of pressure-treated wood may be used for basement or crawl space walls. These walls are framed with lumber and plywood just as are typical above-ground wood frame walls except that the lumber and plywood are pressure treated. To construct a basement with treated wood walls, the ground is excavated, then gravel or crushed stone is spread over the excavation. Next, a treated wood footing plate is placed on the gravel or crushed stone fill. Finally a treated wood stud wall sheathed with treated plywood is set in place on the footing plate.

To construct a crawl space wall of treated wood, a trench is excavated around the perimeter of the house location, gravel is placed in the bottom of the trench, and then a footing plate and wall similar to a basement wall are set on the gravel. After framing the upper portion of the house, a concrete slab is poured in the basement and earth may be backfilled against the wood foundation wall. Crawl space walls are temporarily braced and backfilled immediately after erection.

How long will a treated wood foundation last? Properly pressure-treated wood foundations are expected to last as long or longer than the average life of wood frame houses on masonry or concrete foundations.

Skyscrapers and large highway bridges are often supported by pressure-treated timber pilings that provide many years of service. Some of these pressure treatments are unacceptable for house foundations because of their odor, unsuitable appearance, or capacity to soil clothing or irritate skin when touched.

Quality mark required on lumber or plywood used in residential foundations.

Wood for house foundations pressure-treated with waterborne salt is odor free and clean and has an attractive appearance. The treatment destroys the food value of the wood, making it immune to decay and rot by fungus or to attack by termites. A special quality mark put on each piece of lumber and plywood assures builders and owners that this material has been properly treated for residential wood foundations.

Treated wood foundation basements are more comfortable to live in for several reasons.

Insulation can be added to a wood wall for less than the cost to strip a masonry wall. This provides a wall that has one-fourth the heat loss of a conventional basement wall. Although heating and cooling costs are reduced by a small amount, a more comfortable living space is probably more important to the homeowner.

Walls are easily finished by the owner or the builder because no stripping is required. Paneling or gypsum wallboard can be applied by nailing directly to the studs.

Treated wood foundation basements have proved to be essentially leak free and to provide dry living space below grade; this is attributable to the porous gravel or crushed stone fill under the floor and wall, in combination with a sump where soils are poorly drained. Water from rainstorms cannot be trapped outside the wall, and the ground water table is held well below floor level.

Inspections by the Forest Service found that studs in treated wood foundation walls are nearly as dry as studs in the walls above grade. Occupants of houses with treated wood foundations often stress their satisfaction with a basement that is warm and damp free.

Treated wood foundation walls offer unlimited combinations of attractive wall finishes both inside and out. Inside wall finishes may be essentially the same as used in conventional above-wall wood frame construction. The outside may be brick, stucco, or wood sid-

Finished home with wood frame foundation has appearance of conventional house.

ing or virtually any other finish used in conventional construction. Textured plywood and wood stains make available many combinations of color and texture that are pleasing to look at.

Treated wood foundations are being used in all price classes of homes.

Families have benefited from treated wood foundations in two ways. They have obtained more living space at less cost and their houses are constructed much faster.

The Farmers Home Administration office in Richmond, Va. has recently developed house designs using treated wood foundations. These designs provide 53 percent more living space at only 8 percent more cost than was possible with previous designs.

Crawl space foundation walls have been most typically used to keep structural costs down. By switching to a bi-level design, where the lower level uses treated wood walls, it is possible to provide nearly twice the living space at essentially the same cost as a house on a crawl space. Owners can easily finish off the inside of treated wood foundation walls with gypsum wallboard or wood paneling.

As a result, families now can get more attractive and comfortable living space at less cost.

In Fern Cliff, Va. the Farmers Home Administration demonstrated the speed of constructing a house with treated wood foundations.

Starting in the morning with a raw building lot, a treated wood foundation was installed by 10 a.m. Backfilling was completed by 11 a.m. A sectionalized house had been placed on the foundation by 11:30 a.m.

By mid-afternoon the telephone, water, electricity, and heat systems were in operation. The farm family started moving into their new home at 3:30 p.m. and by 4:30 p.m. the yard had been landscaped.

Treated wood foundations can be installed in approximately one-sixth the time required to install a conventional foundation. Factory fabricated treated wood foundation walls for an entire basement are often erected in only one hour.

As a result, owners and builders benefit by using treated wood foundations because they eliminate costly construction delays at the job site.

An interesting feature of wood foundation walls is their resistance to cracking caused by settling soil. Small amounts of soil settlement under conventional concrete footings can result in unsightly large cracks in conventional

Treated wood foundation, started at 8:30 a.m., has been installed by 10 a.m. Sectionalized house is placed on foundation by 11:30 a.m. Family starts moving in at 3:30 p.m. Landscaping is finished at 4:30 p.m.

masonry or concrete walls. Treated plywood and lumber framing used in wood foundation walls acts like a large diaphragm or deep girder that effectively "bridges" the areas of soil settlement. Cracked wood walls are unheard of.

Often people ask how gravel footings under a basement wall can support the house without settling. No concrete footings are used.

The answer is that soil under the footing ultimately supports the house above. Footings are only as effective as the soil which supports them, regardless of the type of footing used. The footings must be deep and wide enough so downward loads are adequately distributed to the supporting soil.

Coarse sand, washed pea gravel, and ⅜-inch crushed stone are excellent footing material because they are classified as a noncompressive soil. In addition, stone and gravel footings of this type are easily leveled during construction. Because of their porous nature these types of footings are a key factor in preventing water accumulation outside the wall. Preventing such water buildup outside basement walls is important in preventing basement leakage.

You may hear a treated wood foundation referred to as the "All Weather Wood Foundation." Wood foundations can be erected in colder and wetter weather than is possible with conventional systems.

Mortar for masonry block cannot be placed during raining or drizzly weather, and concrete will not cure properly in below freezing temperatures. Muddy sites prevent trucks from delivering heavy masonry or concrete products but do not stop deliveries and installation of prefabricated wood foundations.

As a result, builders using wood foundations have been able to extend their building season into periods of wet and cold weather. Hence the name "All Weather Wood Foundation" accurately describes one advantage of the system.

Wood foundations are usually supplied by qualified fabricators who custom design and fabricate treated wood foundations. All sizes and grades of materials are selected on the basis of the soil characteristics at the site, lateral loads from soil pressure on the walls, downward loads on the structure, and strength properties of the lumber and plywood used in the foundation. Thus, a treated wood foundation is engineered to meet job requirements.

Conventional foundations are usually not selected on the basis of engineering design but rather as specified by the local building code. Because of this, a conventional wall may be stronger than necessary, which is wasteful of material, or may not be strong enough, which results in an unsafe condition.

Collapse of masonry walls during rainstorms—in addition to problems with leakage and cracked walls—led the National Association of Home Builders and the Federal Housing Administration to seek better ways of building basement walls. Research by the Forest Service, the American Wood Preservers Institute, and the National Forest Products Association resulted in the promising new idea of building better foundations by using pressure-treated lumber and plywood.

FURNISHINGS

Esthetics of Color, Texture, and Design

Price, function, and beauty are the most important factors which consumers consider when purchasing home furnishings or clothing.

Price is most frequently determined by the financial situation of the consumer. Function and beauty can be found at almost any price but sometimes beauty is sacrificed for function, or vice versa. Some items are neither functional nor beautiful.

The consumer's task is to find the desired furnishings and clothing that will serve the definite function and at the same time be esthetically pleasing to the eye at a price he or she can pay. This chapter will be devoted to only the esthetic considerations related to clothing and home furnishings—the combination of qualities that please the eye and the mind, because what a person sees can determine what he feels.

Three basic components affecting the appearance of any article are colors, textures, and lines (which determine the spaces, shapes, and forms). The innumerable variations and combinations of these components can produce limitless effects which may delight visually and mentally. On the other hand, unsatisfactory or distasteful visual and emotional responses can be produced. The way that colors, textures, and lines are combined can create optical illusions. For example, the same room can be made to look larger, smaller, wider, or higher simply by changing the lines, colors and textures used. Your personal appearance is affected by the colors, textures, and lines which you wear.

AUTHOR ELEANORE ADAM is Professor and Head of the Department of Clothing and Textiles at Florida State University, Tallahassee.

We have traditionally thought of the designer as the person who originated the idea for a piece of furniture, an article of clothing, or an accessory. But truly the designer of your home and your wardrobe is the person who makes the selections and arrangements of the lines, colors, and textures that develop into the final design.

Your choices and decisions naturally will reflect your needs, likes, and dislikes. But because you want others to enjoy and approve your home decorations and personal appearance, it is wise to employ some accepted principles to guide you in your selections.

You should understand the effect of colors, their values, and intensities on one another, the impressions the various textures produce, and the responses or feelings that different kinds of lines will call to mind. These impressions, responses, and effects are not the same in all situations. But there are some fundamentals you can rely on.

Color has three dimensions: the hue distinguishing one color from another—such as red, green, blue, etc.; the value denoting lightness or darkness; and the intensity—the brightness or dullness.

These hues, values, and intensities can appear to change when used together. Two or more light values combined afford little contrast; nor will darker values in combination provide much interest. But when a light value is used with a dark, the light appears lighter while the dark appears darker.

Intensities also have similar effects. A bright string of beads will appear brighter and will stand out when used with a dress of dull color, as it will produce a spot of interest. In contrast, a few dull-colored pieces of furniture will sink into the background if the room contains brighter colored rugs, draperies, and other furnishings.

Contrasting or opposite hues will emphasize one another. Red with green will make the red look redder and the green appear greener; while similar hues together will seem to change the hues. For example, if a red is used with red-purple, the red will appear more orange—while the red-purple will take on a bluish tone.

Personal coloring must be analyzed before choosing the colors to be worn in order to attain the most flattering effects. For example, bright yellow (blonde) hair will appear more yellow or golden when soft purple, its opposite, is worn. But dull, colorless blonde hair will appear even duller if a bright purple is worn near it.

Dark skin will appear darker when white or light value is worn. To make the skin appear lighter, a darker value in clothing should be used.

There are many ways of combining colors for interest. Related color schemes such as reds, purples, and blues together can produce very pleasing effects. Contrasting hues, such as blues with oranges, can also be combined to give more vibrant results.

Some people enjoy excitement. Advancing colors such as yellow, orange, and red are exciting because they are associated with things like sunshine, fire, heat, and even blood. Receding colors are cooler and calmer, such as green (as grass) or blue (as the ocean).

Colors also have visual weights. Dark and bright appear heavy, while light or dull seem to weigh less.

Line may move in any direction; up or down or in diagonals to form zigzags or curves. Line forms the boundaries which define the shape or silhouette. And within these silhouettes, line divides the whole into parts or spaces. Lines can also be used to decorate, form patterns, to create illusions, or express emotions.

Line can be thick or thin, long or short, straight or curved, clear-cut or fuzzy.

Long slender, vertical lines placed close together give a feeling of dignity, stability, and height. Short, stocky vertical lines may give a feeling of width and stodginess. Curved, flowing lines express grace and rhythm as a bird in flight or the ripples in a stream.

Lines can emphasize shape and form by repetition or, paradoxically, by contrast. Straight lines used on curved fig-ures will emphasize the curves. But rounding, curved lines will also emphasize the curves of a figure (such as curved necklines with a round face, curved yokelines placed at the bustline, or rounded pockets on the hips).

Sharp contrasting lines such as X's and V's will draw attention to the point where these lines reverse direction. But many lines all going in one direction will carry the eye along in that direction to the point where they stop. Upward curving lines give a lift (smile). Downward curving lines express weariness and sadness (drooping shoulders or a sagging couch).

Surface quality—the feel, weight, and hand of an object—is known as texture.

Heavy, bulky, thick, or fuzzy textures in fabrics when used on a large piece of furniture, or on a large person, will definitely increase the apparent size. But when used on a tiny person or small, delicate furniture, the person or furniture will seem to be overburdened by such weight and consequently will appear even smaller and overpowered by the covering.

Shiny textures reflect light. Because of this, the shape or form underneath will stand out.

For example, if shiny satin is worn by a plump person, the light will bounce off in every direction from the curves of the figure. The resulting effect will be one of even greater rotundity. A bony angular person may wish to avoid very shiny fabrics which will emphasize the sharp angles of the figure.

Shiny textures will intensify the color, also. The same fabric will appear brighter in satin than in crepe.

Crisp looking fabrics, especially if dull in color, are good camouflages. They have a tendency to hide the shape underneath because the fabric does not cling and define. Crisp fabrics also give a feeling of neatness and order but they will not fall easily into folds.

If draperies are made of fabrics that are too crisp, they may jut out in an awkward position. Softer, more flexible fabrics are ideal for draped designs. But if the fabric is too thin or sleazy, it

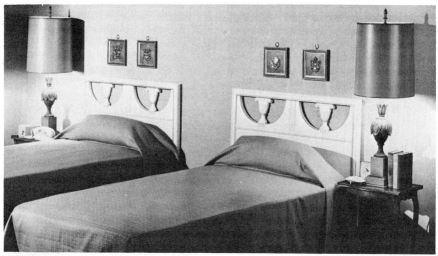

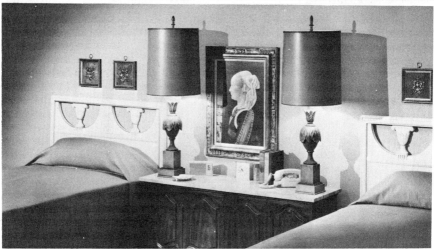

Above, lamps and other items overburden night tables, while unity is lacking. Below, chest, painting, and lamps create a center of interest. Arrangement also provides ample space for the same accessories, besides storage for bed linens and extra blankets.

will eventually hang limp and lifeless.

Nubby textures will soil more quickly. However, they will not show the soil as readily as smooth fabrics, particularly if they contain a mixture of colors.

No hard and fast rules regulate the use of textures in combination. We must become sensitive to harmony in our combinations.

Smooth woods can be used with rough brick. Soft velvets can be combined with crepes which appear to be hard. But in each case, these contrasting textures should be tied together harmoniously.

Unity of color may be the solution, or perhaps, rhythmic lines can draw the two together.

At times, it might be necessary to introduce a third intermediate texture as a transition from one to another.

This technique is often seen in dresses which are designed of two fabrics—one for the bodice, another for

268

the skirt. A belt of a third material (leather, perhaps) can bridge the gap between the two different fabrics.

A nubby chair cover may have a smoother cording around the cushions which would help to tie it to the smoothness of the wood frame.

A sense of order is needed for an esthetically pleasing design. Order can easily be achieved by unity of all parts. But if all parts are exactly alike, monotony or boredom may be the result. Therefore variety must be introduced for interest. The first principle then, can be expressed as *unity with variety.*

An experienced designer is one who knows just how much variety is needed to produce a pleasing effect.

Variations of colors, textures, or lines can be used. But if there are several variations of one of these components, then the others should remain more constant in order to retain the harmony of the whole.

For example, if several colors or many intensities and values of one color are desired, then closely related textures and lines could hold these color variations together.

So the second principle to be considered is *balance* in the use of colors, textures, and lines.

To minimize the confusion that might occur when using a number of colors, textures, and types of lines in room or costume, one dominant idea should be emphasized.

In a room this could be an unusual piece of furniture, occupying a prominent place, a lovely picture on the wall which is first seen when entering the room, a fireplace with logs burning in it, an attractive centerpiece on the table. In costume as well, one feature should be emphasized by the use of color, line, or texture importance.

Briefly, the third principle to remember to employ is the need to maintain

An example of the use of good proportion, or scale.

one *center of interest* instead of many strong features vying for attention.

But this point of emphasis might be too shocking if it actually is so different or unusual in color, line, or texture that it stands out by itself.

Some means of leading the eye to this dominant spot should be used. You can do that in many ways such as grouping smaller or less important articles of furniture or accessories in an attractive arrangement near the main piece; or repeating the color of the main piece in other parts of the room to lead the eye to the dominant point.

The same methods can be adapted to costume.

Another way might be a gradation of color from light to dark or dull to bright to carry the eye to the darkest or the brightest. Gradation of size is also pleasing.

Any method that will lead the eye to the center of interest will produce *rhythm*, the fourth principle that should be considered when creating good design.

The scale of sizes and shapes within a room or design of a garment should be in relation to the whole. For example, a large heavy piece of furniture will dwarf a small room. On the other hand, tiny, insignificant sizes or shapes in a costume will look ridiculous on a large woman.

The fifth principle, the use of good *proportion*, or scale, should never be overlooked when you are choosing the sizes and shapes to be combined.

But use of the knowledge of all these principles in handling the elements (line, texture, and color) will not necessarily produce beautiful results. Imagination, understanding, and personal taste must be developed to a point where the combining of these elements becomes a natural skill instead of a maneuvered or set pattern of arrangements.

Color is one of the most important forces in our lives. It is what we see first when we view any object or scene.

Most people enjoy color because it gives the impression of life. For example, the average person who has had the opportunity to enjoy colored television finds black and white viewing dull. A colored picture seems more real.

Designing through selection and arrangement of colors, textures, lines and shapes is not easy. You must be constantly aware of the effects of each component on the other.

Seeing is not enough. Practice in combining the available elements will result in skillful designing.

If you learn to analyze your mistakes —and even the most experienced designers make errors—you probably will find that your designs will improve, and designing may become fun.

The creative experience of designing through selection and arrangement provides an outlet and fulfills the need to express yourself. At the same time it can bring esthetic pleasure to others.

For further reading:

Bopst, Harland. *Color Personality,* Vantage Press, Inc., New York, 1962.

Brockman, Helen L. *The Theory of Fashion,* John Wiley & Sons, Inc., New York, 1965.

Burnham, R. W., R. M. Hanes, and James C. Bartleson. *Color: A Guide to Basic Facts and Concepts,* John Wiley & Sons, Inc., New York, 1963.

Graves, Maitland. *Color Fundamentals,* McGraw-Hill Book Co., Inc., New York, 1952.

Hillhouse, Marion D. *Dress Selection and Design,* The Macmillan Company, New York, 1963.

Morton, Grace M. *The Arts of Costume and Personal Appearance,* John Wiley & Sons, Inc., New York, 1964.

Floors: Finishes And Coverings

Floors play an important role in the interior housing scene and many treatments are available, but a final decision on what to use and why requires careful consideration of a number of factors. If you are concerned with finishes and maintenance for hard-wood floors or with selection of carpets and rugs, here are facts and suggestions that can help.

Hardwood floors have a natural beauty which should be emphasized and protected by the finish. There are two basic types of floor finishes from which to choose: penetrating seals and surface coatings.

Penetrating seals (with or without stain) soak into the flooring material to form a strong bond with the wood. When you add a good paste or solvent base liquid wax and buff well, the result is a tough floor with a beautiful gloss. Both the wood and the sealer are worn away at the same time, leaving little evidence of wear. When necessary, heavy traffic areas can be repaired with sealer and the floor will not appear spot finished.

The surface coating group includes shellac, varnish, polyurethane, epoxy, and amino resin.

Shellac is the oldest and cheapest of these finishes, but it does not wear as well as the others, especially under heavy traffic. If you do use shellac, buy a four or five pound "cut" and be sure the date on the label is not more than 6 months old.

Varnish will wear well under light use, but will not withstand heavy abra-sion or abuse. In addition, varnish scratches white, making it less desirable in appearance.

Polyurethane, epoxy, and amino resin finishes (plastic finishes) are tough, long wearing, resistant to chemicals, and quick drying. They are also resis-tant to the scratching and marring that are readily apparent with shellac and varnish.

Recent studies at The University of North Carolina at Greensboro indicated plastic varnishes maintained a better appearance under heavy traffic than did the conventional finishes. A two-

AUTHOR NANCY H. HOLMES is a housing research instructor in the School of Home Economics, The University of North Caro-lina, Greensboro.

part amino resin was rated superior in appearance to all other finishes tested. Many textile mills are now using poly-urethane or epoxy floor finishes, anoth-er indication of their toughness.

When you select a finish, choose one that is best suited to your needs. A high quality, "gym-finish" varnish can be very satisfactory in an area of low traffic or little wear (a bedroom with a room-size rug, for instance), and will cost much less than the newer plastic fin-ishes. However, the extra money would be well spent to finish a foyer or hall-way with a tougher plastic finish which may cost from two to three times as much as shellac or varnish.

Some epoxies are very good water-proofers, and I have known people to paint damp basements with epoxy paint and not be bothered by moisture again. Check with local dealers about the waterproofing aspects of epoxy var-nishes and paints.

Most finishes are available in high and low gloss and some in medium gloss; so that you have a choice to make there, too.

Preparation of the floor to be fin-ished is highly important for a satisfac-tory job. Whether you are refinishing an old floor or treating a new one, the floor must first be made smooth. Al-though it is possible to do this by hand, a power sander is generally used. If you have decided to do-it-yourself, rental agencies, paint stores, hardware stores, or lumber and building supply dealers can recommend and supply the proper equipment.

Paint and varnish removers are some-times used to remove old finishes, but power sanding is still considered more practical and effective. When finishing floors, *all* furnishings must be removed from the room and *all* dust (sanding or other) vacuumed away before the finish is applied. Pay particular attention to window ledges and baseboards.

In some situations it may be possible to apply a new finish directly over an old one, particularly if the old finish is in good condition. Again, check finish labels carefully to determine whether

271

this is possible and over which finishes the new one can be applied.

Application of all floor finishes should be made according to the manufacturer's instructions, so read labels or pamphlets thoroughly. They will tell you what to use to apply the finish, whether a wood filler is required, how many coats of finish are necessary, and what to do about waxing. (If a stain is to be used, that is the first step in finishing.)

Generally, penetrating seals are brushed, rolled, or swabbed on the floor and allowed to dry 20 to 30 minutes. The excess is wiped off and the finish allowed to dry according to the label instructions. Shellac and lacquer should be brushed on evenly and sanded with a fine sandpaper before additional coats are applied. Two or three coats are required.

Polyurethane may be applied with a brush or a roller and is also sanded before each additional coat. Clear polyurethane is used for a high gloss or to build the finish, and a low gloss or satin finish is used only as the final coat.

Epoxy and amino resin finishes are brushed on and sanded between coats. Thinning is required before use in some instances. When the two parts of the amino resin are combined, the finish has a short "pot life" so only the quantity needed should be mixed.

Proper maintenance of wood floors is necessary for maximum service and enjoyment. In addition to regular vacuuming to remove dust and heavy grit, I strongly recommend weekly cleaning with a spray-treated dust mop to remove fine particles and dust and to get into corners that are difficult to vacuum.

Occasional damp-mopping with a sponge mop will not harm the floor if the finish is in good condition and provides a good seal. Do not saturate the floor with water.

Periodic buffing will restore the gloss to a floor; if it does not, it is time to rewax.

The main function of a wax is to protect the floor finish. Three basic types available for wood floors are buffable paste, buffable liquid, and self-polish-

ing liquid. Be sure you purchase a wax for wood floors and follow label directions carefully.

Paste waxes are best applied on your hands and knees with a soft cloth. Work with small areas, spreading the wax evenly first across the wood grain and then with the grain. Next, buff with the grain of the wood.

Liquid waxes are poured on the floor in small amounts and spread evenly with a long-handled applicator.

Further research at The University of North Carolina has shown that whether paste or self-polishing liquid wax is used, there is no appreciable difference in the wear of the finish. In addition, finishes waxed with the liquid wax were consistently rated better in appearance than those waxed with a paste wax. Therefore, the self-polishing liquid wax might be a more convenient choice for you.

If you switch from buffable wax to the self-polishing liquid type, however, all old buffable wax must be removed from the floor before applying the new liquid wax because the two types are not compatible. A solvent wood floor cleaner can be used for this purpose.

You will find that proper maintenance and care can be as important to the life and beauty of your floors as the finish.

Carpeting is one of the most expensive items you have in your home, and it should be selected with care. Don't rush into the purchase of carpeting—shop the reputable dealers and compare their products, prices, services, and know-how.

Avoid "fantastic" low prices if they are, in fact, too low to be real, and any questionable "package" deals unless you have thoroughly investigated them.

This does not mean that good buys are not available. You might get a very good price on a carpet that is not a good seller because of color or pattern; but it may fit your needs perfectly.

Before you begin to shop, however, decide on color scheme and mood for the room (formal or informal). Since furnishing styles are being mixed today, you are not bound to an all-traditional or all-modern style unless that is your preference.

Tweeds or shags are usually more informal while plush cut pile, sculptured patterns, and formal designs are best for more formal rooms. Colors of medium intensity show soil the least and usually allow more freedom in the overall color scheme. Plush piles show footprints and traffic patterns more than dense piles of low to medium loops or twists.

Density refers to the amount of pile per square inch of carpeting. To check density, roll the edge of the carpet back to back to see how close the rows and stitches of yarn are. If there are large spaces and the backing is quite evident, the quality is low.

Fiber content is very important to carpet performance, maintenance, and appearance. Wool, the traditional carpet fiber, is resilient, luxurious, resistant to abrasion and soil, warm, and easy to maintain. It is generally higher in cost per square yard ($14 to $25) than the synthetic fibers (nylon, acrylic, polyester).

Acrylic fibers are most nearly like wool. An acrylic carpet is a good choice if you want the look and feel of wool at a lower cost ($8 to $16) and with hypoallergenic properties (having a relatively low capacity to induce hypersensitivity).

Polyesters have the weight and luxury of wool but are shinier and less resilient. They are in the same price range as acrylics.

Nylon is the best wearing fiber of the synthetics. It is tough, resistant to soil, and cleans easily. Static electricity is a problem with some nylons but newer types are available that are static free. Nylon carpets range from $6 to $16 in cost.

Padding (underlay) will lengthen the life of a carpet and add luxury and warmth. I strongly recommend using padding.

Pads may be made of hair, sponge or foam rubber, foam rubber on hair, or jute and hair. Hair is always a good choice except where dampness and mildew is a problem. Foam rubber would be a better choice under these circumstances. Carpet pad prices range from $1.50 to $3.50 per square yard.

Room-size rugs are also very practical, since they can be turned to distribute wear and you can send them out for thorough cleaning. If you buy a good rug, it will last for years and you can take it with you when you move. It is also possible to change color schemes more easily by moving rugs from one room to another. Area rugs are now being used over carpeting for a decorator effect or in areas of heavy traffic.

Whatever your floor needs are, plan, shop, and select carefully, and practice proper maintenance for a more satisfying product.

Window Treatments: Curtains and Drapes

Windows provide ventilation, let in light, and display the view. You can add another dimension by making a window a spot of beauty.

Before you decide what will best enhance your windows, consider the visual effect you want to achieve. The style you select will depend on the type of window, amount of light desired, the view, and style of furnishings.

Treatments to consider might include draperies, sheer curtains, ruffled curtains, cafe curtains, and headings to coordinate with the curtains or draperies you select.

Fabrics you choose for your windows will depend upon the effect you wish to achieve. Sheer curtains covering the window will filter the light to some extent and give you a feeling of privacy in the daytime. You will be able to see out—but others will not be able to see in.

Sheer fabrics which will serve for this

purpose include marquisette, ninon, voile, batiste, and lace. Marquisette and ninon will be the most transparent fabrics. Batiste, voile, and lace are more opaque fabrics and shut out more of the view.

Since sheer fabrics must be made from small yarns, choose fabrics containing strong fibers to obtain the best wearing qualities. Polyester is the most satisfactory fiber for marquisette and ninon fabrics. It has high strength and good resistance to the degradative effects of sunlight and of atmospheric pollutants.

Polyester blended with cotton or with rayon is frequently used in batiste and voile. This blend gives a more opaque fabric which has good wearing qualities and easy-care features.

Marquisette, ninon, batiste, voile, and lace are all soft fabrics. They will give the best appearance when used as straight panels shirred on rods or pinch-pleated for use on traverse rods. They may be used alone or under draperies.

Glass fiber is used in heavier fabrics with an open-weave appearance. Glass fibers have good resistance to sunlight and atmospheric pollutants. However, glass fiber fabrics must be handled with care in laundering. Curtains and draperies containing glass fibers will have a statement on the label cautioning you about their care.

Fabrics for draperies vary from such informal types as homespun and denim to formal ones such as damask and antique satin. Heavyweight, thick fabrics will shut out all light and give privacy at night without the use of additional blinds. Lighter weight fabrics may not give the degree of privacy desired.

Many fibers and blends of fibers are being used for drapery fabrics. Fibers which have given the most satisfaction

when used alone include cotton, acrylic, and glass fibers. Blends of the following types have been satisfactory: cotton and rayon, cotton and polyester, rayon and polyester, and rayon and acetate. Cotton, acrylic, polyester, and glass fibers are more resistant to sunlight degradation than are rayon and acetate.

The kind of care you wish to be able to use will influence your choice of fabrics for curtains and draperies. Many fabrics on the market today are machine washable. Durable press finishes give easy-care qualities to fabrics. These finishes are most satisfactory when used on blends of polyester with cotton or rayon.

Drycleaning is recommended for fabrics of 100 percent rayon, and blends of rayon with cotton or acetate, to prevent shrinkage. Glass fiber fabrics must always be hand washed, since machine washing or drycleaning will cause damage by abrasion in the machine.

Atmospheric pollutants as well as sunlight cause degradation of the fibers. These pollutants are invisible and will not always be accompanied by tiny particles which cause obvious soiling of fabrics. In areas where high levels of pollutants are present, more frequent washing or drycleaning will be necessary to remove the pollutants and give longer life to fabrics.

Dyes used in fabrics are not all equally fast to sunlight and atmospheric pollutants. It is difficult to predict what effect sunlight and atmospheric conditions will have on colors. Undyed fabrics or very light shades of colors may be a better choice for curtains or draperies in areas of intense sunlight as color change will be less noticeable.

Fabric manufactured for apparel purposes will not normally have the colorfastness qualities required in curtains or draperies. Brightly printed percales may fade easily and thus give limited satisfaction.

Linings in draperies, either attached or separate, give protection against

AUTHOR BARBARA DENSMORE is Associate Professor of Clothing and Textiles in the College of Human Development, The Pennsylvania State University, University Park. COAUTHOR MARY ANN ZENTNER is Assistant Professor of Clothing and Textiles.

sunlight damage. Linings can also provide more insulation and light control.

The style of window hangings you choose will determine the type of hardware to purchase. The selection includes cafe-traverse rods, adjustable traverse rods, combination traverse and valance rods, single or double curtain rods, spring-tension cafe rods, and rods that will fit around corners. Rods come in many decorator styles and colors.

You can choose from a wide selection of models in sizes up to 25 feet wide in traverse styles, 12½ feet in cafe rods, and 10 feet in curtain rods. Extension units can be added. For special window areas, rods can be custom cut by stores that offer such services. Check local stores to determine types of fixtures and special services available.

Decide exactly what type fixtures you are going to use and where they are to be placed—on the window frame, above the window, extending beyond the window on each side, or conforming to some special need of your own. Good fixtures are important for they will out-

Drapes reach bottom of window apron.

last several sets of draperies and will be largely responsible for the way the fabric hangs.

When draperies are heavy or constantly opened and closed, be sure the anchorage for the fixtures is firm. If screws go into the window frame there is usually no problem. If fixtures are attached to the wall, toggle bolts may be used. Draperies will cover such devices.

Draperies and curtains may be purchased ready made, or the material may be bought by the yard. The ready mades are the most popular.

Readymade draperies and curtains offer one of the best means for creating very attractive window treatments the quick way.

Use your imagination—add fringes, colored borders, tiebacks, and other decorator touches for your own special creations. If you are so inclined, you can save yourself the price of the workmanship by making them yourself.

After hardware has been selected and installed, measurements can be made. Decide on the length of your draperies. Window hangings may come to the window sill, brushing the sill lightly, or to the bottom of the apron, which is the piece of wood just below the sill. The most practical length for long draperies is one-half to one inch above the floor or carpeting.

For ready mades, measure from the top of the rod to the desired total length. Also measure the length of the rod on the wall. Stores and catalogs provide measurement charts to help in selecting the appropriate size curtain or drapery.

To determine the amount of fabric needed for custom-made draperies, measure the face—including the ends of the rod—and multiply by two for double fullness. To this add the sum of inches in allowance for four side hems, usually 2 inches each. Add 6 inches for standard overlap. The total is the width needed for each pair of draperies. Slightly more or less width can be used by adjusting the pleat size and spacing.

To measure for drapery length, determine the distance from the top of the rod to the bottom of the hem. Add 11 inches for hems. This will give enough fabric for a double 3-inch hem and a generous heading to cover the top of the rod. If the fabric has a large repeat pattern which must be matched, allow one full length of the motif for each cut fabric length required for the draperies.

Consider the width of the fabric when deciding on the number of widths for fullness. Some fabrics may be only 36 inches wide—chintz and some polished cottons, for example. Others may run 40, 48, or even 54 or 60 inches in width. The average is about 48 inches.

Some stores will provide assistance in calculating the amount of fabric needed. Be sure you have taken measurements of the rod and curtain length desired.

Draperies and curtains must be cut on the true lengthwise and crosswise grain of the fabric so when they are hung they will fall straight from the rod in even, graceful folds. Before cutting panels, cut off or pink selvages on both edges to avoid puckering in stitching, drycleaning, or washing.

If you want your draperies to hang in richer and more formal folds, linings will give the needed weight. Linings also give a uniform appearance to the windows from the outside. Some figured fabrics lose their decorative effect when too much light filters through. Linings are usually made from sateen in white or off-white depending upon the background of the fabric used.

Window treatments other than curtains or draperies may be the answer to your problem. There is hardly a window of any size or shape that cannot be covered with an interesting shade. Shades are relatively inexpensive, can block out the light, heat, and cold, and give privacy when needed.

You'll find a selection of textures, interesting colors, and designs that will harmonize with any decorative scheme. There are shade types and brackets to fit almost every window shape, including difficult to treat odd-shaped windows. Shades alone or combined with another window treatment offer numerous ideas.

Venetian blinds are being used in glamorous new treatments. Slats have become slimmer and a wide range of decorator styles is available. Colorful laminated blinds create a new mood in a room where the light must be carefully controlled. Slats can be covered with a pattern to match a wall covering or upholstery design. For large windows, vertical blinds made from lightweight aluminum and steel are appropriate.

Inside shutters can be used next to windows in place of curtains. Some are put under curtains or draperies; others are used cafe-style, either above or beneath cafe curtains.

Shutters may be made from wood or metal. Natural wood tones are often used to enhance the beauty of the shutters. The inside section may be made from any of the following materials: fabric, mesh, cane, grill cloth, or screening. You can purchase shutters at your local hardware store or builder's supply outlet.

When a full window treatment is not desired, you may want to have a valance at the top of your window to harmonize with the decorative scheme of your room. For a kitchen window that faces the children's play area or a wooded area in which the view is important, consider a shirred ruffle hung from a regular curtain rod or a pleated valance suspended from a cafe rod. Use your imagination to create effective treatments when a decorator's touch is needed.

Problem windows are problems only as long as you believe they are. You can discover many ways in which windows can be made to look taller, shorter, wider, or thinner. Their treatment can pose an interesting challenge. You may have several windows in one wall and believe that an impossible task is at hand. Where double or triple windows are close together it may be advisable to treat them as one window and use a single pair of draperies to cover them.

Consider using several pairs of ruffled curtains placed side by side to create an entire unit covering multiple windows and connecting wall areas. Another solution may be to use one long cafe curtain covering the lower half of the windows and a single valance at the top.

When dealing with separated windows on a wall, alternating sections of draperies and sheer curtains may be used to cover the entire wall. Place the draperies over the wall sections between windows; use the sheer curtains over the windows. This technique will give a unified appearance over the entire area.

If light and privacy are needed in the breakfast or dining room, you may want to use a cafe curtain which covers the bottom of the window and panels at the top separated to admit light. Be innovative in your use of available materials to create the desired illusion.

The window treatment that you choose should depend on your personal taste and style of life. Factors to be kept in mind include the desired visual effect, care requirements, and environmental conditions present in your geographical location.

Indoor Lighting— Lamps, Lumens, And Fixtures

Cecile Scott stood amid the store's enormous lamp department utterly confused. Which lamp to buy? She had thought it would be simple to select one but was perplexed by the variety of styles, shapes, and sizes from which to choose. Some didn't resemble a lamp at all. The wide variety of designs made Cecile have second thoughts about what she wanted.

Cecile had made two common mistakes. First, she had not thought of the lighting for the room as a whole. She needed to consider all the lighting in the room so the results would be attractive, yet effectively provide her with comfortable light for all needs. After all, the primary function of most lamps and fixtures is to provide useful light.

Her second mistake was that she had not decided if she wanted the lamp to be decorative or functional or both. Did she want the lamp to be a decorative element or an accessory? Or did she want it to provide good light for seeing?

Needless to say, lamps can be attractive as well as furnish enough comfortable light for difficult tasks such as sewing or studying. Finding these lamps requires knowledge of the requirements of good lighting as well as some knowledge of interior design.

You, too, may be like Cecile when you shop for lighting equipment if you don't first decide what you want it to do.

You will be wise to think of lighting for the entire room, and select equipment that contributes to an effective overall lighting system. If you are building a new home, the design for the lighting should be part of the plans. Therefore, you may want to seek help from someone who knows how to design a good lighting system. Your electric utility or county Extension Service office may be able to refer you to such a person.

A well designed lighting system need not be expensive since modest priced lamps and fixtures can be attractive and effective. However, the lighting may be designed as elaborately and expensively as you want and can afford.

How do you plan your lighting? By providing enough light of the right kind in the right place.

It is not simple to achieve this, and we will be able to discuss only a few of the considerations. Many points will have to be omitted, and some of those included must be oversimplified.

"Enough" light means an adequate

AUTHOR FRANCES FORTENBERRY is Housing and Equipment Specialist, Mississippi Cooperative Extension Service.

amount of light to enable you to see easily and quickly. Although our eyes are very adaptable to low levels, we see better with more light than is found in most homes. Lighting authorities of the Illuminating Engineering Society have determined the minimum amounts of light needed to do different tasks. These amounts are given in terms of foot-candles, which are measured by light meters.

Light meters are not readily available, so you may have to rely on other guides.

Place sources of light everywhere they are needed for seeing, then include others to balance the room lighting. Also include sources for accent and as decorative elements if these fit into your decorating scheme.

Plan for a source of light where you read or study, at the bathroom mirror where you shave, at the kitchen sink where you work, and anywhere you need to be able to see.

Include enough sources so that no part of the room has to be in darkness. Shadows add interest to a room, but too deep shadows become uncomfortable when you are doing difficult seeing over a period of time. USDA Home and Garden Bulletin No. 138 recommends: "Most living rooms need at least five portable lamps, most bedrooms three."

Lamps are no longer considered the only source of task lighting, for fixtures hung on the wall or ceiling or recessed in the ceiling can also provide required light.

Artful use of accent lighting can be an element of the decoration by emphasizing an art object, a picture, a planter, a brick wall, or a mural. This accent lighting adds a touch of glamour and beauty to the room and contributes to the overall amount of light. In addition, lamps or fixtures may be used merely as decorative elements. Since lamps or fixtures to be used primarily for seeing should be effective light sources, you will have to be selective when you buy.

Choose a table lamp with a minimum of 100 watts; 150 watts would be bet-ter. Table lamps used for prolonged periods and floor lamps need 200 or 300 watts. This wattage is in addition to other sources of light in the room. The bulb should be low in the shade so the light strikes the task.

Select a table lamp of good proportion. The size of the lamp should be in relation to the table and chair where it will be used, as the bottom of the lamp shade should be about level with the eyes of a person seated in the chair.

"Enough" light is not the only criterion. The "right kind" or good quality lighting is equally important. Lighting should be comfortable.

Select lamps or fixtures that produce "soft" or diffused light to eliminate glare and contrasts which cause distraction and difficulty in seeing. This is not to imply that "hard" or bright light does not have a place in lighting your home, but it should not be used as a primary source of light.

Study lamp correctly located for a right-handed person. Center of lampshade should be about 15 inches to left of work center, and the lamp about 12 inches back of front edge of table.

All primary sources should have bulbs shielded in some manner, except in sources such as the new see-through lamps or chandeliers which are unshielded. These latter need low wattage bulbs and are often placed on dimmers in order to be visually comfortable.

Look for lamps with under-the-shade devices to provide the comfortable light needed for prolonged difficult tasks. Under-the-shade devices may be diffusing bowls of milk glass or plastic, plastic diffusers, or refracting bowls. Such lamps are not easy to find, but keep looking.

Left, reflector-type fixtures highlight a dining table. Dimmer controls lighting level in these downlights. Valance lighting enhances scenic wallpaper and drapery. Below, flexible lighting for bedroom includes lighted cornice, swing wall lamps, ceiling fixture.

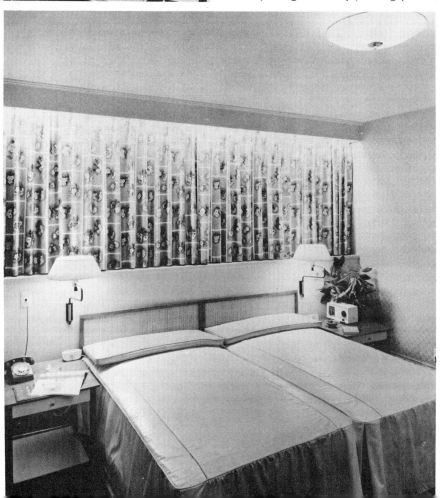

LIGHTING FOR THE HOME

Seeing Task	Primary Task Plane
Dining	15
Grooming, Shaving, Make-Up	50
Handcraft	70
Ordinary seeing tasks	70
Difficult seeing tasks	100
Very difficult seeing tasks	150
Critical seeing tasks	200
Ironing	50
Kitchen Duties	
Food preparation and cleaning, involving difficult seeing tasks	150
Serving and other non-critical tasks	50
Laundry Tasks	
Preparation, sorting, hand wash	50
Washer and dryer areas	30
Reading and Writing	
Handwriting, reproductions, poor copies	70
Books, magazines, and newspapers	30
Reading Piano or Organ Scores	
Advanced (substandard size)	150
Advanced	70
Simple	30
Sewing	
Dark fabrics	200
Medium fabrics	100
Light fabrics	50
Occasional—high contrast	30
Study	70
Table Games	30

Select a lamp shade that blends with the background and transmits some light through the sides. Usually light colored translucent shades are preferred because opaque shades create spots of uncomfortably high brightness above and below the rim of shade. Too thin shades show "hot spots" that are distracting. Avoid narrow, deep shades or those which are too shallow. Be sure the lining is white.

Most lamps will be chosen for decorative suitability and for the amount and quality of light produced. Occasionally you may need a lamp that is primarily functional. One type functional lamp is designed for study desks.

Standards have been established for study lamps in order to meet the Illuminating Engineering Society requirements for comfortable seeing. These include an adequate amount of light (70 foot candles) with light distributed upward, and low contrasts in amounts of light around the task. The lamp should be capable of casting diffused rather than sharp, pencil shadows. The amount of light shining through the shade should be limited (50-150 foot-lamberts, the measurement of brightness) for eye comfort.

Lamps made by any manufacturer that meet these standards are tagged Better Light, Better Sight, study lamps.

You may decide to do-it-yourself and make your lamp or fixture from "scratch." You can buy parts in some hardware, variety, hobby, and lighting equipment stores. Lamp making kits are also available.

You are limited only by your imagination. You can make attractive, unique equipment inexpensively that is decorative, functional, or has both of these features. If the end product is to be functional, consider many of the points that have been discussed previously.

Light in the "right place" is critical if it is to be used for difficult, prolonged tasks. Lighting authorities have worked out measurements for placement of sources in relation to the tasks to be lighted. One rule of thumb for placing a lamp is that the bright inner surface of the shade should never be visible to the user. Tall table lamps and floor lamps are placed at the right or left rear corner and close to the chair.

Don't forget that lamps are not the only way to provide lighting, even task lighting. Consider other ways: pendants, downlights, wall washers, valances, coves, or wall brackets, to name a few.

Ceiling fixtures in the middle of a room became so unpopular they have disappeared from many rooms.

General lighting from other sources

must be provided to compensate for this loss of light.

Fixtures are being moved toward the edges of the room and now may provide both general and task lighting. Chandeliers used in living areas are placed over baby grand pianos, sofas, or other appropriate large pieces of furniture. Pendants, singly or in clusters, placed off center, may be used for task or accent lighting.

Recessed fixtures can create dramatic effects, but you need more fixtures and more total wattage than when other fixtures are used. If a high percentage of light for the room comes from recessed fixtures, you need to nearly double the total wattage. Designed and installed properly, recessed fixtures can light a room attractively and effectively.

Structural lighting, too, is effective if properly designed and installed, but is often disappointing when done without the correct know-how.

Select a fixture that is decoratively suitable for the surroundings, provides enough light without distracting glare or brightness, has enough wattage for the task, and is designed to allow the light to get out and be distributed where it is needed. No part of the fixture should be so bright that you are uncomfortable when you view it directly. There should be no great contrast between the brightness of the fixture and background.

The bulb used in a lamp or fixture is critical to achieving "enough" light of the "right kind." The wrong color fluorescent tube can "kill" the colors in an attractive room. A too small incandescent bulb does not provide the amount of light needed, and a bulb too large for the equipment causes "hot spots" and can melt plastic.

Colored and decorative bulbs need to be used with caution. Inside frosted or white bulbs are preferred for most lamps and fixtures.

A word must be said about fluorescent tube colors: Deluxe warm white (WWX) and deluxe cool white (CWX) are most frequently used in homes. Warm white enhances warm colors and

flatters complexions, but cool white is preferred if blues and/or greens are predominant in the color scheme.

Size of the incandescent bulb is determined by the equipment in which it is to be used.

The wise consumer today takes advantage of information included on the "sleeves" or jackets in which bulbs are packed. Labels list initial "lumens" and bulb life, as well as wattage.

Lumen may be a new word. It means light output—what you get out of the bulb, initially. Fluorescent tubes are more efficient than incandescent bulbs: 40 watt fluorescent = 2,080 initial lumens, 40 watt incandescent = 450 initial lumens. Quite a difference! Some incandescent bulbs of the same wattage are more efficient than others.

Lumens increase as wattage increases —a 100 watt bulb produces 1,700 lumens, while a 200 watt bulb produces 3,900 lumens.

Consumers investing in long life bulbs may not realize they are sacrificing light for a long life. You get longer life, but lose light and pay the same for electricity.

Restrict longer life bulbs to such hard-to-reach spots as a stairwell, attic, or fixture in a high ceiling. Where longer-life bulbs are the primary source of light, use a higher wattage bulb (provided the equipment can accommodate the size and heat) to compensate for the reduced output.

The bulb sleeve includes the average expected life of the bulb before it burns out.

New bulbs on the market are reported to last longer than standard bulbs, with less loss in light output. One, a bulb filled with Krypton gas, is called a "Super Bulb"; another bulb utilizing a "power-coil" filament is called "Soft-White Plus". Both cost more than standard bulbs.

Check lumen rating as well as bulb life before making a choice.

Selecting bulbs and lighting equipment may require more know-how and time than you anticipated.

But the results—more attractive

rooms with comfortable, adequate, visual conditions—make it worth the effort.

To obtain more information on lighting consult your county Extension Service's home economist or the electric utility that serves you.

For further reading:

U.S. Department of Agriculture. *Planning Your Home Lighting*, Home and Garden Bulletin No. 138, Superintendent of Documents, Government Printing Office, Washington, D.C. 20402, 20 cents.

Better Light Better Sight Bureau, *The Facts of Light: The New Language of Light Bulbs: Remodeling Sketchbook* No. B72-580, Box 1647 Grand Central Station, New York, N.Y. 10017. Single copies free.

General Electric Co., The Lumen Calculator, No. 146–0486: *The Light Book:* How to be at Home With Lighting, No. 146–1220; Six booklets in the *Light Makes a Difference* series—In the·Kitchen, No. 230–5520, In the Bathroom, No. 230–5521, In the Family Room, No. 230–5522, In the Living/Dining Room, No. 230–5523, In the Bedroom, No. 230–5524, In Outdoor Living, No. 230–5525, Inquiry Bureau, Nela Park, Cleveland, Ohio 44112. Single copies free.

Illuminating Engineering Society, *Design Criteria for Lighting Interior Living Spaces*, 345 East 47th Street, New York, N.Y. 10017. $4.50 plus $1 service charge on single-copy orders.

Sylvania Lighting Center, *Bright Ideas* Series, Sylvania Electric Products, 100 Endicott Street, Danvers, Mass. 01923. Single copies free.

Portable Storage, Room Dividers

GENERAL BASIC STORAGE in housing units is needed by all families, and different life styles require some individual adaptation of storage. Often there is a sparsity of storage in even the more expensive houses and apartments. Homes occupied by low-income families almost without exception have inadequate storage. The biggest reasons for inadequate storage in residential units are the added cost and a lack of planning at the time of building.

Fortunately, something can be done to improve household storage in owner-occupied and rented units. Portable or movable storage can be designed to fill the need, and constructed either by a cabinetmaker or by a family member who has some knowledge of hand tools and likes to work with his hands. Portable storage units can also be moved with other household goods when the family changes its place of residence.

The following suggestions for storage designs with do-it-yourself construction techniques may be helpful in planning and keeping costs down. Ideas for portable room dividers also are discussed later in the chapter.

Base-type storage units are useful in the home in at least two ways. They serve to store items at the place of use, and the counter top can serve as a work surface for meal preparation and serving, as a dressing table, or as a place for working on or displaying hobbies.

A base cabinet with simple design that will have the fewest parts, and proper use of the least expensive materials may interest families with a small amount of money to invest. Others may elect to use more expensive materials, add drawers and hinged doors for convenience, and apply a fine finish.

A low-cost counter-type storage unit 3 feet high, 2 feet deep and 4 feet long can be used in the kitchen, utility room, bedroom, dining, or living room. A simple design with sliding doors, wood counter top, and no drawers can be relatively inexpensive and easy to construct.

Sides, floor, shelf, and back may be of ⅜-inch particleboard, or plywood—which is more expensive. The base providing toe space is a 1-x4-inch No. 2 pine or fir board.

Parts should be sawed accurately, using an electric saw with a carbide-

AUTHOR WOODLEY C. WARRICK is Specialist in Charge, Housing and House Furnishings, North Carolina Agricultural Extension Service, North Carolina State University, Raleigh.

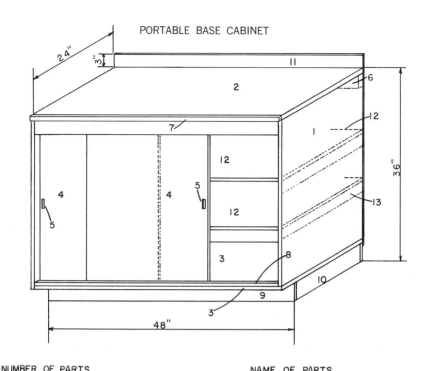

NUMBER OF PARTS	NAME OF PARTS
1	Ends (2) 24" X 31 1/4"
2	Top (1) 24" X 48"
3	Bottom (1) 24" X 48"
4	Door (2) 24" X 30"
11	Back (1) 36" X 48"
12	Shelves (2) 21 3/4" X 46 3/4"
13	Shelf supports (4) 2 1/4" X 21 1/2"
5	Pulls (2) 3/4" X 3"
6	Support top (2) 1" X 4" X 46 3/4"
7	Front trim (1) 1 1/2" X 48"
8	Door guide (1) 3/4" X 46 3/4"
9	Front toe (2) 1" X 4" X 48"
10	Side toe base (2) 1" X 4" X 19 1/2"

tipped blade for particleboard. Holes should be drilled for 4-penny finish nails driven near the edge of the board. A ¼-inch drill, with a regular drill bit, three-fourths the diameter of the nails to be used, is recommended. A finishing nail serves very well in place of a regular drill bit. Glue on both surfaces, in addition to nails, adds strength at the joints.

When varnishing or painting particleboard, use a filler or sanding sealer first, then two finish coats. The satisfactory use of stains with lacquers or varnishes may require some experimentation.

Normal procedure for painting is to use: (1) a filler or sealer, (2) a prime coat, and (3) a finish coat. Paint containing water should not be applied to particleboard which has not first been coated with an appropriate oil base primer or filler.

Apply filler and primer to the back of doors to prevent unbalanced moisture penetration that could cause warping.

A closet for clothes storage is needed by all family members, and of course the more clothes one has the more storage is needed. A clothes closet 2 feet deep inside by 3 feet wide is the

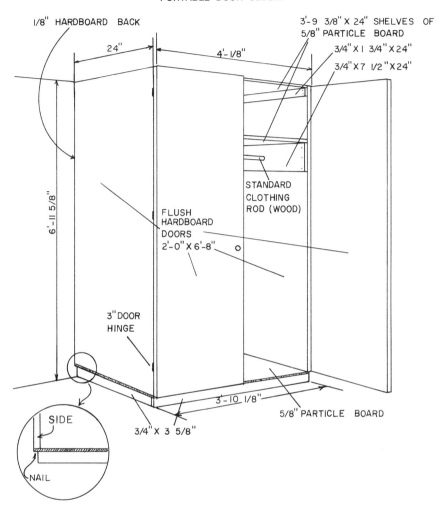

1/8" HARDBOARD BACK

3'-9 3/8" X 24" SHELVES OF 5/8" PARTICLE BOARD

24"

4'-1/8"

3/4" X 1 3/4" X 24"

3/4" X 7 1/2" X 24"

6'-11 5/8"

STANDARD CLOTHING ROD (WOOD)

FLUSH HARDBOARD DOORS 2'-0" X 6'-8"

3" DOOR HINGE

3'-10 1/8"

SIDE

3/4" X 3 5/8"

5/8" PARTICLE BOARD

NAIL

minimum allowed in new homes with loans insured by the Government. An adult needs 4 to 8 feet of rod-hanging space.

Closet space seems limited in most houses and apartments. A simple 2- by 4-foot free-standing unit 6 feet 8 inches high can be quickly and easily constructed by assembling four flush doors. First, a base is made of 1-x4-inch No. 2 pine on edge with a floor of ⅝-inch particleboard nailed to it.

After constructing the base it should

be tapered, if necessary, on the bottom so that the floor of the closet will be level from front to back and side to side. This step is not required where the floor is level at the place of closet use.

Next, nail the shelf and top cleats to the side panel doors, then hinge the front doors to the side panels. Then with the front door laid face down, install the ⅝-inch particleboard shelf, top panel, and base. The base is nailed on the bottom end of the side panels.

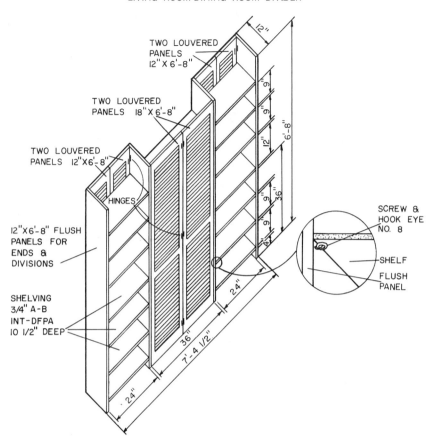

With the unit in this position, nail the ⅛-inch hardboard back which will enclose the back and give rigidity.

The unit is usable in a corner, in the center of a wall or beside the front entrance to serve as a coat closet and room divider when needed and when space permits.

Hardboard hollow-core doors are the least expensive to buy and they paint well. A primer-sealer coat and one semi-gloss enamel coat are suggested for hardboard. Flush wood doors may be selected. Closet width can vary, as the width of stock doors varies in 4-inch increments. Prefinished hardboard doors are available.

Two units together, facing in opposite directions, can be used as a free-standing room divider in a large bedroom for children.

The combination living room-dining room or family room-dining room is designed in some floor plans to economize or for casual living. Families with such arrangements may find that privacy at the table is needed during mealtime, and there may be a need for a shield to obscure a view of dirty dishes from the living area. Privacy can be provided with a room divider that adds graciousness and may even provide needed storage.

A divider may consist of a simple folding screen, cloth panels from floor to ceiling, or a three-dimension unit useful for storage in addition to giving space dimension and sight separation

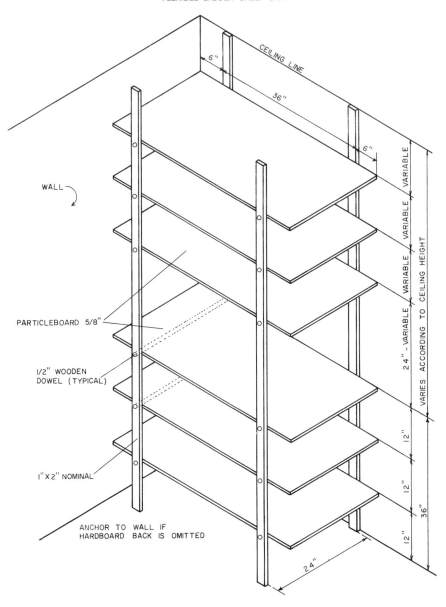

between the living and dining areas. Such a divider can be designed, built, and installed by owner families and even by renters of houses or apartments because no structural changes in the residence are necessary.

A free-standing divider, 12 inches deep, 6 feet 8 inches high and 7 feet 4½ inches long, can be assembled mostly of stock elements. This should assure good appearance.

Selected for an example is a divider consisting of end and division panels 12 inches wide by 6 feet 8 inches high by 1⅛ inches thick, purchased as flush bifold closet doors. For the back panels, bifold louvered closet doors are used. The unit requires four flush panels 12 inches wide, four louvered panels 12 inches wide and two louvered panels 18 inches wide.

Shelving consists of ¾ inch A-B INT-DFPA plywood or shelving board. Shelves 24 inches long are shown in the end sections and 36 inches in the center section. These shelves are 10½ inches deep.

With the use of hinges to attach the side and division panels to the back panels on the shelf side and with the use of screws and hook eyes for shelf supports, the unit can be readied for moving, if necessary, by removing, stacking, and tying the shelves and then folding the panels flat similarly to folding a road map.

One basic design principle for storage that can be adapted to individual family needs for specific purposes would seem to be ideal. Ladder-type supports for shelving approaches this because of the flexibility it provides. It can be moved from room to room, or from one home to another.

Shelving is the basic component of most household storage. Wide, narrow, long, short, flexible spacing, open or closed shelves, variable height, material cost, etc., are considerations in designing shelf storage. A shelf unit should be designed to fit the need and located where the stored items are to be first used.

One example of the ladder-support shelf design may serve to illustrate this storage principle. To construct a floor-to-ceiling unit, cut four pieces of 1x2's of No. 1 pine or fir to the floor-to-ceiling length.

Decide next on the shelf spacing and mark one support. Stack the supports with the marked one on top and drill ½-inch holes to receive ½-inch hardwood dowels for shelf supports.

Build two ladders using the dowels. For 2-foot-deep shelves, cut the dowels to allow shelf to fit on the dowel between the vertical supports. The span

of shelves between the ladder supports should not exceed 30 inches, particularly for heavy storage.

Rear vertical supports must be anchored to the walls at the top. But where the unit is to be free standing, a back of ⅛-inch hardboard can be fastened by screws to the back of the rear vertical supports.

Such a unit can be easily disassembled and moved to a new location, if necessary.

In designing or adapting existing storage to a specific need there are some simple rules to keep in mind. Use of factory components such as the factory-made doors suggested in the closet storage and in the room divider can fairly well determine that the unit will be of acceptable appearance if jointing and finishing are well done.

One should also keep in mind the limitations on the weight shelves will carry. A solid-wood shelf of white pine or most other woods should be supported for at least every four feet of length. Particleboard would be expected to support less weight than plywood or solid wood of the same thickness.

Privacy at the front door plus a chance to create a warm welcome and desired family impressions is sometimes provided by an entrance hall. Some families that do not have an entrance hall may feel a real need for doing something to improve their guest entrance.

Space permitting, privacy at an entrance often can be created by a portable free-standing divider beside the front door. A minimum 4-foot-wide entrance should be allowed at the door.

An entrance unit might be built in the form of exposed bookshelves, using the bottom 3 feet to face the living area.

The space above 3 feet could face the entrance area. In this space a mirror with side lights and a plug-in cord would make the divider functional and attractive to persons coming or going, particularly those who might want to check their appearance. Thickness to accommodate the medicine-cabinet-type

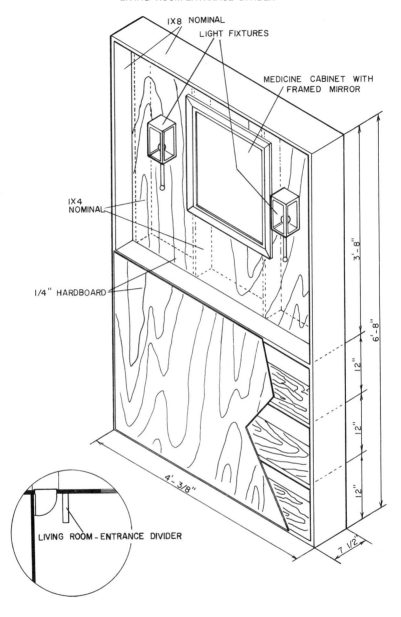

LIVING ROOM - ENTRANCE DIVIDER

mirror and the wiring is provided by the use of 1x4's separating the back surface and the front. A mirror without lights might be the choice of some families.

Overall dimensions for initial consideration could be: 4 feet wide, 6 feet 8 inches high and 7½ inches thick. This thickness will give reasonable stability and provide shelf space deep enough for most books. Moving this unit should not be a problem.

A shelf depth to 12 inches and greater may be desirable where space permits and where the unit is to be permanent.

Side pieces, top, bottom, and shelves should be of No. 1 pine or fir. Back and front panels may be of ¼-inch plywood or hardboard prefinished or unfinished. Unfinished sides and shelves should be finished to match prefinished panels.

A word of caution for do-it-yourselfers is to learn how to use tools. Pick the right tools for the job and keep tools sharp and true. Ragged edges are often the result of dull tools.

Plan work ahead and be accurate in marking, cutting, and nailing. You will cherish the finished product in proportion to the accuracy that you used in constructing it.

Major Appliances For Homemakers

Responsibility for satisfactory performance of major home appliances falls upon three groups: the manufacturer, the retailer, and the family.

The manufacturer must search for better, safer, and more economical appliances to better serve the family. Through the Association of Home Appliance Manufacturers (AHAM), industry is working cooperatively on performance standards and certification programs for home appliances.

Manufacturers make appliance innovations known to the public through advertising and educational programs. Adequate instructions for operating the appliance should be provided with each sale.

Appropriate warranties or guarantees should be provided to protect the consumer who purchases the appliance against faulty merchandise. Replacement parts and training for servicemen must also be made available so that the appliances can serve a long and useful life.

The retailer must provide a suitable selection of each appliance to be sold so that each buyer can find the best appliance to meet his family situation. Salesmen should be trained to understand appliances and appliance features in order to explain them fully to prospective buyers. Such services as delivery, installation, and maintenance of appliances sold should also be provided at costs that are reasonable for the community served.

Additionally, the retailer is charged to serve as a liaison between the family and the manufacturer, seeing that conditions of the warranty are met by the manufacturer and insuring the general satisfaction of the family.

A reliable dealer is likely to retail reliable appliances and stand behind them.

Role of the family in appliance satisfaction is sometimes overlooked. Because appliances are purchased at infrequent intervals, new appliances may be different from what you now have. More choices may be available. You should take time to become fully informed before shopping.

The home economics extension program in most States can provide information on what is available in home appliances, the capabilities and limitations of appliances, and features that may be new to the consumer. Current magazines may also help. Mail order catalogs and information sheets which the dealer has describe the appliance and its features.

Many people rely on information provided by consumer testing groups. This information can be helpful if you recognize that not all models and makes are studied, and then read carefully to make certain that appliances are compared on a basis important to you.

Knowing what appliance variations are available is only half the job. You must also evaluate your family needs,

AUTHOR VIRGINIA PEART is an Associate Professor in the Equipment and Family Housing Department, School of Home Economics, Purdue University, Lafayette, Ind.

at present and projected through the lifetime of the appliance.

• Is your family large or small? What space is available? These may determine appliance size

• What can you afford and how will it be paid for? Spreading payments over a longer period of time may ease the budget temporarily, but in the long run it will cost more for the purchase

• What are the demands on your family time? Time and energy-saving features may help

• What is your family's life style? It is wasteful to purchase an appliance or feature you are unlikely to use.

When shopping for appliances you should ask about the availability and costs of appliance service. Carefully read warranties and check instruction books, too. Make sure the instructions are clear.

The American Gas Association (AGA) Seal certifies that gas appliances have been tested for safety, performance, and durability. The Underwriters Laboratories, Inc. (UL) certifies that electrical appliances have been submitted by the manufacturer for testing and have met standards regarding life, fire, and casualty.

Read credit contracts before signing to be sure all spaces are filled in. It will help you understand what you are paying for.

When the appliance has been selected and installed, the instruction book should be carefully studied and followed. Write the appliance model and serial number on the instruction book so it will be easy to find if you need service.

Instruction book, warranties, and sales receipts should be filed in a safe but handy place. If an appliance problem occurs, check the instruction manual. It will tell you what to do and may even save a service call. When service is required, call the dealer or service agency he recommends.

For service problems that cannot be resolved locally, feel free to write or call the manufacturer, giving all details. His concern for consumer satis-

Above, smooth-top range with touch controls and visual readout. Right, next page, smooth-top range that slides in between kitchen cabinets and looks built-in.

faction will usually help. If not, you can write or call MACAP—Major Appliance Consumer Action Panel, 20 North Wacker Drive, Chicago, Ill. 60606. The phone number is (312) 236-3165.

RANGES: The appliance the homemaker uses most extensively is her range. She and her range form the team that cooks and serves food for the family. Along with cooking, many spills, spatters, and splashes occur, and the homemaker must spend much time and effort keeping her range clean.

When things go well with the homemaker and her range, she is a better cook. So it is important that she select a range that meets her needs and then make the best use of it and its features.

About five electric ranges are bought for every four gas ranges, but the choice is highly individual.

Your satisfaction will depend on the availability and cost of each and your past experiences.

Many of the same features are to be found on either gas or electric ranges.

About 10 percent of the ranges bought are high oven type, usually with two ovens.

A second oven may be useful for a large family, special occasions, or entertaining. This feature is available in both gas and electric models. It requires special space.

290

The upper oven may be smaller. Check size, if it's important to use large roasters or cookie sheets in it.

Look for take-apart units and burners and surface tops that can be lifted for easy cleaning underneath, removable oven doors and oven liners that can be washed at the sink.

Two oven-cleaning arrangements are available in gas and electric ranges.

Self-cleaning ovens use high temperatures to remove oven soils. Insulation should keep surface temperatures at a safe level during cleaning.

Continuous cleaning ovens are lined with a material which encourages the breakdown of oven soils at baking temperatures. More time is needed for cleaning. If spatters occur very frequently, cleaning may have difficulty keeping up.

Programmed cooking is another feature. Delay-cook ovens have been available for some time on electric ranges. Gas range ovens with programmed cooking will usually be the cook-and-keep-warm type. Cooking begins when food is put into the oven. As the end of cooking time approaches, the oven temperature drops to about 170°F. and is held until food is removed.

Smooth-top ranges provide a new look for the kitchen. Glass ceramic materials have been developed to be strong enough to withstand normal banging and bumping and high cooking temperatures. Pans with smooth, flat bottoms should be used. A special product is available to clean cooked-on spots if they occur. The heat-up and cool-down times are longer.

Microwave Ovens are a new way to get heat into foods. Microwave energy, much like radio and TV radiant energy, is produced and directed into the oven.

The oven has special locks and seals designed to keep microwave energy in and protect the user. Materials such as glass, glass ceramic, china, pottery, paper and some plastics allow the energy to flow through and are used for cooking utensils.

Microwave energy enters food directly. Molecular agitation inside the food produces heat. Cooking times are much shorter than usual and browning will not take place, except for something as large as a roast that requires longer to cook.

The family that buys a microwave oven will probably enjoy quick heating and reheating of foods when many busy schedules must be observed. They will also need to spend time and effort to learn to make the best use of it.

Some heart pacemakers are affected by microwave energy, so a pacemaker wearer should consult his physician before purchasing a microwave oven.

New utensils have been developed which absorb the energy, and after preheating will brown foods in the oven while cooking quickly with microwave energy.

Some concern has been voiced about leaks of microwave energy creating hazards. It is important to point out, however, that microwave rays are longer than visible light and their effect is heating. This should not be confused with cosmic rays, gamma rays, X-rays, and ultraviolet rays which are all shorter than visible light and when strong enough can alter living cells.

REFRIGERATORS: The primary function of the refrigerator is to provide storage that will keep foods fresh and safe longer. The size needed will depend on both family size and how frequently you shop.

Since storage space is so important, special attention has been given to shelf and compartment design. Crispers should have tight covers to keep fresh vegetables and fruits from drying out. Adjustable shelves, pullout shelves, and door storage all stretch space.

It's important for the family to consider what they like to put into the refrigerator when they shop—watermelons, turkeys, tall bottles, and other large items can influence their selection.

About a fifth of the refrigerators sold are side-by-side refrigerator-freezers and come in sizes from 30 to 60 inches wide. They offer storage at a convenient height for both refrigerator and freezer. Doors do not require as much space to open because they are narrow. Some have a third door for icecubes.

Flush mount refrigerators are built with the condenser coils (usually on the refrigerator back) under the refrigerator cold-food compartment. This allows the refrigerator to be pushed back against the wall and saves room space. A fan cools the condenser coils when the refrigerator is running.

In frost-free refrigerators the cooling coils are concealed behind the refrigerator and freezer compartments so as

to completely eliminate the defrosting job. Refrigerated air is blown into the compartments.

Temperatures in frost-free refrigerators are even throughout the unit, and foods cool to safe storage temperatures faster. But unless foods are carefully wrapped and sealed they will dehydrate. The cost of operating a frost-free refrigerator may be almost double that of automatic defrost refrigerators with manual defrost freezers.

Icemakers eliminate the tray filling job. Add-on icemakers will be slower than some built-in types.

Compact refrigerators may be useful for the family room or a vacation home. They usually are manual defrost.

Above left, compact refrigerator and freezer may be just the thing for a family room or vacation home. Left, refrigerator-freezer with a third door so you can get out ice without letting warm air into rest of freezer. Above, side-by-side refrigerator with flexible storage shelves and door, automatic icemaker.

FREEZERS: Home freezers are enjoying a spurt in popularity. The types and amounts of frozen foods have more than doubled in the last 10 years. We can expect them to double again in the next 10.

A freezer allows you to shop less

293

frequently. This is important if the supermarket is distant, and it fits with the trend toward busy family lives and more working women.

Many families enjoy freezing fresh foods and preparing foods to freeze for later use as well.

An upright freezer has easy to see and use shelf space. Most are frost free, but may cost more to operate.

A chest type freezer costs less than an upright, but takes more floor space and makes reaching foods at the bottom more difficult. It needs defrosting one to three times a year. Some types have push button flash-defrost and a bottom drain to help.

A compact freezer saves space.

DISHWASHERS were a luxury appliance 10 years ago. Today, one family in four has one and would hesitate to give it up. Estimates are that 40 percent of homes will have a dishwasher in only a few more years. It may be the next new appliance you buy.

Dishwashers are popular for several reasons. They save an important block of time each day. Kitchen space is reserved because used dishes and utensils go right into the dishwasher instead of cluttering the counter. Dishes are cleaner and more sanitary than if hand washed and dried.

The family's role in getting clean dishes is important. Water must be soft and hot (140°-160°F.). The proper detergent and the right amount must be used.

The dishwasher instruction book will say what can and what cannot be washed and provide charts for proper loading of racks.

In the water distribution system, spray arms direct water onto dishes. Water must reach every dish. A spray arm beneath each rack may be best.

Soft food disposers reduce the need for scraping and prerinsing.

Flexible rack designs allow random loading and accommodate mixed loads easily.

You have a number of cycle choices. Regular and Rinse-and-Hold are used the most. Also offered are Soak, Utensil, Short, Gentle, and Fine China cycles.

FOOD WASTE DISPOSERS eliminate the garbage chore and odors once associated with trash cans. To make the best use of a disposer, all wastes should be ground immediately. Foods decay rapidly and the acid that develops can corrode metal disposer parts and cause odors.

Cold water is a must to solidify fats so they won't congeal in drain pipes and clog them. Most disposers will grind small bones, fruit rinds, and seeds but metals, glass, and china should be avoided.

In a continuous feed disposer, wastes can be fed continuously during the disposing process. A batch feed type will operate only with the cover on. It may be safer when the children are around, but may prove to be slower.

Antijamming and reset devices are features which protect the motor from overheating and allow you to get the disposer back into operation when stalled.

WASTE COMPACTORS are a new favorite in many households. They reduce the volume of trash leaving the home and simplify waste disposal. Bottles, cans, cartons, and waste paper can all be compacted. The compactor should be operated after each addition. It takes about a minute for each use.

Large bottles or cans should be laid on their sides near the center of the compactor for compacting. Keep hands and feet out when adding trash because of broken glass and sharp can edges.

Compacting food wastes may cause problems. Odors develop with the decaying process and disinfectant sprays delay but do not stop food decomposition.

Key locks are available on all models. In some they prevent operation of the compactors. On others they prevent opening the door as well.

Special trash bags may be required and can be relatively expensive. Sometimes any standard sized heavy-duty plastic bag can be used.

LAUNDRY APPLIANCES: We expect

Compact washer and dryer combined occupies a space that is 24 inches wide and 60 inches high.

more of laundry appliances than just clean, dry clothes. The family uses many fibers from cotton and wool to polyesters and acrylics. Easy care finishes on clothes are plentiful, too. Laundry appliances must keep them all clean and protect the carefree qualities that are prized so highly.

Many washers and dryers are larger today than they used to be. They can handle more clothes at a time, but larger washers also use more water and need more detergent and other laundry aids to wash big loads.

New washers and dryers offer more flexibility for better laundry results. However, making the best use of them may mean revising laundry practices. Most manufacturers include a laundry handbook with their washers and dryers

to help. Now, 120 volt dryers are also available when a 220 volt circuit is not available. The 120 volt dryers will usually be slower, but are more economical to operate.

Water temperature selector switches allow a choice of wash and rinse water temperatures for many clothes load types.

Water level controls allow small loads to be washed at a water and detergent savings.

Agitation and spin speed selectors give vigorous or gentle action for both normal and special loads.

In fully-programmed controls you select the button for the type of wash load, and the proper temperatures and speeds will automatically be used in the cycle.

In dryers, look for: Lint filters, which make it easy to locate and empty lint. Temperature choice, from air fluff to hot to suit all clothes load types. Fan speed, from gentle to normal for delicate to normal loads. Drying sensors, which stop drying when clothes are just right. A drying rack, to dry such things as canvas shoes without tumbling.

Compact washers and dryers are good for small families with small loads to wash or where space is limited. Compacts do not usually offer as many features as standard-sized washers and dryers.

Washer-dryer combinations are still around and may solve space problems. Both front-loading washers and washer-dryer combinations use much less water and detergent than the top-loading washers do.

For further reading:

The following publications may be obtained from Consumer Information, Public Documents Distribution Center, Pueblo, Colo. 81009:

Dishwashers, 1972, 20 pp. 001A. 70 cents.
Microwave Oven Radiation. 1971. 9 pp. 002A. 15 cents.
Washers and Dryers. 1972. 24 pp. 006A. 45 cents.

Buying Smaller Appliances

YOUR PLEASANT PLIGHT as a consumer might well be expressed like this. You make yourself beautiful, your house clean and comfortable, and your family or friends happy with good food cooked and served anywhere in the house. And it is all done with appliances, most of them portable and quite inexpensive, but sometimes difficult to select because of a great wealth of choices.

This article gives information that hopefully will help you make the best buy. For organizational purposes the appliances are classified as personal care, comfort, and specialty cooking, and are discussed in that order.

As Americans have become "hair conscious," manufacturers have been busy producing appliances to care for it. There is quite an array of combs, brushes, stylers, dryers, hairsetters, and even "portable beauty salons." Confused? You needn't be, if you know what each one is supposed to do.

Electric combs and brushes are especially suitable for hair with "direction" or for the natural look. They may be sold as attachments for styling dryers or as hot combs, which are more light-weight and streamlined than dryers. In any case, they perform the same grooming jobs.

Brushes for shaping and combs for styling produce even drying by lifting and separating the hair. They help control cowlicks, unruly ends, and too curly hair, and at the same time dry quickly and easily.

Most models have two temperatures or speed settings, hot for drying and a cooler one for styling. They may be

AUTHOR DORIS OGLESBY is Extension Home Economist—Housing and Equipment, University of Georgia, Athens.

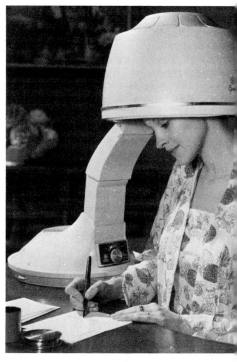

A salon-type mist speed dryer with extra-large tilting hood.

marked "dry" and "style" or "high" and "low." Many models have a mist feature for slightly dampening hair as it is styled, resulting in a better set.

Detanglers are similar in appearance to hot combs but are made especially for combing out snarls and tangles with a gentle vibrating motion. There is a cordless one for use at the beach, pool, or even in the shower.

While hot combs and styling dryers may be used by all members of the family they are often designated by color—pastel for women, dark for men, bright or neutral for the family.

Regular hair dryers are available in bonnet and more expensive salon types. Features of bonnet models are comb and brush, spot curl attachment for quick touchups, "cool" setting for summertime drying, carrying strap and loose-fitting bonnet with detachable featherweight motor floating on top.

Salon-type dryers have such features

as spot mist for touchups, adjustable height, extra-large hood that tilts to allow you to read or sew, remote control, plastic shield for facial saunas, and folding into a compact case.

Hairsetters allow you to roll your hair on heated rollers for a quick set. Some models set hair dry and with mist or conditioner. A set contains about 20 to 27 or more rollers in three sizes.

An electric manicure set consists of a power handle and attachments for shaping, buffing, handling cuticle, and smoothing calluses. The greatest advantage to you, other than saving time and money, is that nail edges are beveled to prevent splitting.

If your children hate to brush their teeth or are in the brace stage, an automatic brush and oral irrigator may be just what they need. Happily, these appliances are geared to family use, so everyone benefits.

Toothbrushes are cordless when in use, but come with a charging unit that must be connected to a live outlet. Don't count on using one that is part of a light fixture unless it operates independently of the light switch. Choose one that has the number of brushes that best suits your family size, and check on local availability of extra brushes.

Some models brush up and down or back and forth at the flick of a switch. Others brush up, down, and around at the same time.

An oral irrigator is designed to supplement brushing. With a pressure control, you send pulsating jets of water into your mouth which clean and stimulate in, around, and between teeth. It is especially good for orthodontic or fixed bridge use.

Rather than two separate appliances, you might prefer having an oral hygiene center that combines the operations of brushing and irrigating.

The best time to buy an air conditioner is when you least need it—in the middle of winter. You have plenty of time then to make a careful selection, and the chances are that you will get a good buy.

Although cost is important, it is not the only factor. An air conditioner must be properly sized for the area it is to cool. When you shop, go armed with information that includes size and shape of the area to be cooled, number of people who normally use the area, exposure, type of windows, amount of glass, and insulation. A dealer then knows what to show you.

You must consider the cost of installation. You may be able to use an existing circuit, but be prepared to pay for additional wiring of perhaps 230 volts.

Operating cost may offset a low purchase price. A simple calculation that takes only a few seconds gives a means of comparing one unit with another. Look for the seal of the Association of Home Appliance Manufacturers which certifies that the BTU rating is correct. Divide this rating by the wattage of the unit to get its efficiency. The most efficient model will cost less to operate.

Look closely at the controls. They should be easy to reach and allow you to tailor the air conditioning to your needs. If you are noise conscious, you will enjoy having several speeds. Direction control louvers for air distribution are important, especially in the larger sizes.

Consider serviceability. Look at it from the repairman's ability to get to and remove the unit if necessary. Also consider filter accessibility because cleaning and changing them is something you will be doing yourself.

As a rule, you won't need a dehumidifier if you have air conditioning. But you may want to consider one if you notice symptoms of excess moisture such as musty, moldy odors, mildew, peeling interior paint, sweating of cold pipes and basement walls, rusty metal objects, warping or swelling of wood.

A dehumidifier works by drawing room air over a cooling coil where it is relieved of some of its moisture. It is then heated slightly and returned to the room at just above its original temperature.

Size depends on a number of factors such as climate, house construction, and where used. But a rough rule of thumb will help you decide. The unit should have the capacity to remove at least a pint of water for every thousand cubic feet of space to be dehumidified.

Look for the Association of Home Appliance Manufacturers' certification of water removal capacity rating.

Cost of the unit depends on its capacity, appearance, and features. Among the features are disposal of water by a drain hose or an easy-to-handle container, automatic shutoff to prevent overflowing, and a signal light telling when the container is full. Others are easily moving wheels, long cord, ease in cleaning, and adjustable controls for operation.

Operating cost is fairly high but a bargain when balanced against moisture damage to your house and furnishings.

A humidifier performs exactly the opposite from a dehumidifier. Signs that you may need one are uncomfortably dry body conditions, static electricity, cracks in house and furniture, and drooping plants.

There is a central type which is installed with a forced hot air furnace and a self-contained console or tabletop appliance. Sizing is determined by size of the house, tightness of construction, amount of moisture from other sources such as laundering, and desired relative humidity.

Your best bet is to follow the manufacturer's recommendations for space a unit will handle. If in doubt, buy an overlarge rather than a too small unit.

Humidifiers operate by evaporation or atomization. The latter may create housecleaning problems because the droplets evaporate, leaving mineral deposits on furniture. An evaporation type emits pure vapor by moving air through or around wet pads or sleeves which must be removed for cleaning about once a month, for replacement about once a year.

Cost of using is very moderate but can be increased considerably if the unit has a heater for offsetting the air cooling effect of operation.

Check these features as you shop—

furniture styling, automatic shutoff, signal light for filling, ease in filling and cleaning, plastic or stainless parts for hard water areas, air-flow louvers, good casters, and flexible controls for humidity and speed.

Your choice of a vacuum cleaner should depend to a great extent on what you want it to do for you. As a rule, canister cleaners are easy to handle and do an adequate job of general housecleaning. Some models feature power attachments that give them increased carpet cleaning efficiency. Uprights are made for carpets, but with a set of attachments they can also houseclean.

Hand vacuums are good for spot cleaning, auto, or other light jobs. They should be used only to supplement full-size cleaners.

Many homes are fully or partially carpeted, some with as many as three or four pile heights. Upright vacuum cleaners that adapt to low (such as indoor-outdoor or kitchen carpet), medium, and shag are desirable for these situations. Some models adapt automatically, others must be set manually.

Standard models can be adjusted by changing the amount of suction to the point that the cleaner moves over the carpet without extra effort or without seeming to skim the surface.

Highest priced models may move around at the touch of a finger, a good point to keep in mind if you are troubled with arthritis or other handicap.

Edge cleaning is a new feature, eliminating the need for using a tool next to walls and pieces of furniture.

You pretty well get what you pay for in a vacuum cleaner, although it is not necessary to buy a very high-priced model that seems out of line with the prices of similar models. Nor should you buy strictly on the basis of low cost. Power, design, and brand reputation are all important, and a good mixture of the three is desirable. Local service is also a plus feature.

Clean, attractive floors are no accident. Whether wood, resilient, carpeted or ceramic, they can be cleaned with an appliance simple and easy to use.

You can buy one that does nothing but shampoo carpets. Another scrubs resilient or ceramic floors, polishes and buffs resilient, ceramic, and wood. It may also apply liquid polishing wax. Still another does all these jobs with a change of brushes and solution.

Prices vary accordingly, and there is no need to pay for one that does more than your need of it. Whatever your choice of floor polishers and shampooers, it should be easy to move around, have controls that are accessible while the appliance is in use, be easy to assemble and to fill during operation, and have a long cord.

It is important that you follow instructions for using in order to achieve good results. Therefore, be sure that the model you select has a good user's manual. For shampooing carpets, it is especially necessary that you follow instructions. The process is basically as follows:

Vacuuming to remove loose soil is the first step. Suds dispensed by the shampooer bring additional soil to the pile surface. The carpet should not be wet excessively and it does not need rinsing. You will notice that the suds disappear rapidly.

After the carpet is thoroughly dry, vacuum to remove soil that the shampooer brought to the surface. It is advisable to vacuum every day for about a week for a thorough cleaning.

A fondue pot is a fun appliance for a specialized type of cooking and a great gift for yourself or someone else. The basic unit consists of a pot, a stand on which it rests, and a burner for cooking or keeping the fondue mixture hot. As you shop you will find many colors, sizes, shapes, and degrees of deluxeness, but all fall into three groups, depending on the type of cooking for which they are suitable. They are metal, ceramic, and dessert.

Meats are cooked in oil and therefore require a metal pot that can withstand high heat. Frequently used metals are stainless steel, plain, enameled or porcelainized aluminum, and copper. By regulating the heat, this type of pot can be used for cheese and dessert mixtures and is the best choice for all-purpose fondue cooking. A heavy-gage metal pot that is larger at the bottom than at the top holds heat well and helps prevent spattering. The interior may have a nonstick coating.

A ceramic pot shaped like a shallow casserole may be used for cheese fondues; it's not suited for hot oil cooking.

Most metal pots have two-quart capacity but a dessert utensil is smaller and may use a candle warmer since sauces require less space and heat than other mixtures. Heat for metal pots is supplied by alcohol, canned heat, or electricity. Candle warmers are for dessert fondues only.

Although alcohol burners have some means of regulating the amount of heat, the electric unit features a thermostat to eliminate guesswork.

Forks, plates, trays, and lazy Susans are accessories that may accompany a fondue set. They can be bought separately.

When making your selection, remember that it will be used on a table by a group of people. Choose a fairly heavy pot with a comfortable, heat-resistant handle that fits securely on its stand. Use it on its own tray or another that protects the tabletop as well as providing a firm foundation.

Although it is more than a toaster, less than a range oven, a toaster-oven is a delightful tabletop appliance that does a variety of cooking jobs. Depending upon the manufacturer, it may broil, bake, roast, or toast. How these jobs are accomplished also varies with the manufacturer.

All the methods are based on one principle. Heat for baking and roasting comes from the bottom. For broiling and top browning, heat comes from the top.

Some toaster ovens have one heating unit but since the entire appliance can be flipped over, the unit is in the top for broiling and toasting, in the bottom for baking and roasting. Another type has both top and bottom units controlled by switches. Select the type of cooking you prefer and the appliance automatically does the rest.

These models generally toast one or both sides, automatically cut off, and may have a bell to signal that toast is ready.

Still another type opens from the front for baking and has slots in the top for popup toasting.

To be certain you know exactly what a particular model is capable of doing, take time to look at the user's book. If it contains no instructions for broiling, the appliance will not broil. If there are no instructions for baking, it will not bake, and so on.

Although the temperature range is from 200°F. to 500°F., baking is necessarily limited by space, even in the largest models. Roasting, where possible, is also limited to small amounts.

As you shop and compare, ask yourself the following questions:

Does the toaster oven perform the jobs you expect of it?

Is the size right for the space you have and the amount you want to cook?

Does it have features such as removable glass door, removable rack, or continuous clean liner to make cleaning reasonably easy?

Does it automatically cut itself off, and is there a signal to tell you that it has cut off?

Does it have adequate instructions for use, care, and service?

A rotisserie cooks meat to a beautiful brown by turning it on a spit in controlled heat. There are two types—open air and covered. Open air models do not have covers, are low in silhouette, store easily, and can be used for broiling. Covered models are larger and more difficult to store but can generally be used for other types of cooking.

Factors to consider when shopping for a rotisserie are:

• What you expect it to do—some models have adjustable heating elements and accessories that allow them to be used as rotisserie, griddle, grille, broiler, and fryer

• Space to use and store it, in relation to the size of the appliance

• Distance between spit and drip pan below, in relation to what you plan to cook

• Features such as removable, immersible parts and continuous clean liner to make cleaning reasonably easy

An electric can opener works on cans of all sizes by piercing the lid, cutting it smoothly, and holding it with a magnet until the operation stops automatically. It may also sharpen smoothedge knives and perhaps scissors, juice fruit, or crush ice. Prices vary considerably, depending on the number of uses. Important features include good balance and stability, cutting assembly easy to take apart for cleaning, and space for excess cord storage.

You may prefer having a separate ice crusher. Features to check are the amount of crushed ice the container will hold, choice of more than one texture of ice, and a powerful but quiet motor.

Mixers and blenders complement each other but one does not replace the other.

Three basic types of mixers are available: standard, heavy duty, and portable. For most families a standard model is the best choice. However, some homemakers prefer the heavy duty because of its strength. Its main limitation is that the motor head may not be detachable for use at the range.

A portable mixer is easy to store and to use at the range but lacks the power to do heavy jobs well. Its very portability can be a tiring liability when you must hold it while mixing a cake or something requiring similar steps.

You may notice a substantial price difference between models made by the same manufacturer. This is sometimes due to the material of which they are made. For example, chrome is more expensive than enamel and glass. There may, however, be a difference in weight, power, number of speeds, or other features.

Some mixers have attachments that usually must be purchased separately. You should ask about this feature if you think that you might be interested at some later date.

Using a blender.

Your one reason for buying a mixer is to be able to mix and beat with ease and efficiency. For this reason, you should check the number and sizes of bowls, number of speeds, power of motor at any speed, coverage of bowl by the beaters, beater insertion and ejection methods, ease of handling, the adequacy of the instruction book, and availability of service and parts.

A blender operates at very high speed, even on the lowest settings, and is especially good for chopping, blending, pureeing, shredding, whipping, grating, and liquefying. It mixes but cannot handle heavy batters. Neither can it beat egg whites or mash potatoes, both jobs that a mixer does easily.

There are many blenders on the market at many prices. Differences are due to materials of which they are made, number of speeds, type of controls, and power of the motor. Also affecting price are size of the container, whether or not there is a timer, attachments, and the amount of research that was done in development of the blender. The latter point shows up as a well made, sturdy appliance with a good instruction book and service available in the region.

All blenders operate in a similar manner but subtle differences are important.

You may, for example, prefer one that has removable blades or that can be used with regular screwtop jars. Design and color of the base, arrangement of pushbuttons, handle and lid style, and shape of the container are other "small differences" which may be of interest to you.

Both the mixer and blender should be kept where they are handy to use. There is a built-in type, with motor installed in the countertop, that has attachments for mixing, blending, juicing, and a number of other operations. The one drawback is not being able to use the appliances elsewhere.

As aromas go, freshly brewed coffee is hard to beat. It is possible to produce the aroma without having good coffee but there is no excuse for it. Delicious coffee depends on a number of factors but first and foremost is a good, scrupulously clean pot.

We cannot say that one type coffeemaker makes better coffee than another because each one has its adherents who swear by it. There are three types—percolator, vacuum, and drip. Differences between the vacuum and drip may not be clear to you.

The vacuum has two bowls that fit tightly together. Cold water in the bottom bowl is heated and rises into the top bowl where it brews for a few minutes until the heat automatically cuts to a keep warm position. The coffee then runs back into the lower bowl where it is kept hot for serving.

The lower part of a drip coffeemaker is empty until hot water runs through the coffee and a filter and drips into it, ready to serve. Recently this type coffeemaker has become popular in a model similar to what is used in restaurants. At the moment, it is somewhat more expensive than other types.

Because spotlessness is so important, you should buy a model that is easy to clean. Regular washing with hot water is a must but special periodic cleaning is determined by the material of the coffeemaker interior.

Oil from the coffee tends to cling to the interior parts and if left, affects the taste of the coffee. It can be removed by going through the brewing process, using a cleanser instead of coffee. For stainless steel or glass, use laundry or dishwasher detergent after removing aluminum parts. For aluminum, use cream of tartar or scrub with a soap-filled steel wool pad.

Buy a coffeemaker that fits the amount you want to make. It is just as important to know how little it will make satisfactorily as how much. Generally the smallest amount is three or four cups. There is, however, a small basket that fits inside the large one for making small amounts in some makes.

The spout of a percolator should pour without dripping and should be accessible for cleaning with a percolator brush. There should be a control that allows for flexibility in strength of the coffee and also allows you to reheat coffee without reperking.

These buying hints are necessarily limited and general in nature.

There are many good appliances on the market and the final choice may be difficult.

All else being equal, let the following factors weigh heavily:

Buy a recognized brand with service available locally or not too far away. Some manufacturers maintain service centers in the larger cities, where appliances can be carried or sent for repair.

Look for the Underwriters' Laboratories, Inc., seal of approval for safety, and Association of Home Appliance Manufacturers' certification of rating for room air conditioners and dehumidifiers.

Take time to look through the instructions, making a quick check for adequacy. This one factor is often a good indication of a quality appliance.

Once you've made your decision, return the warranty card, follow the instructions, and enjoy your new convenience.

For further reading:

The following publications may be obtained from Consumer Information, Public Documents Distribution Center, Pueblo, Colo. 81009:

Automatic Toasters. 1972. 8 pp. 193A. 30 cents.

Room Air Conditioners. 1972. 24 pp. 003A. 45 cents.

Vacuum Cleaners: Their Selection, Use and Care. 1972. 16 pp. 005A. 60 cents.

Purchasing Hi-Fi Systems, TV, and Tape Recorders

IF YOU ARE PAST 60, probably you can remember when family entertainment in the home was reserved for special occasions. If you are under 60, it has been as natural as breathing to turn on entertainment anytime with the flick of a switch.

Time was when Sunday afternoon entertainment consisted of gathering in the living room with aunts, uncles, first cousins, and neighbors to hear Grandpa tell about the old days. And Uncle Harry presided at the phonograph, letting the youngsters take turns cranking after each record to rewind the spring-driven motor.

Ours is the electronic age. The era of radio began in 1920. From then until America's entry into World War II in 1941, 100 million receivers were sold. Amos and Andy, Fibber McGee and Molly, *I Love a Mystery,* Kate Smith, and the *National Farm and Home Hour* were just a few of the great shows.

Music no longer had to be played on the phonograph. Now the big bands and country and western entertainers came into the living room on the radio.

Television was an immediate and fantastic success after 1946. Its impact on America's entertainment habits and family life was revolutionary. TV be-

AUTHOR FOSTER MULLENAX is an electronic communications media specialist, Information Services Staff, Extension Service.

came a "window on the world." No longer was talk allowed in the living room. There was little time for Grandpa to tell about the old days.

At about the same time a new do-it-yourself hobby had developed. It was very much like the pioneering days in radio when listeners wound coils of wire on oatmeal boxes to build their own receiving sets. This new hobby was "hi-fi." Started by engineers who wanted near perfection in their sound reproduction, it soon spread to advanced laymen, who bought their own components—turntables, tuners, amplifiers, speakers—and did the hookups themselves.

This caused major new developments in phonograph records—the 45 rpm and 33⅓ rpm long-playing discs. FM radio started coming into its own among the hi-fi enthusiasts, too.

Tape recorders, color television, stereophonic phonograph, and stereo records all became key home entertainment devices. Then stereo multiplex systems of broadcasting made it possible to hear radio programs as well as records and tapes in stereophonic sound.

Now there is "quad"—quadraphonic sound—the "hottest" thing on the hi-fi scene since stereo. Quadraphonic sound is just what the name implies: four channels of sound, rather than the two of stereo or the one of monophonic sound. With four channels it is possible to pick up the reverberant sounds, which when properly reproduced make you feel as if you are sitting in the room where the music originated.

The effect is most apparent with classical music originating in large live halls.

BUYING HI-FI EQUIPMENT. Whether you need quadraphonic or stereo to fulfill your listening tastes, selecting a high fidelity system from the many makes and models can be a problem. Fortunately, there are lots of choices in range of sophistication and price.

How do you decide what to buy for home listening entertainment? How do you know you will be satisfied with the equipment you choose? Unless you are already well along as a stereo enthusiast, you can't possibly know just what to buy. Since good sound systems are expensive, you will want to consider several important factors which may help you make an intelligent choice.

What you need depends on at least four things. First, what is your minimum sound standard? Second, where do you do your listening? Third, do you have a space problem or installation problem? Fourth, what type of material do you listen to most?

The answers to these questions will help you focus on the least elaborate equipment you can be happy with. Your minimum sound standard might be described as the least good sound you can stand to listen to for an extended period of time without getting tired. This will vary from person to person.

At the extremes are the people who enjoy listening to music on a small transistor radio and the people who can't enjoy anything except live concerts. Most people, probably including you, are in between these extremes.

One major manufacturer of high fidelity equipment suggests some ways to decide where you fit in. First, pick an equipment maker and a dealer you trust. Take your favorite record to your dealer, and ask him to play it on several systems.

You might start with a $150 system. Then ask him to play it on a $300 system by the same maker, one containing the same basic components, but of better quality. Keep moving up in quality until you're satisfied with what you hear.

When you have settled on your minimum sound, listen to the system right above it in price, just to check yourself. Then listen again to the one you chose. If you're still satisfied, you've found your minimum.

Some people suggest you listen to a recorded male speaking voice in making a systems test. The system is pretty good if it reproduces the voice like a man talking before you.

Now, where do you do most of your listening? Chances are you will not always be seated comfortably in a listening room at your house. One room may be the primary place, but you also may want the sound to reach into the kitchen or the bedroom. If so, you may need a system a cut above what you pick in the showroom as your minimum acceptable quality. You'll probably need more power and larger speakers to be happy with the performance in your home.

Third, if you have a space problem, you should consider a compact, which has the receiver and turntable mounted on the same chassis. In a component system, the receiver and turntable are separate. If you plan to install your system in a homemade cabinet, components are perfectly suitable as long as there is adequate ventilation.

A fourth consideration is what you listen to. Do you listen mostly to records? The radio? Tapes? You may find that your minimum system needs only one source, the one that you use most frequently. You can add others later.

Consider home furnishings when you choose your sound system, too. Are you interested only in the sound equipment, or do you want it housed in a cabinet to blend with your furniture style?

Weigh all these factors heavily and take time to shop for your entertainment sound system. Remember that the experts in this field are the manufacturers and reputable dealers. And even they are not expert enough to tell you what you need or will enjoy in your own home. What's right for you must be determined by your own levels of tolerance in high-fidelity.

Ideally, the way to make sure that the system you choose will do the job in your home as well as it did in the showroom is to try it out at home. Some dealers will agree to this arrangement on a 2- or 3-day trial. Both you and the dealer may benefit from this performance test.

TELEVISION. Your TV receiver is probably the most complex device in your home. You depend on it daily for entertainment, news, and information. Because your TV is such an important purchase, a little extra care in its selection will pay dividends in reliability and satisfaction.

There are now TV sets to meet almost every viewing requirement and preference, from ultraminiature "personal" portables to giant-screen color home entertainment centers complete with a stereo phonograph and AM-FM radio. There are sets which can be operated outside from rechargeable batteries, sets with personal-listening earphones, and sets with timers that automatically turn themselves off when you fall asleep.

Color TV is now in the majority of American homes—usually as a furniture-styled console in the living room, sales figures show. Increasing numbers of portables and table models make it possible to have color in many other locations in the house. Black-and-white sets are still in demand, too, largely as "second sets" for the bedroom, the family room, or the kitchen.

Obviously, the type of set you choose should be determined by where you intend to use it. There is no hard and fast guide to screen size in relationship to room size, but sets with screens measuring 18 inches or more (diagonally) generally are considered "family" sets, while those with smaller screens are usually for personal viewing.

The following information supplied by the Electronic Industries Association and the Council of Better Business Bureaus, Inc., may help you choose the right TV set for your home.

Screen size, in inches, is the measurement of the viewable picture from corner to corner, diagonally. Sometimes you will see sets also advertised by square inches of viewable picture. For example, a color set with a 25-inch diagonal screen has a picture measurement of 315 square inches, and a 19-inch screen measures 185 square inches.

Color sets are available in screen sizes ranging from 25 inches diagonally down to 10 inches and even less. Black-and-white sets generally run from about 5 inches diagonally to 22 inches, although some specialized and novelty models are even smaller than 5 inches.

Color sets are much more complex than black-and-white receivers, and because of the extra cost it is particularly important to shop carefully.

All color sets have the same basic controls as black-and-white sets: tuning, brightness, contrast, and volume. In addition there are two other controls. These are color, sometimes called chroma or color intensity, and tint and hue.

A color set is tuned exactly the same way as a black-and-white set, except that the two additional color controls are varied to give the most pleasing picture.

In shopping for a TV set, keep in mind that although the manufacturer stands behind his set through warranty, a reputable dealer can also go far in helping to assure you of satisfaction.

It's often true that TV reception in a store isn't as good as it will be at home, away from the many sources of interference. But the dealer should be able to demonstrate a reasonably good picture to help you with your choice. He also should have a sufficient variety of models to give you a good selection.

Since 1967, "solid-state" color TV sets have been on the market. This innovation in the electronic construction of televisions has eliminated from many models all tubes except the picture tube.

"Solid-state" is a term commonly used to indicate substantial usage of diodes and transistors in radio and TV receivers. Another technical term for all this is the integrated circuit. For the consumer it means some advantages such as smaller size, low power drain, high reliability, and eventually, lower costs to be realized from use in mass production.

Select your set carefully with an eye to crispness and sharpness of picture, pleasing color tones, and lack of distortion. Don't select by picture alone;

turn the sound up to determine whether it is well-balanced and pleasing, particularly in musical passages.

Watching titles or commercials on the screen is a good test. Written matter should be crisp and easily legible, and titles shouldn't "run off the screen" so that the first and last letters of a screen-wide title become invisible.

It's a good idea to measure the distance you will sit from the TV set at home and stand at about that same distance from the sets in the store. The salesman should explain the set's controls and any special features. But try tuning the set yourself to determine how easy it is to bring in a good picture.

Some dealers provide "installation and setup" for color sets without extra charge. This means attaching the set to an existing antenna, making any necessary minor adjustments, and introducing you to the set's operation. This is an added convenience and well worthwhile if it is included in the price of the set, but not strictly necessary with modern color sets.

If you are switching from black-and-white to a color set, you may need a new antenna. Often a worn antenna, particularly one designed for black-and-white reception, will deteriorate the picture or cut out some of the color signal. Try the old antenna, but if you don't get a good picture, have a new one installed.

The warranty is an important feature of your new set, and it varies from one product brand to another and even from dealer to dealer. The basic minimum manufacturer's warranty on a black-and-white set is 90-day coverage of all parts except the picture tube, which is warranted for 1 year. For color sets, parts are covered for a year and the picture tube for 2 years.

Many manufacturers—and dealers—improve on this minimum. Some sets are sold with warranties which include labor for up to a year, so that repairs during the initial period cost nothing at all.

Be certain you understand terms of

the warranty, which should be clearly stated in writing. Save the sales slip or owner warranty certificate, if supplied, as proof of date of purchase. Register the warranty by following the procedure in your instruction book.

A service policy is an extension of the warranty for which you pay extra. It's simply a form of insurance, generally covering all repairs for a specific period of time. Some service policies also cover installation and setup.

TYPES OF RADIOS. No longer is a radio just a radio. The portable radio is by far the most popular, followed in order by auto, clock, and table models. But new specialized types of radios to satisfy varying needs and tastes are gaining in popularity.

The digital clock receiver, for example, indicates the time in numerals rather than on a clock face. It is believed that well over half of all clock radios sold are the digital type.

There are radios which float, cordless travel clock radios, radios combined with flashlights, radios with cigarette lighters, and radios in bicycle headlights.

FM stereo radios, both portable and table models, are at the top of the line, according to the Electronic Industries Association. In 1971, close to 60 percent of all home radios sold were equipped to tune the FM band. Another important specialized line of radios is the world-wide multi-band sets for listening to shortwave broadcasts from points around the world.

TAPE RECORDERS AND TAPE PLAYERS. Today's home entertainment often includes one or more tape machines. There's an almost endless list of uses for tape recorders and players, and the number of models and types available seems just about as endless. Your satisfaction with the unit you finally purchase will depend on quality and reliability and also on how well it is suited to the job you intend it to do.

There are three major types of tape instruments, each of them with its own special uses: reel-to-reel, cartridge, and cassette.

Reel-to-reel is the original type of recorder and the kind still used by recording studios, radio stations, and serious sound hobbyists. The reels, generally 7 inches in diameter, must be placed on the machine and the tape threaded by hand from the "feed reel," across the recording/playback heads, and onto the "take-up-reel."

Quality open-reel recorders usually provide a choice of at least two speeds —3¾ and 7½ inches per second (ips), with speeds of 1⅞ or 15 ips also available. The higher speeds produce higher fidelity, and 7½ ips is regarded as the standard speed for open-reel music recordings.

The eight-track cartridge player is the type commonly used in automobile stereo systems, but it also has become popular for home and portable use. The standard tape cartridge is somewhat larger than a cassette, and its operation is even more automatic. It contains a single reel of ¼-inch-wide tape arranged in an endless loop so that it never needs to be rewound.

The four pairs of stereo tracks are automatically played in sequence—switching from one track to the next is usually automatic. A cartridge can accommodate up to the equivalent of a two-record LP album.

The cassette recorder or player uses a standard thin "compact cassette" which contains two small reels with ⅛-inch-wide tape, designed to travel at 1⅞ inches per second. The cassette snaps into the recorder or player and you never touch the tape itself.

Cassettes are commonly available in 30-, 60-, and 90-minute playing times (known as "C-30," "C-60," and "C-90" cassettes) and are also made with playing time from as little as 15 minutes up to 2 hours or more. The standardized cassette system provides "compatible stereo," which means that a cassette recorded in stereo can be played on a monophonic (non-stereo) player and vice-versa.

For music listening, recorded stereo albums are available for all three types of tape players, with a somewhat wider variety offered in the cartridge format. The eight-track cartridge player is at its best in the presentation of album-length selections of background music, since it plays the album from start to finish without requiring any handling. In fact it can start all over again automatically.

All three tape formats are now recognized as capable of providing high-fidelity stereo reproduction. For listening outdoors, either a cartridge or cassette player—particularly in combination with built-in radio—provides a lightweight, ready-to-go music source.

For recording speech, making "sound snapshots," sound letters, helping with school work, learning languages, and memorizing speeches or dramatic roles, a cassette recorder is ideal. A unit capable of both battery and AC operation is versatile for use both outside and at home.

Most brands of blank (unrecorded) tape come in several quality and price ranges. Off-brand "bargain" tapes may have considerable surface noise, and some can actually damage your recorder. Most brands are available in a "low-noise" version which is highly satisfactory for both speech and music.

Before you buy a tape recorder and player, you should give careful attention to the following:

• Know how you plan to use your tape recorder or player, and select an instrument which meets these requirements

• Cartridge, cassette, and open-reel units have different characteristics and uses. Familiarize yourself with them

• Buy from a reputable dealer. Listen to the instrument and learn to operate it before you buy

• Know and understand terms of the warranty

A lot has happened in the electronics home entertainment field since 1895 when Guglielmo Marconi sent and received the first wireless signals in Italy.

In America we now have more TV sets and more radios in use than washing machines or refrigerators or bathtubs. And the future continues to promise exciting innovations. Videocassette recorders and players, for example, are now available for use in the home.

This opens a whole new world in sight and sound for family participation. The player attaches easily to the home TV set and provides instant playback of recorded movies, drama, concerts, study courses and the like in complete color television. It operates very much like a cartridge tape player.

The videocassette recorder will record your favorite program from your own TV set and play it back for you when you wish to see it at a later time. With a TV camera, you can produce your own home TV shows and play them back on your set.

At present the primary uses for videocassettes are in industry and education. Manufacturers will be making home models and prices will probably be in the range acceptable to most color TV set owners. Program producers have begun to package cassettes for sale, rent, or loan. The potential is exciting and is bound to be almost endless.

You should make a special effort to see demonstrations of the new home entertainment features to help you determine what best suits your tastes and needs. The electronic age of entertainment and recreation is indeed an exciting time to be alive.

For further reading:

What's Being Done About X-rays From Home TV Sets? 1971. 12 pp. 007A. 10 cents. Write to Consumer Information, Public Documents Distribution Center, Pueblo, Colo. 81009:

Electric Sewing Equipment

For the home sewer, the major piece of electrical equipment is of course a sewing machine. This long time investment, if bought from a reputable manufacturer, will last many years with only minor replacement of parts. Usually you can clean, oil, and adjust the machine yourself.

Needs of most home sewers can be filled by a simple sewing machine which does the straight stitch, forward and reverse. With this less expensive machine, attachments are provided or can be purchased to make a zigzag stitch, ruffles, buttonholes, a blind hem, and the like.

A greater variety of stitches is possible with a more costly zigzag machine. It takes some skill to develop a uniform pattern or design. The least expensive zigzag machine is the basic zigzag stitch type. This sews a straight stitch, but can also be set to sew a zigzag stitch with the needle swinging from side to side for overcasting, blind stitching, darning, satin stitch, buttonholing, and sewing on buttons.

A more versatile zigzag machine which is also more expensive offers special stitch possibilities. Besides operating like the simple zigzag machine, this type has from one to 25 or more stitch possibilities. The needle movement is guided by cams, which may be built in or added separately. Some of the special stitches you can make with this machine are blind hem, buttonhole, multiple zigzag, and a variety of decorative stitches.

A fourth type of zigzag machine might be called the most versatile zigzag. This is also the most expensive

type of sewing machine. In most zigzag machines, the needle motion is side to side while the fabric moves under the presser foot. This machine has a mechanism for moving the fabric automatically back and forth while the needle swings from side to side. It makes possible a wide range of practical stitches including some of the special stitches recommended for sewing fabrics. A number of these machines can be updated with cams as new features are developed.

Weigh carefully your decision as to whether you use special stitches often enough to warrant the added cost and the increased amount of service it will possibly need. When buying a zigzag machine, test it for good straight stitch and for ease in switching from straight to zigzag stitching. Although many machines are considered automatic, you will always need a complete knowledge of the machine to make the best use of its varied operation. Be sure to get personal instruction from the seller.

Some makes of machines come in an open arm model. This style allows you to slip tubular parts of a garment, such as a sleeve, pant leg, etc., over the arm in order to sew them more easily.

Machines have been developed for the use of handicapped persons who have impaired vision and for those with limited use of hands, arms, or legs.

For a person with restricted use of the hands, the speed control is designed to be operated by the foot, the arm, or the knee. Knobs are fitted with projecting spokes. Levers have knobs at the end; clamp screws hold the needle in place. A slow speed control makes operating by a handicapped person easier.

A further choice is between a cabinet or a portable model. A cabinet machine has the advantages of being ready to use, and of being more convenient and time saving for anyone who sews frequently. You will probably have several choices of style and price of cabinet for the machine you select. The extra cost of a fancy cabinet may better be invested in useful furniture.

AUTHOR VIRGINIA OGILVY is a Clothing Specialist with the Extension Service.

The portable machine costs less than a cabinet type and requires less space. A portable often is a wise choice since today many people live in small homes and apartments and move from place to place, as our society is a mobile one.

Some portables, though heavy, have the regular sewing head set in a carrying case. It has the advantage of being able to fit into a cabinet if your needs change and you want a cabinet type at a future time.

You should investigate at least three makes of machines to have a basis for comparison. Look them over carefully and *use them yourself.* Try the machine on some of your own fabric. If it is not possible to see and operate every machine being considered, study a catalog description and compare it with ones you have seen.

To have some basis for deciding on a sewing machine, discuss the features with dealers, repairmen, and friends whose opinion you value. The person who uses the machine should be the one to select it, even if it is intended as a gift.

A well-written instruction book with many illustrations should accompany each sewing machine. This should clearly explain how to operate, adjust, and care for it. You are entitled to free, personal instructions on operating your new machine. The more versatile the machine, the more important it is to have this instruction.

If free instruction is not provided with the machine you are considering, it is not a wise choice.

Speed of the sewing machine motor is controlled by a foot pedal or a knee lever. This control mechanism may be either a step control or a carbon control.

The step control changes the speed in a series of steps or intervals, usually from 5 to 8, from slow speed to top speed. With some step controls, the first step does not provide the slow speed you sometimes want in sewing. The carbon control, however, adjusts the speed from slow to fast smoothly and uniformly, especially when starting, and at very slow speed.

Sometimes you need greater power to sew through heavy materials, but you want to sew slowly so that you can place stitches carefully. Full power and slow speed are needed at the same time. There are three ways of doing this available on machines today:

• Controlling speed by withholding electrical current. This will reduce the machine's power as well as the speed

• Control of speed by a transmission with a gear reduction system, which provides slower speed with increased power. This is similar to the gear system in an automobile

• A solid state electronic control system which maintains power at various speeds

On machines which have the electronic feature, you will find a button, dial, or such, usually on the head of the machine. This is in addition to the speed control you operate with your foot or knee.

Know your dealer. Can he give you reliable service? Most dealers who sell sewing machines offer some form of guarantee and free service agreement. The best guarantee is one from the manufacturer. Dealers move, you may move. Buy a machine from a company with service centers in many places. Would you have to pay the cost of shipping the machine to the factory for service? How far away is the factory?

The guarantee protects the buyer for various periods of time after purchase against inferior or defective parts or concealed damage. Make sure this guarantee protects you for a reasonable length of time. These agreements should be in writing.

Understand the total cost; that is, all costs in addition to the retail price. A machine should last for a number of years. Buying from a well established manufacturer will more likely provide a continuing source of parts.

After you make your purchase, take time to study your instruction book and learn its proper use. Otherwise you may damage the machine.

The cost of a secondhand machine is usually much less than that of a new

490-100 O - 73 - 21

one. No machine is a bargain if it is difficult to get parts or fill such simple needs as procuring extra bobbins, needles of correct size, etc. Round bobbin machines are usually preferable to the long-shuttle ones. Most machines today are electric.

The most readily available sources of secondhand machines are stores with secondhand articles, stores which sell both new and reclaimed or trade-in machines, an individual whom you might locate through a want-ad or notice on a neighborhood store bulletin board, or an auction.

It is difficult to decide whether a secondhand machine is worth the selling price. Factors to be considered are whether it meets your sewing needs, its condition, and the cost. A dealer's machines are reconditioned and should carry his service warranty. The price may be higher because of warranty and servicing.

Buying from an individual offers the greatest risk. The price may be lower because the buyer must take the appliance "as is."

A treadle machine is likely to be the least expensive. It is such an old style machine that it may be difficult to find parts when necessary to replace them.

In a secondhand machine, look for signs of abuse such as dents and scratches. Look for signs of wear, such as bare or cracked wires.

Check the machine's operation. Take some fabric and thread with you when you are looking over the machine. Try it out and make sure it sews satisfactorily.

If the machine has been reconditioned by a reputable dealer, it has been cleaned inside and out. Functioning parts of the sewing machine have been checked, adjusted, or repaired, and the machine tested to be sure it is in satisfactory condition.

A manufacturer's instruction book should be available; you would have difficulty operating the machine satisfactorily without it.

Check parts which are apt to show signs of wear or deterioration. If it is

an electric machine the wiring should be in good condition, not with broken insulation exposing bare wires. The belt or chain belt should not be worn, frayed, or loose. The motor pulley should not be glazed or hardened. If the rubber gasket on the bobbin winder is hardened, it should be replaced.

The choice between a portable and a cabinet model depends upon the space available, your budget, and the amount of sewing you anticipate doing. A cabinet model has the advantage of always being ready to use and a sewing surface level with the bed of the machine.

A portable has the advantage of requiring less space for storage. If the convenience of being able to move the sewing machine about is a factor, this is the type for you.

Now let's turn to *shears*. There are both plain electric shears and electric pinking shears. Skill must be developed to use them with any degree of accuracy, as one needs to become accustomed to the speed and the vibration of the shears. Those bothered with arthritis find electric shears easier to use as it is only necessary to hold them, and the joints of the hand need not be moved.

When a great deal of cutting is necessary, especially with heavy fabrics, electric shears can be less tiring to use than ordinary shears. But if the fabric is too heavy or too tough, the blades will jam. Very lightweight fabric such as lingerie fabric can also be a problem.

Some shears are equipped with blades which can easily be sharpened. Others must be returned to the factory for this. There seems to be little difference in original cost.

Shears can be equipped with a light, either over or under the blades. Or there may be none at all. Areas in which one sews must have a good source of light, so this may not be an important factor.

Models are made with a single speed or several speeds. It would seem to be an advantage to have several speeds. There are varying lengths of cord. Though a lightweight extension cord can be used with a small appliance of this kind, it is an advantage to have a reasonably long cord on the shears.

A cordless model is available. You have to plan several hours in advance of use of the shears for charging the battery.

Motors are of the rotary type and the vibrator type. The rotary motor is more expensive. It has the advantage of causing less vibration in the handle of the shears. Vibration can be tiring and annoying.

Size and shape of the handle are of great importance. A small handle can be held comfortably for long periods of time. It may be contoured to provide added comfort.

In some models, the transformer is located at the wall plug instead of in the handle. This enables the manufacturer to provide a handle of considerably smaller size than one which contains the transformer.

Since the need for pinking shears by the home sewer is extremely limited, the added expense of purchasing those with an electric motor should be weighed carefully.

An electric *hand steamer* is another appliance for the home sewer. It is satisfactory in removing soft wrinkles, but not too effective with hard creases. Since it covers only a small area at a time, it would be time consuming to steam an entire garment.

This appliance is effective for what is intended. Consider carefully your need for an item with such a specialized function.

The home sewer should weigh carefully her decisions in selecting all equipment. Cost, the meeting of immediate needs and those of the foreseeable future, ease of operation, skill required to operate—all are factors to consider in choosing equipment.

For further reading:

U.S. Department of Agriculture. *Buying a New Sewing Machine*, Program Aid 1044,

Supt. of Documents, Washington, D.C. 20402, 1973, 25 cents.

Reading the Labels On Apparel and Household Textiles

LABELS AND HANG TAGS on textile products include a wide variety of descriptive terms and instructions to the consumer. This information can be very helpful in selection, in purchase, and during use and care of textile items.

Textile labels can also be confusing and may be ignored by some consumers. So much information is given it may seem overwhelming. The meaning of some technical terms may not be understood. Or the ability to relate textile information to individual needs and wants may be lacking. In some cases labels are actually unclear, containing conflicting instructions or incomplete information.

In general, however, it is not difficult to understand the terms used to describe textiles and their care. Federal legislation and rulings regarding textiles and voluntary efforts by the industry have made it possible to know, for the most part, what to expect on textile labeling. But in rapidly changing markets which are heavily influenced by fashion and by technological changes, the updating of your consumer knowledge is necessary from time to time as new types of textile products become available.

AUTHOR WILLIAM L. MAULDIN is Associate Professor, Department of Clothing, Textiles and Related Art, Virginia Polytechnic Institute and State University, Blacksburg.

COAUTHOR MARIANNE S. BEESON is an Instructor in the same department.

311

Careful attention to labeling can increase satisfaction with apparel and household textile products. Most textiles can be damaged or ruined by improper use and care. This can be a sad experience when a daughter's favorite sweater is no longer wearable. Since some textile items represent a large investment, reduction of wear life can mean a serious financial loss as well. We usually expect such items as carpets, rugs, draperies, curtains, slip covers, upholstery fabrics, bedspreads, and blankets to perform satisfactorily over a period of several years before they have to be replaced.

The information provided on textile labels and hang tags offers factual knowledge about the products, which can make purchasing decisions easier and help you to obtain maximum use and enjoyment.

For those responsible for laundering and cleaning clothes, one of the most common problems used to be knowing exactly what care procedures were required. This information was usually given on hang tags, but they were of course removed by consumers prior to wear. Highly organized individuals were able to file the tags with a description of the garment, but most of us had problems locating the instructions whenever the garment needed cleaning.

A new Federal Trade Commission (FTC) ruling, which went into effect in July 1972, now requires that care instructions be permanently affixed to the garment on a label sewn in, adhered, or stamped onto the garment. Thus, directions for care are located where they can be used most effectively.

The ruling applies to all articles of wearing apparel which require care and to fabrics sold by the yard. Some items are exempt from the ruling: articles priced at $3 or less which are completely washable, footwear, and items to cover the head and hands.

The FTC has granted several additional exemptions upon petition from manufacturers under conditions where "utility or appearance would be substantially impaired by a permanently attached label."

Some of the labels may be fold-over or loop labels on which instructions continue around the loop of the label. Consumers should be sure to read the entire label.

If a garment is packaged and the label not easily visible, the care instructions should be repeated on the package itself or on another prominent tag. Intent of the ruling is to have care instructions available at the time of purchase, as well as the time of actual care, thus making it possible to compare products in terms of care required. The cost and convenience of care should be considered in reaching purchasing decisions.

For piece goods, labels are ordinarily offered to the consumer with the purchase of fabrics. The consumer should check the label to see that it contains the same care instructions as those printed on the fabric bolt or attached hang tag.

One system of label distribution uses a number code. You can check the number code on the end of the fabric bolt to be sure it corresponds to the number on the care label.

Since the care labels for piece goods are usually separate from the fabrics and distributed by the sales person, mistakes can be made. Consumers should ask for a care label if it is not provided. It is the consumer's important responsibility to attach the care label to the garment after it is made.

It is also the home sewer's responsibility to keep track of the label which is intended for a particular fabric. When several different fabrics are purchased at one time or when fabrics are stored before being made into garments, you may find it necessary to tape or pin the appropriate label to the edge of the fabric piece.

Care of the home constructed garment will not be successful unless all

CONSUMER CARE GUIDE FOR APPAREL

American Apparel Manufacturers Association

MACHINE WASHABLE

WHEN LABEL READS:	IT MEANS:
Machine wash	Wash, bleach, dry and press by any customary method including commercial laundering and dry cleaning
Home launder only	Same as above but do not use commercial laundering
No Chlorine Bleach	Do not use chlorine bleach. Oxygen bleach may be used
No bleach	Do not use any type of bleach
Cold wash / Cold rinse	Use cold water from tap or cold washing machine setting
Warm wash / Warm rinse	Use warm water or warm washing machine setting.
Hot wash	Use hot water or hot washing machine setting
No spin	Remove wash load before final machine spin cycle
Delicate cycle / Gentle cycle	Use appropriate machine setting; otherwise wash by hand
Durable press cycle / Permanent press cycle	Use appropriate machine setting; otherwise use warm wash, cold rinse and short spin cycle
Wash separately	Wash alone or with like colors

	WHEN LABEL READS:	IT MEANS:
NON-MACHINE WASHING	Hand wash	Launder only by hand in lukewarm (hand comfortable) water. May be bleached. May be drycleaned
	Hand wash only	Same as above, but do not dryclean
	Hand wash separately	Hand wash alone or with like colors
	No bleach	Do not use bleach
	Damp wipe	Surface clean with damp cloth or sponge
HOME DRYING	Tumble dry	Dry in tumble dryer at specified setting—high, medium, low or no heat
	Tumble dry / Remove promptly	Same as above, but in absence of cool-down cycle remove at once when tumbling stops
	Drip dry	Hang wet and allow to dry with hand shaping only
	Line dry	Hang damp and allow to dry
	No wring / No twist	Hang dry, drip dry or dry flat only. Handle to prevent wrinkles and distortion
	Dry flat	Lay garment on flat surface
	Block to dry	Maintain original size and shape while drying
IRONING OR PRESSING	Cool iron	Set iron at lowest setting
	Warm iron	Set iron at medium setting
	Hot iron	Set iron at hot setting
	Do not iron	Do not iron or press with heat
	Steam iron	Iron or press with steam
	Iron damp	Dampen garment before ironing
MISCELLANEOUS	Dryclean only	Garment should be drycleaned only, including self-service
	Professionally dry clean only	Do not use self-service drycleaning
	No dryclean	Use recommended care instructions. No drycleaning materials to be used.

the fabrics, findings, and trimmings are similar in regard to care. Linings, interfacings, and trims must be selected with care requirements that are compatible with the care needed for the garment fabric. A lining labeled "Do not dryclean" used with a garment fabric labeled "Dryclean only" would cause an obvious problem.

Because care labels on garments are necessarily brief, additional information may be needed in order to know more about garment care. The chart with this chapter may be used as a reference.

The Flammable Fabrics Act (1967) has broadened the scope of textiles legislation to include the development of Department of Commerce (DOC) Flammability Standards for certain textile products.

At the present time children's sleepwear (sizes 0-6x), fabrics intended for children's sleepwear, carpets and rugs, mattresses and mattress pads are covered under standards.

It is expected that additional standards will be developed to apply to other textile products, such as children's sleepwear in sizes 7-14, girls' dresses, blankets, draperies, and upholstered furnishings.

The standards specify laboratory test methods that subject textile products to sources of fire somewhat related to household situations which can cause textiles to burn. For example, burning cigarettes are the source of ignition in the test for mattresses and mattress pads, since smoking in bed is a frequent cause of fires. Textiles which meet the various standards may char, or burn very slowly, or not burn at all under the test conditions.

For products that meet the flammability standards, the consumer may be protected from undue hazard from textiles flammability. However, prevention of burn injuries and deaths will also continue to depend upon safety precautions. Do not become careless about sources of fire just because some textiles on the market are now flame-retardant or resistant to fire.

Flammability is referred to on labeling of textile items covered under the present DOC standards. When a standard becomes effective there is often a "period of grace" during which products may be marketed which do not meet the standard so long as cautionary labeling appears.

In the case of children's sleepwear, prior to July 1973, garments which did not meet the standard were labeled "Flammable (does not meet U.S. DOC Standard FF-3-71). Should not be worn near sources of fire."

Rugs and carpets larger than 24 square feet must meet the flammability standard and will bear a label "Approved. Meets or exceeds Federal Flammability Standard DOC-FF-1-70." Rugs less than 24 square feet and bath mats must carry warning labels if they do not pass the flammability test.

Care instructions on flame resistant textiles should be strictly followed. Characteristics of these products can be changed drastically by improper care, often to the point of making the fabric highly flammable. In particular, the effect of flame-retardant finishes on fabrics can be counteracted by soap and hard water mineral deposits on the fabric.

You may see labels cautioning, "Do not use soap. Launder with phosphate detergent." This procedure is needed in order to allow the flame-retardant finish to remain effective. There is a concern about households in areas which have banned the sale of phosphate detergents in order to lessen water pollution problems. At present the dilemma is not resolved.

To protect consumers from false advertising and misbranding of fiber content of textile products, Congress enacted the Textile Fiber Products Identification Act in 1958. The Act covers wearing apparel and household textiles. An important provision is the requirement that textiles be labeled or otherwise identified by percent of each fiber present, by weight, in amounts of 5 percent or more.

Fibers must be listed in their order

314

of predominance, each fiber designated by its generic name. Cotton, wool, silk, and flax are the names used for the major natural fibers. The Act provided for establishing generic names for the manmade fibers, classifying them according to chemical composition as

acetate	metallic	rayon
acrylic	modacrylic	rubber
anidex	nylon	saran
azlon	nytril	spandex
glass	olefin	triacetate
lastrile	polyester	vinal
		vinyon

Consumers should learn to recognize fiber generic names and realize that there are likely to be several trade names for the same type of fiber.

This knowledge can make comparison shopping easier since the performance and care required for fibers with the same generic name can be expected to be very similar when used in the same type of product. However, keep in mind that fiber content is only one of many factors which determine characteristics of the final product.

Other Federal legislation has been enacted to prevent deception in labeling of furs and wool. The Wool Products Labeling Act of 1939 requires fiber content labeling by wool type as defined below:

• Wool—fiber from the fleece of the sheep or lamb or hair of the Angora or Cashmere goat (or hair of the camel, llama, alpaca, and vicuna) which has never been reclaimed from any woven or felted wool product
• Reprocessed wool—fiber which has previously been manufactured into a wool product but has not been used in any way by the ultimate consumer
• Reused wool—fiber reclaimed from wool products which have been used by the ultimate consumer

The term "virgin wool" was not defined in the original Act, but it is used on labels to refer to new wool fiber which has never been previously processed. None of the terms which describe wool type indicate anything to

the consumer about quality or grade of the wool fiber.

The Fur Products Labeling Act of 1951 prevents deception by requiring labeling of the true English name of the fur-bearing animal and other provisions.

Designation of fabric weight may appear on labels and be useful in comparing textile products or in determining suitability of a fabric to season of the year. Fabrics for men's suits and work clothes, draperies, tents, and camping equipment are sometimes described by weight in ounces per square yard or ounces per linear yard.

Thread count of fabrics is usually given on labels as a single number (for example, 180) representing the total number of warp and filling threads or yarns per square inch, although two numbers may also be used. A thread count of 95 x 85 means 95 warp yarns and 85 filling yarns per square inch.

Thread count is often labeled on sheets, pillowcases, and draperies, and can be used as an indicator of durability in comparing items of the same fiber content and fabric construction.

Often trade names are among the most visibly prominent words on textile labels. The manufacturer of the item may be identified in characteristic printing style and trademark symbols. It is possible for a single item to carry trade name labeling for almost every step in the manufacturing process: fiber trade names, yarn processes or finishes, fabric mill, fabric finishes, and end product. In addition, the retailer's name may be included.

The names, and particularly the mailing addresses, of manufacturers give consumers several sources, in addition to the retailer, from which to seek adjustment in case of product failure. Unsatisfactory performance believed to be the fault of the manufacturer and not due to misuse or improper care by the consumer should be reported.

The best recourse for complaints is usually the store from which the item was purchased. But if this proves unsatisfactory, the manufacturer should be contacted and given a precise and honest account of how the product failed to perform.

Industry representatives repeatedly say that one of their continuing problems is the lack of adequate consumer "feedback." Producers need consumer reaction in order to know how to improve their products.

Product guarantees are relatively new in the textile field. Some textile products carry labels describing terms or conditions of a guarantee. Read carefully! Most of the guarantee programs require you to keep the sales slip and the guarantee tag and return them with the garment in order to claim replacement or money refund if the product fails to perform as stated in the guarantee.

In summary, textile labeling offers a wealth of information to the consumer, whose responsibilities are to read and understand labeling, follow directions given and communicate with retailers and manufacturers regarding performance of their products.

For further reading:

Blanford, Josephine M. and Gurel, Lois M., *Fibers and Fabrics*. NBS Consumer Information Series 1, issued in November, 1970. Available for 65 cents from Superintendent of Documents, U.S. Government Printing Office, Washington, D.C. 20402.

A Dictionary of Textile Terms by Dan River Mills, Inc., eleventh edition, 1971. Single copies available free from: Public Relations Manager, Dan River Mills, Inc., P.O. Box 6126, Station B, Greenville, S.C. 29606.

The following publications may be obtained from Consumer Information, Public Documents Distribution Center, Pueblo, Colo. 81009:

Clothing and Fabric Care Labeling. 1972. 7 pp. 036A. Free.

Look for That Label. 1971. 8 pp. 039A. Free.

Carrying It Off In Style! The Role of Clothing

CLOTHING VIVIDLY reflects one's values and life style. An individual's clothes serve as a kind of "sign language" that transmits a variety of information which usually becomes the basis of our initial impressions of a person.

It doesn't matter if the perceptions are accurate or fair. Whether we like it or not, people make these kinds of judgments about us. And although we may not admit it, we make such judgments about them.

These first impressions are sometimes false, but often amazingly accurate. Thus we should understand the role clothing plays in order to achieve the kind of image that family members desire.

For most people, clothing satisfies the need to be warm and comfortable. But if chosen wisely, it can also make them more attractive, help them feel part of a group, provide social status or prestige, give them individuality, or satisfy the need for creative self-expression.

Such needs will not only vary from individual to individual, but some may even be in conflict. Adolescents in particular—although this is not restricted to youth by any means—will sacrifice comfort, beauty, economy, and even health in order to gain the social approval that comes from conformity to peer group fads and fashions.

Clothing is probably one of the greatest sources of disagreement between parents and children. A conscientious father tries to instill in his son the importance of a neat and well-groomed appearance. The son's preference for patched jeans, sandals, and a wild head of hair not only baffles but outrages the father. He regards such behavior as a blatant violation of values the family holds important: respect for authority, cleanliness, and an appearance of success. The father becomes convinced that young people are against anything traditional, just for the sake of being against it.

For some youth, style of dress does in fact symbolize both a rejection of the middle-class culture and assertion of a counterculture. No doubt the new generation has been strongly influenced by the appearance and lifestyle of those who espouse an antimaterialistic ethic. However, the majority of young people adopted the "look" not for ideological reasons, but for reasons of fashion.

Fashion is a powerful force in human nature. We can't afford to ignore it, nor should we rationalize our fashion motives in the direction of more "logical" reasons. The basic character of human life is expressed in what we call "normal behavior"—a "norm" meaning the typical or common way of responding. Nowhere can such behavior be seen more visually than in the whole fashion process.

We live in an age of volatile fads and rapidly shifting fashions. New styles are quickly diffused via the mass media. This, in turn, encourages the avantgarde to introduce newer styles at an even faster pace.

Changing fashions often make one's clothes old hat before the wear life of a garment is over. An understanding of the fashion cycle—the gradual rise, peaking, and eventual decline in the popular acceptance of a style—will help you be a wise consumer. It may prevent you from investing in quality that will long outlast the fashion value of your clothing.

Remember that a fashion, on its way in, is accepted and worn by the relatively few people who have the re-

sources and the desire to be conspicuously different. As the popularity of a style spreads, more and more people hop on the bandwagon until the style finally snowballs to the peak of acceptance. But once everyone has it, the attraction is past. There is no place left for the style to go but to slide into obsolescence.

Forces that give vent to the rise and fall of fashion are identical with the tensions that exist between the need for conformity and individuality in dress. Conformity, particularly within small social groups, is widespread, and the desire to be like others, to "fit in with the crowd," is strongly reinforced in human interaction.

Beginning at a very early age, most of our social behavior is imitative. As children, we learn a great deal by copying the actions of older persons. Especially at a time when the child becomes concerned about changing body proportions, it is important to make him feel he is no different from others of similar age.

The parent who insists on frilly dresses when all the other little girls are wearing denim pants and cotton T-shirts may unknowingly alienate the child from the group. Undue emphasis placed on the importance of clothes early in life can contribute as much to later personality maladjustments as feelings of clothing deprivation.

While conformity to a given set of clothing norms thus provides for social approval and group belongingness, we all feel the need to achieve some distinction for ourselves as unique individuals. The search for individuality appears to be somewhat more crucial in today's world because of what the economists have termed "the homogenization of the consumer market." The steady growth of our economy and the accompanying diffusion of affluence has made it possible for many, many more people to enjoy the luxuries which only a few decades earlier had been limited to a few.

As a result of the economies of mass

AUTHOR MARILYN J. HORN is a professor in the School of Home Economics at the University of Nevada, Reno. She is the author of The Second Skin: An Interdisciplinary Study of Clothing.

317

Pat Fenley made this cotton pantsuit, and it won first prize in a Progressive Farmer *contest in Texas. This brought Pat $100 and a weekend at Houston's Astrodome for herself and her husband.*

need for people to differentiate themselves from others. This need for self-expression is one of the things at the base of the boom in the home sewing market. We can assess this trend not only in terms of increased sales in yard-goods and sewing machines, but in the accessory field as well, e.g., belts, buckles, hand-tooled leather goods and stitcheries of all kinds.

More and more men's wear patterns are available, and people have taken to sewing their own thing simply because it gives them an opportunity for expressing their individuality.

The decision to make rather than buy much of the family clothing thus has a stronger psychological base than an economic one. If you sew at home, chances are you have a more extensive wardrobe of better quality and fit than the person who spends the same amount for ready-to-wear. But if you value your time, you may want to ask yourself if it is economically worthwhile to make your own garments.

At every stage of development, clothes can help establish one's identity for himself and for those with whom he interacts. The childhood game of "dressing up" in parents' clothes provides the opportunity for the child to practice the roles that he will be expected to play in adult life.

Many "roles" in life can't be carried off successfully without the aid of the "props" of costume. The banker who looks like a rock singer may have considerable difficulty convincing his associates of his financial acumen. The degree to which a person chooses clothes that "fit" the role—whether it's a salesman, a teacher, a cowboy or a college president—will affect the cogency of his performance in that role.

Clothes are, moreover, an important factor in developing feelings of self-confidence and self-respect. When you look good, you feel good. For most people, clothes are often a source of positive reaction from others, since in our culture we are more apt to compliment a person on his appearance than on other aspects of the "self."

production, coupled with increased spending power among the middle income groups, lower income families now have access to the same kinds of fashionable clothes as the families of successful businessmen or professionals.

Out of this homogeneous-looking society comes a deep-seated psychological

318

Most Americans also recognize that a "proper" appearance and "proper" dress are the keys to association with the "right crowd," which in turn opens the door to job advancement, increased income, and greater prestige.

At this point it should be clear that our clothing needs are influenced by a multitude of circumstances. Buying motives are seldom simple, and rarely is the final selection made on completely rational terms. Every day we are faced with a number of choices regarding the selection of apparel.

The first step in the decision-making process is to make a conscious ordering of the things that are important to us. If a person recognizes and accepts the priorities of his values—e.g., that his status and prestige may be more important than his physical comfort or his individuality—his choice of clothing is not only simplified, but more likely to bring him greater satisfaction.

Quality and good workmanship are still important economic considerations. But if we evaluate clothing solely in terms of its economic worth, we may deny ourselves the psychological satisfaction that a seemingly "worthless" garment may provide. No costume or item of clothing will ever meet all our needs, but we might check some of our purchases against the following list of criteria:

Is the outfit compatible with my self-image and style of life?

Does it contribute to my feelings of self-worth and self-esteem?

Will it make me more effective in the performance of my business or social roles?

Will it bring approval from the group I want to belong to?

Does it enhance my physical characteristics and make me more attractive?

Does it provide an outlet for creative expression or a personal identity?

Is it comfortable and functionally designed?

Is the quality and workmanship in keeping with its anticipated fashion life?

Is the cost within the limitations of my income and other financial obligations?

Is it easy to care for?

For further reading:

U.S. Department of Agriculture, *How to Tailor a Woman's Suit*, Home and Garden Bulletin No. 20, Superintendent of Documents, U.S. Government Printing Office, Washington, D.C. 20402—Price 20 cents.

————, *Clothing Repairs*, Home and Garden Bulletin No. 107, Superintendent of Documents, U.S. Government Printing Office, Washington, D.C. 20402—Price 25 cents.

Current Washing Considerations

During the past 10 to 20 years so many new textiles have come into common use that the once simple chore of caring for them has become quite complex. In addition to getting them clean, we now are expected to consider whether our washing methods will harm the environment, the textiles washed, or our washing machines.

Clothing and home furnishings account for two-thirds of the huge amount of textile fibers consumed annually in this country. All become soiled or unattractive when used, so we attempt to restore their new appearance and remove the soil. How you restore them depends on many factors, including the items, the facilities, the quality of your water, and supplies at hand.

Some items require dry cleaning because they are not washable and other items, such as rugs and upholstery, require special care methods because of their size or complexity. However, it is probably no surprise to you—especially not if your regular responsibilities include caring for the textiles in your home—that the vast bulk of all textile items manufactured annually are washable. Thus, washing is overwhelmingly our most used textile care method, so you should be interested in several recent considerations that may influence how you wash.

The first consideration is a government regulation made to provide consumers more information when they purchase textiles, to help whoever does the washing choose the most suitable conditions for each item, and to point out procedures that should not be used. A Federal Trade Commission (FTC) ruling on permanent care labeling went into effect in July of 1972. It requires that most apparel sold in this country carry permanently attached labels giving care instructions for the items.

The ruling applies to both domestic and imported items and includes home sewing fabrics. Those of you buying fabrics for home sewing will be given an appropriate label (according to a number on the bolt end) to be sewn into the finished item. A few items have been exempted from the ruling but only because of a belief at the FTC that the ruling was not really needed for them.

I strongly recommend that you follow the care instruction given. In addition to stating procedures in clear and positive terms, the labels also point out procedures that *must not* be used because of possible damage to the item. If the label reads "Do not use chlorine bleach" or "Hand wash only" or "Dry clean only"—FOLLOW INSTRUCTIONS!

If the care instructions given fail to adequately restore an item to usable condition, or if an item is damaged or degraded as a result of care given, inform the store where you purchased the item and/or the manufacturer who made it. Also tell the FTC what happened so appropriate changes in the

AUTHOR WAYNE L. ST. JOHN is an Associate Professor in the Department of Clothing, Textiles and Interior Design, College of Home Economics, Kansas State University, Manhattan.

ruling may be considered (Federal Trade Commission, Division of Textiles and Furs, Bureau of Consumer Protection, Washington, D. C. 20580).

A second consideration affecting our washing procedures is recent introduction of differently formulated washing products. In the past, such changes evolved as new and better ingredients for products were developed, or as changes in textiles and washing machines suggested different washing product ingredients for better performance.

A little over 20 years ago, washing products were introduced which used a combination of phosphate builders with synthetic detergents in place of soap. That was especially beneficial to those whose water for washing is other than soft. Hardness minerals in water (mainly calcium) react with soap to form insoluble curds or film that build up on fabrics to make them dull and dingy. Phosphates, however, tie up hardness minerals so they do not curd, and a better wash results.

Recently phosphates have been accused by various groups of being a major factor in excessive algal growth in lakes and streams. As a result, the sale of phosphate-containing detergents has been banned in various towns, counties, and even States. This has led to introduction of nonphosphate washing products which provide poorer washing results for many of you and also may cause other problems.

Nonphosphate products have thus far relied mainly on replacement of phosphate with carbonate (washing soda)—which ties up calcium by precipitating it out of the washing solution. Unfortunately the calcium carbonate (limestone) deposits on—and is firmly bound to—textiles, machine parts, and anything else contacted.

This is a minor problem even for those of you whose water is soft because hardness minerals come into the wash water as part of the soil on textiles. However, the problem grows increasingly serious the harder your fresh water is because the deposition of calcium carbonate will become excessive.

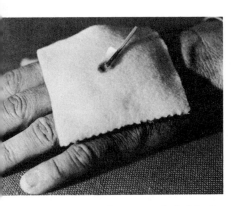

Piece of flame retardant cotton baby blanket withstands a lighted match. Hand underneath blanket is protected from the heat.

If you want to or must use a nonphosphate washing product, ask your water company how hard your water is (or have your water tested) and then take appropriate steps to get the best washing results you can.

If your water is very hard—more than 21 grains per gallon or 360 parts per million (ppm)—you should soften that water used for laundering, even if you use a phosphate-based detergent. If you use soap or a carbonate-based, nonphosphate washing product, you should soften the laundry water if it is other than soft (maximum of 3.5 grains per gallon or 66 ppm).

One consequence of calcium carbonate deposits is that you will spend more of your hard-earned money for washing machine service calls. Deposits on the inside of tubs and outside of agitators do not interfere with the basic operation of most washers, but they mystify the owners and may cause other problems. Variable blade agitators sometimes become locked due to limestone buildup in the vane control mechanism. Excessive buildup on perforated tubs has occurred to the extent that 80 to 90 percent of the holes are plugged so that drainage of wash water and subsequent rinsing are quite incomplete and overall laundry results are poor.

A washer pump is analogous to a human heart and the hoses, etc., are like veins, arteries, and other organs through which blood flows. Therefore it is not surprising that chunks or accumulations of limestone in the water circulation system of a washer have led to machine failure, just as deposits in blood circulation systems have led to heart failure and other problems in humans.

Massive accumulations have also been observed in sewer pipes which receive the wash water. If the slope of a pipe is very slight, the waste water moves so slowly that calcium carbonate tends to deposit. Sewer lines as large as six inches in diameter have been partially or completely plugged. This requires major repair if the plugged sewer line is under a concrete floor such as in a basement.

While deposits on tub and agitator may not interfere with your washer's operation, the deposits do present a rough surface to the textiles being laundered. The result is excessive abrasion of the textiles and consequent shorter useful life for them. This is a problem particularly with textiles that are normally subject to abrasive effects.

Deposits occur on cotton more rapidly than manmade fibers. Towels become scratchy and boardy, colored items appear to lose color as the deposits build up, and some items give off the deposits as dust when shaken. In addition, some of you have reported that durable press items require more touchup ironing when washed with carbonate-based products.

The final consideration also involves calcium carbonate deposits on textiles but is more perplexing because of a conflict between different laws. The banning of phosphate-containing detergents in some cities, counties, and States has already been mentioned. The Federal Trade Commission put into effect a ruling in July of 1972, requiring that children's sleepwear (sizes 0-6X)—and fabrics promoted for use therein—be nonflammable by specified tests and that the garments or fabrics remain nonflammable through 50 launderings.

321

Garments or fabrics made of flame retardant treated cotton flannel satisfied the 50-wash requirement in tests using a phosphate-based washing product, but failed after 10 to 15 washes when a carbonate-based product or soap was used. The failure was due to buildup of calcium carbonate deposits or soap film on the fabric, and it was shown that nonflammability could be restored by just three or four washes with a phosphate-based detergent.

What can you do if you want the extra meaure of safety that nonflammable sleepwear will provide your children when local laws require that you use nonphosphate washing products that will make the sleepwear flammable? No solution is yet certain—you are in a quandary. However, if you must use a non-phosphate product, do not use one with carbonate.

While I have no short-term remedies for the problems that may be caused by nonphosphate detergents, there is something you can do that may help out long-term. Let those responsible for your predicament (local, State, and Federal officials) know that you are unhappy and that you expect them to do something about it.

For further reading:

U.S. Department of Agriculture, *Removing Stains from Fabrics*, Home and Garden Bulletin 62, Washington, D.C. 20250.

————. *Sanitation in Home Laundering*, Home and Garden Bulletin 97, Washington, D.C. 20250.

————. *Soaps and Detergents for Home Laundering*, Home and Garden Bulletin 139, Washington, D.C. 20250.

Specially Designed Clothing Can Be a Boon to the Aging And Handicapped

CLOTHING DESIGNED for people who have special needs can take them off the sidelines and put them in the mainstream of life.

With the ever-increasing life expectancy of people in our society, there is a growing awareness of the importance of considering the needs and interests of our aging population. Careful selection of clothing can provide elderly and handicapped persons with some tangible defenses against aging and physical deformities.

Clothing—besides being as essential to daily life as food and shelter has a special significance in developing new social relationships for older people. It is important for elderly people to create a favorable impression through their personal appearance as well as through their behavior. Clothes help maintain a positive self-image and help provide ego support.

There is a strong tendency in all of us to judge personality on the basis of physique. A person can find himself feeling self-conscious or with low-self-esteem from a physical handicap. The condition may make him dependent on other people.

Dependency on someone else for the daily task of dressing can be demoralizing. Specially designed or carefully selected clothing may serve to camouflage a physical defect or provide ease in dressing that will contribute to an individual's feeling of independence.

Some basic requirements of clothing can be identified for individuals with special needs:

• Clothing must be easy to handle. The elderly and persons with handicaps have limited movement with less than average coordination

• Clothing must provide freedom of movement. Clothes that bind or are tight tend to affect the circulation, which at its best may not be good. Energy is often limited and dressing activities are difficult if clothing does not provide enough room to get in and out of it. Since individuals often must sit or lie down for extended periods, this requires roomy clothing

• Psychological needs are important and can be realized through fashionable designs with interesting and colorful fabrics. A person can minimize to himself and others the visual effects of age or of a disability with a good appearance

• Durability and easy care are required. Crutches and braces add strain and friction which may soil fabrics in given places. The strain on a garment when dressing and undressing is increased with limited body movement. More laundering may be required as a result of accidents with food and incontinence

These basic requirements and many specific clothing needs can be met through careful selection, special designs, and adaptations.

The first consideration in selection is an individual's preference and need. Current fashion is of the utmost importance, with simplicity of design a key factor. A better fit will be likely and alterations more easily managed in a simple design.

Clothing should fit loosely to camouflage a deformity. However, it can fit too loosely and be both uncomfortable and dangerous.

Careful evaluation may have to be made for the wearer who might be unable to assess fit.

If an individual has little feeling he or she may be unaware of a tight-fitting garment or shoes.

Continuous pressure from clothing could cause a cutoff of circulation or lead to a fall. One should be especially careful that shoes, either new or old, assure proper fit. Socks which are too tight can be just as dangerous. Loosely fitting stockings may bunch and cause unnecessary irritations.

Boots present a special problem. Take care to select the long opening type to aid in getting boots on and off.

Two-piece garments may be best for fitting some figure problems and provide comfort for the wheelchair user. They are also easier to cope with when dressing and undressing.

Shift dresses are good for disguising hip and waist irregularities. They are particularly comfortable for a person with a thick waist.

One-piece dresses are easier to take care of and may be easier for some to keep in place.

For the person who is sitting all the time, trousers for both men and women might have to be longer in the back and shorter in the front to provide comfort. Suit jackets need to be short to prevent bunching of excess material. The trouser leg should be longer to accommodate the bend in the knees.

The neckline of a garment is important for comfort and a key to ease of dressing. Avoid large collars and low necklines. They tend to be uncomfortable and require more accurate fitting to look nice. Expandable neck openings without fastenings will be helpful, especially for children. Round and V-necks provide comfort and fewer fitting problems.

Fastenings perhaps cause individuals with special needs more difficulty than any other garment feature. Avoid back openings; they are hard to reach. Features to look for are zippers with long pull tabs, large buttons, large grippers, and Velcro closures.

Blouses and shirts with action pleats help to accommodate extra movements and aid the crutch user. Consider knit garments for ease of movement.

Colors and fabrics are of great significance. Color is an individual thing. Many older men and women have blue as a favorite—perhaps because it is a becoming color with white or gray hair. Very bright colors may be harsh and more difficult to wear. Bright colors tend to emphasize the figure. Darker colors with some pattern will show soil and wrinkles less readily.

Many easy-care garments are on the market today. To keep clothing attractive and fresh looking, give special consideration to the fabric. Serviceability

AUTHOR AUDREY NEWTON is Chairman, Department of Textiles, Clothing and Design, College of Home Economics, University of Nebraska, Lincoln.

of fabrics depends upon fiber content, construction, and finish.

Fibers like cotton, linen, and rayon tend to be absorbent but wrinkle. Thermoplastic fibers like nylon, polyester, and acrylics are lightweight, resist wrinkles, and dry quickly but are not absorbent and tend to build up static electricity. Blends of cotton and polyester, however, will combine characteristics, often with advantages of both.

The manufacturer's label will supply information on performance and directions for care. This information is important for selection and care. Follow directions for the highest degree of satisfaction.

Yarn construction can affect care and serviceability. Loosely twisted yarns tend to soil and snag easily but have a softer hand. Yarns with a high twist are harsh to the touch but tend to wear longer.

Weave construction affects serviceability. Open weaves may snag and hold their shape less well than a firm weave. Loose weaves fray with friction and laundry.

Knitted constructions tend to move and expand with action but also may bag, stretch, and snag.

Many finishes are added to fabrics to increase their functional qualities. Some prevent shrinkage. Flame retardants are used for resistance to burning; water repellent finishes for resistance to stains and water. Special dyes produce colorfastness to light and laundering.

Fabrics laundered frequently need to be colorfast. If the garment will be laundered at high temperatures, light color or white must be considered in selecting garments.

Clothing which might accumulate large numbers of infectious bacteria must have a disinfectant added to the wash water. White sturdy fabrics would be most serviceable. These and many other special finishes may be very important for a particular function and will be identified on the label.

Shopping is often difficult for older people and for the handicapped. Fitting problems take longer, the effort of trying on clothes is tiring, and it is difficult to get to the shops. The utmost care in selection may still demand extensive alteration.

Although it is not economically feasible to mass produce clothing for each handicap and figure irregularity, some merchandisers of special clothing have been moderately successful.

The following firms merchandise a number of garments designed to meet a specific need and also make clothes to order. Catalogs are available and shopping from home is an added convenience.

Leinenweber, W. G. *Men's Fashions for the Wheelchair Set.* Catalog. 69 West Washington Street, Chicago, Ill., 1965.

Odell, V. D. *Fashion-ABLE.* Catalog for clothing and devices for the physically disabled. Rocky Hill, N.J. 1971.

Vocational Guidance and Rehabilitation Services, *Functionally Designed Clothing and Aids for Chronically Ill and Disabled.* Catalog of clothing for the disabled. 2239 East 55th Street, Cleveland, Ohio. 1971.

Cookman, Mrs. Helen. "Functional Fashions". Clothing Research and Development Foundation, Inc., 48 East 66th Street, New York, N.Y. 10021.

Here are some suggested adaptations for ready-to-wear garments to meet special needs:

Velcro to replace hooks for bras, girdles, shirts, and blouses.

Tabs and loops or large hooks to transfer to front opening bras.

Velcro for the fly opening of trousers.

Zippers added to front opening of slips.

Longer placket openings.

Openings in the inseam of pant legs with Velcro tape or zippers for dressing ease and braces.

Large buttons added to zipper pulls.

Button-on pockets.

Elastic in the waistband.

Wider and additional belt loops.

A bias strip in the seam allowance at the knee area of pants.

A gusset added to an underarm seam.

Extra rows of stitching for reinforcement along underarm seams and lines.

Tape added to the seams to prevent stretching and breaking thread.

Adjustable suspenders.

Reinforced openings and pockets.

Reinforcements on the inside or outside of shorts or trousers to prevent wear from braces.

Linings for pants to accommodate added friction from braces.

Terrycloth lined garments for absorbency.

Reinforced knees, elbows.

Proper care and consideration must be given to clothes of all kinds if alterations are to be kept to a minimum. Even with the best of care some alterations will be required. For those who have sewing skills, pattern alterations when making one's own garment might be the answer.

If you agree that appearance reveals one's state of mind, then suitably designed clothes, careful selection, and appropriate encouragement in reaching this goal should be of great significance to the handicapped and the elderly for independence and self-esteem.

For further reading:

Burton, A. M. and V. Y. Trotter. *Easy Fashions For You*, Extension Service at the University of Nebraska, College of Agriculture and Home Economics, Lincoln, Nebr., 1966.

Handmade Fashions In Doubleknit for the Man in Your Life

SEWING FOR THE MAN in your life can bring about interesting results —for both of you! Although construction of men's wear is too detailed for the beginner, the experienced sewer will find it an exciting challenge.

For the first time, easy-care fabrics are available that can be used to give your man a custom-tailored fashion created at home with "TLC" (tender loving care).

A word of caution when undertaking your first fashion-sewing for your man. You may be creating a monster. He may become intoxicated with your success, and want you to sew constantly *just for him!*

Many patterns are now available for men's wear—special ones for double-knits as well as patterns for woven fabrics.

Some are available in proportioned sizes.

Patterns for jackets are purchased by a man's chest size (example: a 40-inch chest calls for size 40 pattern).

Slacks patterns are generally purchased by waist measurement. A man's hip measure is generally 6 inches larger than the waist. If his hip runs larger than this, buy pattern by hip size and make alterations for waist.

For proper shaping, the shoulder length of the jacket back should be about three-eighths inch longer than the jacket front. If it is not, add the amount needed to upper armhole at shoulder, tapering to nothing just above notches. If a long, or extra long size is needed, slash the pattern and add the extra length. To shorten the pattern, fold out excess length. To add to the waistline of a jacket, add to the back side seams below the armhole. To reduce size of the waistline, increase the size of the back side seams below the armhole.

In a slacks pattern, check the crease line. The crease should be in the center of the leg, and on straight of grain. Fold the pattern in half lengthwise, matching the cutting lines at bottom and knee. Redraw the grain line if it is not parallel to the folded edge. (If the grain line is not in line with the creases, it will be noticeable and the slacks will not hang straight.)

Draw a horizontal line across the back of the slacks pattern where the

AUTHORS BOBBIE B. MCFATTER AND EVVA Z. WILSON are clothing specialists of the Cooperative Extension Service, Louisiana State University, Baton Rouge.

490-100 O - 73 - 22

inseam and crotch seams meet. Distance from the waist to this line should equal the man's crotch depth measure.

To lengthen crotch depth, slash the back pattern horizontally between waistline and crotch. Spread the pattern the needed amount. Add the same amount to front pattern piece and fly facing. To shorten crotch depth, make a fold in back, front, and fly facing of the pattern for the needed amount.

Measure stride from where the back crotch seam crosses the inseam to where the waistline and side seam cross. This should equal half the man's hip measurement less one inch.

To alter the stride, slash through the pattern at the center back to, but not through, the side seam. Spread or lap the amount needed and redraw the cutting line.

MEASUREMENTS

Use the following measurements to check fit and ease of the pattern, and determine alterations needed.

For Jacket
Chest—around fullest part of chest, high up under arms and over shoulder blades, and over items normally carried in shirt pockets.
Waist—at natural waistline, over belt.
Hip—(seat) around fullest part, over articles normally carried in pockets.
Sleeve Length—over bent elbow, from end of shoulder to wrist bone, or desired length.
Center Back Length—from nape of neck down to cover seat, plus any extra length man desires.
Shoulder Width—across shoulder blades, from armhole to armhole.
Shoulder Length—from base of neck to end of shoulder bone.
Shoulder Type and Posture—determine the man's shoulder type and posture to help in deciding where alterations may be needed.

For Slacks
Waist—at natural waistline, over shirt and underclothing only.
Hip (seat)—over fullest part, including articles generally carried in pockets.

Inseam—from inner crotch to length desired.
Length—from side waistline seam to length desired.
Total Crotch—from front waist, between legs, to waist at back (or measure a correctly fitted pair of pants—recording both front and back crotch seams).
Crotch Depth—with man sitting on flat surface, measure from waist down side seam to flat surface.
Width at Knee—around knee, at center of knee cap.
Upper Thigh—at fullest part.
Stride—hip measurement divided in half less one inch (Example—40-inch hip $\div$ 2 = 20 inches − 1 inch = 19-inch stride).
Pocket widths—Check pattern to be sure that pockets will accommodate hands and wallets.

To give better fit and drape to slacks—cut with a slight amount of extra width on one side of the front crotch (usually the left). Pin front pattern section to fabric. Draw a line from bottom of fly to three-fourths of an inch above and beyond the original cutting line for the crotch. Continue down inner leg seam, tapering gently back to original cutting line.

To save time, cut both front pants sections from altered pattern, then recut right side separately using original cutting line. Additional fabric is "eased" into seams in making slacks.

For a large abdomen, slash the pattern front about 1½ inches below the waistline—do not slash through the side seam. The pattern can be spread up to one inch, and the cutting line redrawn.

With muslin or old sheet, make up a shell of the garment, using the altered pattern. Fit, and make any additional alterations on the shell. Transfer these to the paper pattern. Save the shell for future use.

In selecting fabrics choose knits that have a firm weave, and do not snag easily. A small patterned design does not need matching and can hide stitching imperfections. Avoid diagonal stripes.

Check for flaws, and make sure the design is on straight of grain. Allow extra fabric for using "with nap" layout so all pattern parts can be laid in the same direction.

The lining should be of fabric that will require the same care as the fashion fabric.

Interfacing of woven fabric gives a soft drape to the garment. Use press-on woven interfacing cut on the bias for the front and collar. Select a woven permanent press fabric without press-on qualities for the back interfacing.

Shoulder shaping may be made of layers of washable nonwoven polyester fleece, or purchased shoulder pads can be used.

Buy twill tape of ¼-inch width.

Fusing material is optional. It is used in hems and welts.

Pick an under-collar fabric of lightweight felt, tightly woven wool flannel, or self-fabric.

Use cotton-covered polyester or all polyester thread for all general seams, buttonhole twist or heavy duty thread for buttonholes.

Buttons with four holes are best for suit jackets.

Front buttons should be three-quarters inch, and sleeve buttons one-half inch to five-eighths inch.

Inside waistbanding can be purchased already prepared, or perma-press interfacing fabric may be used.

For slacks pocket and fly lining fabric, use cotton or cotton/polyester broadcloth, or fabric especially prepared for pocketing.

Get a 9-inch, nonsnag trouser or skirt zipper. Pants hooks can be the sew-on or clamp-on type for use on the waistband.

Construction pressing is most important to achieve a well-tailored garment. A good steam iron, sturdy ironing board, pressing cloth, seam roll, pressing ham, and pounding block are desirable.

Press as you complete each step of construction—pressing on the wrong side of the fabric whenever possible. Use plenty of steam for best results. A pressing cloth helps to reduce "shine"

when necessary to press on right side of fabric.

Doubleknit fabrics should be preshrunk before cutting. To preshrink washable polyester doubleknit fabrics, use detergent and complete washer and dryer cycles. Allow the fabric to "relax" several hours before cutting.

Include lining, twill tape, zipper, pocketing and durable press interfacing in the preshrinking process. Do not preshrink press-on interfacing.

Press out center crease in fabric. If it cannot be removed, refold the fabric so the line will be located in an inconspicuous place on the garment.

Ballpoint needles (machine and hand sewing) and ballpoint pins are available. They do not split the yarns as regular ones do. For maximum results, you may find it is worthwhile to change machine needles after every garment is completed.

Use "with nap" layout in cutting, with all pattern pieces going in the same direction. Cut with sharp shears, wiping the blades often to remove lint.

For marking, a tracing wheel and paper can be used on most firm knits. A tiny clip into the center of the notch is a quick and accurate way to mark pieces to be matched. Tailor's tacks of thread can be used for marking heavy or textured fabrics.

Mark accurately, being especially careful with pocket markings, buttonholes, and lapel roll line.

Lighter machine pressure is generally required for knits. Your machine may respond to a lighter tension when sewing knits.

Ten to 12 stitches per inch are suitable for most stable knits. Stitch in the same direction on each side of front openings and side seams to avoid differences in the shape of the finished product. Stitch from the widest part toward the narrowest part of the garment. Staystitching should be used on curved or bias seam edges to prevent stretching.

Grade enclosed seam allowances to one-quarter inch and three-eighths inch to remove bulk. Slash and trim wide darts. No seam finishes are usually required on doubleknits.

Turn hem up the desired amount, leaving raw edge exposed. Hem with a loose stitch, or use fusing adhesive to hold in place.

Use one-quarter- to three-eighths-inch bar-tacks at ends of pockets and fly of slacks. Place on the crosswise or lengthwise grain, to give strength at points of stress.

In jacket construction, the following tips may not be found on your pattern's sewing guide, but can help you get a professional appearance. Here's how to apply interfacing to jacket front, using iron-on interfacing.

Fit bias interfacing to front of the jacket. Machine stitch on interfacing side one-half inch from cut edge across shoulder, around armhole, along side, and below buttonholes at edge of front. Do not stitch along outside edges of the lapel.

Trim interfacing from stitched seam allowances, close to stitching lines. Do not trim along armholes, as interfacing will help to support sleeve later.

Place twill tape along side of roll line and stitch through tape, interfacing, and fashion fabric. Tape should stop approximately 3 inches above first buttonhole, and approximately 1 inch below neckline seamline.

Press interfacing to the garment, using a pressing cloth. The iron should be lifted up and down without sliding it across fabric. Do not press lapel!

Roll the lapel over your hand with interfacing up. Pin outer edges of the lapel and interfacing together, allowing lapel of fashion fabric to extend beyond interfacing edge as needed.

Fold on roll line and press in a sharp crease just to ends of tape—allowing iron to reach a point only about 1 inch into lapel. Do not press along outside edges of the lapel yet.

Stitch along outer edges of neckline and lapel about a half inch from cut edges—beginning at the widest point of the lapel and stitching toward shoulder. Break the thread and stitch down front. Be sure to stitch both fronts in exactly

the same direction, to prevent them from curling in opposite directions. Trim away interfacing seam allowance close to stitching. Press interfacing to the lapel.

To shape shoulder, stretch upper third of front armhole over narrowest curve of ham, right side of fabric up. Steam this section generously for about 3 inches down from shoulder seam and about 3 inches into body of garment. Remove steam, and continue to stretch and hold in place until completely dry.

To apply back interfacing, stitch the center back seam and side back seams of jacket and press open. Sew interfacing to jacket back and side fronts a half inch from cut edges. Trim interfacing from neckline, shoulder and side seams. Do not trim from armhole.

Bottom of interfacing is not attached to body of jacket, allowing inside edge of interfacing to hang free. Stitch or pink along the free edge to prevent raveling.

In the back, a half lining is usually preferred for knit fabrics. Make a half lining by using a regular pattern piece, cutting it about 13 to 14 inches long at the center back. Make a ½-inch hand- or machine-stitched hem in the bottom edge of the half lining before attaching it to the garment.

For a professional touch at the collar, make a hang loop from twill tape, narrow braid, or bias strip of lining fabric —3 inches long. Attach at neckline over lining, before attaching collar.

Here's the unfinished method for handling the collar. Cut woven press-on interfacing by upper collar pattern (placed on bias). Trim off seam allowances on all edges. Press to underside of upper collar.

Turn under unnotched seam allowances of collar, mitering corners. Press, and baste top and corners in place.

Place right side of upper collar to lining side of jacket, and stitch, clipping jacket neck edge as needed to make collar fit smoothly. Grade seam, and press up toward collar. Fold the ends of collar seam allowances over ends of neckline seam. Baste to hold.

Machine stitch along roll line of under collar. Lay under collar on ironing board. Fold on marked roll line and press in a sharp crease with edge of iron.

Place under collar on pressing ham, stretching outside edges slightly to cause collar ends to curl slightly toward the center. Press with steam and allow to dry before moving. This helps collar fit more closely against jacket when completed.

Fit under collar to upper collar, covering raw edge of upper collar seam allowances. Sew in place using a whipping stitch or catch stitch to hold raw edges of under collar. Stretch outside edges slightly as you sew.

To make sleeve cap smooth, cut a bias strip of permanent press interfacing 2 by 6 inches for each armhole. Make a ½-inch fold on one long edge. Slipstitch folded edge along seam of sleeve cap.

For polyester fleece shapes instead of shoulder pads, use the pattern back and front pieces (pinned together at shoulder) and cut a paper pattern. Follow the shape of the armhole, from notch to notch. Mark shoulder seam on paper pattern and transfer to fleece.

Cut first layer approximately 4 inches wide at shoulder seam, and taper downward to form a crescent. Cut other layers of fleece in decreasing widths until the correct thickness is obtained (three or more layers are normally needed).

Place layers of fleece over seam roll (smallest layer against seam roll) and steam. Hand tack to hold layers together, keeping curled shape. Pin shapes in place with largest size layer next to garment. Attach to armhole and shoulder seam by hand using loose stitches —with edge extending slightly into sleeve, past armhole seam allowance.

In finishing, top stitching helps to hide seam bulk while holding edges in place. It is usually placed about ¼ inch from the edge. Stitch along collar, turn and stitch in "well" of neckline seam, turn and continue down front of jacket.

Rework, by hand, over machine-made buttonholes, using buttonhole twist or heavy-duty thread. Select keyhole buttonhole shape when using buttonhole attachment. Lower buttonhole will be placed slightly closer to outer edge than upper buttonhole when jacket front is rounded at lower edge.

Sew buttons to front and sleeves. Steam press with care, and for best appearance take to a professional pressing shop.

In slacks construction, before making seams, fold leg pieces in half lengthwise with right side of fabric up. Match cutting edges at bottom and knee.

Press from about 9 inches below the waistline to crease front and back, using steam and pressing cloth. Avoid placing the iron directly on fabric. A damp pressing cloth will help give a sharper crease. Allow fabric to dry while flat.

Here's how to shape the back of slacks. With back piece of slacks still on ironing board, pull crotch area at inseam up toward waistline, stretching and steaming. Keep cutting lines of inseams in line with each other.

Belt loops can be applied before the waistband is applied or afterward. Check width and length of loops to be sure they fit belt width.

In finishing slacks, turn up hem. Use a small loose whipping stitch, with stitches close together.

Make a "West Point" hemline for a professional appearance—by making the center back of the pants leg about half an inch longer than the front.

Attach hook and eye at waistline. Press slacks, using steam iron and press cloth.

Your project will have reached the ultimate when his jacket hangs straight from the shoulders in front and back, without wrinkling. Does not look too tight, nor feel too tight when buttoned. Is long enough to cover seat of slacks— and is proportionate to his height. Lapels roll neatly and hold close to the chest. The collar sets close to back of neck. Sleeves hang smoothly and are proportionate length for him.

His slacks should fit smoothly around waist and hips, hang straight from the waist with creases on straight of grain, be comfortable and have a smooth fit through the crotch, have appropriate length for the times and his body build.

For further reading:

Carlin, David. *Alteration of Men's Clothing*, Third edition, Fairchild Publications, Inc., 1962.

Edwards, Delores. *The Delores Edwards Method: Men's Jackets*, Fashion Sewing Institute, Inc., 1972.

Everything About Sewing Menswear, from Vogue Patterns, 1972.

Lawrence, Judy. *Easy Sewing with Knits*, Countryside Press, 1972.

Martensson, Kerstin. *Men's Wear—Kwik Sew Method*, Sew-Knit-N-Stretch Corporation, 1971.

Waisman, A. *Modern Custom Tailoring for Men*, The Master Designer, 1971.

Selection of Luggage For Happy Traveling

Dɪᴅ ʏᴏᴜ ᴇᴠᴇʀ add up the cost of items crowded into your suitcase when you went away for a weekend? Try it; you'll be amazed at the total! Then think of the vacation or business trip when you were traveling for a week or more. Be sure to include your address book and snapshots, and grandmother's brooch which can't be replaced.

I think you will agree that the contents of a packed suitcase are so valuable that purchase of luggage should be regarded as money paid to protect the clothing and other items it will hold. This expenditure is also an investment in durability, ease in use, and attractiveness.

Some people make their selection once in a lifetime. Others, who travel more frequently, choose new luggage every few years.

Both men's and women's bags are available in a wide range of prices, styles, and materials. So it is important for you the consumer to decide what you want, and search until you find it. The total investment may take place in one shopping trip, or it can be a long-term project of collecting specific items as needed and the pocketbook allows.

Many families find the latter practice helpful in preparing for anticipated costs of launching children into marriage, careers, or college. In our mobile society, most people—regardless of age—will need luggage sooner or later. Suitcases already owned are like money in the bank when the time comes to take a trip.

If you decide to buy over a period of time, get basic pieces first, extras later. Although basic needs are determined by the individual, this usually means one bag to accommodate overnight stays, and another larger one for longer trips.

Some couples start by purchasing one bag which the man or woman may use, either singly or together. For them, the pullman case, measuring 25 to 27 inches, may be the best choice. While these are generally designated in the trade as ladies' cases, neither their exterior nor interior look too feminine for men to use if carefully selected.

One early decision is whether to buy a matching set or mixed pieces. The former makes it easier to identify your luggage, which is important if you travel by commercial transportation. It may also reduce the styles available because each manufacturer tends to vary his production.

Most consumers choose between molded luggage and soft-sided or fabric bags. Molded cases are relatively easy to clean and scuff and snag resistant; so they will probably look good in hard use for a longer time. Their frames, usually of lightweight metal, are primarily to support the bags, but may contribute to their rigidity. The

ᴀᴜᴛʜᴏʀ ᴇɴɪᴅ ꜰ. ᴛᴏᴢɪᴇʀ is an Associate Professor in the Clothing, Textiles and Related Art Department, College of Home Economics, Virginia Polytechnic Institute and State University, Blacksburg.

more rigid the frame, the more the bag may be expected to resist crushing or twisting out of alignment.

Soft-sided cases have been increasingly popular since World War II when many people discovered their relatively low cost, capacity for expansion, light weight, and ease in carrying. These are available in a wide range of fabrics, bright colors, and shapes. They can be folded and stored in a small space when not in use, or crammed full without worry about closing. Many have several zipper pockets conveniently placed on the outside.

Some travelers like a combination of rigid and soft-sided luggage. They fold the soft bag and store it in the firm one, ready to be used when the trip makes it necessary.

Frequent air passengers should be aware of the limited size of underseat compartments in planes. The Federal Aviation Agency suggests maximum carry-on luggage dimensions of 23 x 16 x 9 inches. Soft bags may come well within the 9-inch requirement before packing, but be a lot thicker after cramming.

Most international flights still limit first-class passengers to 66 pounds; tourist class is restricted to 44.

Always lift a suitcase before buying it. Could you carry it a fairly long distance when full? Although most of your journeys may be by car, many people also use public transportation for some travel. Porters and red caps are increasingly scarce in motels and transportation terminals, so be sure you can carry your own luggage.

Is the handle comfortable? Indentations for fingers and rounded edges make a full bag easier to carry than a handle which is the wrong size for your hand or which is slippery or cuts into the flesh. Usually, handles are attached at or near the center of a suitcase to help the carrier maintain body balance. An off-center attachment may prevent the bag hitting the body, but it probably will not last as long.

Durable handles are attached to the metal frame or to a substantial metal backing plate. To check this, look and feel both the outside and inside of the case. Inspect the assembly of the handle to see if it will stand picking up and setting down the many times its use will require.

A frequent cause of suitcase deterioration is the handle. Be sure it is reinforced with metal or heavy plastic cord throughout its length, including the part attached to the bag.

Tongue and groove closures are usually considered superior to the overlapping type. Probably neither closes tightly enough to prevent heavy rain from entering the bag eventually; but tongue and groove closures provide more protection, especially when the case is turned so water is deflected from the opening.

Examine zipper closures to see that they are securely sewed to the bag with no dangling threads. Do they run smoothly? Check the operation at curved areas; usually a gentle curve is better than a tight turn. Additional

protection for packed clothing is achieved if the zipper is inserted into the case so that it does not come- in direct contact with contents.

Few locks on suitcases give much protection against theft. Many come with identical keys, or are easily opened with other objects. Some brands open only by dialing a specific combination, but this may be more inconvenient than helpful.

The chief value of any lock is probably the safeguard it provides against accidental latch opening.

Hinges are important to alignment of the frame and to general sturdiness of the bag. Generally, the longer the hinges, the better they perform. Three hinges are better than two, especially if the case is long. Those which are riveted to the bag in several places tend to increase rigidity and security in use.

Skids, the feet on which the bag sits, prevent abrasion wear. Those riveted to the frame will probably remain attached longer than ones which are merely attached to the shell. Most cases have 4 feet, and the wider apart they are, the steadier the luggage will stand.

Suitcases that open flat or a full 180° occupy twice as much space when being packed as those on which the cover only stands upright. Flat ones will never fall shut on your hands; they may be easier to fill, and more convenient to use if you do not completely unpack each night. Since most molded cases usually open only to 90°, at least one stay and preferably two should be attached to hold the lid up.

Most suitcases are lined. Sometimes the lining is backed by a layer of cushioning material, but this is usually so thin that little protection is given. Superior linings are achieved when fabric for sides and flat surfaces are cut separately. Pinch the lining; if wrinkles occur, it is probably attached only at the corners and may soon pull away.

A separate strip of material over the hinge edge will prevent anything slipping into it and straining the bag when it is being closed. However, this should not be so tight that it prevents the case from opening properly.

Both acetate and polypropylene are often used for linings. Acetate is hard to clean and severely degraded when solvents such as nail-polish remover are spilled on it. Polypropylene is stronger, more resistant to wear, and can be scrubbed with soap and water.

Some linings have special finishes to help repel lipstick and other greasy stains. The label may indicate fiber composition and finish treatments.

Pockets, dividers, and hangers are often inside luggage. These cases usually cost more and the accessories may reduce packing space, especially if they cannot be removed. Be sure you really want the extras before you buy. Dividers help protect contents from crushing, and pockets are very useful for controlling small items, especially if they have a zipper closing.

Some pockets have a plastic lining which is water resistant and prevents creamy substances escaping to your clothes. They are rarely waterproof, and can't be relied on to control loosely closed perfumes or thin liquids.

Each suitcase should have the full name and current address of the owner clearly printed and firmly attached to both the inside and outside. A sturdy, free-hanging strap is preferable to a chain-type fastener for the outside as the chain type tends to separate during rough trips. An adhesive backed label stuck inside the lid is double protection against loss.

If identification tags do not come with the bags, they can usually be purchased in luggage or stationery departments.

Choose your luggage according to your needs and budget! Don't be sold items solely because a store just happens to have them in stock. Beware of bags designed to look as if they were reinforced by the use of plastic strips, welting, or mock seams. None of these increase protection for clothes, durability of cases, or ease in use. Care in selection will save money for future travel, and make your trips worry free.

COMMUNITIES

Our Fragmented Community Living: Can We Relate?

THERE IS NO ONE ANSWER to the question, what kind of community do you want? It makes a great deal of difference whom you ask—a businessman, a professional person, a farmer. A family with schoolgoing children has needs greatly different from a retired couple and therefore looks to its community for different services. Families who live in suburban areas with one or more members commuting to work in an urban center or adjacent area have different expectations of their community than families living in a small, quiet, rural town.

One will also get different answers to the question when it is put to planners, legislators, and those who have responsibilities for major policy decisions concerning where roads are to be built, which centers are to be given priority in developing a modern water and sewage system, and where hospitals, schools, and industries are to be located.

It would not be inappropriate to speculate what the answer would be if it were asked of an environmentalist, a person concerned about people living in a healthy, beautiful, and satisfying environment where the air and water are free from pollution and the emphasis is on quality of life and living.

Actually, people identify with more than one community. If they have children of school age, they relate to their school community. In health matters they relate to the location of doctors, dentists, and hospitals. For worship

AUTHOR DOUGLAS ENSMINGER is President of Mid-Missouri Associated Colleges and Universities and Professor, Rural Sociology, University of Missouri—Columbia.

they are members of a church community. Increasingly, people go regularly to a number of centers in satisfying their recreational, personal, family, and business needs.

As people, we have accepted and are caught up in today's high technological advancements in production, transportation, and communication. As human beings, we are presently in search of more ways to satisfy our human relations needs. People are finding it more and more difficult to relate in meaningful ways to multiple communities.

Clearly, Americans are in quest of new values. Some of the more important values we now seek involve being part of a community of people who know who they are, share common values, and can and will work together to achieve and share common goals. And increasingly, we are placing a higher value on the quality of life people enjoy as reflected in the quality of the community in which they live.

Realization of a higher quality of life for everyone won't just happen. There is a need for plans, and plans need to be carried out.

These plans and programs must assure that people will, step by step, move nearer to what now seems likely to become a universal goal—living in communities where they can, through their involvement, contribute toward creating a friendly, hospitable environment which encourages them to participate in community achievements and to take pride in what they can accomplish together for the mutual benefit of all. Desiring a higher quality of life can be accepted as an objective of everyone, regardless of the size of community.

Being part of a community means caring about meeting one's responsibility to the community. It means families and neighbors being concerned about their homes, parks, and playgrounds. Being part of a community means working together to achieve quality of education, medical care, cultural programs, acceptable transportation and public utilities, good police

Combining her talents as gourmet cook and teacher, volunteer Sophie Leavitt holds a class to help needy families prepare nutritious and tasty meals with USDA-donated foods. As a final touch, the group enjoyed lunch using her recipes. Sophie has taken her down-to-earth demonstrations to migrant camps, care centers, homes, and community halls. She even ran a "cooking school" for inner-city youngsters.

and fire protection, employment opportunities, and responsible and responsive government.

In thinking about what kind of community you want, it is wrong to overemphasize physical objects and services such as comfortable, well-kept houses, up-to-the-minute hospitals and schools, magnificent church buildings, paved roads, elaborate libraries and theaters, expensive water and sewage systems, well-stocked stores, and modern industries.

Although these are important to a

community and often are determinants in choosing a place to live, in themselves they do not make a community. Regardless of its cost, a house by itself won't bring a happy home life. The way members of a family relate to each other, their concern and respect for each other, their sacrifices, and the love they express and share are what create a happy home life.

Similarly, what makes a community a desirable place in which to live, to raise a family, to work, and to retire are the quality of human relations and the concerns people have for and about each other.

An area could have from 500 to 100,000 people who want to live unto themselves, who are too busy or indifferent to care about the well-being of others or the quality of life, and it would not be a good community. An area is a desirable community where concerned, considerate people find time to participate in organizations and institutions and to be neighbors.

As people begin thinking and working together to improve "their community," they need to be realistic in accepting the services it can provide and its potential for growth.

The first essential in thinking about a community is to update our thinking and understanding about changes in people's attitudes. It will be important to know what they want and expect of their community and of government.

It will be necessary to understand the changing role of the family, the trend toward specialization of services, and the pressures of a growing population in contributing to pollution.

There should be a realization that today people have more leisure time and increasingly they will place a higher value on leisure and less emphasis on work as a value.

We should expect there will be more challenging of our present patterns of education and, in the future, look to education to contribute to improving the quality of life.

While individuals will continue to place a value on opportunities to earn a living, they will increasingly seek opportunities which offer greater satisfactions in personal, family, and community living in contrast to just getting ahead economically.

Greater emphasis will be placed on cultural programs.

Special consideration must be given to the growing population of the aged who have special needs, one of the most important being meaningful human relationships and being a part of community life.

Help is available to communities that want to get things done. The young mayor of a small Tennessee community, second from left, talks informally to employees of county and State governmental agencies about land use problems.

Planning for the community we want for tomorrow would be meaningless if we did not accept that every community must have an economic reason for its existence. This could be to serve manufacturing, agriculture, recreation, or education.

We can have the kind of community we want to live and work in only if we are prepared to be diligent in applying the findings of both the physical and social sciences concerned with man and his environment, and support expenditure of Federal, State, and local funds. Needed is a commitment to achieve a higher quality of life where people can live, work, and be part of a community that cares.

Some constituents of a vital community are selfless leaders, involved and concerned people, organizations and institutions sensitive to and actively serving the needs of everyone, a readiness on the part of the people to commit resources for solving community problems, and an economic base that can support the needed institutionalized services.

People of the community should think of Federal and State agencies, programs, and funds as resources to help the community help itself. It

makes a world of difference whether the Federal and State agencies join with the community in working on problems the people define as being their priority needs, or the community joins with the agencies in carrying out programs the agencies decide are important.

Community change and improvements cannot be brought about unless people of the community want them and the changes sought are supported by local leaders. A community that lacks local leaders, that lacks concern, that is not ready to work for change, will be indifferent to what people from the outside think to be their needs.

Every community will find it has among its people potential leadership talent. Furthermore, individuals who hold strong views about community problems will find that if they assert themselves and persevere, they can arouse interest within the community and cause action to be taken.

If dormant leadership talent is to be activated, if organizations and institutions are to keep active and focused on priority community needs, and if the people are to develop and maintain interest and involvement in the life of the community, there will be a need for some kind of community-wide organization which might be called a Community Council for Planning and Action.

Without some kind of overview organization like this, the people's expression of concerns will be sporadic, Federal agencies and program activities will dominate, and the element that contributes most to creation and maintenance of a good community—participation—will be lacking.

Only people of a community can decide what kind of community they want. Accepting the different interests and objectives in planning for the kind of community people are now in quest of, some or all of the following should be examined:

If people are to have alternatives to where they live and work, we should strive to develop the community as a place where people's requirements can be met, where they can be employed, and where they can achieve a satisfying life. Needed will be the people's participation in formulating specific programs to create additional employment opportunities and assure that most of the people's needs, services, and cultural programs are met within the community.

If people of all talents and interests are to have a sense of fulfillment, it will be important that the community be concerned, and through its sponsored programs offer opportunities to develop to the fullest the community's human resources.

People of the community should think first about what they can do for the good of the community, decide what they can achieve by working together, and finally, what outside help will be needed if the community is to develop as the people wish it to. Programs for developing the community should seek to harness local energies and be run by local people, who know better than anyone else their problems, their capabilities, and their own priorities.

Since the strength of the community is to be found in individuals and in the people's own institutions—schools, churches, organizations, businesses, and industries—these institutions should serve the needs of everybody.

People can have the kind of communities they want if they will accept and understand the need for continuous concern and involvement. New needs will require new leaders and a continuous commitment on the part of the people to play roles appropriate to each need and situation. Community development must be accepted as a continuous process.

The kind of communities people now seek do not just happen, nor are they beyond the reach of any group of people. In the same way that research and experience have provided guidance for the development of American agriculture and industry, community research must be accepted as a continuous need

338

to provide guidance for planners and organizational, institutional, and community leaders in their common quest to develop tomorrow's community.

It is my view that we need to clarify the objective of rural development as contributing to the development of socially and economically viable rural-urban communities.

Things Get Done
By Communities
Working Together

Is YOUR COMMUNITY forever struggling with the problem of how to accomplish all the things people want done—build an airport, remodel a hospital, provide better fire protection, enlarge the library? Sometimes it seems there is an endless list of community needs, but few resources available to meet them. Improving a community takes time, money, and hard work.

Some communities get a lot more "quality of living" from their resources than others. By pooling hours, dollars and energy to stretch resources, these communities get things done. Cooperation is the key.

Cooperation between—and within—communities is becoming more vital every day. In a recent survey of 1,000 community leaders in Ohio, cooperation between and within communities ranked first among all community problems mentioned.

Increased interdependence between

AUTHOR G. HOWARD PHILLIPS is Professor and Associate Chairman, Department of Agricultural Economics and Rural Sociology, Ohio State University, Columbus.

COAUTHOR JOHN S. BOTTUM is Assistant Administrator, Rural Development, Extension Service, Washington, D.C.

COAUTHOR DONALD L. NELSON is Program Leader, Extension Service.

In central New York State, the MIDNY project is designed to stimulate multicounty community education and to improve regional planning.

communities is one reason community leaders are so concerned about cooperation. For example, school consolidation has increased interdependence and interaction between communities. When our Nation was dotted with one-room schools, there was no great need to cooperate on school issues. Now we often have several communities trying to work together to decide about curriculum, staffing patterns, school location, and financing.

Cooperation means something only when we think about the contrasting concepts of competition and conflict. Competition and conflict are often needed to resolve differences. But a group, a community, or a society cannot live by competition and conflict alone. Cooperation is necessary if a community is to keep going and prosper.

How can people cooperate to get things done?

Here's one example: The county commissioners in a rural Indiana county found that the cost of maintaining a home for the aged was increasing at an alarming rate. In searching for answers, the commissioners visited nearby counties to learn how their fellow commissioners were dealing with the problem.

By joining forces with an adjoining county, they were able to close their own home and send their needy aged people to the facility in the next-door county. This resulted in lower costs for both counties.

In another cooperative project, the people of the cities of Cambridge and Zanesville, Ohio, joined forces to construct an airport. This combined effort provided a quality of service which probably could have never been achieved on a community-by-community basis.

In another instance, cooperation crossed State lines as Marietta, Ohio, and Parkersburg, W. Va., teamed up to build an airport.

In eastern and southern Ohio, several communities have cooperatively established quality water systems not possible on a single community basis. Residents of the small towns have benefited from the cooperative efforts, and residents living in the open country are better off as well.

Another example of community cooperation in action: In Albany County, Wyoming, three communities found a way to get the fire protection they needed. Here, the county Extension agent worked out a Federal-State-rural district plan to purchase 2½-ton trucks with 1,000-gallon capacity tanks from the State forestry department for $250 each.

In the Centennial community, local volunteers worked on the tank. Representatives of the University of Wyoming did all the painting and also built a garage with materials furnished by the local Lions Club. Volunteer firemen

Community cooperation resulted in a coffee house for teenagers in Patrick County, Va. The building was a vacant apple storage shed until converted.

339

Extension community development agent travels between communities in southern Illinois, helping people get things done.

man the truck and attend monthly training sessions.

Similar cooperation got the fire trucks rolling in the Little Laramie and Harmony communities.

People in Clark County, Wis., were quite proud of the organized activity programs they had for different age groups. But one day some of them realized there wasn't much going on for senior citizens to enjoy, even though about a fourth of the county residents were 65 or older.

An Extension home economist in the county decided to try to help with the problem. She talked to members of county homemaker clubs. Women from the clubs made a survey which showed great interest in organized activity for the elderly.

Twenty-two older people attended a planning meeting in September, 1967. Attendance went up every month until more than 100 were soon taking part. The program has continued to grow—there are now 800 elderly people in 10 groups. They meet in churches, halls—anywhere they can·find room.

Cooperation is not necessarily the easiest way to resolve a problem. But, sometimes it is the only way. Cooperation requires understanding, patience, and a willingness to compromise. Cooperation involves sharing. When you share, you don't get all the benefits.

Many community problems involve establishing a physical facility desired by two or more communities (a school, an industry, a library, or a hospital, for instance). Other times, it may mean starting a facility nobody wants (a garbage dump, a sewage disposal unit). But if the needed facility or service is to be developed or the issue resolved, a compromise has to be reached.

Let's look at some reasons why people may not want to cooperate and, consequently, progress is slowed down. Leaders may be unwilling or unable to face issues objectively. In one case, supporting school districts could not agree on a site for a new technical school. After months of controversy, a private research firm was called in to evaluate the proposed sites.

A compromise was reached when facts were substituted for emotions. The stalemate was broken by citizens recommending the outside group as a neutral third party to help identify new factors to be used in reaching a solution.

Another reason communities sometimes fail to cooperate is that leaders and citizens may not know what the real problem is.

Most small communities do not have professional planners, economists, sociologists, psychologists, engineers, biologists, or other specialized occupations to draw on for help and advice. Because of this, the real problem may not be apparent to community leaders.

Communities often try to deal with the symptoms of drug abuse and crime, for instance, rather than trying to dig into the underlying problems.

Citizens and community leaders can broaden their base of expertise by seeking help from private and governmental agencies widely available to most communities on request, such as the Extension Service, the Rural Development Committee, or the planning office.

Cooperation sometimes fails to come about because local residents don't have the kind of organization needed to help them reach community goals.

Most communities *do* have organized groups. However, these groups may not represent a cross section of all residents.

People who are not involved in community groups may resist community progress rather than cooperate. This may be because the non-involved people don't understand the problem or because the proposed solutions are not in the best interest of all the people.

Take this example: A private swimming pool outside of a small town in a Southern State failed to meet the total needs of residents because many of the children had no way to get there. A public pool was eventually built near the center of the town to serve all of the people.

With two full-sized pools in one small community, neither pool could operate efficiently. Cooperation between the private and public sectors of the town could have provided an adequate pool for the community and, probably, additional recreational facilities as well.

Community change does not always benefit people equally. Resistance rather than cooperation sometimes occurs because different groups must take unequal risks. As an example, a manufacturer said he would locate a plant in a small community if the town would provide him with adequate services. A community industrial development group agreed to provide the services.

Upon investigation, the industrial development group found it would have to mortgage a building constructed for

A game developed in Virginia—appropriately called "Community"—helps people see the value of cooperation.

a previous project in order to meet the cost of extending the required services. However, one of the largest stockholders objected.

The group found out that the stockholder was not objecting just to be obstinate. Since the original building was constructed, this stockholder had lost money in other projects. At his advancing age, risking his investment threatened his own future security. The problem was resolved when two community residents bought out his interest.

Sometimes tradition rather than objectivity rules the day. Planning and zoning are current issues confronting many communities.

Population expansion causes a number of communities to "bulge at the city limits." Often, farmers own the land outside of town. Most farming operations do not fit in well with nonfarm activities. Crop dusting, manure spreading, or noisy equipment are some obvious problem areas when farms and residential areas are too close together. Real estate taxing may not be obvious at first, but often arises to create a further division of opinions between farm and home.

As towns and cities reach further out into farmland, a community may be faced with an outright standoff. Compromise is difficult when hostile parties glare at one another across city limits. Communities that are willing to work together tend to get things done.

How can individual citizens and leaders of a community stimulate greater cooperation to stretch their resources?

One of the first steps is to learn the art of cooperation. This means gathering new information about the different problems and issues confronting your community.

Citizens and leaders can learn much from visiting other communities that have dealt with similar problems. Recently, the Cooperative Extension Service helped leaders from a multi-county area in eastern Ohio arrange a tour of communities in Kentucky and Tennessee. The leaders studied several community projects, ranging from sewer

341

systems to beautification. The value of working together toward common objectives was impressively illustrated to these community leaders.

A second step to greater cooperative effort is to learn what is possible. Self-study, bringing in experts, visiting other communities, or a combination of these are just some of the ways to learn what is possible.

A third way to improve cooperation is to play down differences and emphasize likenesses. It is seldom true that everybody in a community or communities thinks alike. There are usually social class, ethnic, religious, racial, economic, and historical differences lurking beneath what may seem to be a smooth surface.

Two communities may have battled over the location of a courthouse 60 or 70 years ago, and the scars of battle are still there. Almost every community in the Nation has had a school consolidation fight.

If these differences aren't played down or efforts made to smooth things over, they can be major stumbling blocks to working together with another community.

The fourth step to closer working relationships between groups is careful planning. People perform better when they know what is expected of them. Projects often flounder because no one knows what to do.

A final step in which *you* can help improve cooperation within and between communities is by selecting, electing, or serving on committees that represent people's needs and interests without ulterior motives. Community cooperation is often bungled by leaders who are serving because it is "expected" by their employer or for motives other than the true purpose of the activity. Community interest must come before self-interest.

Working together toward common goals requires cooperation. The fruits of cooperation are many for the communities willing to compromise, be generous with their neighbors, and learn what is possible. Stretching community resources can greatly extend opportunities and satisfactions to more of a community's people.

Rule-of-Thumb Guides For Evaluating Your Community's Services

IF YOUR COMMUNITY wants to improve its services, it can compare its own with what other places have to offer. Or you can see how your community measures up to what experts say would be desirable for communities about the same size as yours.

Standards from either of these sources provide rough guidelines that may have to be adjusted in particular situations. The experts sometimes differ among themselves regarding details. Nevertheless, these standards provide useful guidance in community planning.

Size of population to be served is one of the important factors involved in determining both adequacy and comparative costs of community services. Accordingly, many standards are expressed in terms of population numbers, such as dollars per capita or amounts per 1,000 persons.

Per capita costs for many services tend to vary inversely with size of community. The larger the community, the lower the cost per capita, at least up to some optimum size, above which higher per capita costs seem to be associated with each successively larger size of community.

Community standards frequently are given either as amounts per capita or a schedule of amounts for specified sizes of places. Still other standards are expressed simply as the minimum population needed to support a given type

AUTHOR STANLEY W. VOELKER is an Agricultural Economist with the Rural Development Service, USDA, stationed at North Dakota State University, Fargo.

The 1972 National Teacher of the Year on the job in Durham (N.C.) High School.

of service. In any event, standards imply some sort of compromise between the ideal or desired quality of service and what it is believed the average community would be willing to pay for.

Every community, for example, is expected to be able to educate its children from kindergarten through at least grade 12. The quality of education is linked to the diversity of the curricula, qualifications of teachers and administrators, salary scales, and amounts spent on buildings and equipment.

Size of attendance area is also a key factor, especially in rural regions. The area should be large enough to provide both the number of pupils and the amount of tax base needed for high quality education at reasonable costs per pupil.

As a practical matter, the size of rural attendance areas is limited by the length of bus routes that school patrons will accept. If it is decided that bus routes should not exceed 60 to 70 minutes travel time, morning and evening, the maximum length of bus route would be about 22 miles, depending somewhat on population densities and traffic conditions.

Even with this limitation on bus routes, it would be geographically possible to have attendance areas as large as 485 square miles, which is considerably larger than average.

You probably will want to consult with the specialists in your State department of public instruction, not only for recommended minimum sizes for school districts and attendance areas, but also for criteria by which the quality of your school system might be judged. These would include the standards used by State and regional school accreditation agencies.

An evaluation tool you might find helpful is "Profiles of Excellence: Recommended Criteria for Evaluating the Quality of a Local School System," published by the National Education Association, 1201 16th Street, N.W., Washington, D.C. 20036.

A public library requires a surprisingly large population base if it is to supply the books, periodicals, pamphlets, documents, audio-visual materials, reference assistance, and other services at a reasonable cost per user. The American Library Association (ALA) recommends a minimum population base of 50,000, but other studies put the figure at 100,000 or more.

To achieve the desired population base, the ALA has long urged that libraries be organized into "systems," of which there are several kinds. They include the main library and several neighborhood branches in a large city; a city-county system in which at least one city library provides a pool of books, materials, and services for bookmobile stops and other local outlets; and regional cooperatives of community libraries for inter-library lending and joint services.

Some State libraries function as Statewide pools of printed materials and audio-visuals to supplement local collections, particularly those of the smaller community libraries.

Not all libraries are included in library systems. So, if you are to appraise the quality of library service in your community, the first step will be to determine the adequacy of the library system. Your local librarian and State library department will gladly help with this.

A set of criteria for library systems

serving specified population sizes, ranging from 150,000 to 1,000,000, will be found in "Minimum Standards for Public Library Systems, 1966," published by ALA.

Criteria for independent community libraries differ considerably from those for members of library systems. Your local librarian and State library department can help you locate the appropriate guides.

If your State library department has not published a set of standards for your State, you may want to follow the guidelines in "Interim Standards for Small Public Libraries: Guidelines Toward Achieving the Goals of Public Library Service," published by ALA in 1962. These standards are by size groups of communities, ranging from 10,000 to 100,000 inhabitants.

These library standards have been updated and extended to both smaller and larger sizes of places by a noted library consultant and published in the *Library Journal* for February 1, 1970.

Per capita costs for police and fire protection, unlike those for many other community services, tend to vary directly with size of community; that is, the larger the community, the higher the costs per capita.

According to the 1967 U.S. Census of Governments, the average annual cost of police protection was $6.40 per capita in cities smaller than 2,500, $13.70 per capita in cities with 25,000 to 50,000 inhabitants, and $24.03 per capita in cities of the 500,000 to 1,000,000 size range.

Similarly, the costs for fire protection were only $2.51 per capita in cities smaller than 2,500, but ranged from $14.32 to $15.10 per capita in groups of cities larger than 100,000. Obviously, factors other than the size of the community are important in planning for the protection of lives and property.

According to the International City Managers Association, the adequacy of police protection depends not only on staff and financing, but also on the amount of crime, the area covered, and geographic peculiarities of the community—such as nearness to a large city, location of schools and hospitals, presence of rivers and lakes, and number and direction of streets.

One of the reasons for higher per capita costs for police and fire protection in larger cities apparently is higher salary scales. Then, too, the larger the community, the larger the number of policemen and firemen per 1,000 people who must be employed.

In 1967, cities smaller than 2,500 employed an average of 1.2 policemen per 1,000 inhabitants. The number employed in cities larger than 50,000 ranged from 2.0 to 3.7 per 1,000 inhabitants.

The American Insurance Association (successor to the National Board of Fire Underwriters) has developed a grading schedule to measure a community's fire defenses. It takes into account the water supply, firefighting staff, alarm system, fire prevention, building laws, structural conditions, and any unusual climatic conditions.

AIA periodically rates the fire defenses of 465 of the larger cities in the country. Fire defenses of all other places are inspected by the official insurance rating bureaus in each State.

If your community wants to find out how it can improve its fire defenses, a first step would be to seek information and advice from the official rating bureau in your State.

Availability of medical services is a concern of every community. On the average, each person visits the doctor 4.5 times a year and the dentist 1.6 times. One person out of 10 probably will be hospitalized at least once in any given year. But there are wide differences between rural areas, small cities, and metropolitan areas in the use people make of health-care services, as well as in the availability and quality of health facilities.

For the country as a whole, there are about four hospital beds, three nurses, and one physician per 1,000 people. The number of general practitioners per 1,000 persons is about the same in rural counties, small cities, and metropolitan areas, but there are nearly 20 times as many specialists and hospital-based physicians per 1,000 people in metropolitan areas as there are in rural counties.

The number of physicians in rural counties is decreasing and their average age is increasing, because these communities are finding it increasingly difficult to attract young doctors to replace those who die or retire.

There are only half as many active nurses per 1,000 people in rural counties as in urban and metropolitan areas. Similar disparities exist in the case of dentists and pharmacists.

The number of hospital beds per 1,000 persons is only slightly less in rural counties than in urban and metropolitan areas. Rural hospitals, however, usually are smaller and are more likely to be inadequately staffed or poorly equipped. Many rural hospitals lack out-patient or extended care facilities.

About 170 comprehensive health planning agencies have been created by local groups with financial assistance from the Federal Government. Areas served by these agencies vary widely, although most are multi-county regions. The governing councils consist of representatives of both the health care professions and the general public.

A comprehensive health planning council provides a clearinghouse for information on health activities within its region. It acts as a forum in which local citizens can determine the health service needs of their communities and how these needs will be met.

If your community wants to improve its health care services and facilities, it might start out by consulting with the staff of the comprehensive health planning agency. If such an organization does not serve your community, you may be able to obtain needed information and advice from your State health department.

Specifications for a community water system are based on the number of people and types of industry, if any, that it is designed to serve. Many factors beside population affect costs, including density of settlement, source of supply, depth to water source, length of supply aqueduct, amount and kind of treatment necessary, and amount of storage needed.

The community has several options to consider in upgrading its existing

Sewage and filtration plant for a small city.

system or in planning a new one, such as fluoridation, water softening, and iron removal. A small community must decide between an overhead storage tank and hydrants for fighting fires or the less costly underground pressure tank which has very limited capability for fire defense.

Because of these factors, the total investment in a complete water supply and distribution system for a small community will vary widely from less than $200 per capita to over $1,000 at 1973 prices.

Investments in community sewer systems also differ greatly, depending upon density of settlement, climate, and type of treatment required. Almost everywhere at least primary and secondary treatment are now mandatory. In some situations, tertiary treatment to remove excessive phosphates and nitrates may also be required.

Where land values are relatively low, a two-stage oxidation lagoon might be the safest, least costly treatment facility. In densely settled areas, with high land values, expensive digesters, aerators, filters, and other mechanical equipment may be necessary.

A small community that hitherto relied on individual septic tanks probably will find that a complete sewage collection and treatment system will require a sizable investment, varying from $300 to $900 per capita.

We have briefly mentioned a few rough, rule-of-thumb criteria for evaluating a community's facilities and services. Community leaders can use these and other standards to pinpoint those areas to be studied for future planning and development.

Leaders should not overlook the possibilities of cooperating with neighboring communities to upgrade deficiencies common to the whole area, to eliminate unnecessary duplication, and to reduce expenditures.

Such interlocal cooperation was mentioned in the case of school consolidation, library systems, and health-care facilities. Other opportunities for interlocal cooperation may be possible in the case of water and sewer systems, fire protection, airports, and even civic buildings.

Citizen Participation Is the Key to Creating Better Communities

INDIVIDUAL CITIZENS and their families play a vital part in influencing the kind of community theirs is to be. Participation is the key.

Millions of citizens in communities across the country, through individual action and by joining with others in associations, are attempting to make their communities better places in which to live and make a living.

They are working for better health services, better education, more humane family services, improvement of government at all levels, a cleaner, safer, pollution-free environment, and sound management of soil, water, and wildlife resources. On a very personal basis they work to ease the pain of their neighbors, and to bring hope to the despairing.

These citizen efforts, directly and through the agencies they create, give meaning, character, and quality to a community. Communities would be drab indeed without such efforts.

Observers of pioneer American communities commented that when people were confronted with problems, they talked across the fence line to their neighbors about them. If the neighbors, too, were concerned, they would form an association of some kind and take action. Work through citizen associations backed up by individual action was an effective way for resolving problems.

AUTHOR EDWARD O. MOE is Principal Sociologist, Cooperative State Research Service, USDA.

Meals on wheels reach Baltimore's aging—thanks to elderly volunteers from a church kitchen. Day's hot meal of fish, rice, and stewed tomatoes is packed by a volunteer as fast as cook can prepare it. Another volunteer delivers it by car to senior citizen who lives alone. He uses food stamps to buy these home-delivered meals, which help him remain self-sufficient in familiar surroundings.

347

Today in many sectors of private and public life, the same processes are encouraged in different settings. We are attempting to get residents in neighborhoods, consumers of health services, and participants in welfare and other programs more actively involved in improving conditions which affect them. This challenges dependence on professionals, and alters existing patterns of agency decision making and control.

In some respects we may be rediscovering the meaning of community. Communities exist because of the relationships that emerge among people as they create, and/or use in common, services, agencies, organizations, and a physical environment. Community is manifest in the functioning of schools, churches, health services, welfare departments, child care centers, employment services, and other institutions and agencies. Through these agencies and services as well as through direct individual action, concern is expressed for other people.

Research to date has neglected to identify the neighborhood or community conditions which tend to produce or support participation. We need to know more about the extent to which organizations and community agencies want bona fide participation, what they do to encourage it, the opportunities they create for participation, and the way people see the organizations responding to participation.

If a person sees his community and its organizations as encouraging participation and responding to it, he will participate.

He will also tend to see it as effective in bringing about change.

When an individual doesn't like the way things are going in his community, he has three options:

He can resign himself to whatever exists or whatever he sees his life chances to be. He can move to another community. Or he can attempt to change the conditions he doesn't like and try to improve things for himself, his family, and his neighbors.

If a person sees that he can't do anything about the problems, and he doesn't have the money or the will to move, he tends to become passive and apathetic.

He may be able, on the other hand, both to do something about the problems or to move. How he acts will depend on what he sees as the best answer for him. If he feels he can do something about his problems, and that this is likely to be effective, he may be more and more disposed, under present conditions, to stay and become active in efforts to improve his community.

Case histories of citizen participation are many. Examples from two States will be cited here.

Researchers examined the health care systems in two rural regions of Michigan, the Grand Traverse area in the Lower Peninsula and the Copper Country in the Upper Peninsula. Grand Traverse has substantial resources and a substantial agriculture. The Copper Country is a mining area which has suffered the consequences of a declining copper industry, the loss of services, and heavy outmigration of people.

Health care systems in the two areas were examined over time. Efficiencies and inefficiencies were analyzed. The role the health industries played in their regional economies was assessed.

There are wide differences in geographic location, climate, population numbers and composition, levels of affluence, management of the health industry. But the study concludes that they were similar in that influential local leadership and citizen support in each case was a major factor in the expansion and improvement of health services.

Through continuing diligent effort, citizen leaders in the Copper Country had replaced the paternal control the mining companies had held over the medical industry.

The following example illustrates the growing number of success stories in rural development. It shows the importance of doing the necessary "homework" so as to be able to respond to opportunity when it comes.

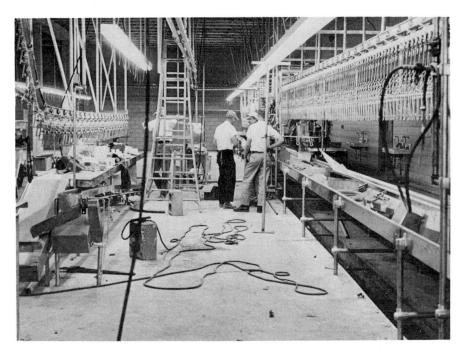

Poultry plant being built as part of a rural development program in West Virginia.

Garrett County had the lowest per capita income in Maryland. It also had the conditions which produced low income and results from it. But in 1959, citizens of the county formed the Garrett County Development Commission. Supported by local, State, and regional agencies they expanded vocational educational facilities, enlarged the county hospital and county library, established a community college, and with the Soil Conservation Service's help developed a flood plan that included a reservoir. They hoped to attract industry. They planned for it.

This opportunity came, and from one of the Nation's top optical firms. In July 1969, an industrial scout told their Development Corporation executive director that his company wanted to buy 90 acres of land as a possible industrial site.

The company would need 800,000 gallons of water a day, and natural gas, electricity, sewage disposal, and access roads.

Adequate community facilities and services would be needed also—public schools, a hospital, a library, opportunity for recreation, and a place to train workers.

If the county could supply these, it might be able to attract the company and the 1,000 jobs projected. The representative wanted to meet with community leaders in 5 days.

All the community leaders, local government officials, and State and Federal agencies working with the county attended the first meeting. The county and its municipalities could meet the conditions. Their years of planning paid off. But they had some conditions also. While they urgently needed jobs, they did not want a company that would pollute their air, water, and soil.

Officials of the unidentified company were impressed.

An agreement was reached, and Bausch and Lomb came to Garrett County.

349

This brings us, then, to what citizens and their agencies can do to help forge a new partnership.

The Individual Citizen Can:

Talk with friends and neighbors about things that concern him.

Raise questions Tell others what he'd like to see happen in the community. Others may want to see something happen, too.

Seek information about action which affects the community and/or his interests. Get to know what his rights are as a citizen. Become informed.

Join organizations or groups which are trying to do something to improve the community or which voice his views on issues.

Seek and/or accept opportunities to serve on committees, councils, boards, and task forces, both in those organizations in which he has membership, and those appointed by public agencies and public officials.

Use all the means available to get his ideas across to agency leaders, local public officials, members of State legislatures, Congress, and the general public—such as personal contacts, letters, petitions, use of mass media, attendance at public hearings.

Help other people become involved where they see their interests at stake.

Help staffs of public and private agencies create opportunities for citizen participation.

Take court action with competent legal assistance, when other options are exhausted and important issues are not resolved.

Action by individuals on their own is highly important.

Individual action channeled through some group or organization is likely to be even more effective—most of the time.

More powerful still are coalitions of individuals, informal groups, and formal organizations and associations which join their resources to achieve clearly specified objectives.

Citizens and organizations working through such coalitions can improve their communities.

Agencies and organizations can do many things to increase citizen participation and make it more effective. Some of these are:

Re-examine existing structures and procedures for involving citizens to make sure they are adequate.

Look at the makeup of existing policy-making and advisory groups—do they accurately represent whatever they are supposed to represent?

Create new opportunities for participation to supplement general advisory and/or policymaking bodies such as policy-recommending groups on special problems or issues; groups to propose compromise solutions between conflicting interests; quality assurance panels to review plans and programs.

Make groups large enough to represent the interests involved. Small groups of three to 15 panel members can reach decisions quickly, but the decisions may not be implemented. Accept larger, more representative groups, devise effective discussion and decision-making procedures.

Involve citizens early and at every step of the processes.

Continually stress the importance of citizen participation through public education and information.

Provide technical help and assistance to citizens to support their participation.

Help participating citizens and groups build their own support systems to deal with criticism and attack.

Build in "feedback" mechanisms so that people participating and the general public know that suggestions and recommendations made by citizens are taken into account.

Give appropriate recognition for participation.

Present concern about quality of life and quality of environment has arisen in part as a citizen protest. Great resources and great opportunities have not been translated into the good life implicit in the American dream. What is at stake is too important to be left to the experts. A new partnership between citizens, their public and private agencies, and their government with widespread citizen participation can lead the way.

For further reading:

Forming Consumer Organizations. 1972. 32 pp. 048A. 35 cents. Write to Consumer Information, Public Documents Distribution Center, Pueblo, Colo. 81009.

How Environmental Planning Can Work

THE TEXTBOOKS don't say it. But most real community planning begins with worry.

"Yes, we were worried," says Mrs. Edith Henderson about the town of Lincoln, Mass. "Our town was changing and we were afraid that our natural resources would disappear under the bulldozer.

"We knew we definitely needed a better environmental base for planning. So we went out looking for it."

Massachusetts is part of the eastern seaboard, the earliest and most densely populated region in the Nation. From Cape Cod to the Berkshire Hills, farmlands are sprouting a new crop of homes, villages are becoming more urban, and speculative eyes are turning toward long-established trails or open woodlands.

By the 1970's it was obvious to the citizens of Massachusetts and surrounding States that land-use changes were accelerating.

But did the changes have to bring water pollution, visual ugliness, threats to health, or a lowered quality of the environment?

Were expensive building or planning mistakes inevitable? Why couldn't more changes result in positive improvements to the environment? And how could ordinary citizens, who had to live with and pay for these changes, become involved and effective?

What we are about to describe is one way that Massachusetts citizens have found to do this. It is not the only possible way. But it is genuinely citizen based, it is going on right now, and it is producing results.

The ingredients are:
• Men and women in a town, or a group of related towns, willing to invest time, money, and effort in their improvement
• An environmental technical team, (ETT), to provide much of the natural resource technical information. The team (sometimes called a natural resources technical team) includes specialists in soil and water resources from the Soil Conservation Service, a resource specialist from the Extension Service, forestry and wildlife experts from the Massachusetts Department of Natural Resources, and a planner from the regional planning commission. It may also include a geologist from the U.S. Coast and Geodetic Survey, a marine fisheries biologist, and a landscape planner
• A local conservation district to help integrate the work of the different groups with the goals of the town

Townspeople must request technical team help through their conservation district.

Many towns are eager to become involved, but money and manpower restrictions limit the number of technical teams.

Townspeople themselves make inventories of their present land and water uses, their agricultural and residential lands, recreation areas, historic sites and so on. The inventory includes streams and rivers (can you fish in them?), wildlife areas (what kinds of wildlife, and are they thriving?) and a classification of land-cover types.

The technical team prepares, or assembles from earlier studies:

–A soil survey of the township, showing the locations and properties of the different soils, and their limitations

AUTHOR BENJAMIN ISGUR is in charge of Soil Conservation Service (SCS) activities in Massachusetts. His office is at Amherst.

COAUTHOR CAROLYN M. JOHNSTON is Chief, Current Information Branch, SCS, in Washington, D.C.

Housing is the new crop on artichoke land in California. Now only a few "choke" plants remain.

Checking a wood duck nesting box on a tree in a beaver impoundment.

New housing crowds in on market garden land in Massachusetts.

352

for housing, roads and other uses. The Soil Conservation Service (SCS) has been making soil surveys for many years, and about 50 percent of Massachusetts is now covered.

—A water impoundment site survey showing where reservoirs exist or can be built. SCS, in cooperation with Massachusetts officials, has inventoried about 75 percent of the State, and plans to complete the job this year.

—Finally, the team makes a natural resource inventory of sites with development potentials.

A reader of the natural resource inventory for Mansfield, Mass., for example, would learn not only that most of the area is in woodland, but what kinds of trees there are, and ways to improve them. He would learn that the town has no formal camping areas but does have a number of good, potential picnic sites as well as several streams that may be impounded to form reservoirs for future water supply and swimming uses.

With a natural resource inventory, a town can visualize the present condition, and the potential of its resources, and can get a general idea of ways to improve.

But this is not yet a resource plan. The human hopes and plans and desires of the townspeople must be added.

All towns have some idea of how they want to shape their future. But for any real planning, townspeople must seriously consider in what direction they want their community to go. Do they want growth, a stabilization at their present level, more or less industry, more recreation—in short, what are the goals?

And how can the town meet these goals without harming its natural resource base?

While the town is looking ahead, the technical team is determining the Environmental Quality Index (EQI) for the area. This is a yardstick by which to assess present environmental quality and to measure future changes.

The EQI measures the extent to which the natural resources of an area

contribute to a quality environment. It presupposes that any quality environment must provide for these guideposts—

1. Man's health
2. Man's esthetic senses
3. His desires and needs for outdoor recreation, and
4. Environmental stability and balance.

The index is based on the study of nine major land and water uses in the area (agriculture, woodland, water for recreation, etc.) and how well they are used when checked against the four guideposts. It does not judge the economic value of the land use. EQI values are based upon the combined judgments of the environmental technicial team members—men and women who have spent their lives working with people and natural resources.

A town's EQI is stated as a percentage (60 percent, 80 percent) of a possible 100 percent.

The town now has factual information on its land and water resources. It has some future social, economic, and environmental goals. It has an environmental quality yardstick by which to judge what will happen as it changes its present land and water uses to meet these goals.

Next comes a period of trade-offs and alternatives.

The town, of course, has economic and social needs, as well as the desire to use its natural resources well. How can its social and economic desires be met without harming the environment?

To simplify—

The town may want a new lake with swimming and camping facilities. Where are the best places for it from a resource standpoint, and what will have to be "traded" in terms of natural resources. Cut down a wooded area? Find new sources for industrial water?

Or another example: The town may want X amount of industry to meet its economic needs. This may require A amount more of water (where will it come from?); B amount of housing (where located?); C amount of new waste disposal facilities; D amount of new roads, schools, recreation areas, and there may possibly be E amount of water pollution as a result.

Considering these and other factors, how can townspeople plan for economic and social development in ways compatible with their natural environment?

A town may deliberately decide to lower its environmental quality in order to meet pressing economic needs. But, if it does, it will know in advance some of the problems that will occur, and possible ways to meet them. It will avoid the common situation of a town and its people up in arms because of unexpected, unplanned, and unwanted changes they had not foreseen.

This give and take will result in planned-for changes on the landscape; new parks, homes, or whatever else is needed. It may also bring changes in local regulations that reflect a better understanding of the natural environment.

Floodplain areas, for instance, might be protected from undesirable uses, or ordinances to reduce sediment going into waterways may be enacted, or perhaps certain areas of land will be bought by the town to preserve a "fragile" land area or an historic landmark.

Land use changes and regulations, and the community attitudes that led to both, are a town's land-use plan in action.

More than a hundred Massachusetts towns use information gained from soil surveys and natural resource inventories. But time and money currently limit full environmental quality planning assistance to six pilot towns and one river basin area. One of these towns is Lincoln, Mass.

This 300-year-old town bordering the metropolitan Boston area is small (5,000 people), with relatively large areas of open space, and with a highly desirable natural environment. It has a very high EQI rating. Population pressures from metro Boston are pressing on it, and Lincoln citizens—like those of many other towns—are seeking some way to retain a desirable community while they face the reality of growth.

In 1971, Lincoln citizens heard about environmental technical teams and asked to join the program.

A former Lincoln citizen, Mrs. Edith Henderson, describes it this way:

"We were worried about the impact of more people on our town, although we knew we needed to change. A study showed that the cost of living in Lincoln was driving out both young couples and old people. We wanted more low and moderate income housing, but we also wanted to stay an attractive town.

"The Town Planning Board formed a group called 'Lincoln by '80' to do some long-range thinking, and I was on it. We held an open town conference to air the concerns of Lincoln people.

"We were looking for a handle—something to work with, so the town could make conscious, intelligent decisions. Lincoln people wanted to regain the feeling that they had some control over their future.

"Then we stumbled upon the Soil Conservation Service and it was a godsend, especially the help of Bob Morehouse, the local SCS conservationist. He became part of our technical team.

"What we particularly liked about the technical team approach was that Lincoln people themselves could—in fact, had to—participate very actively. We wanted to be involved. We formed committees and went to work.

The sign tells the story.

354

Environmental education—indoor classroom study using minnows, and outdoor classroom study starring a pollywog.

"One of the biggest surprises, during the early work, was the lack of communication between different groups even in our small town.

"For example, Lincoln is at the top of a watershed, so our water supply is generated within our boundaries and is of considerable interest to us. One survey showed that the average person in Lincoln used something like 200 gallons of water a day. Some of our health regulations, however, were based on the assumption that the average person used about a fourth of this.

"The whole process of studying our town's natural resources was an education. Even though we think we're a sophisticated group in Lincoln, we really knew very little about our town. But we were pleased when we came out with a high Environmental Quality Index rating.

"I moved away from Lincoln last year, but of course the work continues, and so do the changes. Some 150 units of low-to-moderate income housing are proposed, along with about 75 more expensive housing units, and these will all mean more people.

"The town has adopted new subdivision control regulations and is considering new health regulations. The regulations require a developer to prepare, in effect, an environmental impact statement, for local review, on how his development will affect the area.

"Lincoln has made considerable use of its natural resource inventories. They have made less use of the judgmental aspects of the Environmental Quality Index. However, I'm convinced the EQI is very useful as a standard of quality. I believe that EQI-type standards would be particularly valuable for towns that start with a lower quality environment than Lincoln did, or for towns that are in imminent danger of destructive land use changes.

"In some ways, the environmental planning work in Lincoln is just starting. While I was there, we had discouragements and disappointments, but the town is on the right track. The whole concept of a town studying itself—its physical, social, and economic makeup—is very beneficial.

"Every town has its own problems, priorities, and plans. But any good development must rest on a thorough understanding of the land, water, and other natural resources a town has to work with."

A natural resource plan, of course, does not constitute total planning for a town. Social, economic, and legal

Crackup of a home foundation built on silty hard-pan soils and in an area with a high water table. Soil survey information can help avoid this.

considerations must be added. But while many towns, and all commercial developers, automatically study the economics of their plans, relatively few towns or developers make in-depth studies of what their economic plans will do to the natural elements of the environment.

A natural resource planner says, in effect, "Look at the carrying capacity of your land and water *first*, and use that to plan for development, instead of letting growth occur helter-skelter, and then having to scramble for more resources that may not be available."

Towns can do environmental planning by degrees. With a soil survey—50 percent of Massachusetts is surveyed—a community can find suitable areas for new homes, schools, and public developments. Water impoundment site inventories give a town more information on present and potential water resources. And, with a natural resource inventory, a town can do further planning.

Townspeople require a yardstick to evaluate the present quality of their natural resources. That same yardstick can help people to evaluate alternative ways to maintain or improve their natural environment even as they change it. The Environmental Quality Index is such a yardstick. Its present form

may alter as both towns and technical teams gain more experience.

Technical team people feel that EQI ratings should be made for a larger area than one township. Several towns, tied together by custom or by shared transportation or municipal facilities, would be more desirable. One pilot EQI study has been started on a six-town watershed basis.

Town planners should be encouraged to consider real solutions to problems, instead of transferring the problem elsewhere. If a town imports much of its water from another area and exports its municipal wastes, it is transferring —but not necessarily solving—problems. There is no such thing as a free lunch when dealing with the eco-system.

Technical team planning of the natural resource base has some elements of the "carrying capacity" concept of farm planning. A good farmer knows his soil and water resources, his financial needs and his personal hopes and plans *before* he seeds his cornfield, stocks his range with cattle, builds a waste disposal system, or plants special areas for wildlife. A good farmer also routinely plans for the conservation of soil and water. Towns can hardly afford to do less.

Natural resource planners must be alert to new technological advances. We hope for more direct participation from the academic world in future work.

Milwaukee school system's environmental mobile laboratory. Students get taped instructions through headphones, and try to solve urban planning problems.

Natural resource planning is not elitist. It is designed to provide some rational answers as to what a town can and cannot do with present resources. Environmental facts do not cease to be facts because they are ignored.

Professional consultants and planning organizations help many towns with their social, economic, and legal plans. Technical teams have worked very cooperatively with planning consultants.

The resource inventories used in environmental planning are based on natural resource facts. But the EQI ratings necessarily include some value judgments as to what constitutes a desirable natural environment. Criteria for these judgments are based on the combined opinions of a number of natural resource specialists.

This brief chapter on resource planning in one State may raise more questions than there is space for answers. The first Environmental Quality Planning Handbook, including EQI criteria, was printed this year, and will help answer these questions. A very limited supply is available to public planning agencies from the State office of the Soil Conservation Service in Amherst, Mass.

Environmental planning will always be hard work. It will remain, to some degree, unavoidably imprecise. But once a community knows itself, and feels some control over its future, much of the worry can be removed, and an orderly system of progress can be developed. That's what Massachusetts is working toward.

Cultural Opportunities In Small Communities

THE SMALL COMMUNITY in the United States is often thought of as a "cultural desert". It is not my purpose here to affirm or deny this evaluation, but rather to offer a few suggestions that might be of help in solving the problem to whatever extent it may exist.

It is important to recognize at the outset that never before have opportunities and resources in the cultural arts been more available to small communities in America than they are today. Whether or not small town America takes full advantage of these opportunities and resources is another matter. Let us examine the situation in perspective.

In an earlier "horse and buggy" day, the small community was pretty much on its own, so far as cultural opportunities were concerned. To be sure, frontier America made a considerable effort to develop itself culturally—witness the historic "Opera House" which still stands in many a small town, the Chautauqua programs of yore, and the very substantial variety of "home talent" productions and activities undertaken in schools, churches, and community halls. At best, however, the possibilities for programs in the cultural arts were limited.

Today the situation is quite different. Thanks to modern mobility, the small town no longer needs to rely entirely on its own resources. Progress in transportation has brought a new world of cultural opportunities to its very doorstep.

One might think of an integrated triad of opportunities, as follows. First, there are the cultural opportunities that can be generated locally, their scope and quality naturally depending upon the size, resources, tastes, and ingenuity of the community concerned. Included here would be programs in music, art, literature, and drama; the dance; crafts, museums; pageants; ethnic festivals; and historic commemorations. Even in villages of less than 1,000 people, much can be done along these lines.

Then, there is a second tier of

AUTHOR OTTO G. HOIBERG is Head, Community Development, University Extension Division and Professor of Sociology at the University of Nebraska—Lincoln. He is author of *Exploring the Small Community.*

Top and left, folk festival at the Ozark Folk Culture Center, Mountain View, Ark. Above, paintings at the Prairie Grove (Ark.) Clothesline Fair.

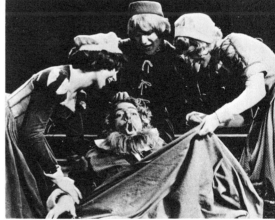

Oregon Shakespearean Festival at Ashland, which began as a community event in the Thirties. It now has an outdoor Elizabethan stagehouse and a modern indoor theater. Top, scene from Henry the Fifth. Above, Falstaff is center of attention in The Merry Wives of Windsor.

359

opportunities that small town citizens can now enjoy. I have in mind a variety of outstanding programs from major urban centers that are booked for appearances in nonmetropolitan trade centers throughout the Nation. Many "growth centers" of 5,000 to 50,000 population arrange for annual program series of this nature; and almost without exception, their intent is to serve the cultural needs, not only of their own municipalities but also of the multi-county rural areas which surround them. Most small towns in the United States are within easy driving range of a trade center of this kind; and where they are not, they can team up and bring in such programs jointly.

The third element of the triad is the large metropolitan center. It is true that people from small towns may have to drive several hundred miles to participate in the cultural bill-of-fare of Seattle, Chicago, Denver, Dallas or the like, but where a few kindred souls can travel together—as thousands unhesitatingly do for athletic contests—the distance is really no great problem.

While increased mobility has been an important factor in enhancing cultural opportunities for rural Americans, the marked advances in communication have also opened up new vistas. Public television, for example, is making significant headway, and there are many programs of distinction also on commercial television. During the week in which these words were written, "the tube" in mid-America featured "Canterbury Tales," "Legacy: Grand Teton National Park," "Snow White" (performed by the Central Children's Theatre of Moscow), "Fiesta Mexicana," "Leonardo," and "Don Giovanni."

It is my feeling, therefore, that no person need suffer cultural malnutrition because he lives on a farm or in a small town of, say, less than 5000 population. A reasonably adequate cultural experience can be enjoyed if he plans his activities well in advance to include active participation in local events, a season ticket to a community concert series in the principal nonmetropolitan

growth center of his area, an occasional trip to a large metropolis for an opera, symphony, play or whatever may suit his taste, and selective television viewing.

Despite this encouraging note, however, the overall situation is still far from ideal. The truism must not be overlooked that an opportunity is really worth very little to an individual unless he recognizes it and chooses to take advantage of it. It is no overstatement that rural America today falls far short of reaching its cultural potentials, in considerable measure because the opportunities available have not yet been fully identified, developed, and used.

In approaching the educational task of building a well-rounded cultural atmosphere in the small community, a logical approach appears to lie in greater emphasis upon cultural orientation in the social institutions which comprise it: homes, schools, churches, business establishments, voluntary associations, and local government. Appreciation of the cultural arts is enhanced by exposing people to them.

Of crucial importance in the home, for instance, is the example set by parents in their choice of music and other expressions of art, as well as in priorities that they reveal by the community activities in which they participate. The influence of "example" upon children, particularly upon teenagers, is often doubted by parents; but in the long run, the fundamental tone of a home tends to manifest itself in the lives of the young people who are exposed to it during their formative years.

Appropriate emphasis must be given to the cultural arts in the schools, as well. Where the arts are regarded as expendable "frills", in contrast to the "solid 3-R's" curriculum, a reorientation of values is in order. To be sure, the tools and skills of the 3-R's are highly essential to a person, but the arts have something to offer in teaching him how to use such tools and skills to optimum personal and social advantage.

Schools also have much to contribute

Is this a prankster's work, or someone's candid opinion of the community where he lives?

through adult education programs. An inventory of artistic talent (crafts, drama, music, etc.) in almost any community will reveal a variety of leaders, most of them amateurs, about whom a worthwhile adult education program in the arts can be built.

Further, a good library can be an important influence. Aside from its traditional collection of books and magazines, a library with adequate personnel and resources may sponsor programs such as film forums, music listening groups and discussion programs for adults, and story hours for children.

The smaller a community, the more difficult the maintenance of an adequate library becomes; but this is where regional, State, and Federal resources come to the rescue. State library commissions and regional bookmobiles often provide helpful services and resources to even the smallest communities.

Of special interest to small towns with high proportions of elderly citizens are free State libraries for the visually impaired. With the assistance of various types of materials obtained through the Library of Congress, these libraries provide books and magazines in large type, in cassette form, and in long-playing records, as well as in Braille. Cassette and record players may also be available on a loan basis where needed.

Voluntary associations of various kinds likewise have much to contribute toward educating their members, and the community as a whole, toward a greater appreciation and support of the cultural arts. Art societies, community choruses, book review clubs, discussion groups, and community theater associations can all help to create an atmosphere conducive to development and use of cultural resources.

Even if all relevant institutions are consciously working toward this goal, however, the community may still fall short of its potentials at any given time. Its status on the cultural development ladder will depend in large measure upon the relative proportions of its people who are found in each of the four general "appreciation categories" that normally exist.

The first category is the "dim viewer" who has no interest whatever in any form of the cultural arts. This is the type of person who unhesitatingly chooses a game of pinochle in preference to a performance of "Hamlet". The second type has no negative orientation toward the cultural arts, but won't go out of his way to participate. If the performance comes at a convenient time, is readily accessible, and some of his friends are going, he will probably plan to attend.

Third, there is the genuinely interested person who keeps an eye open for performances at the local, "growth center," and metropolitan levels and who actively seeks out opportunities for himself and his family.

Fourth, there are those who exercise a leadership function. Locally they may serve on committees or boards to generate programs in the arts; regionally they may help to promote season ticket sales for programs in nearby growth centers; and their hand is often felt in organizing parties to attend performances in metropolitan centers.

One of the continuing tasks of a forward-looking community is to upgrade the tastes of its citizens in the cultural arts—to encourage the "dim viewer" to expose himself at least once in a while to a quality performance; to assure that the "attend-if-convenient" person finds more and more programs conveniently within his reach; and to involve the genuinely interested individual increasingly in leadership roles. As this broad educational task proceeds, enhancing appreciation and involvement among local citizens, the community's cultural profile will gradually improve.

If a rural community is to take full advantage of the potentials available to it in the cultural arts, there are perhaps three major essentials to keep in mind.

It is necessary, first of all, to have at least one local group whose mission in life is to promote the cultural arts for the community. These people may be organized as an arts council, library board, little theater associaton, or in a variety of other ways. The essential thing is that a dedicated, enthusiastic nucleus exists to "carry the ball". The value of an active spearhead of some type has been demonstrated clearly in relation to the business and industrial development of the community. The same applies to the cultural arts.

Next, the rural community must give careful attention to the possibility of developing regional opportunities in the cultural arts.

During recent years, a marked trend toward areawide organizations (county or multi-county) has occurred in regard to health services, recreation, education, law enforcement, sanitary waste disposal, comprehensive planning, and a host of other community services. One reason for this is that we have discovered how small communities can frequently acquire or improve services through joint effort which are not feasible where the communities operate independently of each other.

This principle of "better services and programs through areawide effort" is clearly relevant to the cultural arts. It underlies, for example, the on-going activities of the Sandhills Symphony Orchestra and the McCook Symphony Orchestra in the sparsely populated regions of western Nebraska. Both of these musical groups draw musically talented farmers, ranchers, housewives, students, teachers, lawyers, and other devotees of quality music from wide geographical areas.

A further evidence of the efficacy of areawide orientation is found in the Southwest Women's Association for Fine Arts, Inc. (SWAFA). This voluntary association encompasses a 19-county area of southwestern Minnesota and marshals the energies and resources of culturally interested women from the entire region.

Their most innovative concept to date is perhaps the SWAFA Culture Bank, a fund used to underwrite the presentation of quality concerts, plays, and arts exhibits in small towns where local would-be sponsors are fearful of "going in the red." The local sponsor receives financial assistance from the Culture Bank if a deficit is incurred. The only requirement is that a serious effort be made to cover the expenses involved.

Finally, it is essential for the local community to keep in constant touch with State and national resources in the cultural arts. Prominent among these resources are colleges and universities; statewide and regional arts councils; and relevant State and national voluntary associations. On the Federal level, the National Endowment for the Humanities and the National Endowment for the Arts are of special significance.

Contact with agencies such as these will provide program ideas, calendars of events, and information on the various types of financial supports that are available. Also, it builds a cohesive network of community groups that are dedicated to strengthening the cultural components of the good life for America.

Community Health— Everyone's Concern

COMMUNITY HEALTH is everybody's business. Every man, woman, and child, and every living thing either enhances or detracts from the environment and the well-being of all other life in the community.

That is why so much thought, planning, and effort must go into achieving and maintaining a healthful community. If the delivery of health services breaks down, one person's infectious illness may become the starting point for an epidemic.

Health services include not just curative medicine, but also preventive medicine, sanitation of the environment, health education, and the gathering of vital statistics—including the number of cases of reportable diseases and the number of deaths from all causes.

Private physicians and their associates, public and voluntary health agencies, schools, and various other governmental and social agencies are responsible for delivering these services.

All of the States and territories have public health departments. Many of their counties and cities are covered by local health departments, all backed up by the State agency.

The community is the patient of the public health department.

It is the function of public health departments to know the health situation within their areas and to provide the residents with services that are needed but not otherwise supplied. Emphasis is on the prevention of disease, but treatment is also offered for some diseases, such as tuberculosis and the venereal diseases.

Federal public health agencies provide these guardians of community health with highly specialized services that would be impractical and too costly to maintain on an everyday basis.

These include advanced diagnostic laboratory services, epidemic aid, national and international information on the status of diseases, and many other forms of technical assistance.

Most of the infectious diseases that have been brought under control are those we have learned to prevent. Prevention on a scientific basis is a recent development. It has come, for the most part, within the lifetime of our own elder citizens.

For thousands of years, sick people were isolated to prevent the evil spirits or other mysterious sources of their ailments from reaching more victims.

A few centuries ago, keen observers concluded that filth bred disease. They diverted human and animal wastes from communal water supplies. This provided the first victories over such intestinal diseases as cholera and typhoid fever. Sanitation was the giant step forward in disease prevention. It is still a basic tool.

Following the invention of the compound microscope in 1835, it became possible to study minute forms of life and identify those that were associated with disease.

This opened the door to preventive measures based on understanding how health and disease relate to the biological, social, physical, and economic environment of man.

At the turn of this century, epidemics of smallpox, yellow fever, malaria, cholera, plague, and other dread diseases still ravaged this country. Infectious processes caused one-half of the deaths in our people.

Then bacteriology matured during the first half of this century and virology evolved during the second half. With enlightenment came an explosion in curative and preventive medicine and in environmental sanitation.

Many diseases have now yielded to sanitation, insect and rodent control,

AUTHOR HELEN O. NEFF is a Writer-Editor at the Center for Disease Control, U.S. Public Health Service, Atlanta, Ga.

to the widespread usage of specific vaccines, and to the development and administration of antibiotics and other advanced forms of treatment.

By the late 1960's, communicable diseases accounted for less than one-twelfth of the deaths in the United States. Still the toll in sickness, disability, and death is too heavy, and in light of our present knowledge, too often avoidable.

Many of our infectious disease problems today are related to social and economic problems of our times, to our failure to push preventive measures to the fullest extent, and to our changing life styles.

Venereal diseases have become our Number One epidemic problem, especially gonorrhea. The annual incidence of gonorrhea has more than doubled since 1966, rising to an all-time high of more than 700,000 reported cases in 1972. It is still climbing.

Incidence of infectious syphilis was officially reported as 24,000 cases in 1972. Venereal disease experts of the Center for Disease Control estimate the actual amount of both gonorrhea and syphilis to be at least three to four times higher than reported.

Tragically, the under 24-year-olds account for most of the new cases, with the 20- to 24-year-olds at highest risk.

Yet both of these diseases can be cured quickly, if they are treated soon enough.

Curing the primary cases and tracing and treating their infected contacts will prevent further spread of the diseases, for they can be transmitted only when the organisms that cause them are present. Vaccines are still in the future.

Both viral hepatitis-A (infectious) and -B (serum) are on the upswing. Serum hepatitis has been climbing at a rate of about 33 percent per year, from less than 1,500 reported cases in 1966 to nearly 10,000 in 1971.

Many of the recent cases have been associated with sharing equipment to inject illegal drugs. The malaria parasite has also been passed in this way,

usually by infected Vietnam veterans with the drug habit.

On the brighter side, hepatitis contracted through blood transfusion may well diminish as a result of a newly developed screening test that can indicate the presence in blood of an antigen associated with the disease.

The success of community action has been proved time and again in mass immunization campaigns. Starting with the first licensed polio vaccines in 1955, Federal, State, and local health agencies have worked with private medicine and voluntary and community health organizations to bring down the incidence of a number of diseases with these results:

PARALYTIC POLIO has been brought down from 13,800 cases in 1955 to 17 in 1971.

DIPHTHERIA, in pre-toxoid 1920, affected a quarter of a million people, mostly children. As late as 1940, there were 15,536 cases and 1,454 deaths, dropping to an average of 214 cases per year in recent years—until 1970. At that time, following a letup in immunizations, the incidence rose to 442 cases. Of these, 196 occurred in San Antonio, with a case rate 12.5 times higher for the lower than the higher socioeconomic group.

In 1972 when diphtheria-pertussis-tetanus immunizations were again stressed, the incidence of diphtheria began to drop.

PERTUSSIS (whooping cough) is not reported on a case basis; many victims do not see a doctor. The number of deaths attributed to pertussis have been falling steadily. More than 70 percent of the deaths in recent years have been in children under 1 year of age.

TETANUS is declining slightly each year, but nearly half of the people who contract it die. The value of active immunization with tetanus toxoid was well documented during World War II when only a handful of the wounded military personnel, mostly those who were inadequately immunized, contracted the disease.

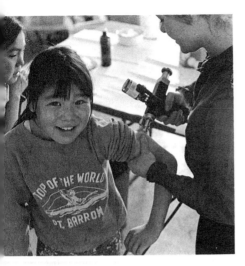

Statewide campaigns to immunize children against Rubella have been conducted in all States—as far west as Hawaii and as far north as Alaska.

MEASLES is not as innocuous a childhood disease as many suppose. It has been estimated that the immunization campaign waged from 1963 through 1968 averted about 10 million acute cases, prevented more than 3,000 cases of mental retardation, and saved 1,000 lives.

In 1970, after the Federal act providing for project grants had expired, the incidence doubled over the previous year. With renewed support and efforts, the incidence again began to decrease.

RUBELLA (German measles) is a disease that is usually mild in children and adults, but it is a killer and a deformer of the unborn. The epidemic of 1964-1965 resulted in 20,000 congenitally malformed children and 30,000 fetal deaths.

In 1969 when the Rubella vaccine was licensed there was an overwhelming public demand for community-based immunization programs to avert a similar tragedy in the 1970's, when another cyclical epidemic could be anticipated.

SMALLPOX, the target of worldwide eradication efforts, was last seen in this country in 1949. Routine vaccination against it is no longer recommended here. It is advised only for people at special risk: For those traveling to infected areas, and for medical and other personnel who might come in contact with a case.

Vaccines exist for other infectious diseases, also; those mentioned above are most commonly used and most effective.

Interest continues to center about influenza vaccines because flu recurs in epidemic form every few years. Flu presents a peculiar problem in respect to immunity and susceptibility.

The two basic types of influenza virus—A and B—undergo continuous changes. From time to time, the A virus changes so greatly that it causes epidemics before the population can build up immunity against it. These changes cannot be anticipated. Production of specific effective vaccines against the new strain comes after the fact.

Improvements in the vaccine are constantly being made, but for the present immunization is recommended only for groups at special risk, such as the elderly and those whose underlying chronic disabilities make them vulnerable to complications.

New active cases of tuberculosis have been decreasing each year for some time. Most patients are now treated as outpatients, or for a short period in general hospitals.

New drugs, such as Isoniazid, have proved very effective in the treatment and prevention of tuberculosis. Patients receiving it, either from public health departments or private physicians, should be watched carefully for liver disease. This is occasionally associated with use of the drug. Every effort must be made to detect this possible complication and discontinue the drug if it develops.

Safe drinking water is one of the first lines of defense against disease.

Urban communities depend on a common source, such as a river, lake,

365

stream or pond, for their municipal water supply.

This water must be treated to offset pollution by human, industrial, and agricultural waste before it is safe to drink.

Because large rivers and bodies of water receive pollutants from their tributaries and from population centers farther upstream, untreated sewage emptied into them becomes a hazard to all communities downstream.

People in rural areas often depend on springs and wells for their water supplies. They should protect their sources from surface drainage and from waste from septic tanks and privies. The water should be tested by State or local health laboratories at regular intervals.

Despite the known relation of water to health, 121 outbreaks of waterborne disease were recorded in this country between 1961 and 1970. More than 46,000 people became ill, mostly with gastrointestinal upsets and sometimes with infectious hepatitis; 14 died.

Both private and public water supplies were at fault. Private systems, serving fewer people, were more frequently involved, but contaminated public supplies, following the breakdown of treatment systems, claimed more victims.

Discharge of untreated human waste into the widely separated Pascagoula and Raritan Bays, coupled with illegal harvesting of shellfish from the contaminated waters, accounted for the first documented outbreaks of viral hepatitis among consumers of the raw delicacies in this country a few years ago.

Foodborne disease outbreaks are irregularly reported and much more numerous than data compiled by local, State, and Federal agencies would indicate.

Most often of bacterial origin, they have been traced to contaminated foods processed commercially and to food mishandled in eating establishments, homes, and catering services.

When a number of people in a community suffer similar gastrointestinal distress simultaneously, local health officials suspect a common source of infection. By thorough investigation, they try to locate the source and stop the further spread of disease. Even a single case of botulism is considered an outbreak.

The healthful community has a stake in maintaining hygienic standards in housing, public institutions, and places of employment. Dry and crumbling paint in dilapidated tenements is the source of many cases of lead poisoning in children, who nibble the flakes.

In this country, the average person rarely considers the possibility of contracting malaria, yellow fever, murine typhus fever, or plague. These diseases have yielded to insect and rodent control measures coupled with sanitation.

Today the most important mosquito-borne diseases are those that attack the central nervous system. These include Eastern, Western, St. Louis, and California encephalitis.

A recent import from south of the border, Venezuelan Equine encephalitis, created an epidemic in Texas in 1971. It caused at least 88 human cases and more than 1,000 deaths in horses before it was brought under control.

The U.S. Department of Agriculture, the Center for Disease Control, and animal and human health agencies in Texas and adjacent States are working together to prevent a recurrence.

The whole question about long-lasting effects of pesticides and herbicides is coming under scrutiny. Pests that endanger agriculture and health must be controlled effectively, yet with minimal damage to the environment.

Although at its best American health care, both curative and preventive, is second to none in the world, it is unequally distributed.

Social, economic, and geographic factors deprive millions of the health services they need.

People in the lower socioeconomic groups have the greatest number of infectious disease and other health problems.

Yet surveys show that about one-half of them consistently fail to utilize available health services, including immunizations, prenatal care, cervical cancer services, dental care, and other programs to protect them from the ravages of disease.

Almost one-half of the 1-to-4-year olds in central city poverty areas were found by the 1971 Immunization Survey to be inadequately immunized against polio, diphtheria, pertussis, tetanus, measles, and rubella.

The health-deprived, including minorities and migrants, have higher infant and maternal mortality rates than more affluent groups. And, in addition to their personal woes, they comprise the principal source of epidemics.

The present era has been described as one of rising expectations. Health is among the good things all people seek.

To meet their aspirations, the delivery of health services is undergoing a major overhaul through the country.

The goal is to improve the quality of medical care; to make it available to all who need it; to find more efficient, effective, and economical ways of providing it; and to bring it within the means of all through a range of prepayment plans.

The action is taking place along the homefront, within individual communities across the land, through the initiative and cooperation of the providers and consumers of health services.

The community is the focal point for services accessible to all. This does not mean that all services must be provided in all localities, no matter how small the population. Not every village and hamlet needs a hospital, for example, but one should be within commuting distance for the population served, with transportation available.

No two communities are identical, nor do they have identical health needs. Determining the needs of a community is as much a partnership venture as supplying them. It is one in which the consumer of health services, the individual, becomes an active participant.

At present there are more than 200 community-based and community-controlled clinics in the United States. They are trying to deliver comprehensive health services and education to inhabitants of ghettos and poor areas.

These clinics are staffed by doctors, psychologists, social workers, dental hygienists, public health nurses, and volunteers, among others.

Volunteers are a largely untapped resource for community health. They have long been utilized in fund-raising campaigns, envelope-stuffing, and routine office work for voluntary agencies.

Now they are working more creatively. They give person-to-person service to young and old, and to the mentally or physically handicapped or disabled. They help with educational campaigns, provide transportation, and form links in the communications chain.

Some have special talents and training that can be put to use. Others can be trained to assist professional personnel.

The amount of time they can give, large or small, depends on their first commitments to family, employer, or other considerations.

The National Center for Voluntary Action helps bring needs and services together.

Many of the more affluent communities enjoy the benefits of private clinics and physician groups with associated services.

In order to furnish health care in the quantity and quality required today, the providers must not only advance and refine treatment, but also use all known tools of prevention and develop new ones.

In this way the preventable diseases, including those of an infectious nature, will truly be prevented.

Curative efforts can then be concentrated on diseases for which no adequate preventive measures exist. And the available medical manpower can then be deployed to best advantage.

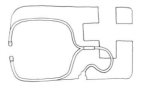

Getting Them Started: Community Water And Sewer Systems

How can a rural community citizen play a leadership role in starting water-sewer facilities? Can it be done alone? Must a coordinated plan be developed?

New central water systems are needed by at least 17,000 of the Nation's rural communities, and another 23,000 need new waste disposal systems. In what category is your community?

Why have so many rural communities felt a need to turn from individual to centralized facilities? How can you determine if your community is one of those in need of a more adequate, centralized water or waste disposal system? And if it is, how can you, as an average rural citizen, go about helping your community obtain one?

The common problems that have caused so many rural areas to seek help for building centralized systems are antiquated wells and septic tanks which are not completely functional, old and inadequate central systems, wells that are polluted, and septic tanks located in soils that will not percolate adequately.

If the well is properly drilled and grouted, it may provide a safe and dependable water supply indefinitely.

Similarly, a septic tank with an adequate absorption field, if properly designed and installed, can be a highly efficient and dependable way of disposing of wastes. This system is particularly effective where liquid flowing from the septic tank can be used on agricultural land or is allowed to seep into sandy or well-drained soils.

AUTHOR CECIL W. ROSE is a Civil Engineer with the Farmers Home Administration.

Why, then, do wells and septic tanks not always provide the answer to rural water and waste disposal problems? Why might a community feel the need to investigate the possibility of installing a central water or waste disposal facility?

Let us examine the most common problems with wells.

In many cases, the water produced from wells contains iron or other impurities which give it an unpleasant taste, or cause it to stain or soil clothes and porcelain fixtures.

Sometimes the well water may contain harmful bacteria or other health hazards. While it may be technically possible for homeowners to drill a well several hundred feet deep to an adequate supply of pure water, it is prohibitively expensive to do so.

In a number of communities there is no absolute or fixed pattern concerning the quality of well water obtained. Some families may have bacteriologically safe water of excellent chemical quality while others must use water of very inferior quality from cisterns.

The use of septic tanks, while providing adequate services in many cases, may also eventually cause problems.

A frequently encountered difficulty occurs with the absorption or percolation field—that land area which must absorb liquid flowing from the top of the tank. Eventually, the land gets saturated and the pores of the soil become plugged, causing polluted and potentially dangerous water to drain into the family's well or to back up into plumbing fixtures.

In other cases the polluted liquid from septic tanks may flow down the road ditch of a county highway, creating odors and potential health hazards.

Some families living on larger parcels of land may have years of trouble-free service from their absorption fields, while others will be confronted with constant expense and irritation because their small lots become saturated.

In the final analysis, this question must be answered: "How can I help determine whether my community needs and can afford a central water supply or waste collection system?" As a partial answer to this question, let's evaluate the nature and extent of the problem.

One must learn whether facilities are providing dependable water supplies and trouble-free absorption fields. On the other hand, it would be a mistake not to determine the number that produce inadequate, unsafe water or troublesome absorption fields.

Often, housing construction is restricted because of inadequate facilities. If so, this may be a factor for determining the adequacy of existing systems.

Comparative costs of individual and central systems can also be a determining factor for a community facility. While initial cost of the installation should not be the only financial consideration, it does form a means of comparison.

If an adequate septic tank and disposal field costs more than $1,200 to $1,500 per family, then it might well be more economical to put in a central sewage system. Similarly, if the individual well is more than 300 feet or so deep and costs more than $1,000 to drill, case, and grout, then a central system might be a bargain.

In some areas water must be treated before it is acceptable or safe.

The most common types of treatment consist of water softening, iron and manganese removal units, and chlorination. Here, again, the cost factor usually weights the decision toward installation of a community treatment system. For while treatment facilities are frequently feasible for the public water system, they often are economically prohibitive for the individual family.

In many areas, a study of the above considerations demonstrates that it is not practical to install water and waste disposal facilities on an individual basis, and that a central water supply or waste collection system would be a better solution. Yet communities still will not have adequate facilities.

Experience shows that because a community is isolated or unincorporated or consists primarily of low-income families, these reasons still do not seem to adequately explain why improvements have not been made.

Frequently the primary problem is the failure of local community leaders to become involved.

When leadership does not readily emerge from the rural community itself due to a lack of knowledge of the problem and the availability of resources, how can you as an individual provide this leadership?

One of the first steps is to determine what services, if any, are required and where. For example, these questions might be asked, "What percent of the families in my community are using water that has been bacteriologically tested and found unsafe? What percent of the families have had problems with plugged up absorption fields within the last year or two? Do some families haul water and, if so, how often?"

If the answers to these questions indicate that a good portion of the community has a common problem, the next question might be, "Would it be more practical for the majority of the people to combine resources and build a public facility rather than continue to rely on outmoded systems?"

The complete answer to this question may require technical professional advice for a final answer, but before this advice is sought, support from a larger segment of the community is needed.

To that end, one of the first steps is to call a meeting of interested citizens. At this meeting, frequently held in an individual's home, a steering committee may be elected.

This committee might be a permanent organization and foundation for a legal association, or a temporary group organized primarily to canvass other families in the area to determine whether or not they would be interested in a central water or waste disposal facility.

At the next meeting, which might be

called in the local school, church, or firehouse, technical assistance could be solicited. For example, the county supervisor of the Farmers Home Administration might be called in to discuss that agency's requirements regarding financing for public water and waste disposal facilities.

Farmers Home is authorized to provide financial assistance to rural "associations" for the purpose of installing community domestic water and waste systems in rural areas.

Associations eligible for this assistance include rural towns, water districts, nonprofit corporations, and other similar groups organized to develop a feasible system to serve farmers and rural residents.

Although the association need not be incorporated to apply for a loan, legal organization must be complete before closing the loan.

Each association is responsible for selecting its engineer, a selection that should be made very carefully.

Ideally, an engineer should be chosen who has successfully designed and completed construction on several systems similar to the one you contemplate building. Any registered engineer, however, who has sufficient experience, capital, equipment, and staff to design the system may contract with the local group.

By working together, the local association, the consulting engineer, and the Farmers Home county supervisor can design, finance, and build a water or waste disposal system that will make life safer, more pleasant, and less worrisome, and at the same time open new possibilities for community growth.

In summary, rural communities can now enjoy the convenience and savings provided by central water and waste disposal facilities formerly enjoyed only by city residents. Simply because the community is small or the families isolated or of low income is not sufficient reason for ruling out a domestic water or waste disposal facility.

Farmers Home has financed many isolated, unincorporated communities with adequate water systems where the families averaged a quarter of a mile apart or more.

Technical and financial assistance can be located, but only after you, the local resident, step forward to provide the community with the leadership it needs to get things started.

Solving Solid Waste Disposal Problems

IT HAS BEEN SAID that man has one foot on the earth, one foot on the moon, and in the meantime is standing knee-deep in garbage. Our situation is not that bizarre, of course, but disposing of solid waste is a serious problem confronting every household, farm, town, city, and county.

Proper disposition of waste is not a new problem—it is one we have always had. Each of us, however, is now creating more waste than ever before in our history. Our increasing population further compounds the burden.

Today we are an affluent nation. Not many years ago materials were scarce and expensive and all items which could be saved and reused were kept. The common practice today is to use it and throw it away.

Each American discards an estimated 5 to 7 pounds of solid waste each day. This amounts to over a ton a year per person. In addition to having more of everything, we also seem to have many items which are as expensive to repair as they are to replace. Naturally, when they break down, they are thrown in the garbage can and become waste items.

About a third of the nation's population lives in rural areas—in open country, unincorporated and incorporated towns and villages with populations of 5,500 or less. Besides the solid waste generated by the rural population, waste and refuse from nearby cities often find their way into rural areas.

Thus more than its share of solid waste is dumped onto rural land.

A national effort is underway to improve solid waste management and reduce environmental problems associated with improper disposal and to conserve our valuable resources.

In thousands of American communities, the most prevalent means of waste disposal today is the open dump. Such dumps are receiving tons of solid wastes each day. Many are allowed to burn, thus polluting the air. Liquids leaching into the soil from the dumps contaminate surface and groundwaters and pollute our sources of water supply.

The Environmental Protection Agency says that only 5 percent of land disposal sites, including open dumps, meet accepted standards. Nearly half contribute to water pollution. Three-fourths pollute the air. Many provide food and harborage for rats, mice, and other pests, and are breeding grounds for disease and accidents.

In 1970, there were some 16,000 authorized land disposal sites, with perhaps 10 times that many unauthorized dumping grounds.

The land pollution problem is very apparent. Abandoned automobiles are an eyesore from coast to coast. Cans, bottles, and papers litter city and country roads.

Rural areas have their problems but the cities, especially, face a crisis in handling solid waste. Urban waste loads are heavy due to population density. Traffic congestion in narrow streets makes garbage and trash collection very difficult and results in inefficient and costly collection problems.

Residential solid wastes are generated and discharged from single family and multifamily dwellings. They include wastes generated both within and outside the dwelling.

In 1968 the Bureau of Solid Waste

AUTHOR JOHN R. BOWLES is a Civil Engineer on the Community Services staff, Farmers Home Administration.

COAUTHOR CHARLES FOGG is a Sanitary Engineer with the Soil Conservation Service.

Management of the Department of Health, Education, and Welfare estimated that 4,340 million tons of solid waste are produced annually in the United States. Two hundred and fifty million tons came from residential, commercial, and institutional sources. Industrial wastes amounted to 110 million tons.

Agricultural wastes amounted to 2,280 million tons. Agriculture by far produces the largest amount of solid waste. These wastes include animal manure, prunings, vegetable crops and greenhouse wastes, and miscellaneous containers.

What can we do to overcome this staggering problem?

As individuals we can't solve the problem on our own. We can, however, join with others in our community to secure approved collection and disposal methods for the wastes we generate. These methods may range from normal trash pickup, provided for a monthly fee by private operators, municipalities, or counties, to other types of community programs that recover values from the disposal process.

We can also urge our community to join with nearby communities to solve solid waste collection and disposal problems on an areawide basis.

The areawide approach is very adaptable to solid waste collection and disposal and usually results in the most efficient operation. Through funds provided by the Farmers Home Administration, several counties in the Nation have used this approach to develop facilities serving an entire county. One project serves four counties.

A typical project might consist of door-to-door collection by private collectors in the rural municipalities, and collection from large containers scattered throughout the sparsely settled sections of the county, with all solid wastes disposed of at a centrally located sanitary landfill. In this way all rural portions of the county receive service from the system. Urban groups may participate also.

Farmers Home funds are used to

371

purchase the compactor trucks which empty the rural containers, the containers themselves, equipment to operate the sanitary landfill, land for the landfill, and other related facilities.

In general, solid waste systems include three basic components: collection, transportation, and disposal. In densely settled areas and in cities and towns, collections are generally made on a twice weekly basis. In sparsely settled rural areas, collection is generally made from strategically located bulk containers.

Collection and transportation are the most expensive phases of solid waste disposal, and may account for as high as 80 percent of total costs of operating the system.

Common acceptable methods for solid waste disposal are recycling, incineration, and use of sanitary landfills. Much effort is concentrated on reduction of wastes generated through convenience packaging and non-returnable beverage containers.

Recycling—such as separating and reusing paper, metals, and glass—should be encouraged. However, recycling is not the total answer to waste disposal. Practical methods for separating and reusing some waste components have yet to be developed, and there are limits to the demand for salvaged materials.

Incineration is very expensive on a per-ton basis.

Both recycling and incineration yield residues that need to be disposed of in other ways.

In rural areas where sufficient land with suitable soils is available, a sanitary landfill is often the best way to dispose of solid wastes.

The American Society of Civil Engineers defines a sanitary landfill as "a method of disposing of refuse on land without creating nuisances or hazards to public health or safety, by utilizing the principles of engineering to confine the refuse to the smallest practical area, to reduce it to the smallest practical volume, and to cover it with a layer of earth at the conclusion of each day's

Top, rubbish fills drainage way leading to a recreation lake. Anyone for a swim? Center, air pollution from a burning dump. Above, spreading solid waste in county-wide sanitary landfill system.

operation or at much more frequent intervals as may be necessary."

When properly designed and operated, the sanitary landfill protects the environment and safely disposes of the waste. But landfill which is improperly designed, constructed, or operated can cause many problems and become a nuisance. Care must be taken in planning and constructing landfills in order to assure adequate and economical waste disposal.

Caution must be used when selecting a landfill site to be sure it complies with air, water, and health regulations. Quite often land can be leased instead of purchased, and the site returned to the owner when the fill is completed, with a substantial cost saving.

Care should be taken not to sign an option on a landfill site or to purchase it until the site has been approved by the health department for landfill purposes.

In planning a solid waste program, take advantage of all technical assistance available.

Farmers Home can provide funds to finance your project and can also render technical advice and guidance.

The Soil Conservation Service can provide soil surveys and interpretations useful in boiling down a number of potential sanitary landfill sites to those warranting detailed study. It can also provide agronomic, drainage, and water and erosion control recommendations for site management, protection, and screening, as well as advice on possible uses of the completed landfill site.

The Environmental Protection Agency can provide current guidelines and technical advice on all aspects of solid waste management including sanitary landfill design, operation, and maintenance.

Your local health department should be consulted on selection of the landfill site and on possible air and water pollution problems. It can help with design of the landfill and make suggestions concerning control of insects, rodents, birds, and other pests. The health department can also assist in evaluating collection, transportation, and disposal costs.

A qualified engineer should take part in selecting the landfill site and in planning and designing the landfill, drainage controls, roads, and utilities.

Quite often the manufacturers of solid waste collection and disposal equipment can provide you sound information on which to base your annual budget.

The ever increasing need for cleaning up the environment is stretching to all facets of community life. If we all work together, we need not stand knee-deep in waste. By working through our community, we can instead provide an adequate collection and disposal system for our solid wastes.

We can also do more to improve our environment. We can provide trash baskets in parks and along our streets and assist in anti-litter drives. Recycling centers can be set up in the community.

Public demand for better service and for proper means of collecting and disposing of solid wastes is increasing the demand for finding ways and means to plan and finance such systems.

Many health hazards are posed by garbage strewn along highways, disposed of in burning dumps, or placed in improperly designed or operated landfills. Garbage thus disposed of contributes to air and water pollution.

Besides tying in to efforts to clean up the environment, the development of an adequate solid waste collection and disposal system is a necessary step which a community must take in providing proper services for its residents.

An adequate solid waste facility is a necessity. Just as a community needs a water system, a sanitary sewer, and electric and gas systems, it also needs an adequate solid waste collection and disposal utility.

You can obtain guidance and information on available assistance from county offices of the Farmers Home Administration, Soil Conservation Service, and Extension Service and from regional offices of the Environmental Protection Agency. They can help you in making first determinations regarding soil suitability, engineering feasibility, the economic soundness, cost estimates, organization, financing, and management in connection with the proposed improvements.

373

Outdoor Recreation Projects on Farms For Fun and Profit

LAND AND OUTDOOR RECREATION go together like apple pie and ice cream. When a body of water goes with the land it's even better. Land and water and trees make a near perfect combination.

If you have one or more of these resources, some U.S. Department of Agriculture agencies will likely be able to help you—or tell who can—help you develop recreational facilities for your rural community.

Some recreational developments are intended for improving the quality of living in a community; others are primarily for profit. But generally the two purposes complement each other.

Take the Rome, Wis., community. Two recreational lake developments were begun there in 1967 when the total assessed property valuation was $1.7 million. This included a valuation of $117,492 for the property on which the lakes were subsequently developed. Four years later the valuation was $12.5 million, of which $9.6 million consisted of the lake developments.

Harold LeJeune, extension resource agent, in a study published in May 1972, concluded that the net gain in tax receipts for all governmental units, after providing the additional services falling under the respective jurisdictions, amounted to nearly $297,000 through the 4 years 1967-1970.

In summarizing overall benefits of such recreational lake developments, LeJeune adds that "When improvements are made, local contractors and

AUTHOR ROBERT S. CRITES is Recreation Specialist with the Resource Management Association Division of the Farmers Home Administration.

suppliers are often employed. The visiting owner buys services, food, gasoline, and other supplies from local merchants. Thus outside money flows into the community, assisting and stimulating the local economy."

He also notes that developers of the Lake Sherwood-Camelot complex designed the project in ways best calculated to preserve and protect the area's natural resources.

Some rural communities learn the value of recreation the hard way. Here is how one chamber of commerce president in a town of 4,000 expressed his feelings on that subject:

". . . . Both of these companies flew their top executives into our community several times concerning locating a new plant here that would have employed 900 men from a five-county area. *We missed this plant and one of the main reasons was lack of recreation for their people.*

"Mr. L. McKay . . . told me, personally, three different times that lack of recreational facilities were weighing heavily against us. I feel very strongly had we such a facility in our county then as we are trying to get now we could have landed this plant and better employment could have been obtained for our people in this area."

It's worth noting that the above letter was written to a consulting engineer. As with any other kind of business, there are failures as well as successes in recreational enterprises. Getting expert advice at the start is a good rule for any community or individual.

Suit the type and size of the recreational facility to a realistic estimate of the number of users. Some communities are too small to support even a small swimming pool. Others may be able to justify a swimming pool but not a golf course. A community might support a 9-hole golf course, but not an 18-hole.

Let's take an example. A 9-hole course can be built in most rural communities for around $250,000, including a modest clubhouse, swimming pool and tennis courts, cost of land, and semi-automatic sprinkling system.

Top, a farm recreation development. Above, water skiing on Lake Thunderhead, community recreational lake development in Missouri assisted by USDA agencies. Right, enjoying farm recreation land and water. Below right, farmer uses his best land for truck crops and converts rest to small lake with sand beach and cabanas.

If the money can be borrowed on terms of 40 years at 5 percent, the annual amortization payment will be around $15,000. Signing up 250 members who will agree to pay $150 a year annual dues will bring in enough, together with the nonmember greens fees, to cover repayment plus annual operating expenses—providing the operations are well managed.

There are some additional costs, however, that you had better not overlook or they will rise up to haunt you later—equipment for maintaining the course, furnishings for the clubhouse, and operating expenses from the start of construction until the course is ready to play (which is generally longer than you think). So you ought to cover those by requiring each member to make an initial contribution of, let's say, not less than $100.

A word of caution. In your planning, strive for utility and modesty; forget about prestige.

Costs need to be based on the lowest common income denominator among the prospective members. When such people as the banker, the lawyer, the doctor, and the dentist dominate the planning committee, they tend to think in terms of their own ability to pay initiation fees and annual dues. Setting these costs too high for the majority of members may doom the project to failure at the start.

Selecting the site for the course is very important. It doesn't have to be the richest agricultural land, and it doesn't have to be rolling. Probably the greatest errors committed in selecting sites are in getting land that is too stony or land that is too steep.

You can get good help in planning a golf course by writing the National Golf Foundation, 707 Merchandise Mart, Chicago, Ill. 60654. The Soil Conservation Service (SCS) district supervisor can assist in all technical matters pertaining to soils and plant materials.

Some individual farmers have converted their farms to profitable golf courses. If a farmer's land is suitable he already has a head start. When he has a good solid barn that can be remodeled into a clubhouse, and his own power equipment for earth moving, he is well on his way to a low cost golf course. He had better get some expert advice, however, on golf course planning and on estimating the amount of patronage.

A fish-out or fee fishing pond can be an income source for a farmer who has plenty of water. "Catfish Farming—A New Farm Crop" is the title of USDA Farmers Bulletin No. 2244. It covers such essential topics as number and size of ponds, water supply ("Well water often has dissolved carbon dioxide or nitrogen but no oxygen—a combination deadly to fish"), brood ponds, feeds and feeding, diseases and parasites, harvesting, and catfish economics.

If you have cool enough water (50° to 70°F.) you may want to check into USDA-SCS Leaflet 552, "Trout Farming." The income per acre from trout is much higher than for catfish. It could run up to $10,000 an acre; but don't let that fool you—acres are not the most important input.

Farmers who have built fish ponds and stocked them with bass and bream for their own use have sometimes turned them into fee fishing enterprises—there's a limit to how much fish one farm family can eat.

Charges for fee fishing can be per pole, per hour, or per pound. If you charge by the pole you can even set up a box with a slot in it at the entrance and depend on the honor system for collecting the fees—fishermen are pretty honest *about money.*

The Farmers Home Administration's Farm Family of the year award in 1972 for the Emporia, Kan., area went to bird farmers Jesse and Flossie Johnson of Bushong. When I visited their farm in 1964 they had just secured a $3,800 recreation loan from Farmers Home, primarily for pheasant raising pens.

The Johnsons started their shooting preserve in 1961. Only 56 hunters patronized them that year. In the fall of 1972 they had 931 customers.

They raise their own pheasants (but buy quail and chukars) and turn them loose in front of the hunters on their 800-acre farm 14 miles west of the Kansas Turnpike.

Your local SCS office is a good place to start looking for expert advice on technical aspects of shooting preserves.

In certain areas of Nebraska, South Dakota, Kansas, and Iowa, pheasants multiply naturally in sufficient numbers to make a mecca for hunters in the fall. Many farmers in those areas earn extra income boarding and lodging hunters.

For those who would escape the asphalt jungles, no better haven can be found than a vacation farm. If you are a farmer, all you really need to start a vacation farm is an extra bedroom, a friendly disposition, and a wife who is a good cook.

Top, drawing bead on a chukar at a shooting preserve, Missouri. Above, girls with mallard ducks shot on a game farm in Wisconsin.

The family should be willing to explain with enthusiasm the many facets of farm life that city folks find exciting, even though they may be commonplace to the farmer, like the farrowing of pigs or the sprouting of seed.

Providing thoughtful little services for the guests will add to their enjoyment and make them want to come back. Treat them like relatives who have arrived for a visit.

Some farmers who lack a spare bedroom have renovated a bunkhouse or built satellite cabins. Indoor plumbing is a requisite, of course.

Farm and Ranch Vacation Guide is put together for Farm & Ranch Vaca-

tions, Inc., by Patricia Dickerman—whose desk is in New York City but whose heart is in the farm fields and in the homes she and her aides carefully inspect before she lists them in her directory.

Size of farm doesn't seem to be a limiting factor. Among the 42 vacation farms listed in New York State in a recent issue of the Guide, one was 2 acres and another 2,000 acres. You can find such intriguing names in the listing as "Stupid Charlie Guest Ranch" in Colorado, and "Big Foot Guest Ranch" in South Dakota.

The county Extension agent and the Extension home agent can give valuable advice on how to operate a vacation farm, and the Farmers Home county supervisor can be helpful with financial problems.

Farmers can do all kinds of things in the recreation field simply because they have *space*. If that's all you've got, just add a little imagination like the Crews family did.

Keith Crews of Interior, S. Dak., is a cattle rancher. The nearest water to his 5,000-acre ranch is several hundred feet underground. You can see 50 miles in any direction, but there are no trees. His ranch is along the main road approaching the entrance to the Badlands National Monument.

On his place was the tumbledown remains of a sod house built by a homesteader in 1909. One day he decided to tidy up the place by bulldozing the old ramshackle remains out of the way and leveling off the site. But then he remembered a conversation he and his mother had one time about the possibility of preserving the "soddy" as a historical curiosity.

So instead of tearing down the sod house he restored it, resurrected some furniture of that period and some old-time farm equipment, paved a parking area, and advertised along the roadside that for $1 per car passersby could visit the homestead. The response exceeded his best expectations.

He has now been in business 10 years, and it improves every year. He

Top, "cowhands" line up for day's operations on a vacation ranch. Above, vacationers retrace the Butterfield Trail through Kansas as the early pioneers did it. This is part of the Wagons Ho recreation project organized by Frank and Ruth Hefner. Right, farm pond used for recreation.

Top, rock formations in Blanchard Springs Caverns, Ozark National Forest, near Mountain View, Ark. Right, the Cathedral Room along the seven-tenths of a mile Dripstone Trail in the caverns. An elevator takes visitors 216 feet down to the trail. Surface activities include an information center, amphitheater, swimming, camping, picknicking, scenic drives, and a nature trail. With the nearby $3.4 million Ozark Folk Culture Center, the caverns are expected to improve the economy of rural Stone County, making the area a tourist magnet. Above, Crow Wing Canoe Trail, Minnesota.

received technical assistance from the local SCS staff.

My wife and I once drove the entire length of one Midwestern State on a primary U.S. highway looking in vain for a place to stop and eat a picnic lunch. Yet I am sure there was a farm woodlot or a small lake on an average of every mile, and each was securely surrounded by a fence and generally had "Keep Out" signs posted.

With very little expense, a farmer could clear out several spots in his woodlot, put in picnic tables, and charge $1 per car. Operate it on the honor system if it can't be attended all the time. SCS people can help design a layout and provide plans for tables.

People who stop at such a picnic area could also be good prospects for home grown farm products.

Wagons Ho, operated by Frank and Ruth Hefner of Quinter, Kan., offers a chance for western buffs to relive the authentic life of a wagon train pioneer.

It's mind-boggling to find that after 3 days of pushing the wagons west at all possible speed you are picked up and taken back to your starting point by auto in 1 hour.

Some ranchers have arranged to take "dudes" along on their regular cattle drives either to summer pasture in the spring or back to the ranch in the fall. The frequency of such drives is limited, of course, as is the number of extra riders, but one rancher permits up to 15 riders on a week's drive at $300 per person.

Farmers and ranchers with initiative have established a place for themselves in almost every type of adventurous sport in the wide open spaces. The Adventure Trip Guide, 36 East 57th Street, New York, N.Y. 10022, lists 20 different categories of adventure trips of which the following are based partially or primarily upon farms and ranches: backpacking, cattle drives, covered wagon trips, 4-wheel-drive trips, hiking, pack trips (by horse), walking trips with packstock, float trips, ski touring and snow camping, and snowmobiling.

Golf clubs in rural areas sometimes make extra income by permitting snowmobiling on their fairways and by activating the clubhouse services for winter sports fans. Individual farmers often get extra income from opening up areas of their farms to snowmobiles.

Almost any farmland (except rice land) can be developed into a camping area which will not only bring some income but will also fill a much needed service to the public. If your farm is near a well traveled highway it has a potential for an overnight camping area. If it is somewhat isolated from the traffic mainstream but has an attraction such as a lake, stream, historic spot, or national park, it may be potentially a destination type camping area.

SCS representatives can give expert advice on camping layouts and building designs, and you may want to consult your Farmers Home county supervisor regarding financial feasibility.

So if you are a farmer with land and time you are not making the best use of, you may want to look into the recreation field. Farmers Home has loaned over $120 million in the last 10 years to enterprising farmers and rural communities for recreational enterprises that are financially capable of repaying the investment. However, due to a current holddown on funds, such lending is now limited to around $2 million per year.

For further reading:

Farm and Ranch Vacation Guide, Farm and Ranch Vacations, Inc., 36 East 57th St., New York, N.Y. 10022. Price $2.50.

Adventure Trip Guide, Farm and Ranch Vacations, Inc., 36 East 57th St., New York, N.Y. 10022. Price $2.95.

Economic Impacts of Artificial Lake Development: Lakes Sherwood and Camelot—A Case History, by Harold Le Jeune, Extension Resource Agent, Environmental Resource Center, University of Wisconsin, Madison, Wis.

U. S. Department of Agriculture, *Be Safe from Insects in Recreation Areas,* Home and Garden Bulletin No. 200, Superintendent of Documents, Washington, D.C. 20402. Price 10 cents.

PHOTOGRAPHY

Pictures are a key part of this Yearbook, and the photographers have made a contribution in many ways as valuable as the authors.

Most of the photos were taken by U.S. Department of Agriculture photographers. They are given individual credits in this section wherever possible (often their names are not known).

Besides what it owes to the valuable work of USDA cameramen, the Yearbook is indebted to many additional photographers, magazines, associations, and other concerns for use of their photos. They also are given credits in this section wherever possible.

Prints of most of the USDA photos may be obtained from the Photography Division, Office of Communication, U.S. Department of Agriculture, Washington, D.C. 20250. In requesting prints, please refer to the 1973 Yearbook, give the page number, and describe the photo briefly if there is more than one photo on the page. Generally there is a reproduction fee.

American Forest Institute, 71
Arkansas Dept. of Parks & Tourism, 358 (all photos)
Morley Baer, California Redwood Assn., 96
O. A. Batcheller, 185 (upper and lower right)
Troy N. Berry, 372 (bottom)
Jean Bethers, *Deseret News,* 109 (bottom)

Illustrations courtesy *Better Homes and Gardens:* 39 (top right), 248 (top), © Meredith Corporation, 1965. 223 (top and lower left), 268 (2 photos), 275, © Meredith Corporation, 1966. 186 (bottom), © Meredith Corporation, 1967. 162, 247 (bottom), © Meredith Corporation, 1968. 226 (2 top photos), © Meredith Corporation, 1969. 269, © Meredith Corporation, 1970. 77 (2 photos), 187, 246 (bottom), © Meredith Corporation, 1971.
Lynn Betts, 356 (bottom)
Leland H. Burgess, 372 (center)
James H. Canterberry, 160 (bottom)
Erwin W. Cole, 160 (top), 372 (top), 375 (center left)
Columbia (Md.), 333
C. J. Deland, 336, 375 (bottom right)
Hank Ernst, 377 (top)
Extension Service Review, 339 (bottom), 340
Family Camping Federation of America, 67
Charles Ford, 355 (right)
Lester Fox, 107
Frigidaire, 290, 293 (lower left), 295
General Electric, 296
Fred Giebel, 352 (bottom)
Cornell Green, Texas Agricultural Extension Service, 24, 26 (3 photos)
L. Hamel, 356 (top)
D. M. Hansen, 110
Harris Seeds, 199
B. C. Haynes, 254 (top right and bottom right)
University of Illinois, 229 (bottom), 233, 234

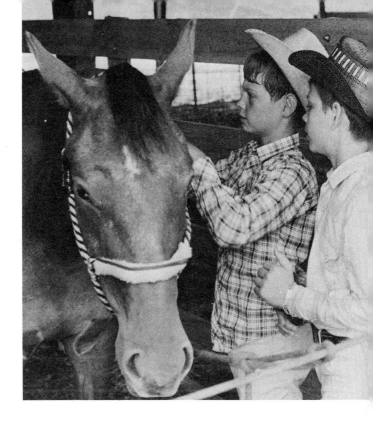

INDEX

GPO : 1973—O–490–100